GENDER IN HISTORY

Series editors:
Lynn Abrams, Cordelia Beattie, Julie Hardwick and Penny Summerfield

The expansion of research into the history of women and gender since the 1970s has changed the face of history. Using the insights of feminist theory and of historians of women, gender historians have explored the configuration in the past of gender identities and relations between the sexes. They have also investigated the history of sexuality and family relations, and analysed ideas and ideals of masculinity and femininity. Yet gender history has not abandoned the original, inspirational project of women's history: to recover and reveal the lived experience of women in the past and the present.

The series Gender in History provides a forum for these developments. Its historical coverage extends from the medieval to the modern periods, and its geographical scope encompasses not only Europe and North America but all corners of the globe. The series aims to investigate the social and cultural constructions of gender in historical sources, as well as the gendering of historical discourse itself. It embraces both detailed case studies of specific regions or periods, and broader treatments of major themes. Gender in History titles are designed to meet the needs of both scholars and students working in this dynamic area of historical research.

Sexual progressives

Manchester University Press

OTHER RECENT BOOKS
IN THE SERIES

The state as master: gender, state formation and commercialisation in urban Sweden, 1650–1780   Maria Ågren

Love, intimacy and power: marriage and patriarchy in Scotland, 1650–1850   Katie Barclay (Winner of the 2012 Women's History Network Book Prize)

Men on trial: performing emotion, embodiment and identity in Ireland, 1800–45   Katie Barclay

Modern women on trial: sexual transgression in the age of the flapper   Lucy Bland

The Women's Liberation Movement in Scotland   Sarah Browne

Modern motherhood: women and family in England, c. 1945–2000   Angela Davis

Women against cruelty: protection of animals in nineteenth-century Britain   Diana Donald

Gender, rhetoric and regulation: women's work in the civil service and the London County Council, 1900–55   Helen Glew

Jewish women in Europe in the Middle Ages: a quiet revolution   Simha Goldin

Women of letters: gender, writing and the life of the mind in early modern England   Leonie Hannan

Women and museums 1850–1914: Modernity and the gendering of knowledge   Kate Hill

The shadow of marriage: singleness in England, 1914–60   Katherine Holden

Women, dowries and agency: marriage in fifteenth-century Valencia   Dana Wessell Lightfoot

Catholic nuns and sisters in a secular age: Britain 1945–90   Carmen Mangion

Medieval women and urban justice: Commerce, crime and community in England, 1300–1500   Teresa Phipps

Women, travel and identity: journeys by rail and sea, 1870–1940   Emma Robinson-Tomsett

Imagining Caribbean womanhood: race, nation and beauty contests, 1929–70   Rochelle Rowe

Infidel feminism: secularism, religion and women's emancipation, England 1830–1914   Laura Schwartz

Women, credit and debt in early modern Scotland   Cathryn Spence

Being boys: youth, leisure and identity in the inter-war years   Melanie Tebbutt

Queen and country: same-sex desire in the British Armed Forces, 1939–45   Emma Vickers

The 'perpetual fair': gender, disorder and urban amusement in eighteenth-century London   Anne Wohlcke

SEXUAL PROGRESSIVES

REIMAGINING INTIMACY

IN SCOTLAND, 1880–1914

↦ Tanya Cheadle ↤

Manchester University Press

Copyright © Tanya Cheadle 2020

The right of Tanya Cheadle to be identified as the author of this work has been asserted by her in accordance with the Copyright, Designs and Patents Act 1988.

Published by Manchester University Press
Oxford Road, Manchester M13 9PL
www.manchesteruniversitypress.co.uk

British Library Cataloguing-in-Publication Data
A catalogue record for this book is available from the British Library

ISBN 978 1 5261 2525 5 hardback
ISBN 978 1 5261 6046 1 paperback

First published 2020

The publisher has no responsibility for the persistence or accuracy of URLs for any external or third-party internet websites referred to in this book, and does not guarantee that any content on such websites is, or will remain, accurate or appropriate.

Typeset
by Toppan Best-set Premedia Limited

Contents

	LIST OF FIGURES	*page* vi
	ACKNOWLEDGEMENTS	viii
	Introduction	1
1	The reach of the 'unco guid'	12
2	Matrons, maidens and new men	42
3	Re-sexing religion in suburban Glasgow	80
4	Realising a more than earthly paradise of love	115
5	Deeds of daring rectitude	156
	Conclusion	197
	SELECT BIBLIOGRAPHY	207
	INDEX	227

Figures

1. The line drawing at the head of 'Lily Bell's' 'Matrons and Maidens' column in the *Labour Leader*, 7 April 1894. Reproduced with the permission of Senate House Library, University of London (14632/2157).   *page* 48
2. Charles William Bream Pearce, photograph in the *Labour Leader*, 27 April 1895. Reproduced with the permission of Senate House Library, University of London (14632/2158).   49
3. Labour Day on Glasgow Green, line drawing in the *Labour Leader*, 8 May 1897. Reproduced with the permission of Senate House Library, University of London (14632/2160).   54
4. Thomas Lake Harris in his late seventies. Reproduced from Herbert W. Schneider and George Lawton, *A Prophet and a Pilgrim: Being the Incredible History of Thomas Lake Harris and Laurence Oliphant; Their Sexual Mysticisms and Utopian Communities Amply Documented to Confound the Skeptic* (New York: Columbia University Press, 1942), p. 424.   83
5. The Brotherhood of the New Life at Fountaingrove (undated). Courtesy of Sonoma State University Special Collections.   85
6. A woman at Fountaingrove (undated). Courtesy of Sonoma State University Special Collections.   89
7. A woman reading at Fountaingrove (undated). Courtesy of Sonoma State University Special Collections.   90
8. Architectural plans for an 'Ideal City' drawn up by Brotherhood disciple Louis Cowles in 1894. Courtesy of Edwin Markham Archive, Horrmann Library, Wagner College.   92
9. An advertisement for a lecture by Charles Pearce in the *Labour Leader*, 25 May 1895. Reproduced with the permission of Senate House Library, University of London (14632/2159).   95
10. Patrick Geddes in 1886 aged 32. Courtesy of Archives and Special Collections, University of Strathclyde Library.   119
11. Programme of the Ruskin Society of Glasgow's excursion to Edinburgh, 1897. Courtesy of Special Collections, University of Glasgow.   122

LIST OF FIGURES

12 Patrick Geddes and John Arthur Thomson's diagrammatic representation of 'Ideal Unity' in *The Evolution of Sex* (London: Walter Scott, 1889), p. 280. — 133

13 Anna Geddes with children Norah, Alasdair and Arthur, May or June 1897. Taken by Robert Smith. Courtesy of Centre for Research Collections, University of Edinburgh. — 136

14 Summer Meeting in Edinburgh, 1894. Courtesy of Archives and Special Collections, University of Strathclyde Library. — 137

15 Jane Hume Clapperton, 1899. Reproduced from *Portrait Album of Who's Who at the International Congress of Women* (London: The Gentlewoman, 1899), p. 20. Image published with permission of ProQuest. Further reproduction is prohibited without permission. — 161

16 Rosehill c. 1850s. Photograph reproduced by kind permission of the Coventry History Centre. — 166

17 George Arthur Gaskell out for a ramble with the Leeds and Bradford branches of the Socialist League, 1886. Reproduced from Fenner Brockway, *Socialism Over Sixty Years: The Life of Jowett of Bradford* (London: George Allen, 1946). — 179

Acknowledgements

Writing this book has taken several years, during which time I have accrued numerous intellectual and emotional debts. The most substantial are to Lynn Abrams and Eleanor Gordon, who have been unfailingly generous with their time and expertise, their insights shaping the project from its inception. Thanks also go to Lucy Bland, Callum Brown, Don Spaeth and Karen Hunt, who read drafts of the manuscript and offered astute commentaries. Funding for the research in its early phase came from the Arts and Humanities Research Council, and I am grateful to them for their support. I am also grateful to Emma Brennan at Manchester University Press, who has displayed patience and understanding as my teaching commitments necessitated considerable delays. In addition, every historian I have approached whose work in some way intersected with my own has either patiently answered my questions or generously shared with me their own research. They include Sheila Rowbotham, Maureen Wright, Siân Reynolds, Chris Renwick, Robert Morris, Brian Dempsey, Dorothy McMillan, Sue Young, Jeff Meek, Irene Mavor, Malcolm Nicolson, Marguerite Dupree, Gayle Davis, Michael Shaw, Kathleen Chater, Rosemary Elliot, Jowita Thor, Mairi Hamilton, Stuart Eagles and Bart Casey. The contribution made by students on my 'Gender, Sexuality and Modernity in Victorian and Edwardian Scotland' honours course at Glasgow should also be acknowledged, with lively seminar discussions on aspects of the book providing valuable new perspectives. Thanks are also due to Maureen Purdie, who generously supplied information on the history of her home, once the summer retreat of Bella Pearce's family, to Christelle Le Riguer for her excellent translating work, and to the book's copyeditor, Caroline Richards, who caught a number of my errors. The responsibility for the remainder lies entirely with myself.

Librarians and archivists at all the institutions I have either visited or contacted have been without exception helpful and knowledgeable. They include staff at the Mitchell Library in Glasgow, the National Library of Scotland in Edinburgh, the Glasgow School of Art, the Women's Library, Senate House Library, Herbert Art Gallery and Museum, and Special Collections at the Universities of Glasgow, Strathclyde, Edinburgh and Liverpool. In America, I have been assisted by Lynn Prime at Sonoma State University Special Collections, Lisa Holland at Wagner College Archives and the staff at Columbia University Library in New York.

In the end stages of the project, colleagues and friends within history at Glasgow kept me going, with Alexander Marshall and Stuart Airlie

ACKNOWLEDGEMENTS

engineering crucial time for me to write. Furthermore, three overlapping networks of women and gender historians have for several years been a vital source of friendship, encouragement and erudition: the Centre for Gender History at the University of Glasgow, the Women's History Network and Women's History Scotland. Together, they constitute my progressive subculture.

Finally, I would like to thank my family. Tomas, Lily and Ivy have grown up with this book in the background of their young lives, it variously providing a source of bemusement and interest. My deepest debt is to Paul, who has in innumerable ways supported the book's research and writing.

Introduction

In 1889, in the popular science book *The Evolution of Sex*, the Edinburgh biologists Patrick Geddes and John Arthur Thomson outlined their vision of a new form of intimacy. While the love shared by the 'poet and his heroine' was currently exceptional, 'these rare fruits of an apparently more than earthly paradise of love' would one day become the reality for all.[1] What was required to achieve such romantic and transcendent unions was evolution assisted by a revised sexual ethic, one in which women's influence was manifest. According to the two natural scientists, nature was not 'red in tooth and claw' as the Darwinist Thomas Huxley had alleged but driven as much by female-coded altruism as male-coded egoism. Women therefore had a crucial role to play in the evolution of sexual relations beyond the crude impulses of lust towards the ideal of co-operative, egalitarian and loving partnerships. Young souls would be duly lifted out of 'the moral mud of modern conditions' and higher, purer, ethical standards achieved.[2]

Five years later, Bella Pearce, a prominent activist for the Independent Labour Party in Glasgow, delivered a strikingly similar message to the readers of her women's column in the socialist newspaper the *Labour Leader*. The future held the real promise of a 'heaven upon earth', when marriage would be 'something very different from now'.[3] For Pearce, its attainment was implicated equally with the progress of the labour movement as with the advance of women's rights, seeing them as 'twin manifestations of the one force which is pressing us forward towards higher conditions of life'.[4] Nonetheless, the 'new life' she sought within the parameters of the ethical socialist movement was founded on comparable principles to that of Geddes and Thomson's evolutionary ideal: sexual equality, mutual respect and elevated standards of morality.

Similar intimations of an imminent utopia of transformed sexual relations were being felt and articulated by other educated, politically radical, middle-class women and men in towns and cities across Britain. In the pages of avant-garde journals, feminist pamphlets and sociological treatises, in lecture halls and drawing rooms, like-minded souls exchanged ideas, consolidated theories and built networks, seeking ultimately to precipitate the dawning of a new, more 'authentic' sexual morality. Concomitantly, some also became intimate with each other, forming passionate friendships, having sex and falling in and out of love. The bold among them embodied their political views in their private lives by choosing not to marry and becoming 'free lovers', or by acknowledging their 'sexual inversion'; the majority confined their reimagining of intimacy to their fictional and non-fictional written work.

Not a cohesive movement, the sexual progressives of the *fin de siècle* were rather a loosely aligned collective of individuals from diverse and overlapping political, social and spiritual affiliations, including feminism, socialism, anarchism, freethought, theosophy and occultism. What united them was the inequity of current sexual and social conventions, which they perceived as hypocritical, immoral and outdated. The precise targets of their reformist zeal varied. For some, the priority was recasting marriage, an institution denounced in the *Westminster Review* in 1888 by feminist writer Mona Caird as a 'vexatious failure', one which enshrined the sexual double standard and was entered into by women educated for little else, often motivated solely by their need for financial security.[5] For others, it was the legions of public, unregulated, female sex workers on Britain's streets, or taboos around the use of birth control, which were the underlying cause of society's myriad ills. For a small minority, such as the socialist and philosopher Edward Carpenter and sexologist Havelock Ellis, a key objective was challenging harsh legal, societal and religious injunctions against homosexual relations.

Whatever the items on their radical manifestos, what was clear to all sexual progressives was the urgent need for change. The existing 'regulative system' was 'no longer fitting for the age', declared Edinburgh feminist freethinker Jane Hume Clapperton, and it was 'more than time that *all* should put their shoulders to the wheel' and formulate a new, 'wide-reaching modern moral code, subserving general happiness'.[6] Critically however, this new code did not sanction amorality; liberation from Victorian bourgeois norms did not mean licence. Instead, the era's sexual rebels sought to replace the strictures of Mrs Grundy, that personification of propriety, with relationships based less on patriarchy, convention and respectability and more on equality, honesty and respect. As Chris Nottingham has demonstrated, the key word here was earnestness.[7] Clapperton was encouraged that the female characters in Henrik Ibsen's

INTRODUCTION

1881 play *Ghosts* spoke about sex with 'a pure, earnest candour', while the Glasgow socialist and 'new man' Charles Pearce was described in the *Labour Leader* as an 'honest, earnest, whole-souled, simple [man]'.[8] His wife Bella Pearce sought out those who were beginning 'to think seriously and earnestly' about female emancipation, while the following conversation appeared in socialist Edith Ellis's fictional, tongue-in-cheek account of an experiment in communal living in London: '"Miss Merton" he said seriously, "you were in dead earnest the other night and I've been in dead earnest for months. As for Mr. Renton, he was in earnest I believe, before he was born."'[9]

Such assertions of sincerity did little to assuage the fears of the respectable bourgeoisie, however. While the borderlines of class were threatened by the violent clashes of Bloody Sunday in November 1887 and the subsequent strikes by match girls and dockers, the borderlines of sexuality and gender were rendered equally vulnerable by the twin perils of the masculine New Woman and effeminate decadent man. The novelist George Gissing, frustrated by what he called the 'crass imbecility of the typical woman', predicted an impending era of 'sexual anarchy', while in *Punch*, a day into Oscar Wilde's first criminal trial, an 'Angry Old Buffer' blustered over the challenge presented by new models of femininity and masculinity:

> WHEN ADAM delved and EVE span,
> No one need ask which was the man.
> Bicycling, footballing, scarce human,
> All wonder now 'Which is the woman?'
> But a new fear my bosom vexes;
> To-morrow there may be *no* sexes!
> Unless, as end to all the pother,
> Each one in fact becomes the other …[10]

In the extant historiography, the primary setting of these culture wars is depicted as London, the city seen to possess a panoply of unique qualities necessary for staging a sexual revolution. Scholarship by Judith Walkowitz, Elaine Showalter, Lucy Bland, Angelique Richardson and Ruth Brandon has meticulously mapped the 'dense cultural grid' of conflicting and overlapping representations of sexuality produced in the late Victorian and Edwardian period by a range of progressive and conservative constituents: in these scholarly accounts, it is the events, individuals and organisations located in England and the English capital which dominate.[11] In addition, in his biography of sexologist Havelock Ellis, Nottingham specifically identifies London as the place in which 'the intellectual leaders of the anti-Victorian revolt' achieved their 'creative identities', the metropolis providing a central meeting point, a source of cheap lodgings and a place of reinvention.[12] It was here, asserts Nottingham, that 'one could join the "New Age" and avoid the eyes of those who might deride a newly assumed identity', and where 'a provincial girl, could, literally, become a "New Woman"', the provinces featuring only as places from which progressive intellectuals escaped or as receptive markets for their ideas.[13] An alternative impression is given by Sheila Rowbotham, who in a series of works provides detailed portraits of those New Women, 'free lovers' and gay rights campaigners who were clustered in 'dissident networks' outside national metropolitan centres and who migrated between Bristol, Belfast, Dunfermline and Sheffield, as well as Massachusetts and California.[14] Progressive lives beyond the metropole are also explored by Harry Cocks, in his analysis of the fellowship of Bolton men who met regularly to discuss the poetry of Walt Whitman during the 1880s and 1890s, expressing a fascination with homosexuality and developing passionate yet unerotic relationships 'through the substitution of inexpressible spiritual communion for "unspeakable" physical possibilities', and by Roy Foster, who in his account of the revolutionary generation in Ireland between 1880 and 1923 acknowledges their exploration of 'other forms of liberation besides the political and national', including their sexual radicalism.[15]

As these studies illustrate, urban centres outside of London were the sites of important and distinctive sexually progressive networks, significant 'constellations', in Matthew Beaumont's words, in the wider 'cosmos' of late Victorian counterculture.[16] This book builds on this work, focusing on Scotland, a nation with a unique moral and religious heritage and in which a pervasive and entrenched Presbyterian religiosity continued to hold sway. Drawing on a diverse array of sources, from private correspondence, memoirs and diaries, to socialist, feminist and avant-garde journals, it provides the first detailed, group portrait of the radical views and intimate relationships of the sexual progressives living and campaigning in Glasgow and Edinburgh between 1880 and the advent of the First World War, including: Bella Pearce (1859–1929); Charles Pearce (1839–1905); Patrick Geddes (1854–1932); Anna Geddes (1857–1917); and Jane Hume Clapperton (1832–1914). With one exception, each has until now been relatively neglected in the historiography. While their published work has been analysed in studies of feminist socialism, New Woman writing, birth control advocacy and secularism, a paucity of contextual information has occluded important connections between their affective lives, political affiliations and written texts.[17] This study endeavours to rectify these elisions, its methodology of collective biography enabling an elucidation of the complex relationship between the radicals' intimate lives and their production of sexual discourse, including the particular conditions necessary for them to 'speak out' about sex. In doing so, it complicates established narratives on radical thought, intimate relations and progressive subcultures in Britain during the period 1880 to 1914, in a number of important ways.

First, studying sexual rebels collectively, as a particular iteration of *fin de siècle* radicalism, highlights that a necessary precondition of progressive thought on intimacy was the rejection of orthodox Christianity. This revolt from established religion tends to be understated in much existing scholarship yet is brought into sharp relief in a study of Scotland, because of the centrality of religion to the nation's sense of its own moral identity. To reimagine sexual relations, all the Scottish progressives necessarily had to break with the Presbyterian religion of their childhoods, choosing from the multitude of propositions vying for cultural authority during the Victorian 'crisis of faith'. Patrick Geddes became a follower of the positivist 'Religion of Humanity' while also interested in theosophy and the occult; Charles and Bella Pearce were early members of the period's pre-eminent magical organisation the Hermetic Order of the Golden Dawn, although their primarily spiritual allegiance was to the American Swedenborgian mystic Thomas Lake Harris; Jane Hume Clapperton was a freethinker, developing her own form of 'religious agnosticism', one which combined religion's emotional and moral qualities with the scientific principles of evolution. It is clear then, that fashioning a new morality required not unbelief, but rather conversion to a new, heterodox belief system. To state therefore, as Cocks has done, that by the early twentieth century, 'religion had come under suspicion and fallen into decay as one of the principal locations for sexual expressions of all kinds', oversimplifies the case.[18] The Scottish evidence demonstrates instead that at a crucial moment of transition, when old moral certainties were being rethought by progressive individuals in a self-conscious process of modernisation, unorthodox faiths provided safe spaces for sexual transgression, as well as rich stores of energising radical ideas.

Second, and relatedly, while progressives may have conceptualised themselves as original, a sense of discontinuity with the past allowing them the freedom to imagine radically new ways of being, the new evidence presented here disrupts the long-standing perception of the era's sexual rebellion as one of generational challenge. Holbrook Jackson, in his 1913 review of the 1890s, described young men revelling in 'smashing up the intellectual and moral furniture of their parents', with 'the snapping of apron-strings' causing 'consternation in many a decent household'.[19] For some English progressives, this will have carried resonance, Edward

Carpenter, for example, recollecting his upbringing in upper middle-class Brighton as a monotonous and vacuous round of shopping, gossiping and socialising, a world he escaped for Whitmanesque comradeship and naked air bathing in a rural retreat near Sheffield.[20] In Scotland, however, the adoption by progressives of sexually radical practices and beliefs drawn from spiritualism, positivism, Swedenborgianism and secularism highlights the importance of considering longer-term continuities across the eighteenth and nineteenth centuries in narratives of sexual change. Furthermore, while these religious heterodoxies may not have been transmitted through the progressives' families, political radicalism certainly was, often providing a pathway to their initial rejection of respectable conformity. For example, the Chartism of Charles Pearce's father and Ruskin Society membership of Bella Pearce's father was formative in both their involvement in 1890s socialism. When ideological dissonance did emerge within the families of Scottish sexual rebels, personal animosity did not necessarily result: while Clapperton clearly waited until her parents' death before publishing her new moral code, Anna Geddes and her mother were able to talk courteously about their differences in opinion on sex and religion, Anna commenting matter-of-factly, 'of course each respected the others opinion & there was no ill feeling'.[21] This relative absence of generational rupture in Scotland may be due in part to another feature which distinguishes them from their English comrades. Nottingham has noted that in London, progressives were united not just by a shared outlook, a preference for the 'new and youthful' over the 'old and established', but by their similarity in age, with Havelock Ellis, Olive Schreiner and Oscar Wilde all born in the mid- to late 1850s.[22] In Scotland, by contrast, the confluence in ages was much less pronounced, with Charles Pearce and Jane Hume Clapperton significantly older and neither of them fulfilling the role of 'rogue uncle' Nottingham ascribes to William Morris and Carpenter.[23]

Finally, while the rigour with which the establishment pursued its course of moral conservatism is well documented, not least in the period's various sexual scandals – including over birth control (the Besant–Bradlaugh trial of 1877), 'free love' unions (the Edith Lanchester case of 1895), male same-sex relationships (Oscar Wilde's trials of 1895), and male prostitution (the Cleveland Street scandal of 1889) – the evidence from Scotland emphasises the additional regulatory role played by socialist and women's suffrage parties. The discourse of respectability was not limited to the 'unco guid', the Scots word for the religiously righteous, but held real purchase within progressive organisations such as the Independent Labour Party (ILP), with widespread reluctance to reinscribe past associations between political radicalism and immorality. The utopian socialists of the

1820s and 1830s had created an enduring link in the public imagination between socialism and the destruction of the family, Robert Owen in his *Lectures on the Marriage of the Priesthood of the Immoral World* advocating 'marriages of Nature' in his New Moral World.[24] In the 1880s and 1890s, any deviation from the appearance of conventional morality was therefore seen within socialism as damaging to electoral prospects, despite its members holding a range of views on issues such as marriage and 'free love'. Ensuring electability required the policing of a strict boundary between public discourse and private behaviour, with intimate relations considered a matter of private conscience rather than party policy.

Sexual progressives in Scotland were therefore required to self-censor their writing. Bella and Charles Pearce, as prominent ILP activists in Glasgow and writers for the *Labour Leader*, chose in their journalism to reframe their Christian sexual mysticism, removing any reference to Thomas Lake Harris's notorious practice of 'conjugial marriage' and instead providing only tantalising hints of a secret sexual knowledge, writing largely in the idiom of contemporary feminism. Only those on the margins of the mainstream progressive movements, or who eschewed them entirely, were able to articulate explicitly radical ideas, although even then the considerable erudition of texts such as Clapperton's *Scientific Meliorism and the Evolution of Happiness* (1885) or the nature metaphors employed by Geddes and Thomson in their essay 'The moral evolution of sex' (1896) projected a convincing air of respectability. Similarly, in the presentation of their intimate lives, all the Scottish progressives appeared conventional. Bella and Charles Pearce married, albeit in an irregular ceremony known as marriage 'before the sheriff', a form valid in Scotland and attractive to those with unorthodox religious beliefs. The exact nature of their relationship is harder to fathom. We know that they had no children together, and may perhaps have been using a sexual technique known as 'karezza', a form of 'coitus reservatus' popular among American sex reformers and possibly used by disciples of Thomas Lake Harris. Patrick and Anna Geddes's marriage followed nineteenth-century companionate and patriarchal lines, the couple most likely spacing the births of their three children through 'marital continence', Patrick expressing profound unease at the sexual misdemeanours of his male students in Edinburgh. Finally, Clapperton, despite championing birth control and female sexual pleasure, and defending those who entered 'free unions', remained unmarried and seemingly celibate throughout her life, although did maintain a close relationship with a fellow neo-Malthusian named George Arthur Gaskell. Scotland's radical voices on the Sex Question may have reimagined new forms of intimacy; living them, however, proved rather more complicated.

In 1889, the poet, literary critic and sex theorist John Addington Symonds wrote, 'We are, all of us, composite beings, made up, heaven knows how, out of the compromises we have effected between our impulses and instincts and the social laws which gird us around.'[25] This book is an examination of this complex dynamic, as it was played out in the lives of Scotland's hitherto under-researched sexual progressives. Before these composite beings are discussed, however, it is first necessary to provide a contextual overview of the regulation of sexuality in nineteenth-century Scotland, a nation with a moral identity engendered by its Calvinist heritage and in which the influence of moral conservatism was particularly pronounced. Chapter 1 provides this context, delineating the legal, cultural and religious discourses by which the sexual lives of Scottish women and men were policed. The institution which formed the centrepiece of this regulatory regime was marriage, although moral panics over illegitimacy and prostitution, along with harsh legal penalties for sodomy, also provided Scots with powerful incentives to adhere to bourgeois norms of respectability. Alternative codes of morality were in circulation, however, in libertine middle-class settings and fishing, farming and urban working-class communities, while the sexual double standard tacitly permitted men of all classes to enjoy 'twilight moments' of transgression.

The book's subsequent chapters are concerned with plotting the sexual discourse and intimate lives of Scotland's diverse sexual progressives. Chapter 2 focuses on Bella and Charles Pearce in Glasgow, political activists for the ILP whose primary forum for their critique of contemporary sexual relations was 'Matrons and Maidens', a pioneering women's column in the socialist newspaper the *Labour Leader*. The disjuncture between this critique and the masculinised rhetoric and class-based analysis which surrounded it indicates the complex negotiations undertaken by feminist activists working within socialism in the 1890s, in their attempts to simultaneously fight patriarchy and wage war on capitalism. Bella abandoned that struggle in the 1900s with the advent of militant suffragism, finding in the Women's Social and Political Union (WSPU) a renewed source of energy and optimism.

The Pearces' narrative does not end there, however. Chapter 3 explores the couple's involvement with the Brotherhood of the New Life, an organisation of Christian mysticism which had its origins in the experimentations with communal living conducted in America during the first half of the nineteenth century. Its leader, Thomas Lake Harris, was a charismatic seer who preached a highly transgressive sexual philosophy based on the practices of 'internal respiration' and 'conjugial marriage', which together allowed followers access to a 'transcendent sexual realm'. The Pearces were key protagonists within a British network of disciples, running a business importing Brotherhood wine, publishing Harris's poetry and disseminating some of their faith's sexually radical ideas in their socialist and feminist journalism, albeit in an anodyne form.

In Chapter 4 the focus of the book moves fifty miles east, to Patrick and Anna Geddes in Edinburgh. A natural scientist by training, Patrick was an intellectual maverick, spearheading a myriad of social, artistic and civic schemes which attracted a coterie of feminists, artists, writers, scientists and social reformers to his base in the city's Old Town. The nature of his relationship with his wife Anna is discussed, as well as with the members of his bohemian subculture, the chapter ascertaining the extent of their influence on his theories on sex. A revised analysis of his highly influential 1889 book *The Evolution of Sex* and its later companion essay, the 1896 'Moral evolution of sex', reveals Patrick's confused and often contradictory attitudes towards both sexuality and feminism, albeit that the texts were both intended and received as significant contributions to progressive sexual and gendered thought.

Finally, Chapter 5 moves from the wynds and closes of Edinburgh's Old Town to Jane Hume Clapperton and the elegant Georgian townhouses of its New Town. Brought up within a wealthy and religiously conventional mercantile family, Clapperton was able to mitigate the constraints of respectable society by seeking out radical, feminist freethinkers from across the country, forming relationships with individuals including Charles Bray and Sara Hennell in Coventry, George Arthur Gaskell in Bradford and the Reverend James Cranbrook in Edinburgh. Their influence, combined with her considerable erudition, facilitated her development of a new, secular ethical code, one which encompassed the dissemination of information on birth control and the acknowledgement of women's right to sexual pleasure.

Notes

1 P. Geddes and J. A. Thomson, *The Evolution of Sex* (London: Walter Scott, 1889), p. 267.
2 P. Geddes and J. A. Thomson, 'The moral evolution of sex', *Evergreen*, 3 (Summer 1896), p. 81.
3 Lily Bell, 'Matrons and Maidens', *Labour Leader*, 1 December 1894, p. 7.
4 Lily Bell, 'Poor Mrs. Fawcett', *Labour Leader*, 30 November 1895, p. 1.
5 M. Caird, 'Marriage', *Westminster Review*, 130:1 (1888), p. 197.
6 J. H. Clapperton, *Scientific Meliorism and the Evolution of Happiness* (London: Kegan Paul, Trench & Co, 1885), p. 12.

7 C. Nottingham, *The Pursuit of Serenity: Havelock Ellis and the New Politics* (Amsterdam: Amsterdam University Press, 1999), p. 97.
8 J. H. Clapperton, *A Vision of the Future based on the Application of Ethical Principles* (London: Swan Sonnenschein, 1904), p. 104; Lily Bell, 'Matrons and Maidens', *Labour Leader*, 21 April 1894, p. 7.
9 'The Independent Labour Party in Camlachie', *Scotsman*, 28 August 1894, p. 6; Mrs Havelock Ellis, *Attainment* (London, 1909), pp. 136-7, quoted in Nottingham, *The Pursuit of Serenity*, p. 98.
10 Letter from George Gissing to Eduard Bertz, 2 June 1893, in A. C. Young (ed.), *The Letters of George Gissing to Eduard Bertz 1887-1903* (London: Constable, 1961), p. 171; 'Sexomania', *Punch*, 27 April 1895, p. 203.
11 J. R. Walkowitz, *City of Dreadful Delight: Narratives of Sexual Danger in Late-Victorian London* (Chicago: University of Chicago Press, 1992), p. 5; E. Showalter, *Sexual Anarchy: Gender and Culture at the Fin de Siècle* (New York: Viking, 1990); L. Bland, *Banishing the Beast: Feminism, Sex and Morality* (London: Penguin, 1995; Tauris Parke, 2002); A. Richardson, *Love and Eugenics in the Late Nineteenth Century: Rational Reproduction and the New Woman* (Oxford: Oxford University Press, 2003); R. Brandon, *The New Women and the Old Men: Love, Sex and the Woman Question* (London: Papermac, 1990).
12 Nottingham, *The Pursuit of Serenity*, p. 101.
13 Ibid., p. 102.
14 S. Rowbotham, *Rebel Crossings: New Women, Free Lovers and Radicals in Britain and the United States* (London: Verso, 2016), p. 3; *Dreamers of a New Day: Women who Invented the Twentieth Century* (London: Verso, 2010); *Edward Carpenter: A Life of Liberty and Love* (London: Verso, 2008).
15 H. Cocks, 'Calamus in Bolton: spirituality and homosexual desire in late Victorian England', *Gender & History*, 13:2 (August 2001), p. 192; R. F. Foster, *Vivid Faces: The Revolutionary Generation in Ireland, 1890-1923* (London: Penguin, 2014), p. 116: see in particular chapter 4 on 'Loving', pp. 115-43.
16 M. Beaumont, 'Socialism and occultism at the fin de siècle: elective affinities', in T. Kontou and S. Willburn (eds), *The Ashgate Companion to Nineteenth Century Spiritualism and the Occult* (Farnham: Ashgate, 2012), p. 170.
17 See for example J. Hannam and K. Hunt, *Socialist Women: Britain, 1880s to 1920s* (London: Routledge, 2002); S. Ledger, *The New Woman: Fiction and Feminism at the Fin de Siècle* (Manchester: Manchester University Press, 1997); K. B. Kalsem, 'Law, literature and libel: Victorian censorship of "dirty filthy" books on birth control', *William and Mary Journal of Women and the Law*, 10:3 (Spring 2004), pp. 533-68; L. Schwartz, *Infidel Feminism: Secularism, Religion and Women's Emancipation, England 1830-1914* (Manchester: Manchester University Press, 2013). The exception is Patrick Geddes, who has had several biographers, and whose wide-ranging intellectual endeavours and interests have featured in histories of sociology, sexual science, urban planning, environmentalism and Celticism.
18 H. G. Cocks, 'Religion and spirituality', in H. G. Cocks and M. Houlbrook (eds), *Palgrave Advances in the Modern History of Sexuality* (Basingstoke: Palgrave Macmillan, 2006), p. 175.

19 H. Jackson, *The 1890s: A Review of Art and Ideas at the Close of the Nineteenth Century* (London: Cresset, 1913, 1988), pp. 154, 33.
20 Rowbotham, *Edward Carpenter*, pp. 11–23.
21 Ibid.
22 Nottingham, *The Pursuit of Serenity*, pp. 89–90, 100.
23 Nottingham describes this role as those who 'have found insufficient honours with their coevals and so enjoy a sweet revenge as the corrupters of youth' (p. 101).
24 K. Hunt, *Equivocal Feminists: The Social Democratic Federation and the Woman Question, 1884–1911* (Cambridge: Cambridge University Press, 1996), p. 82.
25 J. A. Symonds, *Memoirs*, ed. P. Grosskurth (1889; London: Hutchison, 1984).

1

The reach of the 'unco guid'

In 1858, the Registrar General for Scotland released a set of statistics detailing the rate of illegitimate births in Scotland. Part of a new, systematic surveillance of the population's reproductive practices, the figures prompted widespread consternation and collective soul-searching.[1] The 'truth' that had been 'brought before the country' was that 9.7 per cent of births in Scotland were illegitimate, comparing unfavourably to a rate of 6.4 per cent in England and just 3.8 per cent in Ireland.[2] Until that point, according to John M. Strachan, a doctor from Clackmannanshire, 'every Scotchman' had been 'convinced that his own country was the most moral on the face of the globe, and was proud of its superiority'.[3] Now, faced with such damning evidence to the contrary, a variety of explanations were forwarded, of varying plausibility. These included the general illiteracy and intemperance of the working classes, the dangerous commingling of young men and women at hiring markets, and the chemical composition of Scotland's oatmeal, which in Aberdeenshire allegedly contained 'a great deal of phosphorus' and therefore had 'a tendency to inflame the passions'.[4]

Similar convictions of Scotland's superior sexual mores were voiced throughout the nineteenth century often when the behaviour of its female citizens inconveniently and publicly called them into question. In an 1811–12 libel trial, two mistresses at an Edinburgh boarding school were accused of engaging in 'improper and criminal conduct', which included sharing a bed, lying on top of each other, and making a noise akin to 'putting one's finger into the neck of a wet bottle'.[5] However, when the case was reviewed, Lord Woodhouselee, Judge Advocate of Scotland, declared such an 'unnatural commerce' to be 'in this part of the world ... a thing unheard of, – a thing perhaps impossible', while there was real concern that no hint of the trial proceedings be made public and cause 'a general contamination of that innocence of thought which is a distinguished feature of the manners of our country'.[6] The impossibility of sexual vice by respectable Scottish women surfaced again in Edinburgh's High Court in the 1850s. When Madeleine Smith, the daughter of a prominent Glasgow architect, was tried in 1857 for the murder of her lover Pierre Emile L'Angelier, the *Glasgow Herald* laid the blame for their premarital sexual liaison firmly at Emile's door, claiming Madeleine 'fell into the snare planted for her by a vain and boastful braggart' and demurring 'we know not what arts may have been employed to lead her away from the paths of innocence'.[7] In both trials, the reputation of the women accused, and by default of the Scots nation, was preserved by displacing the erotic onto an overtly sexualised, racial 'other': in 1811–12, blame was laid upon the 'tainted imagination' of Jane Cumming, the biracial Indian-born student who had first made the accusations of impropriety against the schoolmistresses;[8] in 1857, it was Madeleine's 'French' lover Emile who was identified by the *Herald* as the source of contagion:

> Though his arts may never be known, it would be of vast importance to ascertain, if it were possible, how much he had acquired of the vile knowledge to effect seduction which is so extensively diffused and put in practice in France. This is no place to enter into details regarding the hideous pollution which is so rife in France, and which has deeply eaten into the moral and social life of Frenchmen. L'Angelier was of French extraction, if not French by birth, and his mind received its first ideas of life and manners in Jersey, which is almost a French colony.[9]

Scotland's claim to moral rectitude as a distinctive national characteristic originated in a particular understanding of its religious heritage. The stark Calvinism instituted by the Scottish Reformation was believed to have lodged a number of characteristics deep within the national psyche. They included an overt attachment to the notion of respectability, an emotional reserve or 'dourness' of manner, and a prudishness over sex, qualities still recognised in the nineteenth century. The biologist John Arthur Thomson, raised in the village of Saltoun in East Lothian during the 1860s and 1870s, described himself as being 'born stiff', while the Leith colourist John Duncan Fergusson wrote with frustration that 'Calvinism has produced a state of mind in Scotland that makes the Scots artist afraid to paint a nude and the Scots buyer afraid to hang one on his wall'.[10] Edinburgh, the 'professional' rival to the 'industrial' city of Glasgow, was by this period home to numerous legal, religious, educational and medical institutions, and was seen as a particular enclave of the 'unco guid', the religiously righteous members of the respectable, urban bourgeoisie. Patrick Geddes railed against the city's 'dull prosperity' and 'soul-deep hypocrisy', while the London man of letters Israel Zangwill was similarly disdainful towards the 'frigid society of Edina', residents of a 'cold and stately' city.[11] Indeed, such stereotypes have proved remarkably enduring, the poet Alastair Reid finding on a visit to Edinburgh in 1968 'The shadow of Calvinism' still lying 'heavy on the land', 'frowning on pleasure, making a barren waste of Sunday, and insisting that life is something to be endured rather than enjoyed'.[12]

Yet, as Callum Brown has noted, this stereotype requires interrogation, not least because during the Victorian period, the austerity and rigorous discipline associated with Calvinism was in decline.[13] Evangelicalism, while no less fervent, was more forgiving and joyful in its doctrines and practice, eschewing hell-fire preaching and beliefs in predestination and an Elect in favour of an Armenian interpretation of atonement and free will, along with shorter sermons, upbeat hymns and an individual commitment to evangelise.[14] This manifested within the urban middle class in an explosion of religious voluntary organisations and publications, with in 1890 over 10,000 Sunday-school teachers in Glasgow alone.[15] Yet if we accept that the 'Calvinist Scot' should be replaced as a representation of national religiosity with the figure of the 'evangelical Scot', this by no means diminishes the degree to which Protestant values permeated people's public and private lives. Despite the constant anxieties voiced by clergymen over the increasingly 'heathen' tendencies of the working classes, Thomas Chalmers railing against the 'deep and dense irreligion' which had 'stolen imperceptibly on the great bulk of our plebeian families', secularisation was neither an inevitable nor a demonstrable consequence of industrialisation and urbanisation.[16] Figures for religious adherence for the period 1880 to 1914 show no appreciable decline, with numbers peaking in 1905, when 50.5 per cent of Scotland's population was affiliated to a church.[17] Religious leaders continued to dominate public discourse on subjects such as housing, temperance and sanitation, with many clergymen and Kirk elders elected to the secular civic bodies formed to administrate the new welfare and educational reforms, such as the School Boards and Town Councils.[18] Furthermore, the oral testimonies of those who were children during the late Victorian and Edwardian era consistently recall their early lives as being 'all religion', with repeated church attendance on Sundays and weekday evenings and participation in organisations such as the Boys' Brigade and the Band of Hope structuring their social and spiritual lives.[19]

An especial focus of Scotland's evangelical zeal was the regulation of sex. The rapidity of the nation's urbanisation, the rate of which exceeded any other European country, encouraged a perception that its towns and cities were hotbeds of immorality, despite evidence that illegitimacy was more prevalent in rural areas.[20] Disciplining the intimate and reproductive lives of the displaced, city-dwelling 'heathen masses' became a national imperative, with the Kirk working through a multitude of local and national state and voluntary agencies to create a formidable 'regime of truth' around the gendered body and its desires.[21] This regime was closely aligned with legal, cultural, medical and scientific discourses also circulating within Scotland, embedding a powerful set of norms structuring and delimiting Scots people's understanding and experience of intimacy. This chapter traces the operation of such norms within four discrete yet inter-relational aspects of sexual behaviour – marriage, illegitimacy, prostitution and same-sex relations – paying particular attention to their gendered aspect. As the trials of both the Edinburgh schoolmistresses and Madeleine Smith indicate, during this period women became the pre-eminent carriers of Scottish national morality, due to evangelical understandings of female piety and chastity, while both patriarchy and the sexual double standard tacitly legitimated a range of men's sexual behaviours outwith the bourgeois code of masculinity.

Marriage

For almost all influential constituents within nineteenth-century Scottish society, from Kirk elders to social purity feminists, the institution which underpinned national morality and the stability of the social fabric was marriage. Defined within Scots law as a consensual, lifelong civil contract between a man and a woman, declared before witnesses, it was only within marriage and for reproductive purposes that sex was considered permissible and moral, and with primogeniture it safeguarded familial property within legitimate, male bloodlines.[22] Virtually all other configurations of intimate relations, including premarital sex, adultery, incest, bigamy and sodomy, were subject to a range of legal, religious and societal injunctions, ranging from the repentance stool at a Kirk session to transportation. As well as being sanctioned by marriage, sex was also an important right and requirement of it. Non-consummation of the matrimonial union, either through the wife's 'frigidity and dislike to connection' or either party's impotence, constituted valid grounds for annulment, while according to a common law rule laid down by Baron David Hume in 1797, sexual consent was assumed upon wedlock, making it impossible for a husband to rape his wife, a judgment not overturned in Scotland until 1989.[23]

Yet despite the centrality of matrimony in the Scottish state's administration of the sexual and reproductive lives of its citizens, compared to

England its laws were relatively liberal. This can be seen in two discrete aspects. First, while south of the border the 1753 Hardwick Act had enforced a stringent set of requirements on the form a marriage could take, which included the reading of banns, a church ceremony conducted by an Anglican celebrant, and parental consent for couples under the age of twenty-one, this legislation did not extend to Scotland.[24] Instead, canon law continued to hold sway, with both regular and irregular forms of matrimony considered legitimate. This meant that in addition to a regular marriage officiated by a Christian minister, either in church or at home, marriage in Scotland could also take place by declaration (*per verba de praesenti*), in which mutual consent was given in verbal or written form; by promise (*per verba de futuro subsequente copula*), in which betrothal was followed by consensual sex; and by cohabitation with habit and repute, in which a couple lived openly and continuously together as husband and wife.[25]

The ambiguity of such arrangements rendered irregular marriage the subject of repeated criticism, with some complaining of 'copious elements of doubt and uncertainty'.[26] Calls for its abolition became particularly acute on two occasions: in the 1830s and 1840s, with the tendering of numerous bills in an attempt to institute civil registration, four of which also contained amendments to marriage law; and in 1865–68, with the appointment of a Royal Commission on marriage to examine the execution of the law in Scotland, England and Ireland.[27] In both instances, however, reform was rejected, due in part to the ambivalence of the Presbyterian churches. Where one might have anticipated objections to the lack of a public church service and the moral difficulties this engendered, instead the churches took a more pragmatic view. Irregular marriage, they argued, allowed them to 'remedy many of the evils resulting from illicit connection between the sexes', for example by forcing a man to acknowledge his betrothed as his lawful wife, or legitimating children who were conceived prior to marriage, and as such was 'favourable to morality and good order'.[28] More cynically, by what Kenneth Boyd terms 'entering into collusion with sinners', the churches could create the appearance, at least, that they remained in control of their parishioners' sexual behaviour, even if the reality was increasingly somewhat different.[29]

The second liberal aspect of Scots law relates to access to divorce. In England, divorce for the vast majority of people did not become possible until the 1857 Matrimonial Causes Act, while in Scotland it had been on the statute books since the 1560 Reformation. Furthermore, while the 1857 English act codified the sexual double standard, allowing husbands to divorce solely on the grounds of adultery but requiring wives to provide further justification, in Scotland, no such contradiction existed. In numerous other ways, however, both the framing and application of Scots law entrenched existing patriarchal inequalities. The condition of coverture meant that, when married, a woman forfeited her independent legal status, becoming effectively 'in a state of wardship or minority under her husband': he was entitled to her heritable and earned property and their children became legally his charges, while the wife lost almost all contractual capacity and relinquished her freedom of movement, being required to live in his house.[30] It was within this context that the Scots-born novelist Margaret Oliphant declared in 1856 that 'marriage is like dying – as distinct, as irrevocable, as complete'.[31] In addition, even though wives may theoretically have been able to divorce when their husbands were adulterous, in practice few did so, preferring to turn a blind eye to indiscretions rather than face economic precarity and the break-up of the family, with only 32 per cent of adultery cases heard at the Court of Session between 1840 and 1880 filed by women.[32] A number of these discriminatory aspects were mitigated to a degree by legislative changes in the second half of the nineteenth century, brought about in part by feminist campaigns, with the *jus mariti*, or wife's automatic loss of property, effectively abolished by 1881; nonetheless, the superiority of the husband in law remained intact.[33]

Patriarchy's tenacity in informing the legal construction of marriage was mirrored by its continued purchase on how it was experienced as an affective relationship. While the longer-term shift from marriage as a primarily economic union to a companionate and romantic one undoubtedly heightened expectations of emotional intimacy and a more egalitarian domestic politics, the fundamentally patriarchal nature of marriage remained. As Katie Barclay has shown with regard to Scottish elite couples, the era's 'new models of loving' tended to identify men as the protagonists and women as the passive and chaste recipients of their attentions; while they may have offered a degree of 'democratic potential', allowing women to destabilise 'lines of power' and open up spaces for negotiations, it was, Barclay asserts, precisely these negotiations that ensured patriarchy's survival, by allowing people to 'relieve tensions and reconcile new experiences with patriarchal values'.[34] Furthermore, while expectations of companionship may have tempered the operation of male authority within the home, obedience was still cited as an important quality in wives. Presbyterian literature emphasised Eve's responsibility for the Fall of humankind as necessitating female subjection, the *Christian Journal* stating in 1840: 'Had [woman] kept her proper place, and been guided by man, instead of attempting to guide him, the great disaster would not have befallen our race.'[35] Memoirs of working- and middle-class Scots contain references to the nineteenth century being a period in which female deference was expected, Fraserburgh fisherwoman Christian Watt recollecting how women 'foolishly believed they must obey their husbands', and Glasgow journalist John Bell that gentlemen still retained a 'lords of creation' air, while ladies were, or seemed to be, 'content to be second'.[36] Such views were buttressed by popular culture, including ballads, plays and music hall 'turns', in which the loss of male authority within marriage was satirised in the comedic figure of the hen-pecked husband. One example from Scotland's theatrical trade press indicates the ubiquity of the trope in everyday humour. When male impersonator Miss Bessie Arthur came on stage at a hall in Bridgeton in the East End of Glasgow in 1888, a couple were overheard commenting on her gender presentation: "'That's a man," said a lady sitting next to me. "I thocht the chairman said a woman." "So it is a woman" replied her husband," "But she's married ye ken, and is wearing the breeks."'[37]

That said, by the late Victorian period, men's behaviour within marriage was undoubtedly the subject of increased scrutiny, from both feminists and the wider public; however, evidence suggests that this had little tangible impact on behaviour.[38] Mona Caird's article, 'Marriage', in the *Westminster Review* in August 1888, in which she declared matrimony a 'vexatious failure' and laid bare an ignominious history of husbands' abuses of power, prompted the *Daily Telegraph* to ask its readers, 'Is marriage a failure?', a question which attracted over 27,000 replies. The 'Great Marriage Debate' resonated in Scotland, Caird's article causing disquiet in the letters page of the *Glasgow Herald*. One correspondent voiced the 'alarm and apprehension' felt by all 'thoughtful men and women' at such an attack on domesticity, while another reflected that Caird's proposals for divorce reform were 'far from being the ideas of a mind afire with love for Jesus'.[39]

Resistance to feminist critiques of male marital behaviour in Scotland can also be seen in the response to domestic violence. According to research by Annmarie Hughes, wife-beating was legitimated by both the judiciary and press as a 'non-criminal' act, suggesting the continued relevance of traditional conceptions of manhood based on violence, workplace reputations and male sociability, alongside the new bourgeois masculine ideal, which espoused instead rationality, domesticity and marital companionship.[40] The 1857 Aggravated Assaults Act for the Prevention and Punishment of Assaults on Wives and Children was not adopted in Scotland, while an increasing number of cases involving 'wife-beating' were prosecuted in the Sherriff, Burgh and Police Courts, rather than the High Courts, limiting the penalties that could be exacted.[41] Provocation by a 'shrewish' or 'slatternly' wife was viewed as an extenuating circumstance, as was the consumption of alcohol, which was normalised as a predicable feature of working-class male culture. This can be seen in the case of Dennis Hickey, who received a two-month prison sentence in 1857 for throwing a kettle of boiling water over his wife; despite having previous convictions for wife-beating, the magistrate accepted his defence that 'when I'm drunk I don't know what I'm doing'.[42] Similarly, in 1871, when the *Scotsman* reported on the case of Daniel Briant, who had beaten his wife to 'within an inch of her life', the newspaper thought fit to ask 'has the wife anything to do with it? There can be no doubt that in many cases if the women managed better they would not fare so badly'.[43] As with patriarchal power more generally, such views were replicated and reinforced in popular culture. In the 1868 ballad 'The Chap That Married Hannah', in common with the male protagonists of numerous similar works, the husband rues the day he married his disobliging and intemperate wife. One evening, fed up and fuelled by Dutch courage, he attempts to reassert his patriarchal authority:

> I took an extra glass one night,
>   And made my mind up,
> That to her I'd show fight,
>   So went in for a wind-up.
> I threw my fists out so *(sparring attitude)*
>   In pugilistic manner;
> She gave me such a blow –
> SPOKEN – Yes, 'twas a regular nosender and no mistake –
> it very nigh settled –
>   The poor chap that married Hannah![44]

The companion discourse to patriarchy in the construction of nineteenth-century Scottish marriage was separate spheres. That husbands should act as breadwinners in an increasingly industrialised public world, while their wives fulfilled a complementary maternal role in the sequestered comforts of the home, was a message repeated so relentlessly it gained the status of common sense, rendering refutation difficult. Accorded a particular significance by evangelicalism, which foregrounded the importance of domestic piety, it harmonised with Enlightenment scientific and medical understandings of the male and female body as fundamentally opposite and incommensurable, and remained compelling throughout the century, an 1894 marriage guide by the well-known author Annie S. Swan warning wives of the serious marital discord that might result from 'ignorance of the prosaic details of housekeeping'.[45] In practice, the discourse was riven with contradictions: working-class women commonly earned a living in public sites such as mills, shops and factories, while the bourgeois home was as much a place of business transactions and status affirmation as a sanctuary from the commercial world. Furthermore, as the century progressed, women increasingly mobilised assumptions about their innate altruism to legitimise their philanthropic, temperance and political work, effectively carving out what Megan Smitley has termed a 'feminine public sphere'.[46] The maintenance of separate spheres was also not without its critics, with the Glasgow poet Marion Bernstein an early feminist voice puncturing the presumption of husbands who wished their wives to 'Be a cheerful companion, whenever desired, / And contentedly toil day and night, if required.'[47]

Despite such inconsistencies, however, the boundary between the two spheres nonetheless required policing, either by wider society or by the women themselves. An obvious and perennial target of censure was the mill girl, whose working life and public demeanour constituted a clear transgression of gender roles, the 'frowsy-haired' and 'bare armed' female jute spinners in the 'woman's town' of Dundee criticised for publicly 'promenading', 'gossiping' and engaging in 'indecent' behaviour with members of the opposite sex.[48] Regulating the femininity of Scotland's legions of middle-class female home missionaries was a more intricate task, which in Foucauldian terms involved mediating in the process of self-formation whereby subjects internalise the disciplinary gaze, performing a variety of operations on their 'own bodies, on their own souls, on their own thoughts, on their own conduct'.[49] More specifically, as an 1844 article in the *Free Church Magazine* titled 'Female methods of usefulness' indicates, it entailed schooling women in the exacting process of emotional self-disciplining, including inculcating an awareness that their actions were to be motivated not by unseemly agency, but rather pious obedience:

> Zeal and activity are, in their own places, excellent and essential qualities; but Christian women require to be very cautious, lest, even in the midst of praiseworthy exertions, they sacrifice those meek and lowly tempers which are so calculated to adorn and promote the cause they love and advocate. Female influence should shed its rays on every circle, but these ought to be felt, rather in their softening effects, than seen by their brilliancy. There are certain duties which sometimes call Christian women out of their quiet domestic circle, where both taste and feeling conspire to make them love to linger; such duties will, we humbly think, be best performed by those who enter this enlarged field, not from any desire of a more public sphere, but because, in obedience to the precepts of their divine Lord, the hungry are to be fed, the sick comforted, the prisoners visited.[50]

It is clear then, that the reach of Scotland's religious, judicial, press and popular prescriptions on marital relations was considerable, extending to numerous aspects of couples' affective, everyday, domestic and working lives. On the practical details of the constitution of their sexual lives, however, the regulatory discourses of bio-power fell silent. Reformed religion taught that conjugal sex should be potentially reproductive, as a fulfilment of the injunction in Genesis to 'increase and multiply': to that end, any use of 'artificial checks to conception', or birth control, was deemed immoral, in that it enabled 'persons to have sexual intercourse and not to have that which in the order of Providence is the natural result of that sexual intercourse'.[51] Beyond that, however, while cautionary tales abounded of the consequences awaiting those who engaged in forbidden sexual acts, any discussion of the productive forms desire *could* take were the subject of a strict taboo and spoken of only in euphemism, if at all. As Simon Szreter notes, this 'withdrawal from usage of the signifying words and linguistic resources' of sex engendered a widespread ignorance of and embarrassment over its mechanics, a public and private inarticulacy which according to Hera Cook reached its apotheosis by the end of the nineteenth century and which necessarily had delimiting effects on people's experience and enjoyment of sexual intimacy.[52]

The ministrations of Mrs Grundy were felt particularly acutely by middle-class young women, who due to societal expectations of female sexual innocence and chastity were often kept unenlightened on the basic facts of sexual intercourse until marriage, the honeymoon then occasioning a profound sense of shock. Indeed, the Banffshire-born feminist Dr Alice Ker, in an 1891 guide to motherhood, referred to cases 'where ignorance has caused the greatest misery and distress', arguing that failing to explain 'the duties of matrimony' to young women was an act of 'great cruelty'.[53] It also ensured that any acts of sexual abuse or violence were effectively silenced. While religious teachings enjoined men to exert sexual self-control – the *British Messenger*, a newspaper produced by the Stirling-based Drummond Tract Enterprise, arguing in 1878 that 'to be a true and real man, we must keep the "body in subjection", put a rein upon the appetites, and a bridle on the passions' – other normative discourses of manhood contradicted this dictate. The more libertine, pleasure-inclined male members of the bourgeoisie, along with young, single men of all classes, ascribed to what Michael Mason has termed 'classic moralism', an uninterrogated set of 'inherited beliefs' which assumed the irrepressible potency of innate male sexuality, a view accorded new legitimacy in the nineteenth century by a range of popular medically-informed texts.[54] In a marriage manual in circulation in Scotland in 1900 and advertised in both the *Scotsman* and the *Christian Leader*, the author, Lyman Beecher Sperry, an American lecturer on 'sanitary science', stated what 'All well informed men' knew, that 'normal, adult males, almost without exception, have strong sexual appetites', while only a minority of women were 'naturally as amorous and as responsive in sexual passion as the average man'.[55] This sexual double standard allowed men not only privileged access to illicit forms of sexual behaviour, such as premarital, adulterous and commercial sex, but to alternative modes of speaking, conceptualising and fantasising about sex, present in pornography and classical Greek and Roman literature, and in the crude humour of male sociability, performed in the gender-segregated worlds of public schools, the armed forces, gentlemen's clubs and certain music halls.

Illicit sex

Marriage then, constituted the centrepiece of Scotland's regulatory discourses on sex: a divinely sanctioned, legally constructed institution which ensured the continuance of monogamy, helped to contain dangerously unbounded sexual desires, and upheld patriarchy, despite a relatively liberal legal framework and shifting expectations of conjugal companionship and the behaviour of husbands. In a country experiencing rapid social change, and in which moral rectitude was perceived as an inherited element of national identity, defending marriage became an imperative. Threats to its dominion were legion and included a disproportionately high incidence of illegitimacy, the 'Great Social Evil' of prostitution, and the 'unspeakable' crime of sodomy. Anxiety over their purported increase periodically erupted into moral panics, with metaphors of contagion deployed to promote fear and reassert social boundaries and normative behaviours.[56] The instigators of such panics were the 'unco guid', whose sense of class differentiation and concomitant authority rested on 'its most vulnerable and therefore most urgently defended point', its sexual code.[57] Reinscribing this differentiation necessitated apportioning blame for the spread of moral disease not on the men from all classes who paid for sex, or on the capitalist practices which had disrupted proletarian courtship patterns, but on the individual, spiritual failings of Scotland's working classes and, more particularly, its women.[58]

Perceptions of an alarming rise in sexual deviance were accompanied by a shift in the mechanisms employed to discipline it. Since the Reformation, the 'sins of the flesh' had been policed in the localised setting of the Kirk session, a church court comprising a parish minister and group of male elders, elected from the local elite, who together investigated sinners, administered fines and enforced public repentance. By the early nineteenth century, however, the efficacy and appropriateness of the session was increasingly called into question, especially in urban areas. In 1811, lawyer William Aiton criticised the Ayrshire clergymen who 'render themselves unhappy, and disturb the peace of their parishioners, by hunting after scandal themselves and employing ten or a dozen of officious elders to assist them in that ridiculous research'.[59] Use of the infamous 'stool of repentance' was gradually superseded by private rebuke, or the expulsion of transgressors from the congregation, so that by 1850, 'Kirk-session justice had lost much of its original role'.[60] In its stead, the urban bourgeoisie, energised by the evangelical call to action, developed a far more expansive, diffuse and in many ways insidious disciplinary regime designed to redeem sinners and mitigate the encroaching moral dissipation. Following Thomas Chalmers's 'aggressive system' of home missionary work, male and female agents were despatched in their thousands to the 'streets, wynds and dens' of Scotland's cities, part of a steady stream of philanthropists who 'went slumming to see for themselves how the poor lived', exercising the 'traditional prerogatives of the privileged urban spectator to act ... as *flaneur*, to stroll across the divided spaces of the metropolis'.[61] There they surveilled working-class people's sexual lives, 'discovered' their 'immorality', and instigated a panoply of lay and religious voluntary organisations and initiatives designed to modify the behaviour of transgressors. In their endeavours, which ranged from Magdalene asylums, mill girls' prayer groups and Sunday schools to the White Cross League, the Girls' Guildry and the Onward and Upward Association, evangelicals were aided by a close working relationship with civic government. As Brown notes, town councillors were invariably church elders, while religious organisations often turned to councils 'for enforcement of moral and religious laws'.[62] The 'polymorphous techniques of power' available to Scotland's evangelical agents of morality can be seen during an 1875 scandal over a risqué music hall act in Glasgow, when a concerned group of influential male citizens, including a wealthy shipping magnate, two directors of the City Mission and a member of the Glasgow School Board, were able to instigate a private meeting with the Lord Provost, mobilise the support of the *North British Daily Mail*, and deliver speeches on the evils of 'singing saloons' at a meeting of the Young Men's Society for Religious Improvement and at the annual soirée of a printing firm.[63]

As the reaction to the 1858 illegitimacy figures indicates, one focus for concern among the 'unco guid' was premarital sex. The revelation that rates were highest in rural areas punctured the myth that the countryside was a place of bucolic 'virtue' and that 'vice' was a singularly urban problem.[64] The ecclesiastical response was spearheaded by James Begg, a Free Church minister and urban *flâneur* who spent his holidays visiting city slums.[65] Within committees at the General Assembly and in the pages of the Free Church newspaper the *Witness*, Begg argued that the primary cause of the 'moral epidemic' of rural illegitimacy was bothies, a form of mixed-sexed farm accommodation.[66] Action was vital, he argued, to avoid an invasion of Scotland's urban areas, claiming that 'at this rate of 10,000 bastards a year, we shall in ten years have nearly 100,000 bastards, or a population of them equal to that of one of our largest cities; a result sufficiently startling, and well-fitted to alarm all classes of moral and social reformers'.[67] To such arguments were added concerns around accommodation shortages for farmworkers, which contracted opportunities for young couples seeking to form independent families, along with the realisation that courtship rituals were distinct from those in urban middle-class families. They included traditional practices such as 'fertility testing' and 'bundling', with investigators shocked to discover that such behaviour was condoned by parents, one commenting, 'I have heard many a mother of this kind say: "It's nae sae bad as stealing or deein' awa' with the puir craters"'.[68] Attempts were made to improve the morality of female farm servants, Lady Aberdeen presiding over the Onward and Upward Association, a 'social exercise in outreach education' in which servants were schooled by their mistresses on Bible history and embroidery, as well as the 'high and dignified' nature of domestic work.[69] However, despite cautionary tales in the association's magazine of girls who had run away to Aberdeen, lost their way and died tragically in childbirth, the 'mischievous craving for independence' continued to entice many to jobs in the towns and cities.[70]

The primary figure upon which moral reformers' anxieties alighted, however, was the female prostitute. Simultaneously evoking feelings of repugnance and sexual frisson, she was a highly visible character in Scotland's increasingly crowded urban landscape, commentators describing noisy, lit-up 'Triple Decker' brothels and open soliciting on the cities' main streets.[71] A walking violation of the bourgeois feminine norms of purity, passivity and domesticity, she was viewed as a constant source of temptation to middle-class sons, a dangerous pollutant of marriage and a threat to the health and stability of society, one of a 'multitudinous amazonian army' keeping the devil 'in constant field service' and making the 'stones seem alive with lust, and the very atmosphere ... tainted'.[72] When the first serious analyses of prostitution were conducted in the 1840s, attempts were made to quantify the danger sex work posed by estimating its prevalence. Their findings did not assuage people's fears, nor indeed were they intended to. Congregationalist minister Ralph Wardlaw, in a series of four lectures delivered to the great and the good of Glasgow in 1842, calculated that around 3,600 women were living on immoral earnings in the city, visited weekly by 36,000 men, statistics which corroborated those produced in 1840 for Edinburgh, evangelical doctor William Tait counting 800 prostitutes working full time, alongside 1,160 'sly' or 'secret' prostitutes selling sex to supplement low wages as domestic servants or seamstresses.[73] Exactly who the reformers counted is a matter of conjecture, however. For Wardlaw, any woman who engaged in 'illicit intercourse' was guilty of prostitution, a view supported by the surgeon of Glasgow's Lock Hospital, who stated that while only one in ten women admitted to the institution gave 'prostitute' as her occupation, 'in the vast majority of those cases the patients were prostitutes of one kind or another, that is to say that they were women consorting with more than one man'.[74] Suspicion could also fall on a young, working-class woman if she had no obvious occupation, was a mill girl or simply behaved immodestly in the street, an ambiguity manifest in an account of the 1863 Glasgow Fair, the observer finding the ground 'teeming with street girls, some of them might be mill-girls … many of them were successful in their attempts to lead lads and boys away with them … Saw 94 prostitutes, also a large number of very young girls like mill workers, scarcely distinguishable from prostitutes in their conduct'.[75]

The causes given for prostitution were multifarious. Economic factors were not ignored, Tait asserting that 'The most distressing causes … are those which arise from poverty – want of employment – and insufficient remuneration for needle and other kinds of work in which females are employed'.[76] However, the weddedness of Scotland's reformers to evangelical understandings of individual responsibility for one's own sin and salvation produced a persistent tension in their accounts between the role of environmental determinants and the women's own moral failings.[77] Clarity in their analyses was further compromised by a tendency to produce long inventories of secondary, contributing factors in young women's ruination, which were an expression more of the alienation felt by middle-class investigators towards working-class culture than any objective attempt to understand the complex mechanisms of causation.[78] For William Logan, a city missionary and seasoned midnight visitor to Glasgow's slums, these included 'obscene books, loose conversation … [and] fondness for dress' as well as Owenite socialism, the keeping of irregular hours and 'walking and visiting public gardens on Sabbath, theatres, and low exhibitions'.[79] It is unsurprising, therefore, given their class and religious outlook, that while evangelical reformers touched upon systemic social problems, such as the economic vulnerability of women under capitalism and their sexual exploitation within patriarchy, ultimately the solutions they proposed were concerned primarily with reasserting the bourgeois sexual code, which entailed identifying 'fallen' working-class women and restoring them to respectability.

For much of the century, these solutions remained piecemeal, voluntary and ameliorative. The first Magdalene home was opened in Edinburgh in 1797, intended 'not only as a place of refuge for [prostitutes] desirous of abandoning their vices, but as a school for training them to industry, to virtue, and to religion'.[80] Similar institutions followed in Glasgow, Aberdeen, Dundee and Greenock; by 1901 there were nine homes in Edinburgh alone. While they varied in size and in the services they provided, they shared certain key characteristics.[81] They were usually lay organisations, charitably funded, in which women fulfilled significant roles as committee members, fundraisers, matrons and supervisors. Attendance was voluntary, with inmates admitted after an interview and medical examination, with those chosen commonly in their late teens, neither pregnant nor suffering from a venereal disease, and who appeared submissive and genuinely contrite. However, the homes were often hard to leave, with women who 'escaped' fined for stealing uniforms and refused the letters of recommendation vital to gain future employment.[82] Inside the homes, a strict daily routine was imposed that comprised religious education and industrial training, often in laundries, designed to instil discipline, promote piety and provide the skills necessary for domestic service. The hope was that on their release back into society, the repentant 'magdalenes' would eschew their previous, deviant sexual behaviour and function instead as 'ideal working-class daughters, wives and mothers: sober, thrifty, chaste and humble Christian women'.[83]

From 1860, however, attitudes appeared to harden, with more interventionist strategies proposed. The Glasgow Magdalene Institution appointed a Repressive Committee, a group of influential, male social purity campaigners, intent on solving the 'great and growing' problem of solicitation.[84] In 1869, they lobbied the city's magistrates, demanding more stringent enforcement of the 1866 Police Act, under which brothels could be closed and prostitutes stopped at will by constables and fined forty shillings or imprisoned for fourteen days. Their demand was met immediately, Alexander McCall, Glasgow's new Chief Constable of Police, instituting a system of repression which Linda Mahood argues was more extreme than that imposed by the Contagious Diseases Acts, which applied only in England and Wales.[85] The number of brothels declined from 204 in 1870 to 22 in 1879, while fines, harassment, stigmatisation and prison sentences forced women off the streets and into the Magdalene homes.[86] Similar measures were adopted in Edinburgh as well as in Manchester and Leeds, and while McCall claimed them a success, in reality they merely forced the trade underground, female sex workers using parks, cabs and closes in less salubrious parts of the city in order to avoid attracting the attention of the police.[87]

While euphemism may have been employed to speak about prostitution, the 'Great Social Evil' was nonetheless discussed ad nauseam in nineteenth-century Scotland, with the regulation of sex work pursued with increasing vigour through a range of religious, medical and state discourses. By contrast, the 'unspeakable' crime of sodomy generated minimal public commentary and according to Lesley Hall was the subject of 'massive agnotological attempts to invisibilize it'.[88] Sodomy trials were not reported in the Scottish newspapers, while legal authorities consistently attempted to avoid such cases reaching the High Court by bailing suspects on the understanding that they would 'quit the country'.[89] This silence was due, argues Sean Brady, to the profound threat sodomy posed to the heteronormative foundations of patriarchal society: while men's recourse to female prostitutes accorded with medical understandings of male hypersexuality, men's sexual relations with men undermined them, destabilising normative masculinity.[90] Legal accounts of sodomy remained vague in Scots law until 1832, when Sir Archibald Alison provided a degree of clarification, describing the crime as entailing unnatural relations between two men during which penetration occurred, with proof of emission not required for a successful conviction.[91] This definition was expanded in 1885, with the introduction of the offence of gross indecency under the UK-wide Criminal Law Amendment Act, which effectively criminalised all forms of sexual contact between men. However, while the death penalty for sodomy remained on the statute in Scotland until 1887, twenty-six years later than in England and Wales, it was not used during the nineteenth century, with those convicted sentenced to either transportation or penal servitude.

The number of High Court trials for sodomy was relatively low, with a yearly average of six between 1839 and 1857, rising to twelve up until 1875.[92] Instead, the vast majority of cases involving male same-sex relations were pursued in the sheriff court as acts of 'public indecency', reflecting in part the injunction to silence and in part the general focus of regulatory attention on encounters in public and semi-public spaces.[93] Almost all men who faced charges were from working-class backgrounds, although as Jeff Meek has asserted, this is reflective not of a preponderance of homosexual behaviour within this social class but rather their restricted access to secure private spaces or the means to travel abroad in pursuit of sexual encounters.[94] While more research needs to be done, to date there is little evidence of the existence in Scotland for this period of gay subcultures, networks of male prostitutes or known cruising sites, with the first case of the use of public toilets as a homosexual meeting point, a feature of queer life elsewhere, not surfacing until 1895.[95] Instead, meetings between men seeking sex appear to have been primarily opportunistic, an illustrative example being the 1845 case of forty-year-old William Simpson, of no fixed residence, and Ralph Dodds, a twenty-three-year-old baker from Dunbar. Arrested in the early hours of the morning in Edinburgh's Old Town by a police officer investigating another matter, they were discovered 'in the act of connection' at the bottom of a common stairwell; while Simpson tried initially to claim they 'had a woman with us' and both that they were drunk, they eventually pled guilty to sodomy or its attempt and were sentenced to ten years' transportation.[96]

Within the middle classes, there exists some disparate evidence of individual men who engaged in same-sex relations, or at least wanted to. While Scotland's cities may not have hosted a decadent subculture comparable to that in London, Oscar Wilde was clearly a source of inspiration, the 'aesthetic mania' of the early 1880s spawning a brief and characteristically Glaswegian iteration, an 'aesthetic' football team who played in a strip of 'immense sunflowers'.[97] During the collapse of Wilde's libel trial in 1895 and his subsequent arrest for 'gross indecency', the Scottish press were universally censorious, the *Scotsman* commenting, 'It is scarcely possible to speak with patience of this creature. He has presented himself as the apostle of "culture." He has set himself up as almost the only man of taste in the country. And all the time he was a beast at heart.'[98]

The most conclusive evidence of male homosexuality, however, relates to members of the progressive social, political and esoteric networks that form the subject of this book. They not only enjoyed a degree of immunity from the censure of the 'unco guid' but had access to national and international currents of ideas and activism around sex, with visiting lecturers providing an important source of knowledge, contacts and companionship. It is telling, however, that on the occasions when same-sex intimate relationships did subsequently form, they took place outside of Scotland. This can be seen with the connections made by the visit in 1886 of socialist philosopher and sex writer Edward Carpenter. As Sheila Rowbotham notes, Carpenter 'played a pivotal role in the cultural networks of homogenic men', acting 'as an exemplar, a confidant, and helpmate'.[99] While in Edinburgh, he met Cecil Reddie, an erstwhile teacher at Fettes College, a private school, who had established a secret sex education society known as 'The Gild of the Laurels', and who with Carpenter's help went on to found a progressive boys' school in Derbyshire.[100] While there is no evidence that Reddie had any sexual relationships during his life, even Carpenter was nervous about the rumours over his 'boy-morals', with questions regarding his 'moral character' eventually precipitating two 'mutinies' by parents at his school, resulting by 1907 in the haemorrhaging of almost half its pupils.[101]

Carpenter also became friends during his 1886 visit with Bob Muirhead, a mathematician and member of the Glasgow Socialist League.[102] A young and clearly attractive Muirhead subsequently stayed with Carpenter at Millthorpe, his house near Sheffield, in 1889 and 1890 becoming entangled in a complex web of comradeship, sexual desire and love involving Carpenter, the New Woman writer Olive Schreiner, and the tailor, theosophist and aspiring poet James Brown, a fellow Glasgow socialist.[103] At one point, Muirhead and Schreiner developed 'tender feelings' for each other, although according to Carpenter they were 'quite apart from sexual'.[104] Their relationship made Brown jealous; he had been enjoying what Carpenter later described as a 'romance of affection' with Muirhead, Brown writing 'in a quake' at the thought of Muirhead going to Africa with Schreiner.[105] How he then reacted to the news that Muirhead and Carpenter had become lovers can only be imagined, in March 1890 Carpenter writing, with what must surely have been unjustified optimism, 'I hope you won't be jealous; but I don't think you are. It was good to have him ... He was very loving and good and we did not forget you.'[106] Three years later, however, Muirhead appears to have drawn a line under his youthful sexual experiences. In 1893 he married a middle-class Scotswoman named Linnie Hurndall; after a brief spot of 'matrimonial trouble', which saw him returning to Carpenter at Millthorpe, the couple settled in Glasgow, raising four children and remaining within progressive circles.[107]

If accounts of male same-sex relations in Scotland are sparse, evidence of sexual relations between women are further obscured in the historical record. This is in part because they were not subject to specific legal penalties in the way that male–male encounters were. On occasion, however, they did reach the courts, Lilian Faderman identifying twelve pre-1900 British court cases involving accusations of lesbianism, with at least two such trials taking place in Scotland.[108] The 1811–12 Woods–Pirie libel suit involving two Edinburgh schoolmistresses, with which this chapter began, reveals the 'central paradox of female same-sex sexuality in the European tradition': that it was known to exist yet simultaneously, and wilfully, denied.[109] Also paradoxical was the fact that anxieties over the behaviour of the women was exacerbated by contemporary society's acceptance of passionate, 'romantic friendships', the boundaries of which were worryingly vague. At the trial's review, the judge Lord Gillies rejected any suggestion that, based on the available evidence, the women had 'indecent carnal knowledge of each other', blustering, 'Are we to say that every woman who has formed an intimate friendship and has slept in the same bed with another is guilty? Where is the innocent woman in Scotland? – If any such is known to your Lordships, she is not known to me.'[110] A more emphatic line could be drawn between guilt and innocence when the sexual act involved vaginal penetration, a long-standing marker of sexual intercourse. This was the case in the second of the Scottish trials, which took place two centuries earlier. In 1649, Maud Galt was investigated by the Kilbarchan Kirk session after one of her servants, Agnes Mitchell, accused her of assaulting her with 'ane peice of clay formed be hir to the liknes of a mans priwie members'; even here, however, the issue appears to have been dropped, with no record of a commission for Galt's trial.[111] Beyond the court records, Scotland's archives hold numerous accounts of eighteenth- and nineteenth-century passionate female friendships, including between the Aberdeenshire gentlewomen Elyza Fraser and Mary Bristow, the pioneering doctor Sophia Jex-Blake and novelist Margaret Todd, and the Aberdeen poet Bessie Craigmyle and teacher Maggie Dale.[112] However, aside from Alison McCall's scholarship on Craigmyle, and that of Faderman, Geraldine Friedman and others on the Woods–Pirie trial, little detailed scholarship exists, with Scotland awaiting its historian of Victorian lesbianism.[113]

Alternative moralities and 'twilight moments'

The influence wielded by the 'unco guid' on the intimate lives of nineteenth-century Scots was considerable. The bourgeois sexual code, which had adapted to encompass evangelical understandings of individual moral responsibility and female sexual purity, was rigidly enforced through the upholding of marriage and the strict proscription of almost all other forms of intimacy. The enacting of this regulatory regime was possible due to the increasing, collective ability of the urban middle-class evangelists to dominate the national conversation in an expanding periodical, local and national press; inform local governmental interventions and initiatives; and disseminate their message through a multiform and pervasive associational culture. It is instructive that Cook cites 1900 as the year in which sexual restraint in Britain was at its height, the same period in which figures for church adherence in Scotland peaked.[114] Yet neither was the reach of the religiously respectable absolute. The sexual progressives analysed in subsequent chapters clearly rejected traditional 'truths' about the body, seeing the exposure of their contingency and proposal of radical new alternatives as a form of progressive political praxis. However, challenge did not rest solely with the era's bohemian intellectuals; neither did it necessarily take the form of a feminist column, a popular scientific treatise or a neo-Malthusian pamphlet. Accepting Foucault's understanding of bio-power as diffuse, fluid and operating at the micro level, resistance to this power can also occur in more mundane, localised and fleeting ways: in the raucous laughter of male clerks at a risqué joke in a Glasgow music hall; a fisherwoman's threat to expose an elder's brothel visits at the Fraserburgh Kirk session; or the promenading, gossiping and flirting of female jute spinners in the streets of Dundee. Such behaviours indicate the existence of alternative moralities in circulation within Scottish society, among 'marginal groups' or 'sexual minorities' who inhabited 'the grey area between the prescriptive ideal and the abject', such as rural farming and fishing communities, the unrespectable urban working class, and libertine bachelors.[115]

The working classes were not passive recipients of bourgeois sexual discourse, and had their own distinctive cultures of intimacy, which informed their ways of talking about, understanding and experiencing sex. These were not uniform but rather varied depending upon occupational group, local custom and material circumstances. In rural communities in northeast Scotland bridal pregnancy was endemic, with couples sharing a bed and having sex before marriage as an age-old form of 'fertility testing'.[116] This contrasts with courtship rituals in Shetland, which had the lowest illegitimacy rates in the country; here, sleeping together did not signify sexual intimacy or betrothal, but was rather reflective of the lack of opportunities to socialise and the inclement weather. George Slater, a Shetlander and retired seventy-five-year-old sea pilot, stated in 1894 that 'It has been the custom for hundreds of years for young men to visit young women at night without any harm being done. It is an old Norwegian or Danish custom. It is often done just for a lark.'[117] A related custom was 'barn bundling', whereby young guests at a country wedding would sleep together on the straw in the hosts' barn, with 'both statistics and the testimony of respectable persons who have taken part in them' witness to the fact that nothing 'immoral' occurred.[118] The sexual culture experienced by the Fraserburgh fisherwoman Christian Watt, born in 1833, was different again. While she had been taught as a child to cultivate 'purity in one's life and thoughts', her everyday encounters were influenced more by the need to mitigate the very real danger of sexual harassment and abuse.[119] When on the road she ensured she was accompanied by 'tinkies' or other fisherwomen and claimed she would not have hesitated to plunge her gutting knife 'into anybody who attempted to molest me'.[120] She employed similarly robust strategies while working as a servant, when she had to deflect the unwelcome advances of her male employers, Watt recounting an incident in which she had 'dug' her 'claws' into the face of one Captain Leslie Melville, costing him 'the skin of his nose', after he had embraced her while she was making the beds.[121] Illegitimacy she viewed not as a stain on her soul but rather a 'folly' to be avoided, arguing 'only the ignorant would put a stigma on any innocent child'.[122] Having learnt the facts of life from a washerwoman when employed in a laundry, when she first had sex it did not occasion the shock experienced by numerous middle-class women on their wedding night; rather, Watt represented it as the culmination of her falling in love with her future husband, describing how 'Life had given me its last and final hidden secret, a moment poets have all written about'.[123]

Alternative codes of sexual morality were also in circulation in Scotland's towns and cities. As Anna Clark notes, 'plebeians often valued other moral virtues more highly than chastity', with evidence from popular and radical culture in early nineteenth-century Glasgow indicating an absence of shame around sex, along with an acceptance of illegitimacy, as long as men fulfilled their financial responsibilities to their new families.[124] In a popular song about a poor unmarried mother, the protagonist Jenny Nettles admonishes the father Robin Rattle to 'Score out the blame, / And shun the shame, / And without mair debate o't / Take home your wain [wee one] / Make Jenny fain [glad] / The leel and leesome gate o't [loyal and lovable way of it].'[125] By the late Victorian period, these attitudes were to a degree reflected on stage in Scotland's music halls, the sexual innuendo integral to the songs and repartee of serio-comics constitutive of a sexual morality diametrically opposed to that of respectable society, as a regular patron of the halls explained in 1875: 'Seduction has many ways of being looked at, the extremes being society's way and the music hall way. Society frowns at it; the music hall laughs at it. Society looks upon it as detestable, and the seducer as a villain; the music hall treats it as a subject for jest, and the seducer as a hero and a conqueror.'[126]

However, acts which entailed female semi-nudity and suggestive dancing, such as burlesque, the 'ballet' and the notorious can-can, and which found an appreciative audience among the city's male clerks, 'mashers', warehouse workers, students and West End voyeurs, can also be read as one example of a libertine culture in which women were not consenting participants in an alternative morality, but rather sexualised commodities staged for male consumption. One 'habitué' of Glasgow's 'singing saloons' was clear that this was the primary draw of the halls, commenting, 'What do we go to the music hall for? for the music! Bless you, no ... It is the ballet we go to see. Not the dancing and tripping and fine attitudes, unless they are of a certain kind: but it is to see the lovely symmetry of the female form; and the more "spiritedly" this is shown, the ballet is all the better and more enticing.'[127] Reports of routine incidents of sexual harassment backstage consolidate the impression of music halls perpetuating a dynamic of sexual antagonism, present from at least the late eighteenth century, between irresponsible, misogynistic young, working-class men and sexually vulnerable young women, a dynamic which Clark argues 'fissured plebeian culture from within.'[128]

Middle-class culture was similarly riven by the sexual double standard. Men visited brothels, kept mistresses, viewed pornography and went to see risqué acts at music halls, while maintaining their position in respectable society. Their behaviour was not condoned, given its flagrant disregard of the bourgeois norms of marital monogamy and sexual self-control, but was instead what Clark has termed 'twilight moments', 'those sexual practices and desires that societies prohibit by law or custom but that people pursue anyhow, whether in secret or an open secret', and did not result in the men's permanent expulsion from society.[129] This was due partly to the medically sanctioned assumption of male hypersexuality, but also to the power structures of patriarchy, with the bourgeois male clientele of plebeian female sex workers complicit in the maintenance of male dominance, rather than challenging its foundations.[130] Bourgeois women, however, were not afforded such latitude. A momentary yielding to adulterous desire, an inappropriate youthful love affair or, much more disturbingly, an incident of rape could result in lifelong stigmatisation, including expulsion from respectability and even incarceration. Among the women living at the Edinburgh Magdalene Asylum in the early 1830s was 'E. H.', who was 'respectably connected, and had received a liberal education' but who had had sex before marriage, compounding her disgrace by behaving with unfeminine ingratitude towards those who had endeavoured to help her, although what that 'help' entailed the Asylum's directors do not make clear in their report.[131] That said, resourceful women who faced social approbation could carve out alternative futures for themselves, if able to find more conducive, less judgemental communities in which to settle. Madeleine Smith is a case in point. During her trial for the murder of her upper-working-class lover L'Angelier, seventy-seven of her love letters were read out in court, her explicit, epistolary accounts telling of her instigation and enjoyment of their illicit sexual encounters. News of her transgressions were circulated to rapt households across Britain and Europe, with even Parisians reportedly taking a great interest in the 'Glasgow Poisoning

Case'.[132] Yet after the 'not proven' verdict, Smith's life continued, after a brief stay at the Devonport vicarage of a couple running a home for 'fallen women', marrying a drawing master called George Wardle with whom she had two children.[133] The couple set up home in Bloomsbury Place in London, becoming part of an artistic, literary and later socialist set which included William Morris, Dante Gabriel Rossetti and Edward Burne-Jones, and among whom her past was an open secret. As Henry James noted, despite her very public breach of sexual proprieties, Madeleine Smith 'precisely *didn't* squalidly suffer', but thrived, as other 'fallen' middle-class women in nineteenth-century Scotland must surely have done.[134]

What united almost all of those who subscribed to alternative moralities, across the social spectrum, was a dislike of the 'unco guid'. Criticisms centred around their humourlessness, their self-righteousness and their hypocrisy. The *Bailie*, a weekly satirical journal published in Glasgow, derided 'respectable Glasgow', representing the young men among them as 'disagreeable prigs' who preferred Shakespeare, sober attire and the Young Men's Christian Association to the pleasures of smoking, music halls and dressing fashionably.[135] Similar opinions were voiced in the *Stage News*, a short-lived theatrical newspaper, which parodied ministers in the form of 'The Reverend Samuel McMeekly of St Vinegar's', who on a Sunday enjoined his congregation to give freely to causes which aided 'moral well-being', while on a Monday instructed his 'man of business' to invest his spare income in breweries, distilleries and music halls, while being careful to omit 'Reverend' from the papers.[136] Elders were the subject of particular scorn. Robert Burns's 'Holy Willie's Prayer' (1785) is an early example of the satire of an elder who excuses his fornication as a trial from God, 'Lest he o'er high and proud shou'd turn, 'Cause he's sae *gifted*', while continuing to bear down with zeal on those who drank, swore, sang and danced.[137] Inspired by William Fisher, a farmer and elder of Mauchline Kirk, some seventy years later, the hypocrisy of elders continued to exercise the ire of parishioners. In 1858 Christian Watt planned to wreck the Fraserburgh Kirk session, if summoned before them for having an illegitimate child, by publicly exposing the elders' duplicity, starting with 'a Fraserburgh business man who had in the past been known to frequent bawdy houses in Aberdeen'.[138]

It was precisely such examples of sanctimoniousness that also exercised the subjects of this book. While both middle- and working-class libertines proffered their critiques of respectability in satirical and trade journals, and alternative codes of morality were lived in fishing, farming and urban proletarian communities in Scotland, the sexual progressives of the radical middle classes tendered a different proposition again. Often already involved in reforming organisations and subcultures, while also disengaged from the beliefs and practices of orthodox Christianity, their rebellion against the 'unco guid' was a more considered and purposeful act. Informed by feminist and socialist thought, they sought to institute a holistic new ethical code or envisage a utopian 'new life' guided by higher standards of morality and gender equality. In each instance, the influences on their thought were eclectic and diverse, reflecting their familial backgrounds, friendship groups and social identities and producing in turn a markedly different iteration of sexually radical thought. It is to the first of these progressive couples that we now turn, examining their very particular melding of ethical socialism, feminism and American sexual mysticism.

Notes

1 The first illegitimacy figures were published in 1855, with the advent of the civil registration of births, marriages and deaths. J. A. D. Blaikie, 'The country and the city: sexuality and social class in Victorian Scotland', in G. Kearns and C. W. J. Withers (eds), *Urbanising Britain: Essays on Class and Community in the Nineteenth Century* (Cambridge: Cambridge University Press, 1991), p. 81.
2 J. M. Strachan, 'Immorality of Scotland', *Scotsman*, 20 May 1870, p. 6.
3 Ibid.
4 An 1870 Royal Commission, quoted in Blaikie, 'The country and the city', p. 86.
5 Trial transcripts, edited and reprinted in L. Faderman, *Scotch Verdict: Miss Pirie and Miss Woods v. Dame Cumming Gordon* (New York: Columbia University Press, 1993), p. 147.
6 Faderman, *Scotch Verdict*, pp. 273, 63.
7 *Glasgow Herald*, 10 July 1857.
8 Faderman, *Scotch Verdict*, p. 273.
9 *Glasgow Herald*, 10 July 1857.
10 Letter from John Arthur Thomson to Patrick Geddes, 10 August 1886, Geddes Papers, NLS, MS 10555, fols 48–9. Quoted in S. Reynolds, *Paris–Edinburgh: Cultural Connections in the Belle Epoque* (Aldershot: Ashgate, 2007), p. 73.
11 P. Geddes, 'The Scots renascence', *Evergreen* (Spring 1895), p. 133; I. Zangwill, 'Without prejudice', *Pall Mall Magazine*, 8:34 (February 1896), p. 329.
12 A. Little, 'The poet who summed up Scotland', in *ScotBuzz*, http://scot-buzz.co.uk/the-poet-who-summed-up-scotland-by-allan-little/ (accessed 11 January 2019).
13 C. G. Brown, *Religion and Society in Scotland since 1707* (Edinburgh: Edinburgh University Press, 1997), p. 187.
14 Brown, *Religion and Society*, p. 117.
15 Ibid., p. 104.
16 T. Chalmers, *The Right Ecclesiastical Economy of a Large Town* (Edinburgh, 1835), p. 21, quoted in Brown, *Religion and Society*, p. 5.

17 Brown, *Religion and Society*, pp. 62–4. See also C. G. Brown, *The Death of Christian Britain: Understanding Secularisation, 1800–2000*, 2nd edn (London: Routledge, 2009).
18 T. M. Devine, *The Scottish Nation: 1700–2000* (London: Penguin, 1999), pp. 364–7.
19 Brown, *Religion and Society*, p. 149.
20 Ibid., p. 96.
21 M. Foucault, *Discipline and Punish. The Birth of the Prison*, trans. A. Sheridan (New York: Vintage Books, 1977), p. 23.
22 F. P. Walton, *A handbook of husband and wife according to the law of Scotland* (Edinburgh: William Green, 1893), p. 1.
23 Ibid., pp. 2–4, 283–4; R. S. Shields, 'Marital rape in Scots law: a further case of interest', *Journal of the Forensic Science Society*, 30:3 (May 1990), pp. 131–4.
24 K. M. Boyd, *Scottish Church Attitudes to Sex, Marriage and the Family, 1850–1914* (Edinburgh: John Donald, 1980), p. 50.
25 E. Gordon, 'Irregular marriage and cohabitation in Scotland, 1855–1939: official policy and popular practice', *The Historical Journal*, 58:4 (2015), p. 1061.
26 Parliamentary Papers, 1868: Royal Commission on the Law of Marriage [RCLM], p. xxi, cited in Boyd, *Scottish Church Attitudes*, p. 53.
27 B. Dempsey, 'Making the Gretna blacksmith redundant: who worried, who spoke, who was heard on the abolition of irregular marriage in Scotland?', *The Journal of Legal History*, 30:1 (2009), p. 27; A. Cameron, 'The establishment of civil registration in Scotland', *The Historical Journal*, 50:2 (June 2007), p. 379.
28 RCLM, evidence of George Dalziel, General Assembly of the Free Church of Scotland, p. 43, cited in Gordon, 'Irregular marriage', p. 1063.
29 Boyd, *Scottish Church Attitudes*, p. 59
30 E. M. Clive, *The Law of Husband and Wife in Scotland*, 2nd edn (Edinburgh, 1982), p. 11, quoted in M. L. Butler, '"Husbands without wives, and wives without husbands": divorce and separation in Scotland, c. 1830–1890' (PhD thesis, University of Glasgow, 2014), p. 29.
31 'The Laws Concerning Women', *Blackwood's Edinburgh Magazine*, 79:486 (April 1856), p. 380.
32 This is from a sample of seventy cases. Butler, 'Husbands without wives', p. 91.
33 The Conjugal Rights Act of 1861, among other provisions, allowed a wife to request custody of her young children during a divorce or separation trial; the Married Women's Property (Scotland) Acts of 1878 and 1881 protected women's earned and inherited property from their husbands.
34 K. Barclay, *Love, Intimacy and Power: Marriage and Patriarchy in Scotland, 1650–1850* (Manchester: Manchester University Press, 2011), pp. 203–4.
35 *Christian Journal* (1840), p. 10, quoted in L. Orr Macdonald, *A Unique and Glorious Mission: Women and Presbyterianism in Scotland, 1830–1930* (Edinburgh: John Donald, 2000), p. 25.
36 *The Christian Watt Papers*, ed. D. Fraser (Edinburgh: Berlinn, 1988), p. 115; J. J. Bell, *I Remember* (Edinburgh: The Porpoise Press, 1932), pp. 114–15.
37 'A Comic Night at the Bridgeton Bursts', *Barr's Monthly Professional and Author's Journal*, 3 November 1888.
38 A. J. Hammerton, *Cruelty and Companionship: Conflict in Nineteenth-Century Married Life* (London: Routledge, 1992, 1995), p. 7.

39 Letter from D. G. Hoey, 'The future of matrimony', *Glasgow Herald*, 21 August 1888; letter from D. Melville Stewart, 'The marriage question', *Glasgow Herald*, 4 September 1888.
40 A. Hughes, 'The "non-criminal" class: wife-beating in Scotland, c. 1800–1949', *Crime, History & Societies*, 14:2 (2010), pp. 31–53.
41 Hughes, 'The "non-criminal" class', p. 36.
42 *Caledonian Mercury*, 5 May 1857, in Hughes, 'The "non-criminal" class', p. 40.
43 *Scotsman*, 13 October 1871, in Hughes, 'The "non-criminal" class', p. 41.
44 'The Chap That Married Hannah' (Glasgow: The Poet's Box, 1868), Bod10227, Broadside Ballads Online, http://ballads.bodleian.ox.ac.uk/view/edition/10227 (accessed 5 December 2018).
45 A. Swan, *Courtship and Marriage and the Gentle Art of Home Making* (London: Hutchinson & Co., 1894), p. 64.
46 M. Smitley, *The Feminine Public Sphere: Middle-class Women and Civic Life in Scotland, c. 1870–1914* (Manchester: Manchester University Press, 2009).
47 Marion Bernstein, 'Wanted a husband', *Glasgow Weekly Mail*, 19 December 1874.
48 Dundee Year Book, 1903, p. 154 and *Dundee Advertiser*, 10 September 1912, quoted in E. M. Wainwright, 'Constructing gendered workplace "types": the weaver–millworker distinction in Dundee's jute industry, c. 1880–1910', *Gender, Place & Culture*, 14:4 (2007), pp. 471, 473.
49 Michel Foucault, 'Howison Lectures', in Paul Rabinow (ed.), *The Foucault Reader* (London: Penguin, 1984), p. 11.
50 *Free Church Magazine*, vol. 6 (1844), p. 171, quoted in Brown, *Religion and Society*, p. 201.
51 R. M. Fagley, 'A Protestant view of population control', *Law and Contemporary Problems*, 25 (1960), p. 474; Solicitor-General at the Besant–Bradlaugh birth control trial of 1877, quoted in L. Bland, *Banishing the Beast: Feminism, Sex and Morality* (London: Penguin, 1995, Tauris Parke 2002), p. 192.
52 S. Szreter, 'Victorian Britain, 1831–1963: towards a social history of sexuality', *Journal of Victorian Culture*, 1:1 (1996), p. 144; H. Cook, 'Demography', in H. G. Cocks and M. Houlbrook (eds), *Palgrave Advances in the Modern History of Sexuality* (Basingstoke: Palgrave Macmillan, 2006), pp. 19–40.
53 Dr A. Ker (Mrs Stewart Ker), *Motherhood: A Book for Every Woman* (Manchester and London: John Heywood, 1891), pp. 30–1.
54 M. Mason, *The Making of Victorian Sexual Attitudes* (Oxford: Oxford University Press, 1994), pp. 49–62.
55 L. B. Sperry, *Confidential Talks with Husband and Wife: A Book of Information and Advice for the Married and Marriageable* (Edinburgh: Oliphant Anderson and Ferrier, 1900), pp. 121, 124.
56 Blaikie, 'The country and the city', pp. 89–90; Boyd, *Scottish Church Attitudes*, pp. 34–6; A. Clark, 'Twilight moments', *Journal of the History of Sexuality*, 14:1/2 (January 2005), p. 144.
57 G. Pollock, 'Feminism/Foucault – surveillance/sexuality', in N. Bryson, M. A. Holly and K. Moxey (eds), *Visual Culture: Images and Interpretations* (Hanover, NH: Wesleyan University Press, 1994), p. 25.
58 Blaikie, 'The country and the city', p. 98.

59 W. Aiton, *General View of Agriculture in the County of Ayr* (1811), p. xiv, quoted in Boyd, *Scottish Church Attitudes*, p. 4.
60 Brown, *Religion and Society*, p. 73.
61 S. Koven, *Slumming: Sexual and Social Politics in Victorian London* (Princeton, NJ: Princeton University Press, 2004), p. 1; J. R. Walkowitz, *City of Dreadful Delight: Narratives of Sexual Danger in Late-Victorian London* (Chicago: University of Chicago Press, 1992), p. 16.
62 Brown, *Religion and Society*, pp. 98–9, 103.
63 M. Foucault, *The History of Sexuality*, Vol. 1: *An Introduction* (London: Penguin, 1990), p. 11; 'The morality of the city. Important deputation to the magistrates', *North British Daily Mail [NBDM]*, 2 March 1875, p. 4; 'Glasgow's Young Men's Society for Religious Improvement', *NBDM*, 4 March 1875, p. 2; 'Baillie Collins of the music halls', *NBDM*, 6 March 1875, p. 4. For a full analysis of the scandal, see T. Cheadle, 'Music hall, "mashers" and the "unco guid": competing masculinities in Victorian Glasgow', in L. Abrams and E. Ewan (eds), *Nine Centuries of Man: Manhood and Masculinities in Scottish History* (Edinburgh: Edinburgh University Press, 2017), pp. 223–41.
64 Blaikie, 'The country and the city', p. 80.
65 Boyd, *Scottish Church Attitudes*, p. 29.
66 Ibid., p. 33.
67 Proceedings and Debates (including Reports) of the General Assembly of the Free Church, 1860, Housing Report, p. 4, quoted in Boyd, *Scottish Church Attitudes*, p. 33.
68 William Cramond, *Illegitimacy in Banffshire: facts, figures and opinions* (Banff, 1888), pp. 47, 49, quoted in Boyd, *Scottish Church Attitudes*, p. 88.
69 Blaikie, 'The country and the city', p. 95.
70 Ibid.
71 L. Mahood, *The Magdalenes: Prostitution in the Nineteenth Century* (London: Routledge, 1990), p. 123.
72 J. Miller, *Prostitution considered in relation to its causes and cure* (Edinburgh: Sutherland and Knox, 1859), p. 5.
73 R. Wardlaw, *Lectures on Female Prostitution: Its Nature, Extent, Effects, Guilt, Causes and Remedy*, 2nd edn (Glasgow: J. Maclehose, 1842), p. 115; W. Tait, *Magdalenism: An Inquiry into the Extent, Causes and Consequences of Prostitution in Edinburgh*, 2nd edn (Edinburgh: P. Richards, 1840), pp. 5–10.
74 Report from the Select Committee on the Contagious Diseases Acts (4 April 1882), pp. 118, 123, quoted in Mahood, *The Magdalenes*, pp. 70–1.
75 Glasgow Magdalene Institution, Report on the Glasgow Fair (1863), p. 9, quoted in Mahood, *The Magdalenes*, p. 71.
76 Tait, *Magdalenism*, p. 279.
77 Mahood, *The Magdalenes*, p. 60.
78 J. Walkowitz, *Prostitution and Victorian Society: Women, Class and the State* (Cambridge: Cambridge University Press, 1980), p. 38.
79 W. Logan, *An exposure from personal observation, of female prostitution in London, Leeds, Rochdale, and especially in the city of Glasgow; with remarks on the cause, extent, results, and remedy of the evil* (Glasgow: Gallie and Fleckfield, 1843), p. 18.

80 *An Address to the Public in Favour of the Magdalene Asylum in Edinburgh instituted in the year 1797* (Edinburgh: printed by James Ballantyne, 1804), p. 5.
81 J. A. Thor, 'Religious and industrial education in the nineteenth-century Magdalene asylums in Scotland', *Studies in Church History*, 55 (2019), pp. 347–62; O. Checkland, *Philanthropy in Victorian Scotland: Social Welfare and the Voluntary Principle* (Edinburgh: John Donald, 1980), pp. 237–8.
82 Thor has pointed out the tension in the use of the word 'escape' in the official reports of Magdalene homes, given their assurance that residency was voluntary. Thor, 'Religious and industrial education', p. 354.
83 B. Littlewood and L. Mahood, 'Prostitutes, magdalenes and wayward girls: dangerous sexualities of working-class women in Victorian Scotland', *Gender & History*, 3:2 (1991), p. 172.
84 Mahood, *The Magdalenes*, pp. 130–6.
85 Ibid., p. 138. According to Barbara Littlewood and Linda Mahood, the Contagious Diseases Acts were seen in Scotland as 'an infringement on the powers and competence of local authorities to handle local problems'. Littlewood and Mahood, 'Prostitutes, magdalenes and wayward girls', p. 164.
86 Mahood, *The Magdalenes*, p. 144.
87 Ibid., pp. 121, 155.
88 L. A. Hall, *Sex, Gender and Social Change in Britain Since 1880*, 2nd edn (London: Palgrave Macmillan, 2013), p. 20.
89 B. Dempsey, '"By the law of this and every other well governed realm": investigating accusations of sodomy in nineteenth-century Scotland', *The Judicial Review*, 2006, part 2, p. 129.
90 S. Brady, *Masculinity and Male Homosexuality in Britain* (Basingstoke: Palgrave Macmillan, 2005), pp. 1–2.
91 J. Meek, *Queer Voices in Post-War Scotland* (Basingstoke: Palgrave Macmillan, 2015), p. 14.
92 Meek, *Queer Voices*, p 19.
93 Hall, *Sex, Gender and Social Change*, p. 20.
94 Meek, *Queer Voices*, pp. 20–2.
95 J. Meek, 'The legal and social construction of the "sodomite" in Scotland, 1885–1930' (MSc thesis, University of Glasgow, 2006), p. 56.
96 Dempsey, 'Investigating accusations of sodomy', pp. 109–10.
97 'Too too!', *Bailie*, 11 January 1882, p. 11; 'Football', *Glasgow Herald*, 2 January 1882, p. 7. The gender challenge inherent in aestheticism and its incompatibility with the masculine sport of football was not lost on the *Bailie*, who commented, 'It would not be easy to think of any two subjects more incongruous than "aestheticism" and football. One had considerable difficulty in conceiving of the die-away disciples of Mr Oscar Wilde plunging through the mud in pursuit of an inflated bladder, and exposing their slender shins to the mercy of their opponent's heavy boots.' According to the *Glasgow Herald*, however, the Aesthetics played a 'creditable game', with the Stewart brothers in particular showing 'great dash and judgement'.
98 Editorial, *Scotsman*, 6 April 1895, p. 8.

99 S. Rowbotham, *Edward Carpenter: A Life of Liberty and Love* (London: Verso, 2008), p. 207.
100 Letter from Edward Carpenter to Robert Muirhead, 4 April 1890, Papers of Robert Muirhead, MS Gen 1767/A, Glasgow University Special Collections; B. M. Ward, *Reddie of Abbotsholme* (London: George Allen & Unwin, 1934), p. 46. For a useful survey of Reddie's influences, which includes a brief discussion of his sexuality, see P. Searby, 'The new school and the new life: Cecil Reddie (1858–1932) and the early years of Abbotsholme School', *History of Education*, 18:1 (1989), pp. 1–21.
101 Ward, *Reddie of Abbotsholme*, p. 97.
102 For an account by Muirhead of his friendship with Carpenter, including their first meeting, see R. F. Muirhead, 'Memories of Edward Carpenter', in G. Beith (ed.), *Edward Carpenter – in Appreciation* (London: George Allen & Unwin, 1931), pp. 155–8.
103 Rowbotham, *Edward Carpenter*, pp. 131–3.
104 Letter from Edward Carpenter to Robert Muirhead, 25 June 1890, papers of Robert Muirhead, MS Gen 1767/A, Glasgow University Special Collections; letter Edward Carpenter to James Brown, 16 January 1890, quoted in Rowbotham, *Edward Carpenter*, p. 132.
105 Edward Carpenter's note on a letter from Robert Muirhead, February 1925, quoted in Rowbotham, *Edward Carpenter*, p. 132; letter from Edward Carpenter to Robert Muirhead, 17 January 1890, papers of Robert Muirhead, MS Gen 1767/A, Glasgow University Special Collections.
106 Letter from Edward Carpenter to James Brown, 2 March 1890, quoted in Rowbotham, *Edward Carpenter*, p. 133.
107 Rowbotham, *Edward Carpenter*, p. 207. When Muirhead was in his sixties, he wrote to Carpenter, reflecting back on his youthful friendships with him and Brown and commenting how 'You and he idealised me a good deal. I am really a very ordinary person, inspite [sic] of my mathematical prowess and philosophic abilities and I daresay I have often been very disappointing to the idealists.' Letter from Robert Muirhead to Edward Carpenter, February 1925, quoted in Rowbotham, *Edward Carpenter*, p. 133.
108 A. Oram and A. Turnbull, *Lesbian History Sourcebook* (London: Routledge, 2001), p. 156.
109 Faderman, *Scotch Verdict*, p. xiv.
110 Ibid., pp. 280–1.
111 Entry for 'Maud Galt' in *The New Biographical Dictionary of Scottish Women*, ed. E. Ewan et al. (Edinburgh: Edinburgh University Press, 2017), p. 155.
112 A. Duncan, '"Old Maids": family and social relationships of never-married Scottish gentlewomen, c. 1740–c.1840' (PhD thesis, University of Aberdeen, 2012), pp. 124–6, 138–43; entry for 'Sophia Louisa Jex-Blake' in *The New Biographical Dictionary of Scottish Women*, pp. 218–19; A. T. McCall, 'The poetry and life of Bessie Craigmyle (1863–1933), the Sappho of Strawberry Bank', *Aberdeen University Review*, 61 (2005), pp. 109–21.
113 McCall, 'The poetry and life of Bessie Craigmyle'; Faderman, *Scotch Verdict*; G. Friedman, 'School for scandal: sexuality, race and national vice and virtue in *Miss Marianne Woods and Miss Jane Pirie Against Lady Helen Cumming Gordon*', *Nineteenth-Century Contexts*, 27:1 (2005), pp. 53–76; M. Vicinus, *Intimate Friends: Women Who Loved*

Women (Chicago: University of Chicago Press, 2004), pp. 63–9; C. Roulston, 'A thing perhaps impossible: the 1811 Woods/ Pirie trial and its legacies', in C. Mounsey (ed.), *Developments in the Histories of Sexualities: In Search of the Normal 1600–1800* (Lewisburg, PA: Bucknell University Press, 2013), pp. 125–44.

114 Cook, 'Demography', p. 27; Brown, *Religion and Society*, pp. 62–4.
115 Clark, 'Twilight moments', pp. 147–8.
116 Blaikie, 'The country and the city', p. 89.
117 Quoted in L. Abrams, *Myth and Materiality in a Woman's World: Shetland 1800–2000* (Manchester: Manchester University Press, 2005), p. 165.
118 R. Cowie, *Shetland: Descriptive and Historical* (Edinburgh: John Menzies and Co., 1st edn 1871), p. 102, quoted in Abrams, *Myth and Materiality*, p. 168.
119 *The Christian Watt Papers*, p. 71.
120 Ibid., p. 36. 'Tinkies' or 'tinkers' are the Scots terms for itinerant traders or merchants.
121 Ibid., pp. 56–7.
122 Ibid., pp. 47, 61.
123 Ibid., p. 92.
124 A. Clark, *The Struggle for the Breeches: Gender and the Making of the British Working Class* (Berkeley: University of California Press, 1995), p. 61.
125 'Jenny Nettles', in *The Wonderful Age* (Glasgow, n.d.), a chapbook of songs, quoted in Clark, *The Struggle for the Breeches*, p. 47.
126 Letter, 'Confessions of a singing saloon habitué', *Glasgow Herald*, 6 March 1875, p. 4.
127 Ibid.
128 In 1886, 'Roving Jack', the gossip columnist for Glasgow's main theatrical trade paper, reported on incidents of sexual harassment, with young girls seemingly particularly at risk. See 'Notes by Roving Jack, an old stager', *Professional and Authors' Journal*, 9 January, 13 March, 15 May and 2 October 1886. Clark, *The Struggle for the Breeches*, p. 44.
129 Clark, 'Twilight moments', p. 140.
130 Ibid., pp. 146–7.
131 Report from the Directors of the Edinburgh Magdalene Asylum for 1830, 1831 and 1832 (Edinburgh, 1833), p. 12, cited in Thor, 'Religious and industrial education', p. 355.
132 *Glasgow Herald*, 10 July 1857, quoted in E. Gordon and G. Nair, *Murder and Morality in Victorian Britain: The Story of Madeleine Smith* (Manchester: Manchester University Press, 2009), p. 133.
133 For a detailed account of Madeleine's Smith life after the trial, see Gordon and Nair, *Murder and Morality*, pp. 174–193.
134 Letter from Henry James to William Roughead, quoted in Gordon and Nair, *Murder and Morality*, p. 189.
135 'Resolutions for the New Year', *Bailie*, 1 January 1873, p. 7; 'What folk are saying', *Bailie*, 3 March 1875, p. 7.
136 'Modern methods', *Stage News*, 8, 24 April 1897.
137 'Holy Willie's Prayer: A Poem', lines 51–2, in R. P. Irvine (ed.), *Robert Burns: Selected Poems and Songs* (Oxford: Oxford University Press, 2013), pp. 230–3.
138 *The Christian Watt Papers*, p. 93.

2

Matrons, maidens and new men

In January 1894, thirty-four-year-old Bella Pearce sat in a packed hall in Glasgow and listened for the first time to a speech by James Keir Hardie, the founding chairman of the Independent Labour Party (ILP). The party had formed in Bradford exactly one year previously, delegates at their inaugural conference identifying their principal objective as securing the collective ownership of the means of production, distribution and exchange. Hardie started his address at the Accountants' Hall on Glasgow's West Nile Street by enumerating the various material benefits that would accrue from such a change in governance. He then went on, however, to issue a warning. Without a corresponding moral transformation within the people themselves, there was a real danger that this change would do more harm than good. Purely economic measures could never hope to precipitate the ultimate goals of socialism, which according to Hardie were no less than the salvation of humanity and the establishment of 'peace on earth and goodwill to all men'.[1] These could only be realised through interior means: love for one's brother and a renewed ethic of altruism. Bella was an immediate convert to the cause:

> I left that meeting ready and willing to join in the work, feeling there was hope for a movement whose leaders had their eyes open to the truth that state Socialism *alone* is powerless to overcome the evils which manifest themselves among us, that without the growth of the spirit of human brotherhood within each one of us personally we cannot even attain the outward ends we seek, or having attained, enjoy them.[2]

Numerous similar accounts of the moment of 'becoming a socialist' can be found in the pages of labour newspapers, socialist memoirs and fictional renderings of the period. As Stephen Yeo has demonstrated, their resemblance to narratives of religious conversion is not incidental, but indicative of the religious character of the emergent phase of late Victorian socialism.³ The movement of the 1880s and 1890s was imbued with an intense idealism and millenarian utopianism, specifying as its ultimate aim a paradisiacal 'new life' comparable to Christianity's promised land. Remembered nostalgically by those involved as a time of untrammelled optimism, it was a moment in which, according to Ruth Livesey, men and women were offered the chance of 'sensing and living through another historical rhythm, the spectre of a future utopian transformation'.⁴ Those contemporaries more sceptical that the mechanics of socialism's imminent new dawn could be conveyed during the course of an evening meeting at a Co-operative Society hall were nonetheless impressed by its dynamism, the Fabian Sidney Webb conceding that the movement might hold the momentum to 'carry us forward more rapidly than any politician foresees'.⁵

Individual motivations for joining the socialist crusade were complex and varied, and encompassed 'poverty, religious eclecticism, unresolved guilt, domestic unhappiness, unfocused indignation, scattered activity, wealthy aimlessness, or social unease'.⁶ For Bella, it was the hope that socialism's promise of a new ethical blueprint for humanity would also include a transformation in sexual and gender relations. Alongside the implementation of a selfless and benevolent fellowship between all their comrades, Bella, along with her husband Charles Pearce, sought a reconceptualisation of the everyday and intimate heterosexual interactions of men and women, based on a recognition of gender equality and of women's essential role in the formation of the 'good time to which we all look forward'.⁷ Achieving this new, female-centred form of intimacy took precedence over other affective and structural changes envisaged by 'new life' socialism and the couple worked determinedly towards this goal.

The predominant way in which the Pearces influenced socialist opinion was through the 'Matrons and Maidens' column in the *Labour Leader*. Bella was the editor from March 1894 to December 1898, Charles filling in enthusiastically as 'Sophia' for an extended period when Bella went on holiday.⁸ The first women's column in a socialist newspaper, it provided a weekly, feminist critique of contemporary sexual relations, addressing topics such as the sexual double standard, prostitution and 'free love'. Often at odds with the masculinised rhetoric which surrounded it, the column engendered a mixed response, some male readers objecting to its feminist politics. Yet alongside like-minded allies within the subculture of Glasgow socialism, the couple persevered with their message, delivering lectures to the Ruskin Society and the Glasgow Women's Labour Party on gender complementarity and debating with fellow *Labour Leader* journalists on the Woman Question, while also manifesting their commitment to progressive gender relations in their marriage, working as equal partners in their political activism and their publishing and wine-importing business.

Themes within the 'Matrons and Maidens' column have been explored in unpublished work by Helen Lintell, the only research focused solely on Bella Pearce and which provides an astute examination of her sexual politics.[9] Further insightful commentary can be found in the scholarship of June Hannam, Karen Hunt and Laura Ugolini on women in the ILP and the Social Democratic Federation (SDF), and this has been invaluable in placing Bella's feminism within the context of the early labour movement.[10] However, the absence of any in-depth, biographical research on the Pearces' lives has necessarily prevented the tracing of key connections between their sexual progressivism and their intimate, political and spiritual lives. This chapter begins to remedy this elision, and in doing so underscores the opportunities present in 'new life' socialism for those advancing a feminist sexual politics, but also the considerable challenges. These included a patronising and infantilising attitude towards female activists, a persistent eliding of gendered issues within a class analytic and, at points, an unabashed male hostility, particularly towards critiques of the sexual double standard and the legislative structures which upheld it.

Beginning with the formation of the Pearces' political consciousnesses in childhood and early adulthood, the chapter then provides a portrait of the subculture of early socialism in 1890s Glasgow, detailing the couple's varied contributions to the administrative, political and financial running of the ILP. An analysis of Bella's journalism follows, situating its discourse on progressive sexuality within both feminist and socialist understandings of intimacy, highlighting the complex and sometimes fractious relationship between the ILP and the women's rights movement during this period. The chapter ends with Bella's transference of allegiance to militant suffragism, her frustrations apparent in her assertion in 1907 that socialists were 'apt to keep their beautiful principles for theoretical use' and when asked to put them into practice, had 'a knack of finding excuses of expediency for delaying that operation until the arrival of some delectable future'.[11] With the advent of the Women's Social and Political Union (WSPU), that future appeared to her to have arrived.

Earliest recollections

Born on 5 May 1859 in Glasgow, Bella Duncan was the third of four children of Margaret Fraser and John Thomson Duncan, her mother the daughter of a land surveyor and her father the son of a weavers' agent from Douglas, a village in Lanarkshire.[12] By her early childhood, the family had settled in a flat in Laurieston, a newly built suburb just south of the River Clyde, its wide streets and Georgian-style tenement blocks designed to attract members of the city's expanding middle classes. The family prospered financially, her father progressing steadily from working as a clerk in a wholesale warehouse to becoming a chartered accountant, his employment providing enough money to enable Bella's mother to remain at home, for them to employ a domestic servant and for all four children to attend school.[13] In 1864, they purchased land on the Rosneath Peninsula, building a substantial summer retreat, a 'beautiful home' according to one visitor, which commanded 'a magnificent view of Loch Long and other waters'.[14] Back in Glasgow, the rapid industrialisation of the neighbouring district of Tradeston was gradually eroding Laurieston's genteel charm, the smoke and fumes of its factories and railways carried in on the prevailing westerly winds. By the time Bella was in her twenties, her family had joined the exodus of middle-class households removing to the South Side and West End of the city, their vacant homes filled by a largely working-class and immigrant population.[15] Relocating just one mile south, the Duncans took up residence at 'Laurentine Villa', a rather grand appellation for what was another tenement flat, albeit a large one within a handsome crescent overlooking the lawns and terraces of Queen's Park.[16]

In gendered terms, Bella's upbringing was typical of a mid-Victorian, middle-class family, with different roles assigned and futures plotted for herself and her sister, in comparison to her two brothers. Her 'earliest recollections in life' were of the resentment and anger she felt over the 'unfair and wholly unjust discrimination made between boys and girls', Bella attracting disapproval and ridicule for refusing to recognise such 'arbitrary differences'.[17] She later claimed to have laid the blame for such attitudes squarely at God's door, in her 'childish ignorance ... foolishly fancying that to His unjust preference for the male human I owed my inferior status in life!'[18] On reaching adulthood, like many nascent feminists of her generation, her first political affiliation was to the Liberal Party. She joined the Scottish Women's Liberal Federation on its formation in 1891, the organisation spearheading the support of female enfranchisement, in its constitution outlining its objectives as securing 'just and equal legislation and representation for women' and the removal of 'all legal disabilities on account of sex'.[19] Bella quickly became disillusioned, however, describing male Liberal politicians as 'always ready to come and make their pretty little speeches at our meetings' and 'only too glad to get all the help we were willing to give them' but who were 'by no means desirous of going further in the matter'.[20] She relinquished the 'last vestiges' of her allegiance to the Liberal leader William Gladstone only a year after joining the federation, when he blocked a bill to extend the franchise to unmarried women over a concern that possessing the vote might cause them 'unwittingly to trespass upon the delicacy, the purity, the refinement, the elevation of [their] own nature, which are the present sources of its power'.[21]

While Bella's passionately felt sense of injustice over women's inferior status positioned her at odds with her family, what they did share was an interest in social reform. Together with her father, brother and sister-in-law, she was a member of the Ruskin Society of Glasgow, attending its 'quiet gatherings' in rooms and halls in the city centre, as well as serving on its committee and eventually becoming its vice president.[22] John Ruskin had first developed his controversial critique of free-market capitalism in the 1850s and 1860s, believing the root cause of the chronic social problems endemic to industrialised Britain to be a utilitarian political economy which had resolutely failed to incorporate social, moral and aesthetic considerations, a philosophy encapsulated in the now celebrated phrase 'THERE IS NO WEALTH BUT LIFE'.[23] By the late 1870s, a new constituency for his civic vision had emerged from among the professional middle classes, who began to found Ruskin Societies in several of Britain's industrial centres, seeking to consolidate their own understanding of 'The Master's' work, disseminate his message to others and launch modest programmes of social reform. The society in Glasgow was the first to be established and was a particularly active organisation, membership rising from sixty-nine in 1881 to nearly two hundred in 1897.[24] Patrick Geddes, the Edinburgh natural scientist and fellow sexual progressive, lectured for them on five separate occasions, while it was the Ruskin Society who organised the 1894 talk which secured Bella's conversion to the socialist cause, Hardie speaking on 'Carlyle and Ruskin: The Pioneers of the Labour Party'.[25] Bella herself gave a lecture for the society, despite considering herself not 'gifted in that direction', in January 1899 speaking on gender relations in a talk entitled 'Duality in Development'.[26]

It may have been at a Ruskin Society meeting that Bella first met her husband. Described as one of the Ruskin Society's 'earliest and most enthusiastic members', Charles William Bream Pearce was an Englishman, born in 1840 in Stockwell, just south of the Thames.[27] His interest in reform politics had been kindled in childhood by his father, a builder and a Chartist, the last and greatest Chartist rally taking place in 1848 on Kennington Common, close to his family home.[28] Charles was also a vocal supporter of women's rights, in March 1893 giving a Ruskin Society lecture on 'The Relation of Woman to the New Age', and two years later delivering what the *Labour Leader* termed 'an exquisite little supplement' to a talk by Ellen Neilson, a fellow Ruskin Society member, in which Charles argued 'that men and women were not meant, and never could be, mentally and physically exactly alike; but would and ought to be perfect equal counterparts one of the other'.[29] Later still, in 1897, his commitment to women's rights was manifested by membership of the Executive of the Male Electors' League for Women's Suffrage, the first male-only society to campaign specifically for female enfranchisement.[30]

By the time he arrived in Glasgow, Charles was working as a fire insurance broker, although he had also tried his hand at dry saltery and commercial travelling. It is equally possible therefore that the couple met through the business interests of Bella's father, who specialised in insurance accountancy. At this point Charles was also married. His wife was Mary Gill, a gentleman's daughter from Yorkshire whom he had married when aged twenty-two, the couple going on to have four children and moving from Norwich to Cambridge and then to Kilburn in Middlesex.[31] However, by 1881, the family had disintegrated: Charles was staying with Bella's father and eldest brother at the Duncans' summer house on the Rosneath Peninsula, while Charles's wife and their three youngest children, aged ten, twelve and fourteen, were lodging at a boarding house in Matlock, Derbyshire.[32] What was behind the separation is unknown. At some point during the next decade, however, Mary died.[33] Now a widower of fifty, on 17 June 1891 Charles married for the second time, to thirty-two-year-old Bella Duncan.[34]

The marriage of a New Woman and a new man

The couple (see figures 1 and 2) wed in an irregular marriage ceremony, a form valid in Scotland and referred to colloquially as marriage 'before the sheriff'. Attractive to those with unorthodox religious views, it required only that the husband and wife sign a declaration of their marital union in front of two witnesses, with all parties then examined by the sheriff under oath.[35] Unlike some of her contemporaries in progressive politics such as Elizabeth Wolstenholme Elmy and Eleanor Marx Aveling, Bella chose not to retain her maiden name and in the 1890s socialist press was variously referred to as Mrs Pearce, Mrs C. W. Pearce and Mrs C. W. Bream Pearce, except when employing her pen-name of 'Lily Bell'. Only after Charles's death in 1905 did she reintroduce her maiden name, using the moniker 'I. D[uncan]. Pearce' in her articles for the *Westminster Review* (1907–8) and letters to the *Freewoman* (1911–12). In her private correspondence she signed herself, and was referred to by friends and family, as Bella. Charles also chose not to incorporate his spouse's maiden name,

1 The line drawing at the head of 'Lily Bell's' 'Matrons and Maidens' column in the *Labour Leader*, 7 April 1894

instead continuing to use the surname 'Bream Pearce', an amalgam of his father and mother's names, in keeping with his family's radical, Chartist associations.

Temperamentally, Bella and Charles appear to have been markedly dissimilar. Bella was passionate and opinionated, known among her friends for sermonising and being easily roused to furious indignation, especially when encountering prejudice towards women. One female colleague commented that while she herself was able to 'listen calmly' during a meeting in which male socialists spoke much 'outrageous nonsense' concerning women's rights, she was certain Bella would have 'relegated every man of them to a furnace seven times heated'.[36] Describing herself as not 'very dependent on company', even when married she holidayed alone, claiming to seldom feel 'the want of a companion'.[37] Yet her social and intellectual self-reliance was tempered by a warm sociability: her

2 Charles William Bream Pearce, photograph in the *Labour Leader*, 27 April 1895

friend the Cheshire-based feminist Elizabeth Wolstenholme Elmy described her as a 'clear-sighted' but also a 'warm-hearted' woman, while an American visitor to her home in 1903 thought her 'a great comfort' and 'a jolly good girl' who was 'a delightful hostess'.[38] Her natural conviviality, coupled with a firm commitment to breaking down 'the unnatural sex barriers' between men and women, enabled her to maintain a sparring camaraderie with the most incorrigibly condescending of her male socialist colleagues. When George A. H. Samuel, who wrote as 'Marxian' in the *Labour Leader*, stayed with the Pearces in Glasgow, they treated him as if he were 'the heir to two or three empires', despite his well-known antipathy to women's rights, Samuel claiming teasingly during his visit to have 'gently disclosed to Mrs. Pearce the true view of the woman question'.[39]

By contrast, Charles was reserved and serious, 'Tricotrin' in the *Labour Leader* describing him as a 'tall, quiet, intuitive, subtle-minded man, who is as just as he is generous'.[40] He was particularly known for his personal integrity, Hardie referring to his 'high conscientiousness' and the Scottish socialist William Haddow believing him 'above reproach'.[41] A frequent public speaker, Charles was viewed as an effective rather than effusive communicator, the *Glasgow Evening News* forming an impression at the 1895 Labour Day rally on Glasgow Green of an 'elderly, bespectacled gentleman' who attracted a good crowd but whose style was insufficiently 'fiery' for the 'ordinary [socialist] enthusiast'.[42] Yet despite the disparity in their personalities, the Pearces' marriage was distinguished by a confluence in their personal politics. Also speaking at the 1895 rally on Glasgow Green, Bella commented that 'They heard a great deal about the new woman. This labour movement showed that they were also hearing a great deal of the new man.'[43] Charles was indisputably one of these 'new men', committed to the cause of women's emancipation and to securing their equal participation in the state, believing that 'the man without the woman is the "very devil" in politics and works discord and war all around and everywhere'.[44]

The couple's involvement in socialist politics was a natural extension of their membership of the Ruskin Society. While the Society was careful to avoid formal affiliation to any one political party, it gave numerous talks to ILP branches under its 'extension lectures' scheme, designed to familiarise the 'intelligent working class' with Ruskin's work, while several individuals were members of both organisations.[45] The decade prior to the ILP's foundation in 1893 had been a time of breathtaking expansion for the labour movement, one commentator describing how, in 1883, 'a socialist movement seemed to break out spontaneously in England', a Labour Day parade in Edinburgh in 1894 attracting 10,000 marchers and approximately 120,000 spectators.[46] Declining at this juncture to tender a detailed and therefore potentially divisive blueprint for the future, socialism instead represented itself as a panacea, a social agency which by its nature alone would rid the world of poverty and its resultant material and moral degradations, and bring about the realisation of a new social ideal. For those involved it was a moment when it seemed as if 'we were all socialists more or less' and was later remembered wistfully as a period of great energy and enthusiasm, akin to a religious revival, when the revolution was believed to be both inevitable and imminent, the ILP propagandist Katharine Bruce Glasier relating how it was as if 'a great window had been flung wide open and the vision of a new world had been shown me: of the earth reborn to beauty and joy'.[47] In part this was due to the severance with past associations that becoming a socialist often entailed, Charles claiming to have lost two thirds of his business in Glasgow once his political affiliations became widely known.[48]

The speech given by Hardie at Glasgow's Accountants' Hall in 1894 was a typical exposition of ethical socialism, a conceptualisation of the labour movement inspired by William Morris and embraced by many members of the ILP during the early 1890s. Within it, socialism was conceived less as a political pressure group campaigning to enact economic reforms and more as the realisation of an ethic of fellowship. It was therefore considered imperative that its members underwent an inner moral reformation prior to or in conjunction with the overthrow of capitalism. The objective was one with which the Pearces were in complete accord, Bella stating the root cause of 'the evils which manifest themselves amongst us' to be man's inherent selfishness, 'a love of self, which makes him look first to his own self interest, careless of that of his brother'.[49] What was required, through the impetus provided by the socialist movement, was a fundamental shift in the way people related to one other, a 'growth in the spirit of human brotherhood', without which the transformation of society was impossible:

> No, it is not "economic" Socialists we are most in need of. We want men and women who are Socialist in their hearts as well as in their heads, who think less of gain and more of truth and right, who feel brotherly towards each other, and therefore desire in all things to act brotherly towards each other – and that is just where true Socialism and religion are indissolubly connected, for religion implies doing good for the love of good, the doing right for the love of right – not for the love of gain in any form.[50]

Bella's assertion of the necessary symbiosis of religion and politics was a defining characteristic of ethical socialism, Robert Blatchford, the editor of the socialist paper the *Clarion*, claiming that the labour movement was 'but one sign of a new spirit at work in many directions throughout human affairs' which it would be 'affectation if not folly to refuse the name of Religion'.[51] Its adherents came from a diverse range of theological and anti-theological backgrounds, including nonconformity, Anglicanism, evangelicalism and Swedenborgianism. The Pearces, as shall be explored in the next chapter, were committed disciples of the American sexual mystic Thomas Lake Harris. Despite their disparate beliefs, what united ethical socialists was a conviction of the necessity for a renewed sense of altruism as a prerequisite of the 'new life', Bella emphatic that 'Socialism, without the true religious spirit inspiring each individual member of society, will never do any great good.'[52]

Between 1894 and 1898, the Pearces were important local activists for the ILP, performing a range of roles and functions.[53] Both were vital members of the local party administration, Bella the treasurer and then vice president of the Glasgow District Council, as well as president of the Cathcart and Govanhill branches.[54] In 1895 and 1896, Bella was president of the Women's Labour Party (WLP) in Glasgow, a pioneering organisation closely affiliated to the ILP, which was established in 1892 as a means of 'educating women in the first principles of Socialism, initiating them into taking their part with men in the general propaganda and preparing them for the time when the franchise shall be fully extended to them'.[55] Its treasurer was Lizzie Glasier, the sister of John Bruce Glasier and a formidable campaigner in her own right, whose work, according to one male associate, was 'more satisfactory and enduring' than her brother's, for while he 'attacks and converts in crowds', she 'attacks only the individual and converts'; Kate Taylor, previously an organiser for the Women's Protective and Provident League, later became its secretary.[56] Flourishing briefly in the middle years of the decade – in 1896 boasting seventy-seven members and its own rooms in Glasgow – by the following year the WLP's numbers were in steep decline, the women 'straining every nerve' just to pay their rent.[57] Nonetheless, when at its peak of activity, the organisation offered an important and vibrant space for socialists of both sexes. During their 'At Homes' on Saturday evenings, male and female comrades could read the labour papers, 'discuss the burning questions of the day', make new friends or enjoy an occasional dance, while their fortnightly lecture series addressed both literary subjects and the Woman Question.[58] Ultimately unsuccessful in its attempts to unionise a group of seamstresses, Bella and her female comrades fared better in drawing in the children of the movement, running a popular Sunday class to teach them 'the rudiments of socialism'.[59] In May 1895 a picnic to Cathkin Braes was organised, the children wearing red 'Labour Crusaders' sashes embroidered by the women of the WLP, returning home to Glasgow in lorries preceded by 'quite a regiment of men on foot' who 'made the distance shorter by singing Socialist songs'.[60]

Charles came to prominence within the ILP when he ran as the parliamentary candidate for Camlachie in the 1895 general election. He had initially refused to stand, after the party's male-dominated shortlist for the Glasgow School Board elections led him to conclude that he did not have them with him 'on the question of the complementary equality of woman with man'.[61] He was clearly brought round, however, accepting his nomination at a 'great meeting' in the Camlachie Institute in August 1894. Attended by an audience 'numbering fully a thousand', he was careful to state that his acceptance was conditional upon a direct acknowledgement that God was 'the father of us all' and that the ultimate end sought was 'the inbringing into the constituency of the fraternal spirit of His social Christ'.[62] According to the *Glasgow Evening News*, he then proceeded to tell 'a very unwashed audience very little about politics and more about Christianity than they had perhaps heard in all their lives before'.[63] After a year of campaigning, however, and with less than two months to the election, he suddenly withdrew his candidature, a decision Hardie condemned as precipitous, regrettable and 'a very bad blunder'.[64] A vehement opponent of anarchism, Charles disagreed with a decision by the ILP's National Administrative Committee (NAC) to delete a clause in its 1895 report disowning it. While Hardie believed it a purely constitutional matter, Charles was concerned it could be interpreted as giving anarchists 'a negative support'.[65] That it prompted him to take such a drastic step reflects his deep commitment to a fraternal, Christian conception of socialism as 'a party working for the realization of the ideal life', believing members of the ILP had a duty to 'unequivocally disown all sympathy with methods whose uttermost weapons are dynamite and the bomb'.[66] The replacement ILP candidate for Camlachie, the trade unionist Robert Smillie, went on to suffer ignominious defeat at the polls, gaining just 696 votes in comparison to the 3,198 cast for the Liberal Unionist candidate Alexander Cross, a result broadly replicated across Britain, with not a single one of the thirty-two socialist candidates gaining a seat. Beatrice Webb dubbed the election 'the most expensive funeral since Napoleon', with even Hardie losing his West Ham seat, attributing his defeat to failing to run an effective local campaign and instead 'taking the country as his parish'.[67]

Despite this debacle, Charles initially remained an active worker for the cause, Hardie having forgiven him enough by the following March to describe him as belonging to the 'thinking, solid element of the movement'.[68] While not on the NAC or among the core of nationally recognised speakers, the couple were nonetheless at the heart of the local movement in Glasgow, contributing in a variety of ways to the dissemination of the socialist message and the necessary party bureaucracy. At the Labour Day rallies on Glasgow Green in 1895 and 1896 (figure 3), both Charles and Bella spoke to crowds of thousands of working men and women, moving resolutions in support of female suffrage, Bella remarking triumphantly that there was 'Not a hand held up in opposition; not a dissenting voice to be heard'.[69] They could also regularly be found on the platform at the numerous meetings of ILP branches, chairing the speeches of prominent propagandists such as Margaret McMillan, Caroline Martyn

3 Labour Day on Glasgow Green, line drawing in the *Labour Leader*, 8 May 1897

and Katharine Bruce Glasier, while also working intensely behind the scenes, attending council meetings, forming new branches and organising visiting speakers, Bella describing herself as 'in the front of the "seat of war"' when the NAC visited Glasgow during the winter of 1894.[70]

With the emphasis of the ILP during this early period as much on 'making socialists' as on formulating policy or winning elections, social events were seen to perform a vital function in the party. The Pearces participated fully in the culture of the 'new life', hosting a tea at the Co-operative Rooms after the 1894 municipal elections, putting up comrades when they arrived in Glasgow, and in 1895 and 1896 travelling to the annual ILP conferences in Newcastle and Nottingham, where Bella 'eloped for three hours' with *Labour Leader* writer 'The Wastrel', taking an evening paddle steamer down the Trent as Archie MacArthur, a fellow Glaswegian Christian socialist, played 'Sweet Maree' and 'Ever of Thee' on the fiddle.[71] The couple were also among the thirty-six guests present at the first *Labour Leader* staff party, described in the *Leader* as a 'great function ... entirely without precedent or rival', where Bella toasted 'The Readers' and Hardie 'The Cause' ('Royalty being "hoff"'). Charles acted as a croupier with John Bruce Glasier, and Hardie's younger brother George played the mandolin, the evening rounded off by a rendition of the ballad of the Irish rebellion 'That Night at Skibbereen'.[72] Despite their occasional differences of opinion, the Pearces were clearly good friends of Hardie, visiting his mother when she was ill, looking after his pair of 'bonny wild birds' in their office and loyally defending him during the frequent internal disputes of the ILP.[73]

'Matrons and Maidens'

Despite the couple's extensive involvement in the financial, political and administrative work of the ILP in Glasgow, Bella's most significant role within the party and the one in which she wielded the greatest influence at a national level, was as the editor of 'Matrons and Maidens', the weekly women's column in the *Labour Leader*. Writing under the pseudonym 'Lily Bell', it was a role she undertook for four years, from the newspaper's inception in March 1894 until her eventual dismissal in December 1898. It is worth pausing at this point, however, to refute earlier suggestions made in the scholarship that Bella was not the sole author of the column. Kenneth Morgan, Christine Collette and Carolyn Steedman have all asserted that 'Matrons and Maidens' was in part authored by Hardie, Steedman referring to 'Lily Bell' in her biography of Margaret McMillan as 's/he'.[74] Carolyn Stevens goes further, claiming that Hardie was the sole author of the column, describing 'Lily Bell' as a 'man in drag' and ascribing the column's feminist opinions to the fact that Hardie was an illegitimate child, thereby transforming 'Matrons and Maidens' into a 'barely disguised lament of a loyal son for his mother's honor'.[75] The precise evidence on which these assertions are based is unclear. All the *Labour Leader* staff writers wrote under a pen-name, their real identities a closely guarded secret, 'Lily Bell' stating in 1894, 'My maidenly modesty ... compels me to decline with thanks all invitations to reveal myself.'[76] The only archival source which could be read to support Hardie's authorship of the column is a letter to the sub-editor David Lowe in June 1896 enclosing copy for the *Labour Leader*, in which Hardie commented, 'I have folded up as one some pars which can be used either in B.O. ['Between Ourselves'] M. M. [presumably 'Maidens and Matrons'] or as featurettes just as you find handiest.'[77]

Directly contradicting this evidence, however, is a wealth of contemporary sources attesting to Bella's authorship of the column. First, Bella was consistently referred to as 'Lily Bell' by close associates within the socialist and feminist movements. The letters of Elizabeth Wolstenholme Elmy contain numerous references to 'Mrs Pearce' being 'Lily Bell', Elmy using the two names interchangeably, while John Bruce Glasier, writing in 1919 when seeking to assert the ILP's early feminist credentials, commented that 'Mrs. Pearce of Glasgow ("Lily Bell") was hammering away at [women's suffrage] week by week in the columns of the *Labour Leader*'.[78] Second, there are countless circumstantial details in 'Matrons and Maidens' which strongly indicate that it was written by Bella. For example, the column contains a full report of the 1896 Women's Emancipation Union (WEU) conference, at which we know Bella gave a paper, but which took place when Hardie was in Bradford fighting the Bradford East by-election.[79] Third, the tone, rhetoric and content are entirely consistent across the four years, the author utilising the same metaphors, revisiting the same themes and deploying the same arguments. Finally, the writing contains authentic personal details that it would be fanciful to believe were fabricated by Hardie in order to construct a believable feminine persona. These include grief at the author's dog dying ('I have lost a friend, one whose faithful affection never wavered and whose welcome was always assured'), accounts of her holidays to Scandinavia, Heligoland and Iceland ('I suppose we Scotch folk are more akin to the North than the South') and a moment of feminist epiphany reading Mona Caird's *The Daughter of Danaus* on a delayed train ('seldom has a day's travelling seemed to pass more quickly').[80] In short, woven into the very fabric of the column are the myriad encounters, episodes and emotions that constitute the texture of an individual life. Added to that, the fact that 'Lily Bell' required hiring and then firing by Hardie; that she continued her column when Hardie toured America but that 'Sophia' took over when 'Lily Bell' went to Iceland ('Sophia' being Bella's husband Charles); that 'Mrs Pearce' and 'C. W. Bream Pearce' attended the *Labour Leader* staff party; that the soubriquet 'Lily Bell' was reprised for *Forward* in 1906–8, a paper Hardie had no involvement in, all indicate not an elaborate case of female impersonation by a busy socialist party leader but that 'Lily Bell' was indeed whom Elmy, Glasier and others said she was. In the event of further doubt, however, it is possible to give Bella the last word on the matter. In her column of 8 September 1894, she related that some 'bright youths' had recently been led to believe that 'Lily Bell' was in fact a man. 'Never mind, old man,' was her rejoinder, 'a woman's a woman for a'that.'[81]

When first asked by Hardie to edit a women's column, Bella was initially unconvinced, complaining that 'You don't set up a special column headed "For men only"', agreeing only on the premise that she used it 'to abuse the men'.[82] Yet while the column's tone was feminist from the outset, Bella's plans for its content were initially relatively modest, envisaging it as a 'sympathetic ear' for women in the movement, a place where they could share problems encountered in their political and domestic lives; she even promised hints on dressmaking and domestic economy.[83] Such advice was never to materialise, however. Instead, as Bella grew in confidence both as a feminist and as a writer, 'Matrons and Maidens' matured into a broad-ranging weekly opinion piece, in which she commented on issues at the fore of contemporary feminist campaigns, including women's suffrage, the sexual division of labour, female entry into higher education, the New Woman and rational dress.

What particularly distinguished the column was its radical critique of contemporary sexual relations. As Lucy Bland has noted, from the 1880s, the consciousness that a double standard of sexual morality existed for men and women became a distinguishing feature in feminist campaigns. Bella's 'Matrons and Maidens' column both reflected and contributed to the increasing prominence accorded the issue, Bella repeatedly denouncing the 'damnable theory' which held that 'sexual vice' was 'an indulgence *necessary* to the human male animal', but which judged harshly any woman who erred from contemporary middle-class sexual norms.[84] Like many feminists, she apportioned much of the blame to the medical profession, asserting that doctors had 'taught our young men, ay, and older ones also, that incontinence is a necessity of their lives, and have encouraged them in the indulgence of their passions as being necessary to health', a position she maintained in the face of fierce criticism from male doctors within her readership.[85] As Bella reiterated on several occasions, it was a discourse of male sexuality which operated within a mutually reinforcing relationship with two similarly egregious facets of hegemonic sexual attitudes: women's sexual objectification and their lack of bodily autonomy. Women, both in cultural and legal terms, were considered to be the possessions of men, their market value determined solely by their ability to satiate male 'bestial lusts': it was as if, Bella noted bitterly, women were 'mere feminine dolls and puppets, whose strings are pulled by the men for whose amusement we caper and dance'.[86]

During her four years as editor of the 'Matrons and Maidens' column, Bella steadily delineated the reach of the sexual double standard in numerous aspects of contemporary society, drawing her readers' attention to its pervasive influence in legal, medical, political and military spheres as well as in the cultural and social world. Contributing to the national debate on marriage, instigated in 1888 by New Woman writer Mona Caird in the *Westminster Review*, Bella was critical of the institution in its current incarnation, although, like Caird, she held back from calling for its dissolution. Decrying it as a 'miserable travesty', she highlighted the inequity of English marriage laws, which decreed that a husband could obtain a divorce solely on the grounds of his spouse's adultery, but not a wife, and which, as in Scots law, made no provision either for marital rape or for the knowing transmission of a venereal disease.[87] Also like Caird, she drew parallels between contemporary marriage and prostitution, construing both as sexual transactions of an inherently commercial nature, commenting in an early column that marriages were often 'little more than "respectable" forms of prostitution, where women sell themselves as freely as their sisters on the streets'.[88] Towards female sex workers themselves, while like many feminists of the period she struggled to perceive them as anything other than passive victims of either male seduction or economic hardship, her writing was free from moral judgement, her column consistently urging compassion towards 'our sisters' and chastising those women who 'held themselves apart in an attitude of pharisaical superiority'.[89] Just like the 'poor girl' driven to take the life of her illegitimate child rather than face 'the shame and disgrace which she knows will be poured upon her in exposure', their plight served to illustrate the faults of the system rather than the failings of the individual, a system 'which sends one sex to the devil and lets the other go scot free'.[90]

When an attempt was made by the Conservative government to reintroduce a system of regulation in India, similar to the notorious Contagious Diseases Acts, after over half the colonial British troops were reported to have contracted a venereal disease, Bella assisted in the vigorous campaign against its authorisation.[91] Indeed, while Kenneth Ballhatchet has downplayed the effectiveness of British anti-regulationism over India, suggesting Lady Henry Somerset's initial support for a new, repressive system of regulation split the movement, Bella's columns depict a vibrant and active propaganda campaign, comprising 'many earnest and indefatigable workers', including the veteran campaigner Josephine Butler, 'on the warpath again – back to her old work, roused up to renewed efforts in the fight for the right by the sight of evil at hand and of fresh dangers ahead'.[92] Referring to the subject in no less than twenty-four of her columns between 1897 and 1898, Bella argued that the Acts would place 'the legal stamp of authoritative approval upon that double code of sexual morality which it should be the undying effort of every honourable man and woman to abolish'.[93] She used her column to fight against their reinstitution, reproducing letters from sympathetic parties, issuing stern rebuttals to more critical correspondents, publicising 'Abolitionist' literature such as Josephine Butler's new paper 'The Storm-Bell', and reporting on the meetings of the organisations spearheading the campaign, the Ladies National Association for the Abolition of Government Regulation of Vice and the Federation for the Abolition of State Regulation of Prostitution.[94]

Indeed, it is plausible that it was her preoccupation with this campaign which led to her dismissal from the *Labour Leader*. It was certainly unlikely to have been a fight that would have particularly engaged grassroots ILP men, who were more concerned with the capitalist exploitation of the proletariat than with male power over women and who in 1897 and 1898 would have been preoccupied with the defeat of the Welsh miners' strikes or with the prospects of forging an alliance with the trade unions.[95] Indeed, several male socialists appear to be been actively hostile to the anti-regulationist propaganda, Bella commenting in February 1898, 'Seemingly my frequent expressions of condemnation of the notorious C.D. Acts have not been at all relished by a number of the male readers of this paper.'[96]

Even Hardie, despite his consistent support of women's suffrage, was liable to foreground class inequities over gender discrimination when considering the issue of prostitution. In doing so, he can be seen to be guilty of enacting the patriarchal power imbalance he elsewhere professed a commitment to overthrowing. This can be evidenced by his response to a scandal that broke in Glasgow in January and February of 1896. It concerned the trial of a Mrs Helen Pollok, a madam who ran a brothel on Great Western Road in the city's middle-class West End. While the *Evening Times* and *Evening News* printed in full the names, addresses, occupations and workplaces of the two girls who had on occasion worked at the brothel and who had been called to give evidence, causing them to be 'shunned as moral lepers by their sanctimonious neighbours', the evening papers withheld the identities of their male clientele.[97] For four weeks Hardie railed against this injustice in the pages of the *Labour Leader*, promising to expose the names of the men. In the process, he precipitated a journalistic sensation comparable to that of W. T. Stead's 1885 exposé of child prostitution in London, 'The Maiden Tribute of Modern Babylon', albeit on a smaller scale. Newsboys were shouting and selling *Labour Leaders* 'by the gross' on every street corner and pandemonium broke out in the newspaper's office as the printers struggled to keep up with demand and members of staff cast lots 'for a few hours sleep'.[98] The paper relished every detail of the drama, relating how bribes were being 'poured out like water to prevent exposure', how their investigator was at times thwarted by 'the emissaries of the ghouls who we are tracking to their doom' and how *Leader* staff themselves were unable to leave the office without being shadowed by private detectives.[99]

Like 'The Maiden Tribute', Hardie's suggestive prose, which at once piqued and censured 'the public taste for prurient and filthy detail', was structured by the narrative form of melodrama, Hardie choosing to represent prostitution as the 'old story of the seduction of poor girls by vicious aristocrats'.[100] Yet while Stead, according to Judith Walkowitz, immediately undercut the narrative's inherent class criticism by a focus on 'sentimental moralism ... passive, innocent, female victims and individual evil men', Hardie, in 'The Glasgow Scandal', repeatedly laid emphasis on the material wealth and social standing of the 'rich seducer', in contrast to the poverty of 'the victim whom he lured by his gold to her ruin', thereby creating a salacious tale of unrivalled aristocratic and ecclesiastical debauchery and hypocrisy.[101] Indeed, the whole episode, according to Hardie, smacked of a class cover-up on a grand scale, with the police, courts and media all implicated:

> Bailies, religious philanthropists who hold their head high in society, lawyers, business men, great employers of labour, clergymen, and men of title *are known to the authorities* as being among those who would have been dragged through the mire, and because of this the matter was hushed up. Had they been poor people, then – then there would have been no reserve. But the rich, the great, the religious! 'Twere sacrilege to lay hands on these.[102]

The brothel's madam Mrs Pollock was depicted as their accomplice, a 'she-devil' whose stock instrument of torture, the abortionist's speculum, caused 'piercing screams and heavy groans' which alarmed the neighbours, while the girls themselves were transformed into the narrative's victims, variously described as 'weak', 'poor' and 'hapless'. Despite the testimony from an ex-councillor of Glasgow that the girls 'went to Mrs. Pollock's of their own free will fully conscious of what they were going for' and, indeed, 'seemed to be on the best terms with Mrs. Pollock', in Hardie's account they were stripped of all sexual or economic autonomy, repeatedly referred to as the daughters of working men, despite Hardie acknowledging that they were themselves 'working girls'.[103] This left the working-class man, embodied by Hardie and his male *Labour Leader* staff, to fulfil the role of hero, struggling against the dangers of libel action and bankruptcy to 'do our duty by the class to which we belong' and tear aside 'the veil which hides the vice of our wealthy classes'.[104]

Hardie's championing of the working-class man in his narrative of prostitution reflects what several scholars have identified as the inherent masculinity of socialism during this period. Livesey argues that for middle-class men of letters at least, 'socialism became a site for the reclamation of manhood lost within capitalist modernity', concluding that 'if late nineteenth-century socialism had a sex, it was male'.[105] It is clear that, by contrast, the sexual script utilised by Bella in her columns on the Contagious Diseases Acts would have struck a strikingly discordant note.[106] Her reading of prostitution in India as the sexual exploitation of native Indian women by the working-class British male soldiery was clearly incompatible with Hardie's melodrama of the aristocratic seduction of working men's daughters.

The incongruity of their interpretations of prostitution reflects the uneasy relationship between socialism and the women's rights movement during the 1890s, a relationship being negotiated by men and women within socialist parties and organisations throughout Europe.[107] The terms of the debate had initially been set by two texts with 'canonical status' within the movement: Frederick Engels's *The Origin of the Family, Private Property, and the State* (1884) and August Bebel's *Woman Under Socialism* (1879, revised 1883 and 1891).[108] Broadly speaking, their central argument was that female oppression had an economic cause: patriarchy was a product of capitalism and its overthrow could therefore only be realised with the cessation of class society. Hunt has argued that, by eliding the subjugation of women within a class analytic in this way, 'socialist theory both recognised and then effectively shelved the question' of female emancipation, leaving a raft of 'ambiguities, absences and limitations' around the role of women in a future socialist state and how sexual equality was to be achieved.[109] The resolution of such issues fell primarily to female activists like Bella working within the socialist movement during the 1890s and early 1900s, who 'struggled to translate the tension between socialism and feminism into a creative political practice'.[110] Their challenge was twofold: to find a legitimate role for themselves as women within the socialist movement and to simultaneously rewrite the language of socialism to fully incorporate a gendered analysis – both difficult undertakings, especially prior to the advent of a cohesive, national and politically efficacious women's movement. Bella commented in 1895: 'I doubt whether there are many amongst us who are yet able to realise all that is involved in this question of the position of women in the Socialist movement.'[111] It involved not only challenging the 'masculinist rhetoric and practice' of contemporary socialism, a movement which persisted in imagining its adherents as 'Young Men in a Hurry', but also creating sanctioned spaces in which to articulate such challenges.[112] While other socialist newspapers followed the *Labour Leader* in publishing women's columns, including 'Our Woman's Letter' penned by 'Julia Dawson' in the *Clarion* between 1895 and 1911 and 'Iona's' later column in the *Leader*,[113] several women found fiction a more hospital genre than male-edited socialist journalism for exploring the more transgressive implications of socialist politics, with Isabella Ford, Katharine Bruce Glasier and Ethel Carnie Holdsworth all writing novels critiquing current gender relations.[114]

According to Hannam and Hunt, that such attempts were permitted at all was due to the fact that prior to 1905 and the advent of suffrage militancy, the Woman Question 'had few immediate political implications'.[115] Even so, the frank and repeated criticism of the behaviour of male socialists in 'Matrons and Maidens' proved controversial, with Bella criticised for being 'too hard on the men', although in her typically dry manner she professed herself unlikely 'to be disturbed by any qualms of conscience on that score'.[116] Yet forming a more precise assessment of the column's reception and significance within the early British labour movement is problematic. While we know that during this period the *Labour Leader* was the most widely read of the weekly socialist newspapers, its circulation in 1894 exceeding 40,000 copies – compared to 34,000 sold by the *Clarion* and between 2,000 and 3,000 by *Justice* and the *Commonweal* – such figures indicate the potential rather than actual readership of the 'Matrons and Maidens' column.[117] Bearing in mind Bella's own misgivings about the provision of a 'special column for women', some ILP men are likely to have ignored 'Matrons and Maidens', seeing it as irrelevant to their concerns, one male correspondent viewing his interest in it as so exceptional as to require an apology.[118] Furthermore, the principal source for ascertaining how the column was received by those who did read it are the readers' letters that Bella chose to publish in the column, the vast majority of which are supportive. While acknowledging these limitations, however, it is possible to draw two tentative conclusions.

The first is that the column was welcomed by women within the movement, who used it as a forum for publicising a wide range of women-focused events, organisations and literature. While some of the female correspondents were prominent within the socialist and women's rights movements, including the Edinburgh feminist freethinker and birth control campaigner Jane Hume Clapperton (the subject of Chapter 5), Elizabeth Wolstenholme Elmy, Isabella O. Ford, Katharine Bruce Glasier, Edith Ellis, Sophia Jex-Blake and Mona Caird, the vast majority of letters came from local ILP branch activists. For such women the column performed a vital supportive, coordinating and unifying role, providing them with a space to vent their frustrations about socialist men, as well as to share advice, request information, report on meetings and appeal for funds. The second conclusion to be drawn is that among male readers the column divided opinion. While several men wrote to pledge their support to the cause of women's emancipation, specific feminist issues such as the medical perpetuation of the sexual double standard or the campaign against the reinstatement of the Contagious Diseases Act in India triggered a flurry of negative responses, one male reader, a 'Hater of Cant', expressing his incredulity that Hardie tolerated 'Lily Bell's' 'column and a half of bigoted cant week after week'.[119]

An uneasy alliance

Hardie stood by her, initially at least. Indeed, it is clear the editorial team of the *Labour Leader* viewed 'Matrons and Maidens' as providing valuable evidence of the paper's pioneering feminist credentials, in an 1895 publicity notice stating how it had 'from the first recognized the importance of the woman's side of the labour movement, and made special provision for a full and fair presentation of their views', praising 'Lily Bell's' 'fearless and intelligent handling of women's interests'.[120] Nearly two decades later, members of the ILP leadership would reflect back with pride on the party's early, enlightened attitude to the Woman Question, Hardie claiming in 1913 that 'ours is the one political organization wherein women stand on terms of perfect equality with men' and John Bruce Glasier in 1919 that 'the women's political agitation, like the political labour movement, may be said to have been cradled in the ILP'.[121] In actuality, however, as work by Hannam has demonstrated, the position of the ILP towards both women and women's suffrage was not uniform, but instead marked by contradiction, inconsistency and ambiguity, in both its rhetoric and practice.[122] There are several telling illustrations of this. First, the *Labour Leader*, while accommodating Bella's weekly critique of male power, also contained highly patronising accounts of women by male socialist writers, who persisted in both infantilising and sexualising ILP female propagandists, sometimes simultaneously. One particularly notorious offender was 'Marxian' (George A. H. Samuel), a well-known and popular columnist on the paper who was on good terms with Hardie and who made no secret of his ambivalence towards women's rights, ranking the issue of marriage along with 'religion, vegetarianism, hypnotism [and] cold baths' as individual idiosyncrasies that socialism should have nothing to do with.[123] After arriving nearly two hours late for a Sunday night meeting in Tottenham, and delivering what he described as 'an atrociously bad lecture', he turned his attention to the chairperson, 'Miss Vida Knight', whom he chose to describe in the following piquant terms:

> Occupying the chair shone a bright-eyed, vivacious little girl, who handled the meeting as though it were her mother's nursery, and made me feel thankful that I did not get a box on my ear for general ignorance, timidity, and incompetence ... If you imagine a chic, brown-haired creature with the healthy grace and assurance of an American girl, the knowledge of an average man, and the years and artless beauty of a child, you may be able to form some idea of what Miss Knight is.[124]

Unsurprisingly, some women activists deeply resented the condescending tone of such articles, the Leeds socialist Lizzie Maguire reacting angrily when described by *Leader* writer Jim Connell as 'irritating, fascinating, exasperating, beautiful'; she protested indignantly to 'Lily Bell', 'He actually admits we are intelligent and then writes such stuff!', and asserted that the women of Leeds were 'far too rational and far too much interested in Socialism to appreciate such folly'.[125] Bella was forced to act as an intermediary between the two parties, in her column warning Connell that while his article may have been written 'in a spirit of fun', 'women resent even the appearance of not being taken seriously, and are much more quick to suspect the presence of an underlying element of contempt in the "chaff" to which they are subjected than might be supposed from the fact that they so often allow it to pass unchallenged'.[126]

Second, while in theory there were no barriers to women holding office within the ILP, with Enid Stacy, Emmeline Pankhurst, Isabella Ford, Katharine Bruce Glasier and Caroline Martyn all serving on the NAC during the 1890s and 1900s, little was done to actively encourage women to become members. Although there were undoubtedly local variations, with branches in Glasgow among the more proactive in facilitating female participation, women were often restricted to organising social events and, overall, numbers remained at a low level, with women comprising approximately 10 per cent of the delegates to the annual conferences.[127] Bella herself occasionally expressed impatience at women's apparent lack of interest in politics, although she understood the considerable impediments on women's time and was sympathetic to how their domestic responsibilities kept them 'on the grind from morning to night without cessation, and without question as to the justice of it'.[128]

Finally, while on paper the ILP was committed to female suffrage, in practice it avoided campaigning directly on the issue. The inclusion of female enfranchisement in the party's constitution can be directly attributed to Bella herself, as a representative of the Women's Labour Party moving a resolution at the 1895 annual conference in Newcastle which sought to clarify that ILP support for extending electoral rights encompassed 'both men and women'.[129] Yet she was well aware of the issue's divisiveness within the party, overhearing some prominent party workers 'deprecating "the lowering of the beautiful ideal of Socialism" (!), which, they considered, would be the result of what they called "dragging in the question of women's suffrage"'.[130] According to research by Ugolini, such views became increasingly commonplace after the election defeat of 1895, which resulted in a major shift in ILP party ideology towards an emphasis on a 'working-class, masculine, trade unionist "Labour" and a concentration on workplace, economic changes'.[131] Although there were undoubtedly still exceptions, Ugolini argues that overall this resulted in a greater tendency amongst male ILP members to view women's suffrage variously as a middle-class issue, an irrelevant 'fad' or as an impediment to socialism, 'C. H.' suggesting in a letter to 'Lily Bell' that as women were 'generally more conservative than men', their enfranchisement might inadvertently result in the maintenance of 'such orthodoxies as the monarchy, the Church, the parson, etc.'[132]

As Margaret McMillan noted, 'the Independent Labour Party was not formed to champion women. It was born to make war on capitalism and competition'.[133] During its early history, the ILP chose to emphasise class unity above gender disunity, and capitalist rather than patriarchal exploitation. As such, socialist women often found themselves engaged in a process of negotiation between loyalty to their gender and loyalty to their class, with a diverse range of positions taken. Bella, despite her sincere belief that 'The cause of women and the cause of labour were indissolubly connected', often chose to prioritise women's rights issues, declaring in 1895 in response to what she perceived to be the sycophantism and misplaced loyalty of Liberal ladies towards the male politicians they supported, 'I hope our Socialist women will never forget that *they* are "women first and Socialists afterwards"'.[134]

Indeed, Bella's emphasis on issues of sexuality and gender can be seen as integral to her understanding of socialism. As an ethical socialist, she was deeply committed to the individual moral regeneration that would result ultimately in a socialist utopia. Critically, however, like other 'new life' female socialists working within the ILP, including Isabella Ford and Enid Stacy, Bella held the movement's reconceptualisation of personal relations to encompass not just an emphasis on selflessness and altruism but the transformation of relations between the sexes.[135] True comradeship, she argued, was impossible while exchanges between socialist men and women were governed by the sex instinct. Instead, Bella envisaged a new model of relations between women and men, one based not on flirtation but on rationality and mutual respect. A necessary precursor to this more 'natural relationship between the sexes', and consequently to the sought-for fellowship and fraternity of ethical socialism, was the securing of female emancipation.[136] 'Until we have free women', Bella urged, 'we may dream of obtaining socialism, but it will continue to remain a dream', its attainment impossible 'so long as any of the existing sex barriers remain.'[137] Indeed, she commented, even if such a utopia were achievable, its realisation would be patently undesirable, for 'Socialist men are pretty much like other men, and their Socialist "heaven upon earth" would be a male heaven only!'[138]

The principal burden of responsibility in securing women's rights she placed on women themselves, believing that until they learnt to assert their own needs, socialist men could hardly be expected to take them seriously.[139] Freedom, she stated, 'does not come to us, we must take it and keep it for ourselves', and in order to do this, she proposed the formation of a national, independent association of women, 'drawing together into one whole all those who are beginning to think seriously and earnestly, or to feel that they have their share in the work that is to be done.'[140] Until then, if ILP men persisted in sidelining women's issues and confining them to auxiliary roles, socialist women should go on strike, 'refuse to do their [i.e., the men's] work without the full recognition we claim, and meantime to go on with our own', a statement prophetic of the later controversial actions of Christabel Pankhurst at the Cockermouth by-election in 1906, when she withdrew the support of the WSPU from the ILP candidate.[141]

Prior to the advent of the national, militant women's suffrage movement, however, the balance of power lay with the ILP. By 1898, its chairman decided its newspaper could do without its 'Matrons and Maidens' columnist. On 3 February, Hardie wrote to David Lowe agreeing with him that 'L.B.' was 'hopeless', before writing three weeks later to give her notice.[142] How Bella reacted to the news is not known. She continued to contribute occasional columns until the end of the year, her final piece appearing on 17 December 1898, reiterating the plight of '"The Queen's Daughters in India" ... so cruelly oppressed by the workings of the Contagious Diseases Acts.'[143] With her departure, the *Labour Leader* lost its only consistent, formalised connection to the women's rights movement, with no section specifically for women included again until 1906, when Katharine Bruce Glasier, writing under the pseudonym 'Iona', began 'Women's Outlook', a column described by Hannam as 'often condescending' and which emphasised women's role in the domestic sphere.[144]

Conclusion

Bella Pearce's rise and fall as an influential feminist socialist commentator within the ILP during the 1890s is illustrative of both the productiveness and divisiveness of 'new life' socialism as a space for the articulation of a women's rights discourse during this period. It necessitated a delicate process of negotiation, which was rendered further complex in Bella's case by the issues of sexual progressivism to the fore of her feminist agenda, notably the pervasive influence of the sexual double standard, the inequity of marriage in its current form, and female sex work and its regulation by the state. At times, she felt progress had been made, in 1894 reflecting that 'considering that there has been so little time for evolution out of the old order of things, we do seem to be making some advance'.[145] With the 1900s, however, came an irrevocable shift in her thinking. The increasing emphasis placed by some socialists, from the end of 1904 onwards, on the attainment of adult suffrage as an alternative to women's suffrage left her exasperated; she interpreted it as an underhand attempt to block the enfranchisement of women by tendering a remote and impractical alternative. The political landscape had shifted and votes for women now appeared a real and immediate possibility. The ILP's failure to grasp the nettle and declare itself 'openly and boldly for the women' was the deciding factor in ensuring Bella's withdrawal from socialist politics.[146] According to her, the ILP had 'proven itself to be first and foremost a man's party, in which, as in the other political parties, women are a secondary consideration'.[147]

Instead, she transferred her energies and resources to the militant women's suffrage movement, whose protagonists she heralded as 'women who dare to fight for their rights, and will plead for them never again!'[148] Since 1895 she had been an active member of the WEU, a cross-party radical feminist organisation founded by Elizabeth Wolstenholme Elmy and which lobbied on a range of issues.[149] However, it was with the explosion onto the political scene of the WSPU in 1905 that Bella felt the greatest sense of excitement, believing it to be 'exactly the kind of party – a woman's party – that I advocated long ago, and hoped some day to see'.[150] In June 1907 she was appointed honorary treasurer of its Scottish Council, an organisation composed of delegates from each of the Scottish branches of the WSPU and which for a brief period functioned as a self-supporting body independent of the Pankhursts in London, establishing headquarters in Glasgow, opening a branch in Edinburgh and even contemplating publishing its own edition of *Votes for Women*.[151] Helen Fraser, an old friend of Bella's, was its principal organiser, and Teresa Billington-Greig its honorary secretary, the Council seeing its main duty as 'the supervision and direction of propaganda work'.[152] On 5 October 1907, it staged Scotland's first large-scale suffrage demonstration in Edinburgh, over a thousand representatives from both militant and constitutional

Scottish suffrage societies processing down Princes Street in fifty decorated 'carriages, cabs, char-a-bancs, brakes and other vehicles, including one motor car'. According to the *Scotsman*, over 10,000 spectators turned out to watch the spectacle, 'some sympathetic, a few playfully hostile, the majority stolidly apathetic'.[153]

Smaller-scale public meetings were staged throughout Scotland. Between July and December 1907 Bella overcame her reservations about public speaking and addressed audiences in Rothesay, Millport, Largs, Langside, Larkhall and Stirling, battling the elements in open-air meetings 'where the roar of the winds and waves makes your voice inaudible at two yards, and when intermittent deluges of rain send all the promenaders scurrying pell-mell to the nearest shelter!'[154] It was clearly an exhilarating time, the experience of intense collaboration towards a shared and passionately held goal facilitating the forging of close personal ties. In February 1907 Teresa Billington married her husband Fred Greig from Bella's house in Langside, with the reception at Helen Fraser's art studio cum suffrage office in town.[155] An Edinburgh WSPU activist later commented how, during this period, 'everything else was gradually swamped and I lived and moved and seemed to have my being in working for votes for women', while Bella wrote to a friend in America describing how she was 'devoting all my spare time to work in the Women's Movement here which is going just as I wd wish – means a big influx of life pouring in, to the astonishment of many who think the women have gone crazy'.[156]

Although she appears never to have engaged in militancy herself, Bella supported the actions of her WSPU colleagues, in direct contrast to her husband Charles's earlier antipathy towards the violent methods of anarchism. In a series of three articles in *Forward* in 1906, later reprinted as a one-penny pamphlet entitled 'The strike of a sex', she argued that by failing to accede to their demands for female enfranchisement, the Liberal government had left women with little alternative but to 'declare war to the death – or to victory', dismissing perfunctorily the criticism that the use of force was damaging the women's movement:

> What idiotic nonsense to prate of putting back the 'cause' for years! It has made a live thing instead of a dead shell, a movement of the people which will not stop until it has carried them to the top of the ascent, out of the valley of humiliation in which the degradation of their womanhood has held them.[157]

The Edwardian militant suffrage movement marked, for Bella, the exciting pinnacle of a lifetime's advocacy of feminist claims. Yet the Pearces' story does not end there. In addition to their involvement with the Glasgow

Ruskin Society, the ILP, the WEU, the Male Electors League for Women's Suffrage and the WSPU, the couple were committed disciples of another organisation, entitled the Brotherhood of the New Life. A relatively small, millenarian, Christian group, with utopian communities in New York state and California, the Brotherhood preached a distinctive and unorthodox set of beliefs regarding sex which rendered it notoriously transgressive by contemporary standards of respectability. It is the Pearces' assimilation, reinterpretation and subsequent dissemination of these beliefs which render them particularly fascinating protagonists in late Victorian and Edwardian sexual radicalism, complicating our sense of the interplay between the discourses of faith and progressive politics. It is to their involvement with this form of Christian sexual mysticism that this book now turns.

Notes

1 Lily Bell, 'Matrons and Maidens', *Labour Leader*, 23 November 1895, p. 2.
2 Ibid.; Lily Bell, 'Woman and socialism. A reply to Miss Bondfield', *Forward*, 9 February 1907, p. 3.
3 S. Yeo, 'A new life: the religion of socialism in Britain, 1883–1896', *History Workshop Journal*, 4 (1977), pp. 5–56.
4 R. Livesey, *Socialism, Sex, and the Culture of Aestheticism in Britain, 1880–1914* (Oxford: Oxford University Press, 2007), p. 47.
5 Quoted in Yeo, 'A new life', p. 8.
6 Yeo, 'A new life', p. 10.
7 Lily Bell, 'Matrons and Maidens', *Labour Leader*, 21 April 1894, p. 7.
8 Charles wrote nine 'Matrons and Maidens' columns as 'Sophia' between 24 July and 25 September 1897, commenting on the reimposition of the Contagious Diseases Acts in India, the 1897 Women's Suffrage Bill and Edward Carpenter's *Love's Coming of Age*. He also penned a three-part explication of his Christian mysticism (see Chapter 3). We know that Charles wrote as 'Sophia' because of a letter from Elizabeth Wolstenholme Elmy to Harriet McIlquham, in which she states, 'Lily Bell is home again and I send a note from Her. "Sophia," the modern Sophia, by the way, is Mr. Pearce.' Letter from Elmy to Harriet McIlquham, 15 August 1897, Elizabeth Wolstenholme Elmy Papers, British Library (BL), Add.Mss. 47449–55, fol. 126. I am indebted to Maureen Wright for providing transcripts of the relevant letters from the Elizabeth Wolstenholme Elmy Papers.
9 H. Lintell, 'Lily Bell: Socialist and Feminist, 1894–8' (Master's dissertation, Bristol Polytechnic, 1990).
10 J. Hannam, '"In the comradeship of the sexes lies the hope of progress and social regeneration": women in the West Riding ILP, c. 1890–1914', in J. Rendall (ed.), *Equal or Different: Women's Politics, 1800–1914* (Oxford: Blackwell, 1987), pp. 214–38; J. Hannam, *Isabella Ford, 1855–1924* (Oxford: Blackwell, 1989); J. Hannam, 'Women and the ILP, 1890–1914', in D. James, T. Jowitt and K. Laybourn (eds), *The Centennial*

History of the Independent Labour Party (Halifax: Ryburn, 1992), pp. 205–28; J. Hannam and K. Hunt 'Propagandising as socialist women', in B. Taithe and T. Thornton (eds), *Propaganda: Political Rhetoric and Systems of Belief* (Stroud: Sutton Publishing, 1999), pp. 167–82; J. Hannam and K. Hunt, *Socialist Women: Britain, 1880s to 1920s* (London: Routledge, 2002); K. Hunt, *Equivocal Feminists: The Social Democratic Federation and the Woman Question, 1884–1911* (Cambridge: Cambridge University Press, 1996); L. Ugolini, '"It is only justice to grant women's suffrage": Independent Labour Party men and women's suffrage 1893–1905', in C. Eustance, J. Ryan and L. Ugolini (eds), *A Suffrage Reader: Charting Directions in British Suffrage History* (London: Leicester University Press, 2000), pp. 126–44.

11 Lily Bell, 'Woman and socialism: a reply to Miss Bondfield', *Forward*, 9 February 1907, p. 3.
12 Birth certificate, Isabella Duncan; death certificates Margaret Duncan and John Thomson Duncan.
13 Scotland Census, 1851–1901; birth certificate, Isabella Duncan.
14 Diary of Jane Lee Waring, 19 August 1903, Thomas Lake Harris Papers, Columbia University, reel 13, section 314 (hereafter TLH Papers reel/section). Maureen Purdie, the current owner of 'Lucerne', generously provided me with information relating to the deeds of the home.
15 E. Eunson, *The Gorbals: An Illustrated History* (Catrine: Richard Stenlake Publishing, 1996), p. 17.
16 I. Marshall and R. Smith, *Queen's Park Historical Guide and Heritage Walk* (Glasgow: Glasgow City Council, 1997), p. 16.
17 Lily Bell, 'The women's fight for freedom', *Forward*, 17 November 1906, p. 7.
18 Ibid.
19 Scottish Women's Liberal Federation, *Minutes*, 1891, quoted in M. K. Smitley, *The Feminine Public Sphere: Middle-Class Women and Civic Life in Scotland: 1870–1914* (Manchester: Manchester University Press, 2009), p. 110.
20 Lily Bell, 'Maidens and Matrons', *Labour Leader*, 19 May 1894, p. 10.
21 Letter from William Gladstone to Samuel Smith, MP, 11 April 1892, in S. G. Bell and K. M. Offen (eds), *Women, The Family and Freedom: The Debate in Documents*, Vol. 2: *1880–1950* (Stanford: Stanford University Press, 1983), pp. 221–5.
22 'A Ruskin Meeting. (By a lady representative.)', in the Ruskin Society of Glasgow Minute Book 1891–9, Papers of the Ruskin Society of Glasgow, University of Glasgow Special Collections, MS Gen 1093, fol. 2 (hereafter RSG Papers MS/folio).
23 From *Unto This Last*, quoted in S. Eagles, *After Ruskin: The Social and Political Legacies of a Victorian Prophet, 1870–1920* (Oxford: Oxford University Press, 2011), p. 27.
24 Eagles, *After Ruskin*, p. 153; press report of the Ruskin Society of Glasgow 'At Home' in the Cockburn Hotel, 25 October 1897, Minute Book 1891–9, RSG Papers, MS Gen 1093/2.
25 Minute Book 1891–9, RSG Papers, MS Gen 1093/43.
26 Minute Book 1891–9, RSG Papers, MS Gen 1093/2; Lily Bell, 'Matrons and Maidens', *Labour Leader*, 3 November 1894, p. 7.
27 'Death of Mr. Bream Pearce', *Labour Leader*, 20 October 1905, p. 349.

28 'Chats with I. L. P. Candidates', *Labour Leader*, 27 April 1895, p. 7.
29 Session Programme, 1892-3, Ruskin Society of Glasgow Minute Book 1891-9, MS Gen 1093/2, RSG Papers; Omni, 'I. L. P. Notes and News', *Labour Leader*, 30 November 1895, p. 10. In 1896, Charles Pearce also gave a talk to the Glasgow Women's Labour Party on marriage. See Omni, 'I. L. P. Notes and News', *Labour Leader*, 18 January 1896, p. 23.
30 Sophia [Charles Pearce], 'Matrons and Maidens', *Labour Leader*, 31 July 1897, p. 254; M. Wright, *Elizabeth Wolstenholme Elmy and the Victorian Feminist Movement: The Biography of an Insurgent Woman* (Manchester: Manchester University Press, 2011), pp. 163, 196; entry on 'Male Electors' League for Women's Suffrage', in E. Crawford, *The Women's Suffrage Movement: A Reference Guide, 1866-1928* (London: Routledge, 1999, 2001), p. 366. While Charles hoped to bring 'actual electoral pressure on members of Parliament or candidates', in reality, the League's impact on the political establishment appears to have been minimal, their propaganda activities seemingly restricted to the distribution of literature at WSPU and Women's Trade and Labour Council meetings.
31 Marriage Certificate of Charles William Pearce and Mary Gill, 25 August 1863, Princes Street Chapel, Norwich.
32 England and Scotland Census, 1881.
33 Charles remained in contact with his children after the death of his first wife. His eldest son Charles lived in Essex and worked as a fire insurance clerk, suggesting his father's involvement in his career path (England Census 1891, 1901). His youngest son Ernest emigrated to America in 1889, settling in San Francisco and also working in insurance (US Federal Census 1910, 1930). Bella left three of Charles's children bequests in her will, with details given of spouses and children, suggesting continued and friendly relations (will of Isabella Pearce, lodged 24 April 1930).
34 Marriage certificate of Charles William Pearce and Isabella Duncan, 17 June 1891.
35 E. Gordon, 'Irregular marriage', podcast on website of AHRC-funded project, 'A History of Working-Class Marriage', University of Glasgow, http://workingclassmarriage.gla.ac.uk/wp-content/uploads/2013/03/Prof-Eleanor-Gordon.mp3 (accessed 3 January 2019).
36 Lily Bell, 'Matrons and Maidens', *Labour Leader*, 17 April 1897, p. 128.
37 Lily Bell, 'Matrons and Maidens', *Labour Leader*, 1 August 1896, p. 262.
38 Letter from Elizabeth Wolstenholme Elmy to Harriet McIlquham, 23 November 1908, Elizabeth Wolstenholme Elmy Papers, BL, Add.Mss. 47449-55, fol. 218; letter from 'Dovie' (Jane Lee Waring) to 'My dearest Son', 22 September 1903, TLH Papers 12/237; letter from 'Dovie' (Jane Lee Waring) to 'Blessed Son', 9 July 1903, TLH Papers 14/315.
39 Marxian, 'Scotland's London', *Labour Leader*, 4 April 1896, p. 117.
40 Tricotrin, 'Chats with I.L.P Candidates', *Labour Leader*, 27 April 1895, p. 7.
41 J. K. Hardie, 'Between ourselves', *Labour Leader*, 8 June 1895, p. 2; W. Haddow, *My Seventy Years* (Glasgow: Robert Gibson, 1943).
42 'A modern maying. Yesterday at the Green', *Glasgow Evening News*, 6 May 1895.
43 *Glasgow Herald*, 6 May 1895.

44 Letter from Charles Pearce to Hardie, 9 March 1894, Francis Johnson Correspondence (hereafter FJC), ILP Archives, reel 2, 1894/42, National Library of Scotland (hereafter NLS).

45 Letter from James G. Borland to John Ruskin, 8 February 1896, in 'The Ruskin Society of Glasgow Correspondence Book', RSG Papers, MS Gen 1093/1. Charles Pearce was responsible for nominating Hardie for membership of the Ruskin Society.

46 J. Rae, *Contemporary Socialism* (1884, 1891), cited in Yeo, 'A new life', pp. 7, 28.

47 I. O. Ford, *On the Threshold* (1895), quoted in Livesey, *Socialism, Sex, and the Culture of Aestheticism*, pp. 104; L. Thompson, *The Enthusiasts: A Biography of John and Katharine Bruce Glasier* (London: Victor Gollancz, 1971), p. 66.

48 William Morris, 'The prospects of architecture in civilization' (lecture to London Institute, 1881), in N. Kelvin (ed.), *William Morris on Art and Socialism* (Toronto: Dover, 1999); *Glasgow Herald*, 8 April 1896.

49 Lily Bell, 'Matrons and Maidens', *Labour Leader*, 23 November 1895, p. 2.

50 Ibid.

51 From an article published in April 1897 in the *Labour Prophet*, the journal of the Labour Church movement, quoted in Yeo, 'A new life', p. 6. Yeo was the first to give the 'religion of socialism' serious attention, challenging the prevailing orthodoxy that the period from the mid-1880s to the mid-1890s was merely a 'backwater' or 'tributary' feeding into the 'mainstream' of a more pragmatic and ideologically sound materialist labour politics, Yeo arguing instead that it constituted a distinctive and important phase in the social history of socialism. Subsequent studies on the Labour Church movement, the Fellowship of the New Life and the Tolstoyan communities in Purleigh, Whiteway and elsewhere, have served to illustrate the pervasiveness of religious and ethical thinking within socialism at this time, as well as emphasise its continued presence within the labour movement, albeit in attenuated forms. See Yeo, 'A new life'; M. Bevir, 'The Labour Church movement, 1891–1902', *Journal of British Studies*, 38:2 (April 1999), pp. 217–45; K. Manton, 'The Fellowship of the New Life: English ethical socialism reconsidered', *History of Political Thought*, 24:2 (Summer 2003), pp. 282–304; W. H. G. Armytage, 'J. C. Kenworthy and the Tolstoyan communities in England', in W. G. Jones (ed.), *Tolstoi and Britain* (Berg: Oxford, 1995), pp. 135–51; D. Maltz, 'Ardent service: female eroticism and new life ethics in Gertrude Dix's *The Image Breakers* (1900)', *Journal of Victorian Culture* (2012), pp. 1–17; D. Maltz, 'The newer new life: A. S. Byatt, E. Nesbit and socialist subculture', *Journal of Victorian Culture*, 17:1 (2012), pp. 79–84; D. Maltz, 'Living by design: C. R. Ashbee's Guild of Handicraft and two English Tolstoyan communities, 1897–1907', *Victorian Literature and Culture*, 39 (2011), pp. 409–26; Livesey, *Socialism, Sex, and the Culture of Aestheticism*.

52 Lily Bell, 'Matrons and Maidens', *Labour Leader*, 25 August 1894, p. 7.

53 During the years 1894–8, Bella Pearce also sat on the Cathcart School Board, serving two successive terms. She was presumably elected on an ILP or a women's platform, overseeing the building of a new school, promoting the use of Swedish drill as a form of exercise for girls and attempting, unsuccessfully, to get the shorter catechism removed from the syllabus, an indication of her unorthodox Christian beliefs. Bella also appears

to have resisted the focus on domestic education adopted by the majority of female school board members, questioning the remit of the Industrial Work and Domestic Economy Committee, of which she had initially been appointed convenor, and instead in her second term rising to become the convenor both of the Finance Committee and the Mount Florida School Committee. L. Glasier, 'The Woman's Labour Party, Glasgow', *Labour Leader*, 13 April 1895, p. 4; 'Women and Local Boards', *Glasgow Herald*, 24 May 1894; Cathcart Parish School Board Minute Book no. 2, 1894–8, D-Ed. 1/2/1, Strathclyde Regional Archives, Mitchell Library, Glasgow; J. McDermid, 'School board women and active citizenship in Scotland, 1873–1919', *History of Education*, 38:3 (May 2009), pp. 333–47.

54 Bella Pearce was also the convenor of the finance committee charged with inquiring into the accounts of the Scottish Labour Party (SLP) following its amalgamation with the ILP in January 1895. The SLP had been running since 1888.

55 L. Glasier, 'The Woman's Labour Party in Glasgow', *Labour Leader*, 13 April 1895. The series of articles continued on 27 April 1895 (p. 9) and concluded on 25 May 1895 (p. 5).

56 Tom Wilson, 'Women's Labour Party', *Labour Leader*, 8 June 1895, p. 5; L. Glasier, 'The Woman's Labour Party, Glasgow', *Labour Leader*, 13 April 1895, p. 4.

57 By April 1897 the membership of the Women's Labour Party had dropped to twenty-nine and they were unable to afford their monthly affiliation fee to the ILP. See letters from Maude Bruce, 1 April 1897 and 5 August 1897, FJC, reel 3, 1897/13 and 1897/51, ILP Archives, NLS.

58 L. Glasier, 'The Woman's Labour Party, Glasgow', *Labour Leader*, 25 May 1895, p. 5.

59 Bella and Charles were on the planning committee for the Sunday children's classes. Omni, 'I. L. P. Notes and News', *Labour Leader*, 25 January 1896, p. 31.

60 Omni, 'I. L. P. Notes and News', *Labour Leader*, 25 May 1895, p. 5.

61 Letter from Charles Pearce to Hardie, 9 March 1894, reel 2 1894/42, FJC, ILP Archives. The failure of the ILP's District Council in Glasgow to include more women on the School Board shortlist was clearly a source of frustration for some female socialists, although for Lizzie Glasier, treasurer of the Glasgow Women's Labour Party, it was not the ILP but the prospective female candidates who were to blame, for their 'discreditable negligence and apathy' in not lobbying harder for their nomination. See L. Glasier, 'The Woman's Labour Party, Glasgow', *Labour Leader*, 13 April 1895, p. 4.

62 'The Independent Labour Party in Camlachie', *Scotsman*, 28 August 1894, p. 6; letter by C. W. Bream-Pearce, 'Camlachie candidature', *Labour Leader*, 1 June 1895, p. 10.

63 The Lorgnette, *Glasgow Evening News*, 5 April 1895, p. 1.

64 J. K. Hardie, 'Between ourselves', *Labour Leader*, 8 June 1895, p. 2.

65 *Labour Leader*, 1 June 1895, p. 6.

66 Letter by C. W. Bream-Pearce, 'Camlachie candidature', *Labour Leader*, 1 June 1895, p. 10.

67 Beatrice Webb's diary, 10 July 1895, quoted in K. Laybourn, *The Rise of Socialism in Britain c. 1881–1951* (Stroud: Sutton Publishing, 1997); *Labour Leader*, 20 July 1895, p. 2. Yeo argues that the defeat marked a watershed in the labour movement, with the emphasis in the 1880s and early 1890s on personal ethics and fraternity replaced

increasingly by the exigencies of electioneering and party bureaucracy, although Kevin Manton and Mark Bevir stress the continuities between the two periods. See Yeo, 'A new life'; Manton, 'The Fellowship of the New Life'; Bevir, 'The Labour Church movement'.

68 J. K. Hardie, 'Between ourselves', *Labour Leader*, 7 March 1896.
69 Lily Bell, 'Matrons and Maidens', *Labour Leader*, 18 May 1895, p. 4.
70 Lily Bell, 'Matrons and Maidens', *Labour Leader*, 8 December 1894, p. 5.
71 Charles was clearly present too. 'The Wastrel' joked, 'In the evening – shall I say it? – Lily Bell and I eloped for three hours. There was another man present. Here you have another innovation of this nineteenth century – to wit, the personally conducted elopement.' The tone of the piece is of mild flirtation, typical of male *Labour Leader* writers during the 1890s when describing encounters with their female associates. The Wastrel, 'On the dander', *Labour Leader*, 11 April 1896, p. 121.
72 *Labour Leader*, 9 February 1895, p. 4.
73 In a letter of March 1894, Charles used his report on the condition of Hardie's birds to reiterate the need for the ILP to commit to female equality, commenting, 'The little man sings freely and sweetly & brings the "music of the spheres" into our office very often – and well he may for his mate is as free as he is & <u>she</u> educates the children to his joy.' Letters from Charles Pearce to Hardie, 9 March 1894, 13 February 1895 and 22 February 1895, FJC reel 2: 1894/42, 1895/32 and 1895/35, ILP Archives, NLS. See also Lily Bell, 'Matrons and Maidens', *Labour Leader*, 31 March 1894, p. 7. For Charles's involvement in two significant ILP internal disputes, both in 1895, see T. Cheadle, '"Realizing a more than earthly paradise of love": Scotland's sexual progressives, 1880–1914' (PhD thesis, University of Glasgow, 2014), pp. 32–4.
74 K. O. Morgan, *Keir Hardie: Radical and Socialist* (London: Weidenfeld & Nicolson, 1975), p. 66; C. Collette, 'Socialism and scandal: the sexual politics of the early labour movement', *History Workshop*, 23 (Spring 1987), p. 105. Steedman harboured 'some suspicion that on occasion Hardie wrote this column, in transmogrification from his "Daddy Time" children's column'. C. Steedman, *Childhood, Culture and Class in Britain: Margaret McMillan, 1860–1931* (London: Virago, 1990), pp. 130–1, 291n.45.
75 C. Stevens, 'The objections of "queer Hardie", "Lily Bell" and the suffragettes' friend to Queen Victoria's Jubilee, 1897', *Victorian Periodicals Review*, 21:3 (1988), pp. 108–14.
76 Lily Bell, 'Matrons and Maidens', *Labour Leader*, 7 April 1894, p. 6.
77 Letter from Hardie to David Lowe, June 1896, reel 3, 1896/63, FJC, ILP Archives.
78 Letters of Elizabeth Wolstenholme Elmy to Harriet McIlquham, 11 December 1895, 15 August 1897, 18 September 1898 and 26 April 1904, Elizabeth Wolstenholme Elmy Papers; J. Bruce Glasier, *James Keir Hardie: A Memorial* (Manchester: National Labour Press, 1919), p. 38. Furthermore, in 1907, Teresa Billington-Greig unwittingly 'outed' Lily Bell in the pages of *Forward*, referring to an article of hers in the previous week as being by 'Mrs. Pearce', while David Lowe, in his 1923 biography of Hardie, stated simply that 'Lily Bell hid the name of Mrs. Bream Pearce'. T. Billington-Greig, 'The difference in the women's movement: autocracy or democracy', *Forward*, 23 (November 1907), 2:7, p. 1; D. Lowe, *From Pit to Parliament: The Story of the Early Life of James Keir Hardie* (London: Labour Publishing Company, 1923), pp. 42, 94.

79 Lily Bell, 'Matrons and Maidens', *Labour Leader*, 24 October 1896; C. Benn, *Keir Hardie* (London: Hutchinson, 1992), pp. 201–2; Wright, *Elizabeth Wolstenholme Elmy*, pp. 167–8, 175n.108; Morgan, *Keir Hardie*, pp. 91–2, 301n.28.

80 Lily Bell, 'Matrons and Maidens', *Labour Leader*, 26 October 1895, p. 3; 11 December 1897, p. 405; 5 January 1895, p. 2.

81 Lily Bell, 'Matrons and Maidens', *Labour Leader*, 1 September 1894, p. 7.

82 Lily Bell, 'Matrons and Maidens', *Labour Leader*, 31 March 1894, p. 7.

83 Ibid.

84 Lily Bell, 'Matrons and Maidens', *Labour Leader*, 10 April 1897, p. 114.

85 Lily Bell, 'Matrons and Maidens', *Labour Leader*, 22 February 1896, p. 68, 29 February 1896, p. 76 and 7 March 1896, p. 82.

86 Lily Bell, 'Matrons and Maidens', *Labour Leader*, 20 March 1897, p. 90.

87 Lily Bell, 'Matrons and Maidens', *Labour Leader*, 15 February 1896, p. 58, 16 June 1894, p. 11 and 16 October 1897, p. 338.

88 Lily Bell, 'Matrons and Maidens', *Labour Leader*, 26 May 1894, p. 11.

89 Ibid. While Bella Pearce did write a column in support of the National Vigilance Association, she referred only to the non-repressive aspects of its work, such as putting posters in steamers warning girls of the dangers of sex trafficking and its provision of legal fees in cases of underage sex. See Lily Bell, 'Matrons and Maidens', *Labour Leader*, 28 May 1898, p. 183. See also L. Bland, *Banishing the Beast: Feminism, Sex and Morality* (London: Penguin 1995, Tauris Parke, 2002), pp. 95–123.

90 Lily Bell, 'Matrons and Maidens', *Labour Leader*, 12 September 1896, p. 316.

91 According to a report by the government of India published in November 1896, annual venereal disease admissions among British troops had risen to 522.3 per 1,000, although this figure included readmissions, a fact not widely publicised at the time. See K. Ballhatchet, *Race, Sex and Class under the Raj: Imperial Attitudes and Policies and their Critics, 1793–1905* (Weidenfeld & Nicolson: London, 1980), pp. 88, 90.

92 Lily Bell, 'Matrons and Maidens', *Labour Leader*, 23 July 1898, p. 245 and 29 January 1898, p. 38. As Ballhatchet notes, however, the campaign was ultimately unsuccessful – with the imposition of a new policy of regulation in India the military authorities were winning 'the last battle in a long campaign'. Ballhatchet, *Race, Sex and Class under the Raj*, p. 95.

93 Lily Bell, 'Matrons and Maidens', *Labour Leader*, 20 March 1897, p. 90.

94 The two organisations merged in 1915 to become the Association for Moral and Social Hygiene.

95 Hannam, 'Women and the ILP, 1890–1914', p. 214; Morgan, *Keir Hardie*, pp. 96–8.

96 Lily Bell, 'Matrons and Maidens', *Labour Leader*, 12 February 1898, p. 50.

97 J. K. Hardie, 'In militant mood', *Labour Leader*, 1 February 1896, p. 35.

98 Omni, 'I. L. P. Notes and News', *Labour Leader*, 15 February 1896, p. 57; J. K. Hardie, 'In militant mood', *Labour Leader*, 22 February 1896, p. 61.

99 'Glasgow West-End scandal: notice to our readers', *Labour Leader*, 29 February 1896, p. 73.

100 Ibid.; J. R. Walkowitz, *City of Dreadful Delight: Narratives of Sexual Danger in Late-Victorian London* (Chicago: University of Chicago Press, 1992), pp. 85–6.

101 Walkowitz, *City of Dreadful Delight*, p. 94; J. K. Hardie, 'In militant mood', *Labour Leader*, 1 February 1896, p. 35.
102 J. K. Hardie, 'In militant mood', *Labour Leader*, 1 February 1896, p. 35. Hardie's reading of the brothel scandal as one of aristocratic sexual exploitation is reinforced elsewhere in the paper, 'Omni' in 'I. L. P. Notes and News' justifying the *Leader's* sensationalist coverage solely on the basis of the story's class dimension, asserting that 'Simply because two girls were poor their names were blazoned forth to the world and branded as prostitutes, and simply because their seducer is rich his name was screened, and this being purely a workers' question the *Labour Leader* took the matter up, and hence the enormous sale.' Omni, 'I. L. P. Notes and News', *Labour Leader*, 15 February 1896, p. 57.
103 Letter from George MacFarlane to Hardie; 'In militant mood', *Labour Leader*, 1 February 1896, p. 35.
104 'The Glasgow scandal. astounding revelations', *Labour Leader*, 8 February 1986, p. 47.
105 Livesey, *Socialism, Sex and the Culture of Aestheticism*, pp. 11–12. See also Hannam and Hunt, *Socialist Women*, pp. 57–63.
106 Walkowitz, *City of Dreadful Delight*, p. 97.
107 See M. J. Boxer and J. H. Quataert (eds), *Socialist Women: European Socialist Feminism in the Nineteenth and Early Twentieth Century* (New York: Elsevier, 1978).
108 G. Lichtheim, *Marxism: An Historical and Critical Study* (New York, 1961), p. 241, quoted in Boxer and Quataert, *Socialist Women*, p. 10.
109 Hunt, *Equivocal Feminists*, pp. 26, 24.
110 Hannam and Hunt, *Socialist Women*, p. 2.
111 Lily Bell, 'Matrons and Maidens', *Labour Leader*, 27 April 1895.
112 Hannam and Hunt, *Socialist Women*, p. 61. In 1897, Hardie published extracts of his book in the *Labour Leader* entitled 'A Chronicle of the Sayings and Doings of the Young Men in a Hurry'.
113 'Julia Dawson' was the pen-name of Mrs D. Middleton Worrall. For an extended discussion of the women's columns, see Hannam and Hunt, 'Propagandising as socialist women', pp. 167–82.
114 C. Waters, 'New Women and socialist-feminist fiction: the novels of Isabella Ford and Katharine Bruce Glasier' and P. Fox, 'Ethel Carnie Holdsworth's "revolt of the gentle": romance and the politics of resistance in working-class women's writing', both in A. Ingram and D. Patai (eds), *Rediscovering Forgotten Radicals: British Women Writers, 1889–1939* (Chapel Hill: University of North Carolina Press, 1993), pp. 25–42 and 57–74.
115 Hannam and Hunt, 'Propagandising as socialist women', p. 179.
116 Lily Bell, 'Matrons and Maidens', *Labour Leader*, 23 May 1896, p. 174.
117 The *Labour Leader* circulation figures are from a letter to Hardie from the newspaper's printers fulfilling his request for a sales statement. See letter from George Mitchell, Labour Literature Society to Hardie, 21 May 1894, FJC, reel 2 1894/98, ILP Archives, NLS. For *Clarion* circulation figures see 'Clarion (1891–1934)', L. Brake and M. Demoor (eds), *Dictionary of Nineteenth-Century Journalism in Great Britain and Ireland* (London: British Library/Academia Press, 2009), pp. 122–3. For *Justice* and *Commonweal* circulation figures, see T. Lloyd, 'Morris v. Hyndman "Commonweal" and "Justice"', *Victorian*

Periodicals Newsletter, 9:4 (December 1976), pp. 119–28, especially pp. 122, 124 and 126. Kenneth Morgan believed the *Labour Leader* to be 'the most effective, because the most authoritative, vehicle for the social democratic cause', reaching thousands of working people and radical middle-class sympathisers. See Morgan, *Keir Hardie*, p. 67. By the turn of the century, however, its circulation figures had tailed off, and by the time it was taken over by the ILP in 1904, weekly sales had fallen to just below 12,000. Hannam and Hunt, 'Propagandising as socialist women', p. 168.

118 Lily Bell, 'Matrons and Maidens', *Labour Leader*, 31 March 1894, p. 7; 15 September 1894, p. 7.

119 Bella Pearce responded by suggesting her correspondent find a suitable replacement among 'the more tractable specimens of the feminine', stating her editor was 'well aware of my willingness to withdraw at any time'. Lily Bell, 'Matrons and Maidens', *Labour Leader*, 2 February 1895, p. 4.

120 'The Labour Leader. Programme for 1896', *Labour Leader*, 21 December 1895, p. 8.

121 J. K. Hardie, *After Twenty Years: All About the ILP* (1913), p. 13, quoted in Hannam, 'Women and the ILP, 1890–1914', p. 205. Bruce Glasier, *James Keir Hardie*, p. 38.

122 Hannam, 'Women and the ILP, 1890–1914'.

123 Marxian, 'Lanchester and Manchester', *Labour Leader*, 9 November 1895, p. 1. On Marxian's popularity, see J. Connell, 'Women's rights: Lizzie Maguire and Marxian', *Labour Leader*, 20 February 1897, p. 63; on his relationship with Hardie, see Lintell, 'Lily Bell', pp. 85–6; on his views on women's rights, see Marxian, 'Scotland's London', *Labour Leader*, 4 April 1896, p. 117.

124 Marxian, 'Mere egotism', *Labour Leader*, 15 May 1897, p. 165.

125 J. Connell, 'Women's rights: Lizzie Maguire and Marxian', *Labour Leader*, 20 February 1897, p. 63; Lily Bell, 'Matrons and Maidens', *Labour Leader*, 13 March 1897, p. 86.

126 Lily Bell, 'Matrons and Maidens', *Labour Leader*, 13 March 1897, p. 86; J. Connell, 'Queer conduct exposed', *The Labour Leader*, 8 May 1897, p. 158; J. Connell, 'The Leeds New Woman', *Labour Leader*, 8 July 1897, p. 223.

127 Hannam, 'Women and the ILP, 1890–1914', pp. 214–15, 226n.45.

128 Bella Pearce also understood that women without business experience might lack the confidence to speak up at meetings, advocating separate ILP women's groups for this reason. See Lily Bell, 'Matrons and Maidens', *Labour Leader*, 15 December 1894, p. 6 and 11 April 1896, p. 126.

129 Minutes of the ILP Annual Conference, Series 2, Part 1, Card 4 1895 24–5, ILP Archives, NLS; 'Women's rights', *Labour Leader*, 20 April 1895, p. 9.

130 Lily Bell, 'Matrons and Maidens', *Labour Leader*, 27 April 1895, p. 4.

131 Ugolini, '"It is only justice to grant women's suffrage"', p. 134.

132 Lily Bell, 'Matrons and Maidens', *Labour Leader*, 5 December 1896, p. 416.

133 Quoted in Hannam, 'Women and the ILP, 1890–1914', p. 214.

134 'Labour Day celebrations', *Glasgow Herald*, 6 May 1895; Lily Bell, 'Matrons and Maidens', *Labour Leader*, 13 April 1895, p. 4.

135 Lily Bell, 'Matrons and Maidens', *Labour Leader*, 21 April 1894, p. 7.

136 Lily Bell, 'Matrons and Maidens', *Labour Leader*, 1 December 1894, p. 7.

137 Lily Bell, 'Matrons and Maidens', *Labour Leader*, 31 October 1896, p. 382.

138 Lily Bell, 'Matrons and Maidens', *Labour Leader*, 5 December 1896, p. 416.
139 Lily Bell, 'Matrons and Maidens', *Labour Leader*, 17 August 1895, p. 4.
140 Ibid. and 21 April 1894, p. 7.
141 Lily Bell, 'Women and work', *Labour Leader*, 12 December 1896, p. 424. Bella Pearce thought the WSPU was entirely justified in its action at Cockermouth, arguing that women's suffrage should not be viewed as merely a plank in the Labour platform and reiterating that 'a Socialist regime which is not founded upon the principle of sex equality, if it were possible to institute it, would be a danger to society'. Lily Bell, 'The lesson of Cockermouth', *Forward*, 27 October 1906, p. 2.
142 Letters from Hardie to David Lowe, 3 February 1898 and 24 April 1898, 1898/11 and 1898/20, FJC, ILP Archives, NLS.
143 Lily Bell, 'Matrons and Maidens', *Labour Leader*, 17 December 1898, p. 415.
144 Hannam, 'Women and the ILP, 1890–1914', p. 211. In a later analysis, Hannam and Hunt are more generous towards Iona's 'Women's Outlook', describing it as a column which 'raised a wide range of issues concerning women's emancipation and the basis on which they should engage in socialist politics'. See Hannam and Hunt, *Socialist Women*, p. 50.
145 Lily Bell, 'Matrons and Maidens', *Labour Leader*, 1 December 1894, p. 7.
146 Lily Bell, 'Women and the Labour Party', *Forward*, 12 January 1907, p. 6.
147 Lily Bell, 'The suffrage question', *Forward*, 9 March 1907, p. 8.
148 Lily Bell, 'Women's view. "The strike of a sex"', *Forward*, 3 November 1906, p. 4.
149 Wright, *Elizabeth Wolstenholme Elmy*, pp. 152–3. Bella Pearce delivered a paper at the WEU 1896 conference titled 'Women and factory legislation', and at one point, Elmy considered her for the WEU's Council, although whether this transpired is not known. Letter from Elizabeth Wolstenholme Elmy to Harriet McIlquham, 18 September 1898, Elizabeth Wolstenholme Elmy Papers, BL, Add.Mss. 47449–55, fol. 253; Wright, *Elizabeth Wolstenholme Elmy*, pp. 167–8, 175n.108.
150 Lily Bell, 'The suffrage question', *Forward*, 9 March 1907, p. 8.
151 Entry 'Helen Fraser' in Crawford, *The Women's Suffrage Movement: A Reference Guide*, pp. 230–2; E. Crawford, *The Women's Suffrage Movement in Britain and Ireland: A Regional Survey* (London and New York: Routledge, 2006), pp. 240–1.
152 Helen Fraser described Bella Pearce as one of her 'older friends' and the two appear to have been close, Bella loaning Helen £300 towards the purchase of her London house and introducing her to both Billington Greig and Hardie. Disappointingly, however, she makes only fleeting references to her in her memoirs and oral history interviews. Will of Isabella Duncan Pearce, lodged 24 April 1930; Brian Harrison taped interviews with Helen Fraser Moyes, 19 August and 18 September 1975, The Women's Library (TWL), London Metropolitan University, 8SUF/B/054; H. Moyes, *A Woman in a Man's World* (Alpha Books: Sydney, 1971), p. 73. For the composition of the Scottish Council, see M. Phillips, 'Woman's point of view', *Forward*, 22 June 1907, p. 3.
153 'Women's social and political union', *Forward*, 22 June 1907, p. 3; M. Phillips, 'Woman's point of view', *Forward*, 12 October 1907, p. 5; 'Scottish women suffragists. Demonstration in Edinburgh', *Scotsman*, 7 October 1907, p. 8.
154 M. Phillips, 'Votes for women', *Forward*, 17 August 1907, p. 4.

155 Wedding programme of Teresa Billington and Frederick Lewis Greig, Teresa Billington-Greig Papers, 7TBG/3/2/2, TWL; Brian Harrison taped interviews with Helen Fraser Moyes, 19 August and 18 September 1975, 8SUF/B/054, TWL.
156 L. Leneman, *The Scottish Suffragettes* (Edinburgh: NMS Publishing Ltd, 2000), p. 47; letter from Bella Pearce to Brother Robert [Hart], 21 November 1906, TLH Papers 9/ 235.
157 Bella Pearce was asked to cover the women's column in *Forward* for Teresa Billington, who was arrested and sentenced to two months' imprisonment in Holloway after attending a WSPU demonstration at the opening of Parliament. The three articles in *Forward* later reprinted as a pamphlet were Lily Bell, 'Women's View. "The strike of a sex"', 3 November 1906, p. 4; 'The women's movement. News and review', 10 November 1906, p. 8; and 'The women's fight for freedom', 17 November 1906, p. 7.

3

Re-sexing religion in suburban Glasgow

In June 1903, Bella and Charles Pearce played host to an American couple at 'Nithsdale', their large stone villa in the middle-class Glasgow suburb of Langside. The man was Thomas Lake Harris, an imposing, eighty-year-old Christian mystic and the spiritual leader of the Brotherhood of the New Life, a millenarian organisation behind two utopian communities in New York state and California. The woman was Jane Lee Waring, a seventy-three-year-old heiress, originally from New York City, who had joined the Brotherhood in her thirties, fulfilling the role of Harris's chief amanuensis and, more recently, that of his third wife.

The American couple had crossed the Atlantic for a very specific purpose. Harris had founded the Brotherhood over fifty years previously, yet despite attracting the occasional, sympathetic curiosity of public figures such as the British journalist W. T. Stead, the popular novelist Marie Corelli and the American poet Edwin Markham, Harris's teachings had never won a broad-based popular support, in Britain or America. Even Arthur Cuthbert, one of his closest disciples, was forced to concede that 'Notwithstanding all the manifest eloquence of his discourses, he never did at any time appeal to the popular ear, as such.'[1] The previous month, however, Harris had received a revelation from God that it was time for him to enter the wider public arena, to declare himself and 'go forth and bear the message to the world'.[2] The Pearces were allocated a pivotal role in this evangelising mission. Both Bella and Charles were committed followers of Harris, his wife Jane describing them as 'staunch and true to the Core', Charles having first encountered Harris's teachings when in his early thirties.[3] Their house now became the British operational headquarters for the dissemination of Harris's message, the prophet renaming Nithsdale 'Battle Abbey', with Bella as the abbess and Charles the curate.[4] Charles was said by Jane to know 'all of the most advanced men in the new thought in Glasgow' and he began assembling 'an audience of eager enquirers' for the prophet's public lectures.[5] As news of the American visitors spread, letters began to arrive from Harris's small number of dispersed and disparate supporters in Britain, while a reporter from the *Glasgow Evening News* turned up to take down the story of Harris's life.[6] Finally, and most auspiciously, the house received a visitation from Harris's spiritual wife, an angelic being called 'Queen Lily', who materialised in the Pearces' breakfast room to proclaim 'this is good. The Kingdom of Heaven has found its central home and service point'.[7]

The 1903 visit marked the exciting pinnacle of what, for Charles in particular, had been a long and careful study of Harris's esoteric teachings, which had their roots in the philosophy of the eighteenth-century Swedish mystic Emanuel Swedenborg. Yet in his deep interest in arcane Christian mysticism, Charles was neither an isolated nor a particularly unusual figure in Glasgow's progressive subculture. As the eagerness of other Scottish 'advanced men' (and women) to hear Harris speak indicates, many of those involved in the emancipatory movements of socialism and feminism embraced the unconventional and eclectic religious theologies and practices that were circulating in late Victorian Britain, which together constituted a significant and enduring 'mystical revival' that lasted well into the Edwardian age.[8] As Alex Owen notes, 'It was considered perfectly feasible at the turn of the century to adhere to a communitarian vision and socialist principles while espousing a belief in an unseen spirit world', with particular enthusiasm reserved for theosophy, occultism, spiritualism and mysticism, all of which drew in varying degrees from heterodox Christianity, paganism and Eastern religion.[9] Indeed, the willingness of progressive individuals to embrace an 'eclectic collation of belief systems' is held to be a defining characteristic of the times, Ruth Livesey asserting that radical critics of late nineteenth-century capitalism exhibited a 'remarkable disregard ... of boundaries that over a century later seemed impassable divides'.[10] For example, Annie Besant was a socialist attached to the Fabian Society, yet was also a dedicated member of Helena Blavatsky's Theosophical Society, later taking over as president, while George Bernard Shaw claimed, during the course of one eventful evening, to have 'attended a Fabian meeting, gone on to hear the end of a Psychical Research one, and finished by sleeping in a haunted house with a committee of ghost hunters'.[11]

What marks out Charles and Bella Pearce's discipleship of Thomas Lake Harris, amidst the *fin de siècle* melee of socialist and spiritual interchange, is Harris's highly unorthodox teachings on sex. What exactly those teachings were, and the manner in which the Pearces interpreted, assimilated and reconfigured them in both their discourse and their intimate lives, forms the subject of this chapter. In essence, however, what their connection to the Brotherhood of the New Life reveals is the circulation, albeit in a modified form, of a radical, transatlantic, Christian doctrine of sexual mysticism within the heart of 'new life' socialist and feminist circles in Glasgow during the 1890s and 1900s, something that complicates our understanding of the sexual conservatism which predominated in such networks. As work by Lucy Bland, Barbara Taylor, Ginger Frost, Karen Hunt and others has shown, while late Victorian ethical socialists and feminists were highly critical of marriage, unlike their Owenite predecessors, the majority saw public advocacy of radical alternatives to marriage such as 'free love' not as the justifiable renunciation of a patriarchal and/or bourgeois institution, but as either an excuse for male sexual licence or a threat to the respectability and political efficacy of their movements.[12] As Frost states, 'most radicals of the end of the century theorised for the future, but lived respectably in the present'.[13] The evidence relating to the Pearces is inconclusive, with few personal papers surviving: the possibility remains, however, that along with the period's small number of 'free lovers', anarchists and secularists, the couple may have been among the few to turn sexually progressive theory into practice.

The Brotherhood of the New Life

To modern sensibilities, Thomas Lake Harris, the patriarch of the Brotherhood of the New Life, appears the very embodiment of a nineteenth-century religious prophet (see figure 4). An intelligent, charismatic, domineering man, with a flowing, patriarchal beard and an overhanging brow, contemporaries commented on his piercing deep-set eyes and the hypnotic qualities of his voice. According to his most famous British disciple, the aristocrat and diplomat Laurence Oliphant, his eyes were 'like revolving lights in two dark caverns', while his voice 'seemed pitched in two different keys', one 'near', rapid and vivacious and one 'far-off', solemn and impressive, Harris switching between the two to calculated effect.[14]

He first visited Scotland in 1860, staying for the greater part of a year. At that time, he was the pastor of the Church of the Good Shepherd, an unofficial Swedenborgian 'New Church' in New York. He had come to Scotland from London, where his reception had been warm, the 'pronounced, arcane element' of Swedenborg's teachings appealing to 'the intellectual, philosophical, and religious proclivities of a well-educated elite', and in Scotland he continued to attract disciples from the middle and upper-middle classes.[15] However, Harris's claims to insights beyond those that had been enjoyed by Swedenborg, combined with his continuing

4 Thomas Lake Harris in his late seventies

emphasis on spiritualism, gradually became unpalatable to many New Church ministers. Soon, he was denounced in England and America as 'an habitual and systematic deceiver' with 'blasphemous pretensions'.[16] Breaking with the New Church, he returned to America, where he established a new religious organisation, claiming the Brotherhood of the New Life would restore a 'paradisiacal order upon the planet' and, in time, precipitate the Second Coming of Christ.[17] It is clear he took some of his Scottish disciples with him: some forty years later, the *Glasgow Evening News* was still bemoaning the city's loss of 'two or three of the most highly-connected and promising young men', who had left the country with Harris 'for the purpose of forming some weird, impossible colony of communistic cranks a generation or so ago'.[18] The men to whom the newspaper referred were in all probability Arthur Cuthbert, later a close friend of the Pearces, who was eventually to contribute $4,000 annually to the Brotherhood of the New Life (the equivalent of $110,000 in 2019), and James A. Fowler and his wife, who were also in possession of 'considerable means'.[19]

Declaring himself the 'pivotal man' of this new religious body, Harris first led his followers north into the farmlands of Dutchess County in New York state, forming a settlement in the hamlet of Wassaic. When numbers grew, the small band of 'chosen ones' moved four miles up the valley, to a larger farm in nearby Amenia; by 1867, the group had relocated again, this time to Brocton, a village on the shores of Lake Erie. Aided by the personal fortune of Laurence Oliphant and his mother Lady Maria, who together contributed in excess of $100,000 (approximately $2.8 million in 2019), Harris purchased roughly 2,000 acres of farmland. Clearly a shrewd businessman as well as a penetrating mystic, his negotiations were apparently blessed by divine intervention, Oliphant relating to friends in England how 'a wonderful special influx' had given Harris 'great power over external people, so that even though they may not want to sell, they cannot resist his influence when he proposes to them to do so'.[20]

From this point on, the main industry of the Brotherhood was viticulture, the disciples planting vines and assembling the infrastructure necessary to manufacture and sell wine. The Scottish disciple Arthur Cuthbert justified the production of alcohol by arguing that as the wine was produced by consecrated hands, it carried with it a 'Divine and celestial energy', through which 'the curse that attends the abuse of wine is occultly met and counteracted'.[21] The number of settlers now fluctuated between seventy-five and one hundred, the majority originating from the southern states, along with a small number of converts from England, Scotland, Germany and Japan. In 1876, after experiencing a vision of 'great forests of sequoia, near the Pacific, where, mingled with the sighing winds among the evergreens, might be heard the murmur of the not far distant ocean', Harris founded his fourth and final Brotherhood settlement, his 'Eden in the West', an estate of 1,700 acres in the low foothills of Santa Rosa, California, named 'Fountaingrove' (see figure 5).[22]

Charles Pearce first became interested in the Brotherhood in the early 1870s. Then married to his first wife Mary, with four young children, he was living in Kilburn in Middlesex and working as an insurance broker.

5 The Brotherhood of the New Life at Fountaingrove

He was also heavily involved in spiritualism, caught up in the huge wave of popular interest that had swept Britain since its arrival from America in the early 1850s. A member of the Kilburn Society of Spiritualists, he organised séances and gave lectures on spiritualism, including on its compatibility with the teachings of Christianity, while also being a medium in his own right.[23] His friend, the spiritualist Edmund Dawson Rogers, a founder member of the British National Association of Spiritualists who would later play a key role in the establishment of the Society for Psychical Research, described his mediumship as 'of a peculiar character'; according to Rogers, Charles 'would sit at the table, and thoughts and ideas would come to him, whereupon the table would move to confirm what was in his mind'.[24] The exact circumstances of Charles's introduction to the Brotherhood is unknown. By 1872, however, he had become a sincere and committed convert, writing to ask whether he and his family could join the community in Brocton. He was to be disappointed, however. Harris replied stating that, regrettably, the timing of Charles's approach was inopportune. While outwardly all was peaceful at the colony, the disciples going about their daily tasks, internally a fierce, apocalyptic battle was taking place between the chosen ones and 'a vast gathering of the Aggressive Kings of Evil'. According to Harris, he alone, in 'these days of mortal anguish and conflict', was keeping them alive, constantly reinforcing and reinvigorating them by the 'Arch-natural elements' which flowed through and matured in his 'transformed bi-sexual personality':

> The members of my Society, relieved of every non-combattant [sic], and trained and prepared for the issue, stand at their posts prepared to perish if need be, but holding in an hitherto impenetrable form. To hold them in the body as one after another is for the time disabled, to open avenues of new life as the old avenues are closed against them, taxes to the utmost my vast resources of arch-natural substance. Obviously, therefore, you should not think of placing yourself, with your dear wife and family, in the midst of this terrific storm.[25]

A more cynical interpretation is that Charles Pearce lacked the requisite funds to make him and his family attractive to Harris as initiates. The majority of Brotherhood disciples signed across their capital to Harris on their arrival at his communities; without money, suggest Harris's biographers, applicants were often turned away.[26]

Internal respiration and conjugial marriage

A core belief within Brotherhood theology was that sex was the elemental life-force behind human and divine existence, the regenerative energy that, harnessed by Harris and aided by 'New Age angels', would banish disease and sin and ultimately precipitate the Second Coming.[27] In its sacred and sanctified state, sex powered the altruistic tendencies of humankind, its sphere of influence stretching far beyond its simple reproductive functions. It was intrinsic to the very nature of God, who declared in his new Gospel (as revised by Harris): 'I am Sex. Whosoever receiveth me, though he were born impotent, shall receive my potency; and though he had become dead, yet shall he revive in my potency, and my potency is eternal life.'[28] The human sex instinct was therefore the most important of all the senses, the 'pivotal sense' which, if suitably honed and perfected through certain practices, including a kind of holy breathing called 'internal respiration' and a spiritual-sexual act termed 'conjugial marriage', could enable the disciple to achieve divine communion and access a 'transcendent sexual realm'.[29]

Underpinning these ideas was a belief in the androgynous nature of the godhead, Harris asserting that God and Jesus were 'bisexual' and referring to them as the 'Twain-in-One', 'Lord Jesus-Lady Yessa' and 'Christus-Christa'. He appears to have derived the concept from the teachings of his former mentor Andrew Jackson Davis, the self-educated American spiritualist and clairvoyant known as the 'Poughkeepsie Seer', as well as from the writings of Swedenborg, which also contained the idea of the divine as Father and Mother.[30] However, the notion of an androgynous deity also had wider currency within late eighteenth- and early nineteenth-century religious and radical thought in Britain, surfacing in the discourse of the Shakers, Southcottians and Saint-Simoneons.[31] According to Harris's imaginative rendering of Genesis, it followed that as God had created man in his own image, prelapsarian humankind had also been androgynous. The principal objective for Brotherhood disciples was to locate their spiritual other halves, the male or female 'counterparts' from whom they had been sundered at the time of the Fall.[32]

Finding one's counterpart was believed to be greatly facilitated by 'internal respiration', a practice known also as open, inner or divine breathing and which equated to the Christian notion of the Holy Spirit or Holy Ghost.[33] Understood not as a learned technique but rather as a gift, divinely bestowed on the worthy, it was nonetheless experienced as an altered physiological state, during which God's breath literally flowed through one's body. A Brotherhood disciple named 'Mrs. L–' described how 'Such a tenderness of Love to the Lord' was 'borne in with the breath' that when she contemplated his suffering she was moved to tears,[34] an intensity of experience echoed in the testimony of Mrs Cuthbert, who declared: 'What shall not be found to result from having the palpitating Breath of God heaving in our bosom, giving us the momentary assurance of His presence and His love, whilst our demon foes tremble and retire before it.'[35] Achieving open breathing was seen as a key attainment within the Brotherhood, a rite of passage, enabling the disciple to progress up the spiritual hierarchy. It was undertaken in conjunction with other 'demagnetising' and 'energising' rituals, including massages and healing baths which the male and female disciples gave naked to one another, Harris reportedly believing that 'before we can be in any true condition we must all be so innocent that we can stand naked before each other without a thought of shame, and wash and dress each other'.[36] Men and boys within the Brotherhood were apparently kept 'demagnetised' by such baths, the mothers of the society struggling valiantly to cure cases of nymphomania and sexual insanity by undertaking the scrubbing 'with a will'.[37]

The ultimate objective of initiates was to consummate their (re)union with their counterpart through 'conjugial marriage', a term Harris borrowed from Swedenborg and used to refer to the sexual consummation of a relationship with a spiritual counterpart. This sacred union, like internal respiration, was experienced as an intensely pleasurable, physical encounter, despite the counterpart's non-physical form, the angelic beings literally entering the disciple's body and sending through it vibrations, flutterings and pulsations, all of which left the disciple exhausted, as the account of one 'sister in the New Life' testifies:

> This morning for the first time, I felt [my counterpart] enter my head and also pass into my thighs. The first time that it came into my body, that is the trunk, it seemed to enter through the generative organs, and with it came the thought, this is like sexual intercourse, only infinitely more so, in that every atom of your frame enters into union with another atom to the furthest extremity of your body. I am sure I never had such a thought before, nor supposed that anything could be of such infinite magnitude. I felt infinitely calm and peaceful, nothing turbulent and passionate about it, and my only desire was to constantly pray in thankfulness.[38]

Harris's own counterpart was called Queen Lily, whom Harris visited in his dreams and trances regularly throughout his life, relaying her divine insights in a voluminous output totalling over forty published works of mystical poetry and prose, as well as innumerable unpublished manuscripts. As Chrysantheus-Chrysanthea, Harris and Lily ruled over the communities of the Brotherhood and 'Lilistan', the heavenly realm closest to the earth, even having two spiritual children together. His poetical account of their conjugial marriage is strikingly sensual, with references to pillowing his head on her 'translucent breast', being kissed by her 'rose-golden' lips and together them sharing in sweet communion 'unspoken thought and ecstasies divine'.[39]

Sex with a counterpart was a sacramental rite, a way to achieve divine communion. Through it, not only could disciples emulate the androgynous form of the godhead, but by harnessing the pleasures engendered by their 'pure sexual fire', they could transcend their isolated selves and worldly existences and realise a higher consciousness of the divine.[40] For example, when recounting the ecstasies of her counterpartal consummation, the 'sister in the New Life' described feeling herself 'desolving', [sic] 'going to pieces and being drawn into something else', while for Arthur Cuthbert, by entering into a conjugial marriage, you were effectively marrying God, for 'God himself is the only real Bridegroom, God herself is the only real Bride'.[41] Religion had until now failed to acknowledge these truths, thinking to deny sexuality rather than work to purify it, and as a result it had become sterile, as Harris depicted in his 1872–73 poem 'Life One Twain':

> .... Unsexed existence weaves but desolation;
> It ends in pallid stone;
> 'Tis only through perpetual infloration,
> That endless life is known.

As frozen seas upon the barren beaches,
Unsexed Religions are:
The lifeless faith Monasticism teaches
Puts very Heaven afar.[42]

Arthur Cuthbert reiterated Harris's argument, claiming in his biography of Harris that the 'monkish ascetic habit' of the early Christians and Buddhists was based on a mistaken understanding of God as 'sexless'. The opposite was in fact true and it was now the role of religion to acknowledge and harness the sexual power of the divine, to 'find God in sex again', Cuthbert identifying this as 'the problem of problems that must be solved'.[43]

Women were accorded a pivotal role in the re-sexing of religion, for, according to Harris, 'If our Lord is the door, He has placed the key of

6 A woman at Fountaingrove

7 A woman reading at Fountaingrove

that door in the keeping of woman's hands' (figures 6 and 7). This key, also referred to as the 'Woman's Word', could alone unlock the door to heaven and eternal life and constituted the 'deepest of all knowledge'.[44] As the chief intermediary between heaven and earth, Harris was enlightened in this secret female wisdom to some degree, in 1882 becoming initiated into the 'woman's way', a process which entailed approaching heaven not through masculine rationality but through female love, and which culminated in him returning to the womb of the Divine Mother, Jesus's counterpart, Lady Yessa.[45] However, the revelation of the 'Woman's Word' would only be made to the wider world when the end was at hand, when women would inaugurate the great spiritual whirlwind of Judgement Day. Indeed, Harris believed this process was already becoming manifest in the aims and actions of the women's movement, a 'holy cause' with which he had a great deal of sympathy.

Unsurprisingly, the Brotherhood's American settlements were under continual threat from scandal, a letter by Harris written in 1892 stating that, 'For the last 30 or 40 years I have been followed … by a stream of diabolical insinuations', adding resignedly that 'Rotted minds must vent their depravity'.[46] What particularly exercised such 'rotted minds' was how conjugial marriage worked in practice. The suspicion was that counterpartal consummation was neither a solitary nor a solely spiritual activity, but involved Brotherhood disciples, both married and unmarried, having sex with other disciples, in the belief that their spiritual counterparts had descended into each other's bodies. In December 1891, the *San Francisco Chronicle* reported on the unorthodox sexual behaviour they believed to be taking place in its local utopian community, explaining that at Fountaingrove, 'After a man has been separated from his wife and has been taken into the inner circle he is given a heavenly counterpart, which after a time is permitted by the prophet to descend and take material form in whatever woman he may see fit to designate as the affinity of the disciple, although this is, of course, all inside the community'.[47] While the *Chronicle* concluded that the morals of the disciples were 'vile', describing them as 'refined sensualism', another local newspaper went further, the editor of the *Wave* pronouncing Fountaingrove an 'idealized house of sin; a den of iniquitous debauchees, whose only religion is the satisfaction of the passions, where there are no ties of affection, and where both sexes of one family bed together like dogs in a kennel'.[48]

A further piece of evidence of the physical enactment of conjugial marriage within the Brotherhood can be found in the architectural notes and plans for an 'Ideal City', drawn up by the Brotherhood disciple and architect Louis Cowles in the 1890s (figure 8).[49] Cowles was clearly aware of their controversial nature, cautioning a fellow disciple, the poet Edwin Markham, not to show them to anyone else, stating they had a tendency to induce 'curious effects on people's minds', with some 'excited to dislike, hatred and angry opposition'.[50] They included plans for a spectacular 'Social Palace', a meeting place for the hundred male and female inhabitants, with 'a pool of crystal water, 220 feet in length and 50 wide, under a canopy of tinted glass, where ladies with their knights together bath in joyous innocence', and around the sides, arranged in three tiers, '100 bowers of love's repose', presumably the settings for counterpartal sexual unions.[51] That prototypes of such spaces existed on the Brotherhood communities is hinted at in the testimony of Christian evangelist Hannah Whitall Smith, who twice visited Harris at Fountaingrove, describing a bathroom lined with marble wash basins in order that the disciples might wash themselves free of corruptions, and rooms with no doors, 'but simply little recesses where beds were placed, because in the new order of things their ideal was that there was to be no need for secrecy, but every one could be open and above board with all they did'.[52]

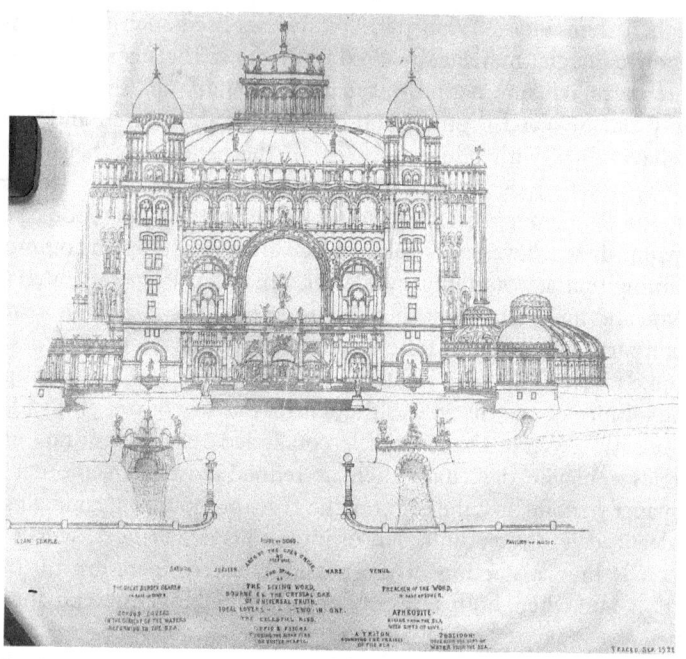

8 Architectural plans for an 'Ideal City' drawn up by Brotherhood disciple Louis Cowles in 1894

Even Harris's closest disciples did not deny that the Brotherhood members had sex. Jane Lee Waring described Harris to her brother as 'no ascetic', while Arthur Cuthbert alluded to their 'Breath-house' (i.e. the community buildings at Fountaingrove and Brocton) as 'no Monastery', going on to state that 'the problem is to be solved by the purification of sex, and not by its abrogation'.[53] It is true however, that very few children were born at any of the Brotherhood communities, Harris believing that reproduction should not take place until men and women had evolved 'into structural, bisexual completeness'. Only then would they be capable of producing 'the Crowning race of humankind's children', sinless and immortal, who would make 'of this sad planet more than a Paradise'.[54]

One solution to the conundrum of the simultaneous existence within the Brotherhood of the small number of births, a theology centred around the divine potency of pleasurable sex and the self-perception amongst disciples that they were chaste and morally pure is that they were practising a sexual technique known as 'coitus reservatus' or 'male continence', later known as 'karezza'.[55] In common parlance, the term 'continence' generally denoted sexual abstinence except for procreation, and it is undoubtedly this meaning which Jane Lee Waring anticipated would be inferred from her statement in 1891 that 'absolute continence' was a 'fundamental law rigidly enforced' in all Brotherhood families.[56] However, during the second half of the nineteenth century, 'continence' was increasingly used by a number of American sex reformers to mean prolonged sexual intercourse without male ejaculation, suggesting Waring's phrase contained a degree of ambiguity and may have held a second, illicit meaning.[57]

Harris's unorthodox sexual ideas eventually led to his undoing. His nemesis came in the form of Alzire Chevallier, a 'woman suffragist, sociologist, spiritual scientist, philanthropist, nationalist, magazine writer and reformer' from Boston, who arrived at Fountaingrove with her mother in June 1891 in order to 'enjoy the society of the "Primate" of the Brotherhood of the New Life, to receive spiritual illumination from him and to obtain the "divine breath" or "open respiration" which Harris professes to be able to impart, he being the sole representative of God on Earth'.[58] On her departure six months later, she vowed to break up the 'licentious' community, making a series of allegations in the *San Francisco Chronicle* and at local public lectures concerning the 'hierarch of Fountaingrove' and his 'accursed doctrine of the counterparts'. This doctrine, she claimed, was worse than that of the Oneida Perfectionists or the polygamous Mormons; it was no less than 'a new sexology, holding the virus of a refined and subtle sensualism in whose web many a pure soul has become hopelessly entangled'.[59] In the same year, a sympathetic biography of Laurence Oliphant by his distant relative, the novelist and biographer Margaret Oliphant, portrayed Harris as a 'spiritual despot', if one possessed of 'extraordinary and imposing gifts of character'.[60] Within months, the hierarch had been hounded from his Eden in the West. On 27 February 1892, Harris married Jane Lee Waring, leaving Fountaingrove shortly afterwards, never to return.

The Department of Great Britain

In the period since his visits to Britain in the 1860s, Harris had faded from the British public consciousness, Margaret Oliphant describing him as 'a teacher who never touched the sphere of fashion, or became a public celebrity'.[61] However, the disclosures of 1891 and 1892 propelled him from obscurity to notoriety. Chevallier's accusations were reprinted widely in British newspapers, while the biography of Laurence Oliphant was an immediate success, running to seven editions in the first year. Spiritualists and theosophers moved quickly to disassociate themselves from Harris.

The spiritualist journal *Medium and Daybreak* dismissed him as a dishonest humbug, while the theosophical journal the *Path* warned its readership to beware of his work, claiming it had 'the usual broad hint of sexual affinities and such disgusting doctrines'.[62] Theosophers were particularly incensed by the repeated connection made in the press between their spiritual leader Helena Blavatsky and Harris, the *Pall Mall Gazette* labelling both 'religious imposters', albeit ones that many people had found 'an aid to a higher life'.[63] Annie Besant, recently appointed chief secretary of the secret Inner Group of the Esoteric Section, the Theosophical Society's school of practical occultism, responded by devoting a whole article in *Lucifer* to differentiating between Harris's 'false mysticism' and the 'true mysticism' of Blavatsky, a distinction she drew entirely on their differing attitudes towards sex. According to Besant, the keynote of the 'true mysticism' of theosophy was asceticism, the 'whole tendency' of its teachings 'towards the destruction of the sex-instinct', with Blavatsky ruthlessly trampling on the 'slightest indication of transferring sex to the astral plane'. However, the 'false mysticism' of Harris deified sex and glorified the sexual emotions, Besant decrying 'Always this mania for dwelling on the sex-idea; no thought that does not centre in sex, revolve round sex.'[64]

Charles Pearce was not deterred by such damaging publicity, however. After being refused admission to the Brotherhood community at Brocton in 1872, he had continued his discipleship remotely from Britain, forced to content himself with occasional visits to the American settlements. His first was in 1885, when he received a warm welcome from Harris, Charles writing how 'Father ... threw both his arms around me, & drew me closely to him, & said "my dear young brother" – making me feel at ease at once.'[65] He stayed for over a fortnight, declaring himself 'altogether happy' and 'at home', meeting members whom he had only read about in letters and clearly revelling in the novelty of Brotherhood community life.[66] The brethren were equally taken with him, Arthur Cuthbert declaring that they all loved him 'beyond measure'.[67]

His commitment to the Brotherhood continued undiminished with the commencement of his second marriage, Bella embracing her husband's Christian mysticism. Despite a period in which the couple also became involved in occultism, in December 1889 both joining the London Isis-Urania Temple No. 3 of the Hermetic Order of the Golden Dawn and later petitioning for a temple to be founded in Edinburgh, their main spiritual affiliation remained to the Brotherhood.[68] After leaving Fountaingrove in 1892, Harris and his wife Jane had settled in an apartment in New York, a city they believed to be the Mother God's kingdom (San Francisco belonging to the Father God).[69] In 1900, Bella made her own pilgrimage to see them, finding Harris to be a 'grand man' in possession of 'the most beautiful head and face I have ever seen', Mrs Harris in turn calling her 'a dear and true sister'.[70] Back in Glasgow, the couple became key figures within a network of disciples in Glasgow, which included individuals who had encountered Harris during his visit to the city in 1860 and who had sustained a groundswell of interest in his work.

Despite Harris's notoriety, the Pearces did not shy away from publicly acknowledging their connection to the Brotherhood, Charles proclaiming his discipleship in the socialist press, giving lectures to the local Spiritualists' Association on Harris's poetry (see figure 9) and even organising a trip to Fountaingrove for Hardie during his 1895 American tour.[71] The subsequent report of the visit in the *Labour Leader* made no reference to past scandals, the writer emphasising instead the colony's communitarian credentials, seeing in Fountaingrove 'an object lesson of how, inspired by noble spirit and example, men can live together in harmony', the only disappointment being that Harris, the 'chief engineer of the many wonders', was, of course, by that time, absent.[72] Bella and Charles were two of a handful of Brotherhood disciples in Britain who actively defended Harris's reputation in the press, a loyal group known as the 'Department of Great Britain of the Brotherhood of the New Life', which included Arthur Cuthbert, who had moved back to England in 1885, the journalist J. Cunningham Walters, the occultist Edward Berridge and the Tolstoyan William Swainson.[73] In December 1891, Charles wrote to the Glasgow

9 An advertisement for a lecture by Charles Pearce in the *Labour Leader*, 25 May 1895

Evening Citizen, denouncing Chevallier's accusations as 'a tissue of falsehoods from beginning to end', while later, in 1906, Bella wrote to the *British Weekly* berating their thoughtless perpetuation of 'ancient slanders' in a recent article, questioning whether it had occurred to them 'to think of the pain they inflict upon the friends of the man they malign', adding, 'By them he is loved and revered.' Crucially, she did not dismiss the significance of his radical sexual ideas, but rather claimed that it was his 'bold and fearless handling of sexual subjects' that had led to him being misrepresented.[74]

In what Harris termed the 'external' or public realm, the couple chose to manifest their faith in several different ways. The first was through political action, their faith exercising a direct influence on the pivotal decisions of Charles's ILP career. In 1894, Charles consulted Harris when deciding whether to stand as the parliamentary candidate for Camlachie. While Harris initially cabled 'Stand', his ambivalence towards socialism was reflected in the letter which followed, in which he warned that 'If the mania [of the Proletariat] should be liberated into a revolutionary whirl, the political system of Great Britain will go up in a blaze, and blood will flow in rivers', cautioning Charles that he was 'going into a powder mine' and that he therefore needed to keep his 'garments clear of proprium [selfishness] – probrium that if it [once] ignites will generate the explosion.'[75] Charles clearly took Harris's warning to heart. A year later, when he was led to believe that the actions of the ILP's NAC (National Administrative Committee) amounted to a tacit support of anarchism, he immediately withdrew from the election, in a letter to the *Labour Leader* stating explicitly that 'Anarchism, in its principles and methods', was in direct conflict with the doctrines of 'another society – located all over the world – known as the B.N.L or Brotherhood of the New Life', to which he owed his 'first allegiance'.[76]

Another significant way in which the Pearces demonstrated their commitment to the Brotherhood was by importing and selling the wine produced at Fountaingrove. This was done through C. W. Pearce & Co., the company which Bella and Charles founded in 1892 and subsequently ran as joint business partners, becoming part of a worldwide distribution network dedicated to ensuring the widespread dissemination of the Brotherhood's sanctified wine, with similar trading bases seemingly in London, France, Germany, Spain, Portugal and Australia.[77] Some of the wine even found its way to the home of the women's suffrage campaigner Elizabeth Wolstenholme Elmy in Cheshire, Charles sending it to her husband Ben when he was severely ill with a bronchial infection. While there is no evidence that the Elmys were aware of the 'Divine and celestial energy' with which the wine was imbued, Elizabeth reported that it had done her husband 'more good than anything yet'.[78]

The objective of the wine-selling operation appears to have been twofold. First, by distributing Fountaingrove wine, disciples such as the Pearces, living at a distance from the communities in America, were able to participate in the Brotherhood's work, thereby becoming, in Charles's words, 'in essence' part of the 'commune'.[79] Second, and more straightforwardly, the profits of the business were used to fund social causes with which the Brotherhood had sympathy, Charles relating that members were obliged, after deducting working and living expenses, to 'spend whatever profits are made for theo-social purposes'.[80] Charles doesn't specify what he interpreted those 'theo-social purposes' to be, but it is logical to assume they were the socialist, feminist and social reform organisations with which the Pearces were involved. During the 1890s, the Pearces made regular financial donations to Hardie and the ILP, raising the intriguing possibility that the Glasgow socialist movement was in a small way funded by the Brotherhood of the New Life.

The Pearces also used their business to publish several of Harris's later works of poetry, an arrangement initiated during Harris and his wife Jane's visit to Glasgow in 1903. Harris had recently completed two volumes of poetry, *The Triumph of Life* and *Song of Theos*, and had initially planned to stay first in London and then with Arthur Cuthbert in Wales to oversee their publication. Waiting for them at Liverpool, however, was an invitation from Bella and Charles putting themselves and their house at their disposal. In the end, the visit lasted for almost four months, Charles assisting Harris with the preparation of the manuscripts, Jane writing that he was proving to be 'a strong prop to Father' and that he had 'grown wonderfully since we met him last 17 years ago'.[81] Bella was also considered 'most precious', with both held to be 'alive & growing' in their faith.[82] In line with the Brotherhood tradition of assigning disciples particularly apt or aspirational epithets, Charles was christened 'Sir Steadfast Hold Strong' and Bella simply 'Lady Bella', while Harris was 'Faithful' and Mrs Harris 'Lady Dovie'.[83] When not working on the poetry books, the American couple received a steady stream of visitors, took walks in nearby Queen's Park and went on sightseeing trips with the Pearces to Loch Lomond, Edinburgh and the Rosneath Peninsula, visiting the Duncans' summer house in Cove.[84]

The visit began well, Jane writing home wistfully that Fountaingrove seemed 'nearer to Glasgow than it did in New York'.[85] Also staying with them was Charles's young niece, Annie Wood (who would later become their housekeeper), who described how 'quite often while we were at breakfast the Fairies would speak through Mr Harris', generating a lifelong interest in spiritualism.[86] The Harrises' optimism quickly gave way to disillusionment, however. The calibre of visitors calling on Harris proved disappointing, Jane writing in her diary that all seemed to be 'fastened into their old conditions' and that 'only a portion of them could in the least understand'.[87] Harris's only scheduled public talk, to the Glasgow Spiritualist Society, fell through, some of the committee members displaying justified reluctance to host a man who had long since denigrated secular or 'naturalistic' spiritualism as inherently corrupting, while the promised *Evening News* article never materialised. The Glasgow visit, however, was not completely futile. As well as coordinating the publication of his poetry, Harris and his wife took a new convert home to New York, sixty-two-year-old Jessie Donaldson, whom Jane described as 'a great acquisition, a ripe, rich soul, weighs about 200 lbs and is 6.3 and a fine pianist'.[88]

Lost in translation

The story of the Pearces' involvement with the Brotherhood doesn't end there, however. Bella and Charles also used their socialist and feminist journalism to ensure that Harris's message of divine sexuality was communicated to the wider British public, albeit in a modified form. Between 1894 and 1912, Bella and Charles disseminated their own rewriting of Brotherhood sexual theology in their articles, columns and letters for the *Labour Leader*, *Forward*, the *Westminster Review* and the *Freewoman*. While several articles dealt directly with their faith (though not mentioning it by name), Brotherhood concepts and terminology infused their columns, with the use of key words such as 'internal', 'external', 'planes', 'spheres', 'selfhood' and 'ultimation' revealing the mystical provenance of their ideas. It is even possible that the pseudonym 'Lily Bell', the name by which Bella was known by socialists across Britain, was a reference to her discipleship of Harris, 'Lily' corresponding to Harris's spiritual counterpart, Queen Lily, with 'Bell' a shortening of her own first name.[89]

Yet despite the Pearces' proven and sincere commitment to Harris and his sexual philosophy, in translating his discourse for a British socialist and feminist audience they also subjected it to a substantial process of revision. This was due, in part, to the different contexts in which Harris and the Pearces operated. The first Brotherhood settlements were formed in the 1860s in the remote, rural districts of northern and western New York state, the crucible for several millenarian, utopian communities. According to Lawrence Foster, participants in such communities were experimenting with new social and sexual structures in response to deep anxieties over the perceived disintegration of social and familial relationships in frontier America, the Shakers advocating celibacy, the Oneida Perfectionists complex marriage and the Mormons polygamy.[90] Harris's project of counterpartal marriage can therefore be seen as a product of a time and place in which small-scale and contained experimentation with marriage, sex and reproduction was tacitly permitted, the Brotherhood communities thriving for thirty years before scandal finally dethroned their spiritual leader.

In the social and ideological space inhabited by the Pearces, however – that of the progressive politics of 1890s and 1900s Glasgow – there was much less tolerance for unconventional sexuality. This was due in part to a desire to ensure the political efficacy of their campaigns. The seemingly intractable association in the public's mind between socialism and the destruction of the family, a legacy of the Owenism of the 1820s and 1830s, had meant that, as Karen Hunt asserts, 'moving beyond a defensive position proved particularly difficult for socialists when it came to the range of issues most closely associated with the private sphere', with silence often viewed by party officials as the best policy.[91] However, feminists also had very real concerns over female sexual exploitation and marital desertion in an era of uneven access to reliable birth control and poor educational and employment opportunities for women. A pertinent example is the reaction of contemporary feminists and socialists to the ideas of the aural surgeon and social prophet James Hinton. Described by Seth Koven as a 'philanthropic hedonist', certain aspects of Hinton's philosophy bear a striking resemblance to that of Harris's.[92] Perhaps most saliently, Hinton like Harris made a connection between selfless love and sensual pleasure, believing that human desires needed to be trained to serve others, and that doing so would result in the liberation of the natural 'pleasures, instincts, impulses' that society was determined to repress, an attitude Hinton encapsulated in his injunction to 'love and do as you like'.[93] How he anticipated this would be translated in terms of particular sexual behaviours is far from clear but he appeared to advocate both polygamy, with men permitted to take several 'spiritual wives', and female nakedness, due to the positive 'moral and aesthetic influence' he believed it had on men.[94] The nature and importance of Hinton's legacy to progressive thought is a point of contention, and more research needs to be done.[95] Koven argues that his ideas made a substantial contribution to both philanthropic movements and social purity crusades, as well as forming part of 'the intellectual lineage of ethical socialism, radical sex reform, and the "science" of sexuality', citing his influence on individuals such as Havelock Ellis,

Ellice Hopkins, Arnold Toynbee, Edith Ellis, Roden Noel, Berkeley Wriothesley and Charles Ashbee.[96] For Chris Nottingham, however, he was a highly divisive figure within progressive circles in London, with Olive Schreiner developing a profound unease over the personal ethics of a man rumoured to have used his status amongst his coterie of female admirers to make inappropriate sexual advances. Nottingham noted that 'Even in the heart of progressive London a decent distinction was drawn between professing unconventional views and their practice.'[97]

There are numerous other examples of the need for socialists and feminists during this period to maintain a strict boundary between public discourse and private behaviour. They include the 'fluttering in the suffrage dovecotes' caused in 1872 by the pregnancy out of wedlock of Elizabeth Wolstenholme (later Elmy), who was subsequently forced by her feminist colleagues to choose between her 'free love' principles and her political career;[98] the resignations from the Legitimation League in 1897 following its change in agenda from securing rights for illegitimate children to promoting 'freedom in sexual relations';[99] and the deep ambivalence felt by many female members of the Men and Women's Club towards alternatives to marriage beyond spinsterhood.[100]

There were a small number of exceptions, however. The 'tiny, radical minority' of feminists, socialists, anarchists and freethinkers, blessed with sufficiently robust personalities and supportive local networks to break ranks and risk forging 'free unions', saw their relationships, in the words of Diana Maltz, 'not as private romances, but as part of an ideological praxis, a way that one might perform one's ethics'.[101] As well as individual couples such as Elizabeth Wolstenholme and Ben Elmy and the anarchist-communists Guy Aldred and Rose Witkop, they included residents of the handful of utopian communities founded in England at the turn of the century. The most prominent was the settlement of Tolstoyan anarchists established in Whiteway in Gloucester in 1898, in which eleven couples formed 'free unions', Nellie Shaw living in an unmarried union with Francis Sedlak for thirty-three years.[102] Despite the overwhelmingly monogamous character of such relationships, to outsiders their unconventional behaviour served only to reinforce the public preconception that utopian communities were synonymous with sexual promiscuity, a financial backer of a settlement in Gertrude Dix's *The Image Breakers* at one point screeching 'I knew it! ... People are talking of free love. Everyone is falling in love with everyone else, as always happens on a mixed colony.'[103]

The tenor of opinion within Charles and Bella's particular network can be gauged very effectively by the reaction to the Edith Lanchester case, the 'free love' cause célèbre of the 1890s.[104] Lanchester was a twenty-four-year-old, educated, middle-class political activist for the SDF (Social Democratic Federation) who began a relationship with James Sullivan, a working-class man and an active member of the Battersea SDF. Ideologically opposed to marriage, the couple announced that on 26 October 1895 they would enter a 'free love' union. The day before, her father and brothers succeeded in having her committed to a lunatic asylum, the doctor who signed the necessary certificate concluding that 'She had a monomania on the subject of marriage, and I believed her brain had been turned by Socialist meetings and writings, and that she was quite unfit to take care of herself.'[105] After four days, the lobbying of her friends and the local MP had secured her release, but not before the case had triggered widespread public commentary. The official response by the SDF was to distance themselves from her actions, expressing considerable pique, in *Justice*, that the marriage question had been 'publicly raised in an acute form by an official member of the SDF, without any conference whatever with other comrades'.[106] Opinion in the *Labour Leader* was mixed. The two female commentators on the case, Bella Pearce and Caroline Martyn, supported Lanchester, praising her for highlighting the inequity of existing marriage law and having the courage to act on her principles.[107] Other commentators were less sympathetic, however. Hardie expressed concern about the damage the case would do to socialism, as did the author of the 'London Letter', who stated: 'If half a dozen young women, connected with the Socialist movement, fired up by a desire for freedom, were to emulate her example it would do the movement incalculable harm.' This position was broadly endorsed by 'Marxian', who dismissed marriage reform as a private issue, marginal to the more important economic aims of socialism, namely 'the transfer of some millions and acres of property ... from class to communal ownership.'[108]

Assuming therefore, that the Pearces desired to enlighten their *Labour Leader* and *Forward* readership on the sexual aspects of their faith, a degree of circumspection was clearly required. Yet despite the hostile environment to sexually radical practices, several of Harris's beliefs, albeit not the most controversial ones, were translated intact onto the pages of the socialist press. First, both Bella and Charles alluded in their writing to the androgynous nature of the deity, Charles, for example, writing as 'Sophia' in the *Labour Leader*, stating that 'sex is God in two opposite finite modes of manifestation. Woman is the mother mode of God ... Man is the male mode of God'.[109] Later in the same article, Charles was also explicit on the androgynous nature of prelapsarian humankind, explaining how the 'ancient people known as the Adamic race ... was hermaphroditic or bi-sexual. Each person was a complex of the two sexes in one bodily form of woman-man, and the reproduction of the race was by a wholly different mode of generation than now obtains'.[110]

Second, like Harris, the Pearces drew a distinction between selfish, 'natural' love, directed covetously towards individual human beings, and selfless, divine love expended for the good of the whole of God's people. In the *Labour Leader* in 1894, Bella, as Swedenborg had done over a hundred years previously in *Conjugial Love*, employed a water metaphor in order to help elucidate the difference between the two. While Swedenborg conceptualised the love of the opposite sex as a fountain, from which selfish and selfless love could be drawn, for Bella love was an inner divine spring, the flowing of which humankind had mistakenly tried to restrict, railing that 'We have damned up the outlets of our hearts, thinking, poor fools that we are, to make for ourselves private reservoirs of our own, but succeeding only in turning the living waters into stagnant pools, where the corruptions of our self-life have choked up the springs of the God-life that is within'.[111] Yet while she claimed that 'help *is* coming', that 'New light is beginning to shine in upon us and new hopes to fill our hearts', she did not develop this into a practical statement on the need for a radical restructuring of the family, as Harris had attempted on Brotherhood settlements, referring to the potential of unselfish '*sex-life*' to 'achieve great things' as one 'of the mysteries of life of which we have yet more to learn'.[112] She did, however, endorse someone else's fictional representation of what unselfish love might resemble, expressing her approval of the portrayal of a commune in the novel *Margaret Dunmore*, sent to her by the author, the Edinburgh feminist freethinker Jane Hume Clapperton (see Chapter 5).[113]

Finally, also like Harris, the Pearces believed the women's movement had a critical role to play in the regeneration of humanity. Bella repeatedly refers to the feminist movement as a divine cause, asserting that Salvation will come 'through the feminine'.[114] Indeed, in a letter to the *Freewoman* in 1911 she hints that women's compulsion to participate in feminism was fuelled by a 'mysterious force', an 'occult power outside the usual experience', while in an article in *Forward* in 1906 she makes the striking assertion that the women's movement was in fact the Second Coming of Christ.[115] Radically reinterpreting the crucifixion story, Bella describes how, during Christ's first appearance on earth, it was the female qualities within a dual-gendered Jesus that were ultimately rejected and nailed to the cross. She asks her readers:

> Now, just think for a moment what it was that was rejected in Christ – that was crucified in Him. Christ stands for the Divine-feminine

qualities in Man, for Love and Gentleness, for Peace and Harmony, for Innocence and Purity, and for these qualities as embodied in Him was no place found in Judea.

It was the Woman in man that was crucified on that Cross, and She has not yet been taken down. No place has yet been found for Her here!'[116]

She goes on to suggest that Christ has indeed come again, 'not in the form of one man, but in, and through, the women of the people'. It is therefore with purely feminist aims, such as the acknowledgement of women's influence in society, the removal of sex restrictions and the prioritisation of women's rights, that the Christian Church must now concern itself. Speaking with an eschatological fervour to rival that of her spiritual leader, she asserts that a 'crisis state in the world's history' has been reached, 'when the parting of the waves is before us'. Either humankind 'must receive and give welcome to the new Spirit' of the Feminine or, 'by despising and rejecting the same, cast ourselves into the Hell of its perversion. Which is it to be?'[117]

It is in the Pearces' portrayal of both current and future sexual relations, however, that a divergence from the doctrines of the Brotherhood becomes apparent. Despite expressing deep dissatisfaction with sex in its current form, neither Bella nor Charles go beyond tantalising suggestions of a secret knowledge relating to a radical alternative. Women and men are described by Bella as living 'in a woeful state of ignorance' regarding their 'true relations to each other', with only a few having risen to a 'higher conception' of their sexual life.[118] Yet what this 'higher conception' entails is never fully explained, Bella only stating that it will occur in the future, that it will be very different from present-day marriage and that out of it will come the 'true regeneration of the race'.[119] Nowhere are these future sexual relationships referred to by the Brotherhood terminology of conjugial or counterpartal marriages, phrases that would immediately have conjured transgressive associations in the minds of her readership. Indeed, at times her conceptualisation of an ideal sexual relationship as 'the outward ultimation of a true spiritual union of love' reads as little more than the conventional Victorian understanding of marriage as a 'communion of souls'.[120]

Furthermore, in their discussions on sex the Pearces incorporate other discourses circulating in late Victorian Britain, principally that of evolutionary biology. We know that Bella attended a series of lectures given by the American utopian feminist and social reformer Charlotte Perkins Stetson (later Gilman) when on a visit to Britain in 1896, and was receptive to her feminist revision of Darwinian evolution.[121] We also know that the Edinburgh natural scientist and social reformer Patrick Geddes lectured on several occasions to the Ruskin Society of Glasgow, an organisation with which the Pearces were closely involved. In addition, in a series of *Labour Leader* articles in 1897 on 'The sexes, what they are, and their relationship to each other', Charles cites Henry Drummond, the populariser of Christian evolutionary science whose 1894 *Ascent of Man* relied heavily on Geddes and Thomson's influential 1889 *Evolution of Sex*.[122] In this text, Geddes and Thomson argued that the physiology and psychology of sexual difference could be explained by an 'organic see-saw' between the twin dynamics of 'katabolism' and 'anabolism': while the male katabolic habit dissipated energy and transmitted variation, the female anabolic habit conserved energy and maintained the stability of the organism (see Chapter 4).[123] Bella and Charles's understanding of sex bears a striking resemblance to this hypothesis, the only distinction being that, for the Pearces, sex was not merely a phenomenon of the natural world but a creation of God, as Charles made explicit in his series on 'The sexes':

> "In the beginning," when the Creative Spirit of God had re-endowed the undifferentiated cosmic substance with creative energy, the law of the newly quickened life was manifested in two opposite but absolutely complementary motions – one positive, energetic, flowing away from the centre; the other negative, energetic, drawing back to the centre. The positive was the mode of the male, or paternal or creative method; the negative was the mode of the female, or maternal or sustaining method. Hence the creative operation of the Invisible God was seen to evolve by a law of complementary opposites.[124]

If the God-given force of life was constituted by the harmonious operation of two opposite but complementary sexes, it followed logically that the disorder and chaos in which the world currently found itself was the result of a critical imbalance in this equilibrium. Not only had masculine rule caused the growth of individual women to become stunted, so that they no longer resembled in outward form the 'God within', but by denying the feminine element its 'true place and power in Society', civilisation had dealt itself a potentially fatal blow.[125] Again melding faith with evolutionary biology, Bella argued that a direct result of this sexual dissymmetry was the supremacy of the 'Masculine principle' of natural selection, or the 'struggle for life' as an evolutionary dynamic in society, implying that racial progress would only be possible with the reinstitution of its 'complementary companion', the feminine principle of altruism or 'the struggle for the life of others'.[126] This contains another strong echo of Geddes, whose appeal to many feminists was rooted in his foregrounding of female-coded altruism in his regendering of the process of evolution.

Another difference between the sexual discourse of the Pearces and that of Harris is in their use of language. While in Harris's poetry and prose, the prefix 'sex-' is ubiquitous, and is used when describing both holy and unholy acts, persons, organs and illnesses, the Pearces use it rarely, instead peppering their journalism with the conventional binary of love/lust. Furthermore, while for Harris, women are often the active agents in sexual, sensuous encounters, either as counterpartal queens or infernal whores, the Pearces reinstate women as the guardians of pure, spiritual, asexual love, with men relegated to its antithesis, the hell of lower, sinful, sexual, animal lust. Charles, for example, bewails the effect of the 'brutal lust of the dominant male' on women who would otherwise be 'sweet and pure in their bodies as when they descended fresh from the heavens through the sacred gate of motherhood to gain an earthly experience'.[127] Similarly, according to Bella, 'Love, which is the true feminine, hasn't had a chance to develop – it is so choked up by the overflow of animal sexuality, which parades through the world ever taking its sacred name in vain.'[128]

Finally, what is resolutely excised from the Pearces' texts is any sense of sex as a source of sensual pleasure. While for Harris, sex, even when conducted with a spiritual being, was an intensely physical and pleasurable activity, for Bella and Charles it was something to be warned against and avoided, or else regulated and controlled. The perpetrators of the majority of sexual evils were men, deceived by the medical profession into believing that the free indulgence of their passions was necessary to their health. Instead, their 'uncontrolled excesses' had entailed 'untold suffering and sacrifice of life' on women, and on the unwanted children their 'animal sensuality' had produced, born into an inheritance of degraded sexuality.[129] The solution was the institution of a single code of sexual morality and the securing of bodily autonomy for women. It is this understanding of sex, drawn from the discourse of feminism, which underpins the Pearces' advocacy of a series of reforms including the legal recognition of marital rape, the provision of sex education for girls and equality of access to divorce.

Conclusion

The Pearces were loyal and devoted disciples of the Brotherhood of the New Life, publishing several volumes of Harris's esoteric poetry, running a business selling his wine and defending his radical sexual beliefs in the local and national press. Yet they were also active participants in the British ethical socialist movement of the 1890s and the women's suffrage movement of the 1890s and 1900s. While socialists attempted to draw a divide between public and private behaviour, considering issues such as marriage, sexuality and 'free love' matters for individual conscience, the emphasis within feminist discourse was less on the power of sex to transform society and more on the need for men to be sexually disempowered, for their oppressive sexual behaviours to be proscribed. It is no real surprise, therefore, that when the Pearces translated Harris's theology for their progressive readership, what began as a doctrine of divine transcendence through sensual pleasure – the creation of a millenarian preacher steeped in the mysticism of Swedenborg – became transformed into a critique of the sexual double standard. While they retained recognisable, if relatively innocuous elements of Brotherhood theology, such as a belief in an androgynous deity, a distinction between selfish and altruistic love and a sense of the divine mission of an awakened womanhood, they also incorporated ideas circulating in their own sociopolitical context, principally that of equal rights feminism, social purity and evolutionary biology. While the language they used was at times deceptively similar to that of Harris, silences and subtle changes in emphasis fundamentally altered its meaning, allowing their discourse to quietly take its place, unnoticed by Mrs Grundy, in the columns of the late nineteenth- and early twentieth-century socialist and feminist press.

The extent to which the Pearces applied Harris's sexual theology in their own intimate lives is harder to fathom. Jane Lee Waring was categorical that 'absolute continence' was a 'fundamental law rigidly enforced in all the families in this country and abroad, where the principles of the B.N.L. are accepted as the guide to life', yet how the Pearces interpreted 'continence' is uncertain.[130] Few of their personal papers survive, a large number destroyed after Bella's death by Annie Wood, her long-term housekeeper and the executor of her estate, who thought them either too personal or no longer required.[131] We know that together they had no children, which could perhaps indicate that they were practising the sexual technique of 'karezza', although we have no evidence for this.

It could, of course, be the case that conjugial marriage, the sexual act at the heart of Harris's doctrine, did not equate to the transgressive practice that outsiders presumed. Despite the accumulation of evidence, including the architectural plans for '100 bowers of love's repose' and the lurid rumours spread by Chevallier, there is still no hard proof that counterpartal encounters were anything other than solitary experiences, or that continence, when referred to by Brotherhood disciples, meant sexual intercourse without orgasm rather than no sex at all.[132] It could also be the case that even if unorthodox sexual relationships were conducted on Brotherhood settlements, the Pearces were unaware of it.[133] Neither Charles nor Bella lived on a settlement, Charles only visiting Fountaingrove periodically and Bella's involvement with the organisation dating from after Harris's deposal. Although Bella alluded in her journalism to a 'higher conception' of selfless sexual relations, a knowledge known only to 'very few', but which would ultimately lead to 'the true regeneration of the race', she may well have been hypothesising about an imagined future rather than hinting at secret knowledge of an illicit present.[134]

It seems unlikely, however, that the Pearces, experts on Harris's sexual theology and key members of the Brotherhood's 'Department of Great Britain', would not have been at least partially aware of any practical experiments made with the sexual order on the American settlements. Promoting such experiments openly within the progressive circles of late Victorian and Edwardian Glasgow would have been a different matter, however.

Notes

1. A. A. Cuthbert, *The Life and World-Work of Thomas Lake Harris* (Glasgow: C. W. Pearce & Co., 1908), p. 183.
2. Letter from Robert Hart to Nagasawa Kanaye, 11 June 1903, TLH Papers 14/313, X. 57; diary of Jane Harris (*née* Lee Waring), 5 May 1903, TLH Papers 14/314.
3. Letter from Jane Harris to 'Darlings All', 11 October 1903, TLH Papers 9/237.
4. Letter from Jane Harris to 'My dearest Son', 22 September 1903, TLH Papers 9/237.
5. Letter from Jane Harris to 'Blessed Son', 9 July 1903, TLH Papers 14/315.
6. Diary entry of Jane Harris, 24 June 1903, TLH Papers 14/314.
7. Diary entry of Jane Harris, 8 July 1903, TLH Papers 14/314.
8. For an extended discussion of the relationship between the *fin de siècle* occult revival and humanitarian and socialist endeavours, see A. Owen, *The Place of Enchantment: British Occultism and the Culture of the Modern* (Chicago: University of Chicago, 2004), pp. 17–50.
9. Owen, *The Place of Enchantment*, p. 25.
10. R. Livesey, *Socialism, Sex and the Culture of Aestheticism in Britain, 1880–1914* (Oxford: Oxford University Press, 2007), p. 6.
11. A. Taylor, 'Besant [née Wood], Annie (1847–1933), theosophist and politician in India', *ODNB*; letter to Archibald Henderson, 3 January 1905, quoted in Owen, *The Place of Enchantment*, p. 24.
12. L. Bland, *Banishing the Beast: Feminism, Sex and Morality* (London: Penguin 1995, Tauris Parke, 2002), pp. 124–85; B. Taylor, *Eve and the New Jerusalem: Socialism and Feminism in the Nineteenth Century* (London: Virago, 1983), pp. 261–87; G. Frost, *Living in Sin: Cohabiting as Husband and Wife in Nineteenth-Century England* (Manchester: Manchester University Press, 2008), pp. 195–224; K. Hunt, *Equivocal Feminists:*

Feminists: The Social Democratic Federation and the Woman Question, 1884–1911 (Cambridge: Cambridge University Press, 1996), pp. 81–117; J. Weeks, *Sex, Politics and Society: The Regulation of Sexuality since 1800*, 3rd edn (Harlow: Pearson, 2012), pp. 205–30.

13 Frost, *Living in Sin*, p. 196.
14 Oliphant's description of Harris comes from a novel written after his defection from the Brotherhood, in which Harris is portrayed as the eponymous 'Masollam', a false and manipulative prophet. L. Oliphant, *Masollam: A Problem of the Period* (Leipzig: Bernhard Tauchnitz, 1886), p. 28. For an analysis of *Masollam*, and of Oliphant's non-fictional texts concerning heterodox spirituality, see J. Chajes, 'Alice and Laurence Oliphant's divine androgyne and "The Woman Question"', *Journal of the American Academy of Religion*, 84:2 (2016), pp. 498–529.
15 A. Owen, *The Darkened Room: Women, Power and Spiritualism in Late Victorian England* (London: Virago, 1989), p. 21.
16 E. Brotherton, *Spiritualism, Swedenborg and the New Church: An Examination of Claims* (London: William White, 1860), p. 5.
17 T. L. Harris, *The Apocalypse* (1867), quoted in H. W. Schneider and G. Lawton, *A Prophet and a Pilgrim: Being the Incredible History of Thomas Lake Harris and Laurence Oliphant; Their Sexual Mysticisms and Utopian Communities Amply Documented to Confound the Skeptic* (New York: Columbia University Press, 1942), pp. 57, 59.
18 'The Lorgnette', *Glasgow Evening News*, 24 June 1903, p. 2.
19 Letter from Jane Harris to Edwin Markham, 25 March 1911, TLH Papers 13/302; Schneider and Lawton, *A Prophet and a Pilgrim*, p. 149.
20 Letter from Laurence Oliphant to William Francis Cooper, 6 October 1867, quoted in Schneider and Lawton, *A Prophet and a Pilgrim*, p. 146.
21 Cuthbert, *The Life and World-Work of Thomas Lake Harris*, p. 55.
22 T. L. Harris, 'Localities: march of events' [undated, unpublished manuscript], quoted in Schneider and Lawton, *A Prophet and a Pilgrim*, p. 276; T. L. Harris, *Star-Flowers; a Poem of the Woman's Mystery* (1886–7), quoted in R. V. Hine, *California's Utopian Colonies* (New Haven, CT: Yale University, 1966), p. 18.
23 *Spiritual Magazine*, 1 July 1871, pp. 290–1.
24 E. D. Rogers, *Life and Experiences of Edmund Dawson Rogers, Spiritualist and Journalist* (London: Office of Light, [1911]), pp. 34–5.
25 Letter from Thomas Lake Harris to Charles Pearce [n.d., marked as possibly 1872], TLH Papers 8/235.
26 This is substantiated by Hannah Whitall Smith, the Christian evangelist who visited Harris twice at Fountaingrove and suspected his attentiveness was due to the fact that he thought she was rich. See R. Strachey (ed.), *Religious Fanaticism: Extracts from the Papers of Hannah Whitall Smith* (London: Faber & Gwyer, 1928), pp. 213–18. The biggest donor was said to be Jane Lee Waring, who contributed between $250,000 and $500,000 to the Brotherhood (between $7 million and $14 million in 2019). See Schneider and Lawton, *A Prophet and a Pilgrim*, pp. 152, 163.
27 The phrase 'New Age angels' comes from a letter from disciple Charles D. Hunter to his sister, 26 July 1881, in Schneider and Lawton, *A Prophet and a Pilgrim*, p. 317.

28 T. L. Harris, *The Lord: the Two-in-One, Declared, Manifested, and Glorified* (Fountain Grove, 1876), quoted in Cuthbert, *The Life and World-Work of Thomas Lake Harris*, p. 258.
29 The most straightforward explanation by Harris of the role of sex within his theology can be found in a letter written in response to a query by a sympathetic Episcopalian minister in 1892. The letter was one of several copied and circulated amongst Harris's close associates. Letter from Thomas Lake Harris to Rev Dr —, 18 January 1892, TLH Papers 9/238.
30 Davis's 'Harmonial Philosophy' was based on the idea of a union between Father-God (love) and Mother-Nature (substance). See Schneider and Lawton, *A Prophet and a Pilgrim*, p. 6. Swedenborg, however, was much less explicit regarding the dual-gendered nature of God, and Harris's reading of this aspect of his work was controversial, one New Church critic labelling it 'sheer nonsense'. See Brotherton, *Spiritualism, Swedenborg and the New Church*, pp. 32–3.
31 Taylor, *Eve and the New Jerusalem*, pp. 161–9. For similar beliefs in an androgynous divinity in occult circles in *fin de siècle* Britain, see Owen, *The Place of Enchantment*, p. 110.
32 Window bill for 'The Marriage of Heaven and Earth' and 'The Triumph of Life', written by Charles Pearce in 1903 and approved by Harris, TLH Papers 9/241.
33 Cuthbert, *The Life and World-Work of Thomas Lake Harris*, pp. 11–12.
34 'From one of the B. N. L. to Mrs Fawcett', quoted in Schneider and Lawton, *A Prophet and a Pilgrim*, p. 175.
35 'From Mrs Cuthbert [n.d.]', quoted in Schneider and Lawton, *A Prophet and a Pilgrim*, p. 168.
36 'Experiences of a sister in the New Life', Schneider and Lawton, *A Prophet and a Pilgrim*, p. 519.
37 Letter from Jane Lee Waring to her brother George, 18 December 1891, TLH Papers 9/238.
38 Quoted in Schneider and Lawton, *A Prophet and a Pilgrim*, p. 511. The account is an extract from a series of letters transcribed in copy books within the TLH papers and labelled 'Experiences of a sister in the New Life' or 'Extracts from a lady in San Francisco to a friend in England'. The author is not known but the letters were reproduced several times and circulated among the members of the Brotherhood.
39 T. L. Harris, *A Lyric of the Morning Land* (New York: Partridge and Brittan, 1854), pp. 49, 99.
40 Cuthbert, *The Life and World-Work of Thomas Lake Harris*, p. 157.
41 'Sister in the new life', quoted in Schneider and Lawton, *A Prophet and a Pilgrim*, p. 511; Cuthbert, *The Life and World-Work of Thomas Lake Harris*, p. 157.
42 T. L. Harris, *The Marriage of Heaven and Earth: Verified Realities* (Glasgow: C. W. Pearce & Co., 1903), p. 234.
43 Cuthbert, *The Life and World-Work of Thomas Lake Harris*, p. 86.
44 T. L. Harris, *Wisdom of Adepts* (printed for private circulation, 1884), quoted in Cuthbert, *The Life and World-Work of Thomas Lake Harris*, pp. 333–5.
45 Schneider and Lawton, *A Prophet and a Pilgrim*, pp. 303, 309, 362–3.

46 Letter from Thomas Lake Harris to Mr G. S. Weller, publisher of Swedenborgian journal *New Church Independent*, Chicago, 11 February 1892, TLH Papers 9/238.
47 'Hypnotic Harris. Miss Chevallier's Strange Story. She Runs Away from the Primate. Now She Vows That She Will Break Up the Licentious Community', *San Francisco Chronicle*, 13 December 1891, quoted in G. LeBaron, 'Serpent in Eden: the final utopia of Thomas Lake Harris and what happened there', *The Markham Review*, 4 (February 1969), p. 19.
48 Editorial, *The Wave*, 13 February 1892, from an extract printed in Schneider and Lawton, *A Prophet and a Pilgrim*, p. 556.
49 The architectural plans appear to have been drawn up in 1894 and the notes written in 1898.
50 Letter from Louis Cowles to Edwin Markham, 12 August 1921, TLH Papers 13/307.
51 Ibid.
52 Strachey, *Religious Fanaticism*, pp. 214, 216.
53 Letter from Jane Lee Waring to George Waring, 18 December 1891, TLH Papers 9/238; Cuthbert, *The Life and World-Work of Thomas Lake Harris*, p. 80.
54 Undated statement by Harris, quoted in Schneider and Lawton, *A Prophet and a Pilgrim*, p. 181; letter from Thomas Lake Harris to Rev Dr —, 18 January 1892, TLH Papers 9/238.
55 Ellic Howe and Alex Owen both believe Harris advocated a form of 'karezza'. See E. Howe, *The Magicians of the Golden Dawn: A Documentary History of a Magical Order, 1887–1923* (London: Routledge & Kegan Paul, 1972), p. 65n2; Owen, *A Place of Enchantment*, p. 100.
56 Letter from Jane Lee Waring to George Waring, 18 December 1891, TLH Papers 9/238.
57 The method was initially 'discovered' by John Humphrey Noyes, the leader of the Perfectionist community at Oneida. His publications on 'male continence' inspired the development of a range of similar techniques, key variants including Henry M. Parkhurst's 'Diana' (1882), George Noyes Miller's 'Zugassent's Discovery' (1895) and Alice B. Stockham's 'Karezza' (1897), each of which placed a varying degree of emphasis on the experience of divine transcendence engendered by the prolonged sexual encounter and the felicitous birth control consequences that also resulted. See T. Stoehr, *Free Love in America: A Documentary History* (New York: AMS Press, 1979), pp. 53–71, 549–635.
58 'Hypnotic Harris', *San Francisco Chronicle*, 13 December 1891, quoted in Schneider and Lawton, *A Prophet and a Pilgrim*, p. 534.
59 LeBaron, 'Serpent in Eden', pp. 14–24.
60 M. Oliphant, *Memoir of the Life of Laurence Oliphant and of Alice Oliphant, His Wife*, 2 vols (Edinburgh: William Blackwood and Sons, 1891), vol. 2, pp. 118, 124.
61 Oliphant, *Memoir of the Life of Laurence Oliphant*, vol. 2, p. 2.
62 *Medium and Daybreak*, 2 October 1891, p. 631 and 6 November 1891, p. 716; W. Q. Judge, 'The Brotherhood of the New Life', *The Path*, February 1891, pp. 346–7.
63 'A word for religious imposters', *Pall Mall Gazette*, 4 September 1891. See also 'The Prophet Harris at home', *Pall Mall Gazette*, 8 September 1891 and letter from B. A. Cantab, 'The Theosophists and T.L. Harris', *Pall Mall Gazette*, 28 November 1891.

64 A. Besant, 'Mysticism, true and false', *Lucifer*, 15 November 1891, pp. 178, 180, 181.
65 Letter from C. W. P., Santa Rosa, 29 June 1885, TLH Papers 14/315.
66 Ibid.
67 Letter from A. A. C. to Dr Berridge, 22 July 1885, TLH Papers 14/315.
68 The Pearces joined the Hermetic Order of the Golden Dawn eighteen months prior to their marriage. Golden Dawn Address Book, GD 2/1/2, p. 177b, Library and Museum of Freemasonry; R. A. Gilbert, *The Golden Dawn Companion: A Guide to the History, Structure and Workings of the Hermetic Order of the Golden Dawn* (Wellingborough: Aquarian, 1986), pp. 37, 143.
69 Cuthbert, *The Life and World-Work of Thomas Lake Harris*, p. 389.
70 Letter from Mrs Pearce, 14 July 1900, TLH Papers 14/313, X.38; diary entry of Jane Harris, 21 June 1900, TLH Papers 14/314.
71 Tricotrin, 'Chats with I.L.P. candidates', *Labour Leader*, 27 April 1895, p. 7; Letter from C. W. Bream-Pearce, 'Camlachie candidature', *Labour Leader*, 1 June 1895, p. 10; advert for lecture, 'Poetry of Thomas Lake Harris', *Labour Leader*, 25 May 1895, p. 5.
72 'America: The Chief's Tour. By a Special Correspondent', *Labour* Leader, 2 November 1895, p. 5. Hardie and Frank Smith gave a similarly effusive report of the Mormon community at Salt Lake City, downplaying their practice of 'matrimonial multiplicity', and arguing that their consistent and practical application of the 'principles of Brotherhood' were 'of far more value' than 'so-called orthodoxy' over sexual relations. The American reports provide an interesting counterpoint to the more hostile coverage of the 'free love' union of Edith Lanchester, a domestic example of sexual unorthodoxy, which ran simultaneously in the *Labour Leader*. See 'America: The Chief's Tour', *Labour Leader*, 19 October 1895, p. 5.
73 Schneider and Lawton, *A Prophet and a Pilgrim*, p. 459. William Swainson was on the committee of the Tolstoyan John Coleman Kenworthy's (unrelated) Brotherhood Church, who met at the Salvation Army barracks in West Croydon. In April 1895, Swainson delivered a paper to the Brotherhood Church Social Conference entitled 'Thomas Lake Harris: Mad or Inspired?'. He later wrote a biography of Harris. W. H. G. Armytage, 'J. C. Kenworthy and the Tolstoyan communities in England', in W. G. Jones (ed.), *Tolstoi and Britain* (Berg: Oxford, 1995), p. 137; M. J. de K. Holman, 'The Purleigh colony: Tolstoyan togetherness in the late 1890s', M. Jones (ed.), *New Essays on Tolstoy* (Cambridge: Cambridge University Press, 1978), p. 196.
74 Letter signed C. W. Pearce, 'T. L. Harris', Glasgow *Evening Citizen*, 29 December 1891; letter from Isabella D. Pearce to the editor of the *British Weekly* [undated, probably written after Harris's death in 1906], TLH Papers 13/302. Bella's letter was not published; in a letter to J. Cumming Walters, Bella accused the *British Weekly* of 'taking advantage of an editorially autocratic position to prevent the possibility of his friends protecting him'. Letter from I. D. Pearce to Mr Walters, 27 August 1906, TLH Papers 13/302.
75 'Reply to the letter of a British friend who asked T.L.H. to cable advice about his standing as Labor candidate for Parliament', TLH Papers 9/235 and TLH Papers 13/302. A note on a separate page states: 'Copy of a letter to Chas & Bella Pearce in answer to whether he should run/stand for Parliament a telegram having been sent day before saying "Stand".'

76 Letter from C. W. Bream-Pearce, 'Camlachie candidature. Bream-Pearce withdraws – explanatory letter to the branch', *Labour Leader*, 1 June 1895, p. 10.
77 Post Office Glasgow Directory, 1892–1904, Strathclyde Regional Archives, Mitchell Library, Glasgow.
78 M. Wright, *Elizabeth Wolstenholme Elmy and the Victorian Feminist Movement: The Biography of an Insurgent Woman* (Manchester: Manchester University Press, 2011), p. 163.
79 'Chats with I.L.P. candidates', *Labour Leader*, 27 April 1895, p. 7.
80 Ibid.
81 Letter from 'Dovie' [Jane Harris] to 'My dearest Son', 22 September 1903, TLH Papers 9/237; diary entry of Jane Harris, 18 July 1903, TLH Papers 14/314.
82 Diary entry of Jane Harris, 18 July 1903, TLH Papers 14/314; letter from Jane Harris to Robert and Dolly Hart, 3 July 1903, TLH Papers 14/315.
83 Letter from 'Dovie' [Jane Harris] to 'My dearest Son', 22 September 1903, TLH Papers 9/237.
84 Diary entries of Jane Harris, 1903, TLH Papers 14/313-14.
85 Letter from 'Dovie' [Jane Harris] to 'Blessed Son', 9 July 1903, TLH Papers 14/315.
86 Letter from Annie Wood to George Lawton, 23 July 1930, TLH Papers 13/308.
87 Diary entries of Jane Harris, 3 July 1903 and 4 August 1903, TLH Papers 14/314.
88 Another new believer, Grace Macgregor, also wanted to go back with the Harrises to America but was prevented by her husband. See letter from Jane Harris to Nagasawa Kanaye, 13 December 1903, TLH Papers 9/237.
89 It could also have been the case that the pen-name was assigned to her by Hardie.
90 L. Foster, *Religion and Sexuality: The Shakers, the Mormons, and the Oneida Communities* (Champaign: University of Illinois Press, 1984), pp. 3–20.
91 Hunt, *Equivocal Feminists*, p. 100.
92 S. Koven, *Slumming: Sexual and Social Politics in Victorian London* (Princeton, NJ: Princeton University Press, 2004), p. 16.
93 Ibid.
94 C. Nottingham, *The Pursuit of Serenity: Havelock Ellis and the New Politics* (Amsterdam: Amsterdam University Press, 1999), pp. 47, 49.
95 Koven puts the lack of scholarly interest in Hinton down to the opacity of his prose, his lack of a coherent philosophy and the disappearance of his unpublished manuscripts, autobiography and letters. See Koven, *Slumming*, pp. 17, 300n59.
96 Koven, *Slumming*, pp. 16–18.
97 Nottingham, *The Pursuit of Serenity*, pp. 47, 50.
98 E. S. Pankhurst, *The Suffragette Movement: An Intimate Account of Persons and Ideals* (1931; London: Virago, 1977), p. 31, quoted in Bland, *Banishing the Beast*, p. 155. For a full consideration of the circumstances surrounding Elmy's marriage, see Wright, *Elizabeth Wolstenholme Elmy*, pp. 97–101 and S. S. Holton, 'Free love and Victorian feminism: the divers matrimonials of Elizabeth Wolstenholme Elmy and Ben Elmy', *Victorian Studies*, 37:2 (Winter 1994), pp. 199–222.
99 Bland, *Banishing the Beast*, pp. 156–9; Frost, *Living in Sin*, pp. 211–13.

100 Bland, *Banishing the Beast*, p. 151; J. R. Walkowitz, *City of Dreadful Delight: Narratives of Sexual Danger in Late-Victorian London* (Chicago: University of Chicago Press, 1992), p. 155. See also C. Collette, 'Socialism and scandal: the sexual politics of the early labour movement', *History Workshop*, 23 (Spring 1987), pp. 102–11; Hunt, *Equivocal Feminists*, pp. 86–94; Frost, *Living in Sin*, pp. 199–211.
101 D. Maltz, 'Ardent service: female eroticism and new life ethics in Gertrude Dix's *The Image Breakers* (1900)', *Journal of Victorian Culture* (2012), p. 5.
102 Frost, *Living in Sin*, p. 214.
103 G. Dix, *The Image Breakers* (1900), pp. 86, 87; Maltz, 'Ardent service', pp. 8–9.
104 Hunt, *Equivocal Feminists*, pp. 94–106; Bland, *Banishing the Beast*, 159–61; Frost, *Living in Sin*, pp. 209–11.
105 Quoted in Hunt, *Equivocal Feminists*, p. 96.
106 *Justice*, 2 November 1895, quoted in ibid., p. 99.
107 Lily Bell, 'Matrons and Maidens', *Labour Leader*, 9 November 1895, p. 3, and 22 February 1896, p. 68; C. E. D. Martyn, 'Edith Lanchester', *Labour Leader*, 15 February 1896, p. 52.
108 Hardie quoted in Hunt, *Equivocal Feminists*, p. 102; 'Our London Letter', *Labour Leader*, 2 November 1895, p. 3; Marxian, 'Lanchester and Manchester', *Labour Leader*, 9 November 1895, p. 1.
109 Lily Bell, 'Christ's "Second Coming"', *Forward*, 24 November 1906; Sophia, 'Matrons and Maidens: The sexes, what they are, and their relationship to each other – Part III', *Labour Leader*, 25 September 1897, p. 318.
110 Sophia, 'Matrons and Maidens: The sexes, what they are, and their relationship to each other – Part III', *Labour Leader*, 25 September 1897, p. 318.
111 Lily Bell, 'Matrons and Maidens', *Labour Leader*, 26 May 1894, p. 11.
112 Lily Bell, 'Matrons and Maidens', *Labour Leader*, 26 May 1894, p. 11; 1 December 1894, p. 7.
113 Lily Bell, 'Matrons and Maidens', *Labour Leader*, 1 December 1894, p. 7.
114 Lily Bell, 'Christ's "Second Coming"', *Forward*, 24 November 1906, p. 5.
115 Letter from I. D. Pearce, *Freewoman*, 28 December 1911, p. 112; Lily Bell, 'Christ's "Second Coming"', *Forward*, 24 November 1906, p. 5.
116 Lily Bell, 'Christ's "Second Coming"', *Forward*, 24 November 1906, p. 5.
117 Ibid.
118 Lily Bell, 'Matrons and Maidens', *Labour Leader*, 27 June 1896, p. 224.
119 Lily Bell, 'Matrons and Maidens', *Labour Leader*, 1 December 1894, p. 7.
120 Ibid.; S. Seidman, 'The power of desire and the danger of pleasure: Victorian sexuality reconsidered', *Journal of Social History*, 24:1 (Autumn 1990).
121 'Women in evolution', *Labour Leader*, 28 November 1896, p. 412. For an analysis of Gilman's appropriation of Darwinian evolution, see P. Deutscher, 'The descent of man and the evolution of woman: Antoinette Blackwell, Charlotte Perkins Gilman and Eliza Gamble', *Hypatia*, 19:2 (Spring 2004), pp. 35–55.
122 Sophia, 'Matrons and Maidens: The sexes, what they are, and their relationship to each other', *Labour Leader*, 25 September 1897, p. 318.
123 P. Geddes and J. A. Thomson, *The Evolution of Sex* (London: Walter Scott, 1889), pp. 123, 271.

124 Sophia, 'Matrons and Maidens: The sexes, what they are, and their relationship to each other – Part III', *Labour Leader*, 11 September 1897, p. 302. For Bella's evolutionary interpretation of sexual difference, see Lily Bell, 'Women and the race', *Forward*, 1 December 1906, p. 4.

125 Lily Bell, 'The women's movement. news and reviews', *Forward*, 10 November 1906, p. 8; Lily Bell, 'Women and adult suffrage', *Forward*, 15 December 1906, p. 5.

126 Lily Bell, 'The women's fight for freedom', *Forward*, 17 November 1906, p. 7.

127 Sophia, 'Matrons and Maidens', *Labour Leader*, 31 July 1897, p. 254.

128 Lily Bell, 'Matrons and Maidens', *Labour Leader*, 19 October 1895, p. 4.

129 Letter from I. D. Pearce, *Freewoman*, 14 December 1911, p. 71; Lily Bell, 'Matrons and Maidens', *Labour Leader*, 8 June 1895, p. 4.

130 Letter from Jane Lee Waring to 'Dear One' [George Waring], 18 December 1891, TLH Papers 9/238.

131 Letters from Annie Wood to George Lawton, 15 July 1930 and 23 July 1930, TLH Papers 13/308. However, Annie Wood did, in conjunction with Bella's younger brother James R. H. Duncan, bequeath ninety-three volumes of Harris's works to the Library of Congress in Washington.

132 Letter from Louis Cowles to Edwin Markham, 12 March 1922, TLH 13/307.

133 Letter from J. M. Shepherd to James Barr, 8 August 1885, quoted in Schneider and Lawton, *A Prophet and a Pilgrim*, pp. 463–4. Shepherd was a friend of Rev. A. W. Manning. The letter substantiates the Brotherhood practice of naked, communal bathing, Shepherd reporting that 'One man states that the men and women washed each other in a *complete nude state*' (his italics).

134 Lily Bell, 'Matrons and Maidens', *Labour Leader*, 1 December 1894, p. 7; 27 June 1896, p. 224.

4

Realising a more than earthly paradise of love

If within the progressive subculture of Glasgow, the Pearces discussed the Sex Question largely in the language of feminism, in Edinburgh, its principal idiom was science. This is because the personality leading the anti-Victorian revolt in Scotland's 'east windy west endy' capital was Patrick Geddes. A natural scientist by training, having studied under the anatomist and Darwinist Thomas Huxley, Geddes was a progressive by inclination. As well as holding down a part-time professorship in botany at the University of Dundee, he instigated numerous civic, educational and artistic projects in his home city of Edinburgh. These included a programme of sympathetic slum regeneration, an annual summer school inspired by the university extension movement, a pioneering sociological museum, a Celtic avant-garde journal and publishing house, and a number of university halls of residence. Yet no matter in which language issues relating to sex were aired, it remained a delicate subject, as an anecdote related by Geddes's daughter Norah illustrates:

> At U. C. D. [University College Dundee] in the garden one day [Geddes] heard his old friend and colleague, Professor Steggall (Mathematics), murmuring:
> 'I always stood up for you, old chap.'
> 'What do you say?'
> 'Oh, nothing.'
> 'Yes, but tell me.'
> 'I only said I always stood up for you.'
> 'But why and when?'
> 'Oh, you know, the book on Sex. But I always told them you'd given up that sort of thing long ago.'[1]

The book was the 1889 *Evolution of Sex*, written by Geddes in collaboration with his former pupil, the biologist John Arthur Thomson.[2] It was the first in a new series of cheap and accessible science volumes, edited by the future sexologist Havelock Ellis, and designed 'to bring within general reach of the English-speaking public the best that is known and thought in all departments of modern scientific research'.[3] By the 1880s, science, and in particular the life sciences, wielded an unprecedented authority within Victorian thought and culture. As Frank Turner has shown, during the second half of the nineteenth century, a newly legitimised scientific profession was highly successful in 'combining research, polemic wit and literary eloquence' to press the superior claims of 'the scientifically educated against the resistance of religious orthodoxy, received opinion, and intellectual obscurantism', addressing audiences ranging from skilled mechanics to the aristocracy.[4] The methodology upon which scientists based their claims for cultural dominance was empiricism, an objective and secular approach which, through its meticulous, patient and exhaustive uncovering of the facts, promised to reveal the fundamental truths of existence, what Thomas Huxley phrased as 'the resolute facing of the world as it is, when the garment of make-believe, by which pious hands have hidden its uglier features, is stripped off'.[5] With the growth in the new social sciences of anthropology, sociology and psychology, human behaviour was increasingly understood to have biological foundations, leading a generation of progressives and conservatives alike to seek solutions to ethical, social and political problems by recourse to the laws of the natural world.[6] Indeed, according to one contributor to the American *Popular Science Monthly* in 1882, classifying phenomena 'as manifestations of a universal law' had become 'the intellectual pastime of the nineteenth century'.[7] While remaining contentious, the theory of organic evolution was particularly pervasive, permeating many such attempts to draw ideological conclusions from biological evidence. For example, the freethinking Edinburgh feminist Jane Hume Clapperton, the subject of the next chapter, was emphatic in her belief in its deterministic status, declaring that 'the doctrine of evolution ... must be regarded as explanatory of things as they are, and prophetic of things as they will be, and should be'.[8]

One of the issues on which the new 'ethical naturalists' believed themselves uniquely qualified to pronounce was the role of women.[9] Commentators from a variety of scientific as well as political and personal standpoints extrapolated on the implications for womankind of the new evolutionary knowledge, with individuals including the naturalist Charles Darwin, anthropologist Paul Broca, psychologist George John Romanes, asylum physician Thomas Clouston and eugenicist Karl Pearson together creating the field of 'sexual science', an in-depth and sustained examination of the biological origins of sexual difference.[10] Geddes and Thomson's *Evolution of Sex* was in conversation with this body of literature, introducing an original hypothesis on the evolutionary process behind sexual differentiation that was intended to supersede 'the bewildering superabundance of widely different theories' currently in circulation, and fulfil the urgent need for 'an explanation at once rational and ultimate, to comprehend and underlie all the preceding ones'.[11]

In addition, however, the text, in conjunction with its 1896 companion essay 'The moral evolution of sex', also addressed the subject of sexuality, speaking to the more marginal, predominantly medical discourse of sexology. Emergent in Britain during the 1890s, sexology was concerned broadly with the analysis of sexual behaviour, and more particularly with the taxonomy and terminology of aberrant psycho-sexual identities such as homosexuality, lesbianism, paedophilia, sado-masochism, nymphomania, transvestism and zoophilia.[12] In its new, medicalised way of speaking about sexuality, it constituted a significant marker of modernity, a discourse within which, as Rita Felski has noted, 'the vocabulary of morality and religion ceded ground to the discourse of science' and 'homosexuality was redefined as an inborn condition, a medical aberration rather than a form of sin'.[13] While Geddes and Thomson confined themselves to the study of heterosexual pairings, their advanced ideas on sexual ethics, 'romantic eugenics' and birth control nonetheless constituted an important contribution to turn-of-the-century sexological ideas.

The international significance of Geddes's scientific work on both the Sex Question and the Woman Question is readily acknowledged, his ideas influencing scientific, feminist and popular opinion in both Britain and America. What is often overlooked, or questioned, are his progressive credentials. Susan Sleeth Mosedale thought him a 'spinner of speculative webs' who 'misused reason' to insist upon 'the opposite traits and capacities of men and women', while Lucy Bland similarly referenced the 'deeply conservative' logic of his arguments and inferred a degree of scepticism towards his 'professed support for women's rights'.[14] This chapter offers a comprehensive revision of this historiography. First, it situates Geddes more precisely within the conflicting and overlapping scientific, medical, feminist and anti-feminist representations of sexuality within the late Victorian period, acknowledging that his work, like that of other scientific commentators such as Havelock Ellis and Edward Carpenter, was 'quite unmistakably intended to serve radical purposes'.[15] Second, it considers Geddes's scientific work in conjunction with his intimate, familial and social life, examining the complex dynamics between his scientific ideas, his upbringing, his relationship with his wife, and his interactions with the scientists, artists and feminists who peopled the bohemian subculture with which he surrounded himself in Edinburgh. In doing so, Geddes emerges as an important, if complex, multifaceted and at times inconsistent, late Victorian sexually progressive voice – like Havelock Ellis, 'a transitional figure', unavoidably limited by the discourse of his historical present, yet nonetheless 'consciously striving for modernity'.[16]

Biosocial beginnings

Born in Ballater in west Aberdeenshire in 1854, Patrick Geddes was the youngest son of Alexander Geddes, a semi-retired Black Watch sergeant major and Janet Stevenson, a former schoolmistress. When three years old, his parents moved to Perth, and it was here, in a hillside cottage just outside the town, that Geddes spent the remainder of what he later described as a 'rarely fortunate and happy childhood with the best of parents, passed in neither poverty nor riches'.[17] His one sister and two brothers were much older, and, in gendered terms, conformed to conventional, lower middle-class expectations, his brothers carving out careers abroad in trade and banking, and his sister Jessie remaining at home after the death of her fiancé.[18] The roles adopted by his parents were similarly unexceptional, his father's family moniker of 'General' and his mother's nickname of 'Chancellor of the Exchequer' indicating a conventional sexual division of labour.[19] Geddes remembered his father as an attentive and affectionate if still authoritarian presence; as the youngest son, Geddes benefited from 'a modifying if not relaxing of parental supervision'.[20] As Eleanor Gordon has commented, there were 'many different ways of being a father' in nineteenth-century Scotland, and Alexander Geddes was far removed from 'the dour, aloof or drunken figure of the popular stereotypes', reading aloud from the Bible after supper (he was an elder in the Free Kirk), taking Geddes on long countryside walks and closely involving him in the family garden.[21] A precocious child, Geddes at aged nine was 'dux' or first in his class 'almost every day', devouring the contents of the local Mechanics Library and winning numerous prizes during his school career at Perth Academy.[22]

Abandoning a degree course in botany at the University of Edinburgh after just one week, Geddes instead sought out tuition in London from Thomas Huxley, the celebrated champion of Darwinian evolution and notorious agnostic, who was currently teaching an intensive five-month course in the natural sciences at the Royal School of Mines. For the next two years Huxley employed Geddes as a demonstrator on the course, as well as sending him on research trips to Cambridge University, where he worked under the leading embryologists Michael Foster and Francis Balfour, and to the University of Paris's marine biological station at Roscoff

10 Patrick Geddes in 1886 aged 32

in north-west Brittany. In 1881, his work on 'reciprocal accommodation' in a simple marine organism known as a radiolarian was awarded the Ellis Physiology Prize by the University of Edinburgh and was subsequently published in *Nature*, securing his reputation as a young biologist of considerable talent and promise (see figure 10).[23]

Despite this early scientific success, however, Geddes was increasingly drawn towards utilising the insights he had gained from evolutionary biology for the betterment of human society. This impulse was part of what Thomson and William Macdonald termed the late Victorian 'communal quickening of the conscience', which manifested itself within the scientific world as a growing tendency by a new generation of naturalists to seek solutions to social problems within their own discipline.[24] In part, this was based on the ideas of Auguste Comte, the French historian and philosopher, who in his six-volume *Cours de Philosophie Positive* asserted the existence of a 'Hierarchy of Sciences', beginning with mathematics and rising through the other 'preliminary sciences' of astronomy, physics, chemistry and biology, before reaching the pinnacle of the study of society or 'sociology', a term originated by Comte.[25] The philosophical school that developed around this scientific study of humanity Comte termed 'positivism', summarising its moral code as 'living for others' or 'altruism' (another Comtean neologism), and asserting that biology should 'indicate the germ of this principle, presenting it in a form uncomplicated by disturbing influences'.[26] While Huxley was antipathetic towards any such attempts to accord the workings of animal organisms an explanatory power in human society, in his 'Lay Sermons' deriding positivism as merely 'Catholicism minus Christianity', Geddes was less dismissive, believing Huxley's criticisms 'were somehow missing the essential significance of this new doctrine'.[27] Instead, Geddes became one of several late Victorian intellectuals 'more or less sympathetic to the Positivist cause while uncommitted to its details',[28] for a brief period attending the 'bright week-night meetings' of the London Positivist Society and later converting his fiancée Anna to the positivist 'Religion of Humanity'.[29]

It was in Edinburgh that Geddes was to test the practical value of these ideas. In the 1880s and 1890s he developed a portfolio of diverse yet interrelated schemes, which he instigated in the tenement slums of the city's impoverished Old Town, a place deserted by the city's middle classes for the elegant Georgian terraces of the New Town, and where, according to the political economist James Mavor, 'unredeemed squalor had reigned for at least half a century'.[30] The schemes were of both a social and a cultural nature, and included an extensive programme of slum clearance and rebuilding work under the Town and Gown Association; the publication of four issues of a Celtic literary and artistic journal called the *Evergreen*, dubbed by *The Times* a northern 'Yellow Book';[31] the establishment of a Celtic publishing house and art school; an annual science and arts 'Summer Meeting' attracting up to 150 students from Britain, Europe and America; a regional and civic museum known as the Outlook Tower; and the establishment of a number of university halls of residence. Geddes envisaged that this work would simultaneously create an environment in which Edinburgh's inhabitants could achieve their evolutionary potential, while also reinstating the city as one of Europe's foremost 'Powers of Culture'.[32]

Believing that lasting social and cultural change could come about only through relatively modest, practical schemes, gradually implemented at a local level, Geddes professed a 'total dissent from contemporary political methods'.[33] Refusing to affiliate himself with any one political party, the one organisation Geddes did maintain a prolonged association with was the non-partisan Ruskin Society of Glasgow. Between 1886 and 1898, Geddes lectured for them on five separate occasions, his topics including 'Population, Progress and Poverty' and 'Some Adaptations of Ruskin's Ideals to Practice'.[34] He also conducted a personal tour of his various civic initiatives as part of a specially organised visit to Edinburgh, an additional carriage having to be put on the one o'clock train from Glasgow in order to accommodate the large numbers of Ruskin Society members on the excursion (figure 11).[35] Given Bella and Charles Pearce's active involvement in the administration of the Society, is seems likely that Geddes would have met the Pearces at least once, although all that can be verified is that Charles was present at Geddes's lecture in Glasgow in February 1896.[36]

Geddes's partner in all his endeavours was his wife Anna, the daughter of an affluent Liverpool merchant whom he married in 1886. The epitome of what Clare Jones has termed the 'Ruskinian ideal of women as supporters and enablers of men', Anna worked tirelessly researching, administrating and facilitating Geddes's work.[37] They had met through the educationalist James Oliphant, one of Geddes's 'select friends' with whom he would discuss solutions to the social problems of Edinburgh 'far into the night'.[38] After three years of friendship, during which time both Anna and Geddes withheld their feelings of increasing attraction, the moment of disclosure came in January 1886. Geddes was invited on a European tour by his childhood friend and benefactor Martin White, and the prospect of their imminent departure forced him to act. Inviting Anna to the Edinburgh Botanic Gardens one Sunday morning when they were closed to the public, he proposed, in a typically eccentric gesture breaking in half a piece of opal from a trip to Mexico with a geological hammer and giving Anna half in lieu of an engagement ring.[39] She accepted, although sought reassurance from Geddes that by becoming his wife, she would be 'a help & not a hindrance' to his work.[40]

Her insecurity is indicative of the gendered power imbalance that structured their early relationship and is further reflected in her letters to Geddes written during their engagement. While Anna emerges as a confident, teasing and solicitous fiancée, her correspondence also conveys a reverence for Geddes's opinions and a diffidence concerning her own. She refers to him as her 'severe old lecturer', promises to pass the time apart thinking of 'what you want me to think about' and anticipates him teaching her how to better articulate her thoughts.[41] When Geddes makes what she refers to as some 'wise speculations' in one of his letters, she hesitates to comment, despite rereading it several times, saying she needs

The Ruskin Society of Glasgow
(Society of the Rose.)

Professor Geddes has invited the members to visit The Outlook Tower, University Hall, Edinburgh. *(Now in course of arrangement)* on Saturday afternoon, 9th October, 1897.

It is proposed to leave Queen Street Station by one o'clock train to Edinburgh, and members will please procure their own railway tickets.

Programme.

2-30. Meet on Outlook Tower (549 Castlehill).

2-30-3-30. Camera and Prospect (weather permitting.) Relief Models. Orientation Table. Episcope. Dials. etc. Collection of Photographs, etc., illustrative of Old and New Edinburgh.

3-30-4-0. Tea on Roof.

4-0-6-0. General Explanation by (by Prof. Geddes) of plan of arrangement to be carried out in Tower (storey by storey), with discussion.

Members intending to be present are requested to send their names to the Secretary, in order that Professor Geddes may have some idea of the number to prepare for.

WILLIAM SINCLAIR,
Hon. Secy.

923 Govan Road,
4th Oct., 1897

11 Programme of the Ruskin Society of Glasgow's excursion to Edinburgh, 1897 time to 'grasp it all' and 'take it all in'.⁴² Conversely, she is 'half shy' about articulating her own feelings, concerned that Geddes will disparage or reprove her.⁴³ Indeed, on one occasion Geddes does grumble about the quality and quantity of her letters, Anna responding defensively that preparations for the wedding combined with an unaccustomed lack of sleep have left her tired, and meant that she has 'been very stupid sometimes I know, but I think we shall be all right when you come back, shan't we?' and saying that by contrast his letters had been 'everything' to her.⁴⁴ Drawing on an image common in Victorian culture of the husband as a stalwart oak tree and the wife as a clinging vine, she describes how she sometimes had the feeling of 'a piece of ivy that has been trailing on the ground amongst the damp grass and out of the sun, but that at last has found the tree that it can twine itself around & grow into and by which it gets into the sunshine'.⁴⁵

Anna's sense of her lack of self-determination and her seeming embrace of a simultaneously patriarchal and companionate model of marriage was the result of two things. First, she had clearly absorbed the normative gendered attitudes which had structured her respectable, middle-class, mid-Victorian upbringing, her expectations of life circumscribed by precisely the 'ice-barriers of masculine authority and conventionality' railed against by Bella Pearce in her *Labour Leader* columns.⁴⁶ Her father came from a strict Presbyterian family and had 'very definite opinions … on the conduct becoming to (even very) young ladies', not permitting his daughters to climb or jump from walls or engage extensively in sports or games.⁴⁷ Their mother, while less strict in this regard, looking on their physical play 'with an indulgent eye when father was safely at business', was nonetheless unyielding in her compliance with other social proprieties, Anna referring to her mother's terror least unconventional behaviour led to 'any talk about a girl'.⁴⁸ Unlike Bella, however, there is no suggestion that Anna Morton rebelled against such gendered restrictions. After attending boarding school, she nurtured her talent for the acceptably feminine accomplishment of music, studying piano, German and singing in Dresden for a year before becoming a music teacher. Still unmarried at the age of twenty-six, she struggled to resign herself to the prospect of a lifetime of 'living alone', later recollecting her frequent feelings of loneliness and discontentedness, frustrated by her emotional dependency 'on the people I liked best' but with no obvious way of achieving the 'fuller better life' of which she dreamed.⁴⁹

Second, however, Anna's intellectual and emotional deference to Geddes can be read as one example of the pupil–teacher dynamic that structured many of Geddes's relationships. The French sociologist Edmond

Demolins commented that he had 'rarely met a man with such an ability to attract people and retain them once he has conquered them', although a fictional rendering of Geddes by a former acolyte offers a less sympathetic portrait.[50] In Riccardo Stephens's gothic novel *The Cruciform Mark*, Geddes is depicted as 'Professor Grosvenor', a brilliant if unscrupulous professor of psychology in possession of a number of characteristically Geddesian traits, including a love of symbolism, an impressionistic manner of speech and a compulsion to persuade young students to participate in his numerous, transitory enthusiasms. The narrator relates how 'Women hung round him and protested that he was "so suggestive" – of what, they could rarely say. Men were attracted also; there were always one or two at his feet, but as a rule they presently got up and went away, laughing or angry, leaving their places to be immediately filled by younger and more enthusiastic fellows.'[51] This depiction is corroborated by the numerous expressions of affection, allegiance and gratitude contained within letters written to Geddes over his lifetime. His wide-ranging intellect, infectious idealism and emotional expressiveness (the result, according to one friend, of his 'man. woman soul' [*sic*]), appear to have engendered epiphanic moments of revelation from both men and women. The painter John Duncan professed himself 'your very faithful disciple', claiming that he carried Geddes's notes with him 'as my Scriptures' and would 'diligently strive to live up to them', a task that would 'come all the easier as they so completely coincide with my own aspirations – aspirations which you have evoked in me.'[52] Ernst Grosse, a German ethnologist from Freiberg whom Geddes appeared to have visited around 1891, described how, since Geddes had left, he had 'wandered once more through the new world of ideas you opened for me', admitting that he was 'writing like a boy of sixteen', but asking Geddes not to laugh at him, 'for if my soul is aflame, my dear friend, it is all your work.'[53] Similarly, the kindergarten teacher Fanny Franks, who had attended Geddes's summer school in Edinburgh in 1903, likened consuming Geddes's glittering and elusive philosophy to 'something like the baby [must feel] when it is drinking in the mothers milk. It knows nothing of the elements of which it is made – nor of the effects it is to produce; but merely feels "that is the food for me!"'[54]

On occasion, the expressions of devotion are sufficiently ambiguous to raise the suspicion that disciples of both genders occasionally misread Geddes's intensity as a sexual invitation. This was certainly the case with Anne Murray, a nurse and sister of a friend whom Geddes met prior to his engagement to Anna.[55] In a letter written in June 1885, she claimed to be 'no longer the meek woman who was learning to be content to be the very commonplace person she had so long bemoaned herself to be', warning Geddes teasingly 'Are you not afraid of your own creation', before three weeks later writing more earnestly that it was 'a very great matter to me to hear you talk in a way that I never heard from any other', and that she owed Geddes 'a great deal'.[56] Similarly heartfelt is the early correspondence of Alex Michael, a young printer who had undertaken some work for Geddes during the late 1870s and was endeavouring to better himself through 'book-learning' and the 'regulation of his habits'.[57] In a letter sent in 1885, he stated that while Geddes 'may have reasons for wishing not to hear from me again', he never saw his name without feeling 'the liveliest emotion', treasuring an 'odd part' of the journal *Nature* because it contained some of his writing, and stating that his devotion to him was 'unequalled in my life and unquenchable in itself'.[58] Finally, in 1895, Geddes received a letter from the Fabian socialist Harry Lowerison from Barnet in Hertfordshire, who confessed to being nervous as he prepared to visit Geddes in Edinburgh during the Easter break, quoting the beginning of a poem by Walt Whitman:

> "Are you the new person drawn towards me?
> To begin with, take warning, for
> I am really far different to what you suppose"
> You remember Whitman?
> Still I am drawn to you.
> H 'L'[59]

Published first in 1860 in the third edition of *Leaves of Grass*, the poem was one of forty-five within the 'Calamus' cluster, which was concerned with 'comradeship' or love between men. While the precise context of the poem is unclear and could equally constitute a warning from a master to a disciple as from a man to his prospective male lover, its position within the Calamus series suggests the latter. In the poem directly preceding it, Whitman describes his joyful anticipation of the arrival of his 'dear friend, my lover', culminating in a moment of perfect happiness as he contemplates the 'one I love most' sleeping next to him: 'In the stillness, in the autumn moonbeams, his face was inclined toward me, / And his arm lay lightly around my breast'.[60] It is still impossible to assert with confidence whether Lowerison's choice of poem indicated a homoerotic interest in Geddes, and in turn whether Geddes would have correctly interpreted its significance. All that can be averred is that the letters of both Lowerison and Alex Michael present the intriguing possibility that within the progressive circle surrounding Geddes in Edinburgh in the 1880s and 1890s there may have existed a space and a language in which to speak tentatively of male same-sex love.

Regendering evolution: a vast mothers' meeting

Geddes's investment in his numerous projects of urban regeneration and cultural renewal in Edinburgh meant that he failed to realise his professional potential in the natural sciences. Despite references from naturalists Charles Darwin, August Weismann and Alfred Russell Wallace, the latter asserting that Geddes was 'well known as an original thinker and worker in some of the most interesting and difficult branches of biological study', he was turned down for professorial posts in natural history and botany at the University of Edinburgh in 1882 and 1888.[61] His scientific publications were scarce, the American sociologist Lewis Mumford referring to his books as 'but notes written on the margins of his thinking'.[62] The one subject on which Geddes did publish extensively, however, was sex. His first work, the 1889 *Evolution of Sex*, was arguably his most controversial, both scientifically and morally, *Nature* cautioning that while it contained many 'useful and suggestive' theories for advanced biology students, it constituted wholly inappropriate reading material for the general reader.[63] According to the science journal, the authors, rather than providing a balanced, reliable synthesis of well-respected opinion, had instead forwarded their own, highly conjectural hypothesis:

> General readers demand, with right, that those who speak to them with the voice of authority shall give them the authoritative views. Controversial matter they are not remotely interested in, and when it cannot be avoided they must have it carefully distinguished from matter beyond controversy. These authors are controversialists from the first page of their book to the last: they are partisan controversialists offering their wares and their wisdom as accredited doctrine and determined result.[64]

The 'controversial matter' that so exercised *Nature* was a new theory concerning the origins and nature of sexual difference, a subject currently of intense debate. While a broad consensus had begun to emerge among biologists that the constitution, age, sex and environment of the parents might be influencing factors in determining the sex of the foetus, there nonetheless existed a confusing number of widely differing theories. What was needed, according to Geddes, was a rational and definitive explanation to supersede all the preceding ones, an explanation he believed his theory provided. He had already sketched the key points in a paper to the Royal Society of Edinburgh in 1886 and in his entries on 'Reproduction' and 'Sex' in the *Encyclopaedia Britannica*.[65] In the *Evolution of Sex* he substantiated them, by providing a detailed compendium of evidence from the natural world. Drawing on a new understanding of cell metabolism, which envisaged organisms as in a continual state of chemical flux, Geddes argued that the physiology of all living matter, including the phenomena of sex, could be explained by an 'organic see-saw' between the twin dynamics of 'anabolism' and 'katabolism'.[66] When a mother had enough to eat, the result was female offspring with an 'anabolic' habit, under which energy was conserved and the stability of the organism maintained. Poor nutritive conditions, however, generated male offspring with a 'katabolic' habit, with a tendency to dissipate energy and transmit variation. This constitutional difference at the cellular level was responsible, asserted Geddes, not just for the structure of the different sex organs, sperm being katabolically small, active and flagellate, and the ovum anabolically large, passive and quiescent, but for a panoply of psychological differences between the sexes:

> The feminine [anabolic] passivity is expressed in greater patience, more open-mindedness, greater appreciation of subtle details, and consequently what we call more rapid intuition. The masculine [katabolic] activity lends a greater power of maximum effort, of scientific insight, or cerebral experiment with impressions, and is associated with an unobservant or impatient disregard of minute details, but with a stronger grasp of generalities. Man thinks more, woman feels more. He discovers more, but remembers less; she is more receptive, and less forgetful.[67]

His hypothesis marked a radical departure from the Darwinian explanation for secondary sexual characteristics, which conceptualised them not as constitutional and static, but as functional and dynamic, the outcome of a long process of natural and sexual selection.[68] Generation after generation, argued Darwin, birds and animals in possession of attributes most useful for attracting mates or seeing off rivals, such as elaborate plumage or large antlers, were more likely to succeed in reproducing and, when they did, they transmitted their superior attributes to their offspring.[69] Yet with the assumption that sexual differentiation was a process that occurred over time came the possibility that evolution could potentially take a different course. For those unnerved by the perceived conflation of the sexes by *fin de siècle* New Women and decadent men, this raised the terrifying prospect of racial degeneration, in which civilised, sexually segregated society regressed to a prior, barbaric and hermaphroditic ancestry.[70] Conversely, eugenic feminists seized the opportunity such a discursive loophole presented, positing women as powerful agents of change in a very different biological destiny to that envisaged by Darwin.[71] The metabolic essentialism of Geddes and Thomson, however, admitted neither outcome. While the physical, intellectual and emotional differences between the sexes 'may be exaggerated or lessened', they argued, 'to obliterate them it would be necessary to have all the evolution over again on a new basis'.[72]

Yet the challenge to contemporary scientific opinion presented by the *Evolution of Sex* lay not just in its belief in the intrinsic and immutable nature of sexual dimorphism but in its emphasis on the extent to which difference suffused the body. Thomas Laqueur, Londa Schiebinger and Cynthia Eagle Russett have asserted that, prior to around 1750, the influence of an Aristotelian–Galenic humoral model of the cosmos meant that women were considered similar if inferior beings to men, merely deficient in the requisite heat necessary to achieve metaphysical male perfection.[73] This is what Laqueur refers to as the 'one-sex', hierarchical understanding of men and women, within which sexual difference was confined to the reproductive organs, with the first detailed illustration of a discrete female skeleton appearing in 1759.[74] After 1800, however, according to Laqueur, a 'two-sex' model of sexual difference predominated, in which the sexes were seen as fundamentally incommensurable. This historical interpretation of changing attitudes towards sexed bodies has not gone uncontested. Sally Shuttleworth has suggested that Laqueur was 'too easily seduced by the economy of his central thesis', while Karen Harvey and Mary Fissell have criticised his reliance on scientific and medical texts produced by and for a social elite, arguing instead that ordinary people will have made use of a wide range of sources, from erotica to public executions, to make sense of their bodies.[75] Utilising such sources, they have advanced evidence to suggest, for example, that in the eighteenth century male and female genitals were thought of as both similar and different, sometimes within the same text. What is certain, however, is that the mid- to late Victorian period saw the emergence of a newly authoritative discourse of sexual science, one which asserted with increasing confidence that men and women were fundamentally, innately different.

The organ recognised as increasingly critical was the brain. In an influential 1887 journal article, the psychologist George John Romanes added an evolutionary rationale to already well-established arguments regarding the existence of conspicuous, scientifically verifiable disparities in men and women's 'intellect, emotion and will', which were of such magnitude that the author believed males should be classified 'in one psychological species and the females in another'. The underlying cause was women's relatively smaller brain size, the psychologist dismissing as unscholarly the 'small section of the public' who believed the absence of female geniuses in history to be due to deficiencies in women's education:

> Although it is usually a matter of much difficulty to distinguish between nature and nurture, or between the results of inborn faculty and those of acquired knowledge, in the present instance no such difficulty obtains ... Women by tens of thousands have enjoyed better educational as well

as better social advantages than a Burns, a Keats, or a Faraday; and yet we have neither heard their voices nor seen their work.[76]

While the *British Medical Journal* disagreed with Romanes over the significance of the 'missing five ounces' of women's brain matter, stating cerebral physiology was not yet sufficiently advanced to permit a conclusive verdict, it was nonetheless 'thoroughly with him in his condemnation of the fatuous notion of some feather-brained reformers that there is no such thing as sex in mind'.[77] For Geddes and Thomson, however, Romanes did not go nearly far enough. Sexual distinctions, according to their new theory, went way beyond 'a mere matter of muscular strength or weight of brain'; instead, they were a manifest expression of the anabolic or katabolic tendencies of each microscopic cell in the body, 'the highest outcome of the whole activities of the organism – the literal blossoming of the individual life'.[78]

As Angelique Richardson has demonstrated, anti-feminist sexual scientists such as Romanes did not hold the monopoly on the belief in the biological basis of sexual difference. Eugenic feminists similarly understood sex and society to be biologically determined, although they believed that 'feminism might work *with* rather than against nature, intervening in the process of biological evolution in order to alter biological destiny'.[79] However, the uncompromising totalitarianism of Geddes's biological account certainly constituted the antithesis of the environmental feminism advanced by John Stuart Mill, who, in his 1869 essay *The Subjection of Women*, queried whether 'any one knows, or can know, the nature of the two sexes, as long as they have only been seen in their present relation to one another', and argued instead for the current artificiality of women's natures, 'the result of forced repression in some directions, unnatural stimulation in others'.[80]

In the *Evolution of Sex*, Geddes chose to question several key tenets of environmental feminism, what Sandra Holton has termed the 'humanistic' or egalitarian faction of the woman's movement.[81] It reflects an indecision over feminism that was still present twenty years later in 1909, when Geddes refused an offer by Charlotte Despard to speak at a meeting of the Women's Freedom League.[82] First, Geddes categorically rejected female suffrage as a panacea, based on his understanding of the 'deep difference' between men and women, declaring infamously that 'what was decided among the prehistoric Protozoa cannot be annulled by Act of Parliament'.[83] Second, he opposed women engaging in paid work, claiming the increasing 'inter-sexual competition for subsistence' was having 'complexly ruinous results ... upon both sexes and upon family life'. Instead, he promoted a vague increasing 'civicism' of women, presumably referring to female participation in schemes of urban regeneration and social housing similar to those he and Anna were engaged with in Edinburgh.[84] Finally, he provided a biological rationale for patriarchy, arguing that the conventional sexual division of labour was not 'a mere product of masculine bullying', as some feminists suggested, but instead a rational response to organic difference. He gave as an example the 'poor [male] savage, who lies idling in the sun for days after his return from the hunting, whilst his heavy-laden wife toils and moils without complaint or cease', arguing that this constituted an entirely rational domestic economy, considering the 'extreme burst of exertion which such a life of incessant struggle with nature' required of men.[85]

Yet, despite its inclusion of such arguments, throughout the 1890s feminists from a range of ideological traditions, in particular eugenics and social purity, responded favourably to *The Evolution of Sex*. This was in part due to the strategic way individuals within the women's movement selected, appropriated and subverted discrete and sometimes contradictory ideas from a wide spectrum of scientific opinion. It was also, no doubt, because of inherent ambiguities and inconsistencies within Geddes's work, which facilitated multiple interpretations. Nevertheless, there were three interrelated aspects of his treatise on sexual difference that rendered it a genuinely useful piece of science for the women's movement.

The first was Geddes's sincere commitment to the idea that women, while different, were fundamentally equal to men. This was a commitment he shared with the *Evolution of Sex*'s editor, Havelock Ellis, who in *Man and Woman*, his 1894 study of the secondary sexual characteristics, dismissed the 'everlasting discussion regarding the "alleged inferiority of women"' as 'absolutely futile and foolish'.[86] Within the conservative rhetoric of evolutionary biology such convictions of sexual equality were manifestly progressive, as Geddes himself was keen to emphasise, stating that 'few maintain that the sexes are essentially equal, still fewer that the females excel', the vast majority of authorities presupposing male superiority.[87] In *The Descent of Man*, Darwin had maintained that civilised, modern man enjoyed a decided intellectual pre-eminence in whatever he chose to take up and that this was an inevitable consequence of natural and sexual selection. The struggles by males of successive generations for subsistence and over rivals had necessitated the development of courage, pugnacity, competitiveness, strength and, indeed, genius.[88] According to Darwin, due to the laws of inheritance these attributes, because acquired during maturity, were then 'transmitted more fully to the male than to the female offspring'; indeed, it was fortunate that man had not become 'as superior in mental endowment to woman, as the peacock is in ornamental plumage to the peahen'.[89] Herbert Spencer elaborated on Darwin's hypothesis, detailing a litany of distinctive mental traits acquired by the 'weaker sex' as survival techniques in their relationships with the 'aggressive, unscrupulous, intensely egoistic' males of early, barbaric tribes. These included persuasion, deception, intuition, a love of approbation and a fascination with power (which accounted for female religiosity), all of which had enabled women and the race to prosper. Crucially, however, Spencer also attributed the restricted growth of women's nervo-muscular system to the early cessation of their individual evolutionary development, in order to ensure the preservation of vital energy for the fulfilment of their reproductive functions.[90] As Geddes put it, if Darwin's man was an 'evolved woman', Spencer's woman was an 'arrested man', analogous to children and the lower races in her deficiency in the 'latest products of human evolution' – specifically, abstract reasoning and the sentiment of justice.[91]

Geddes rejected both Darwin's and Spencer's hypotheses, later referring to the use of 'epigrams' such as 'evolved woman' and 'undeveloped man' to sum up sexual difference as crude, unscientific and 'practically dangerous' generalisations, their threat presumably residing in the easy ammunition they provided those in search of scientific justifications for discrimination against women.[92] In contrast, he expounded a scientific reconfiguration of the notion of sexual complementarity, stating that 'to dispute whether males or females are the higher, is like disputing the relative superiority of animals or plants. Each is higher in its own way, and the two are complementary'.[93] This is not to deny that alongside his explicit professions of belief in female equality nestled, unscrutinised, an assumption of sexual hierarchy, as this prior passage hints at. Most would surely consider it preferable to be an animal rather than a plant, just as katabolic man's 'greater cerebral ... originality' and 'scientific insight' were clearly of a higher status than anabolic woman's 'common sense' and 'greater patience', however sincere Geddes's rhetoric of equality.[94] Indeed, it was his failure to scrutinise the implicit values inscribed within his lists of secondary sexual characteristics that made his work vulnerable to later criticism. The Franco-Polish feminist and pacifist Jean Finot, for example, illustrated the spuriousness of Geddes's assignation of anabolic and katabolic traits, in his 1913 *Problems of the Sexes* outlining a set of diametrically opposite conclusions, which, he argued, possessed an equal chance of being truthful:

> Let us take up the argumentation without allowing ourselves to be disturbed by all those which have made it deviate. Does not the spermatozoon of man, smaller, more variable, already indicate the versatility, the fickleness and the weakness of man? The passive ovule incarnates

seriousness and weight. The government of men and affairs should belong to woman; for since she is more balanced, more reflective, more stable, she will be able to perform her duties with continuity in her ideas and proceedings. Distrust arises concerning the spermatozoon ... He must be regarded with suspicion and kept away from commanding positions. Nature herself has indicated our path. Woman must rule, and man has only to submit to her laws and inspiration. Thus for whole pages, we could continue to demonstrate the superiority of woman and the necessity for the slavery of man.[95]

What Finot misunderstood was that in the context of 1890s debates about sexual difference, Geddes was neither intentionally anti-feminist nor indeed interpreted as being so. Many feminists ascribed to similar views of the natural, sexed qualities of men and women, with New Woman writer Sarah Grand stating in 1892 that 'Womanhood is a constitutional difference which cannot be altered' and suffrage campaigner Millicent Garrett Fawcett similarly asserting in 1889 that 'We do not want women to be bad imitations of men; we neither deny nor minimise the differences between men and women', and that, to a large extent, the claim of women to representation depended on those differences.[96]

The second element within *The Evolution of Sex* which resonated with 1890s feminists was the emphasis that Geddes placed on female-coded altruism and its role in the future evolution of the race. His early biological research on 'reciprocal accommodation', along with his commitment to the evolutionary philosophy of Spencer and the positivism of Comte, had led him to challenge the primacy of natural selection. According to Geddes, nature was not 'red in tooth and claw', as his first teacher, Huxley, had asserted, although neither was it 'one hymn of love', propelled by what has more recently been termed 'the survival of the nicest'.[97] Instead Geddes conceptualised evolution as entailing the coexistence of 'two divergent lines of emotional and practical activity', egoism, which he equated with hunger and nutrition, and altruism, which he associated with love and reproduction (see figure 12).[98] As his diagrammatic representation of this process illustrates, progress was held to be dependent on a symbiotic and increasingly intricate relationship between these two streams, before reaching an 'ideal unity' in which the two became harmoniously entwined.

Yet inherent within the diagram is an ambiguity, which the accompanying text does little to resolve. First, no explanation is provided for egoism and altruism's dramatic coming together, after previously following increasingly divergent trajectories. Second, while diagrammatically each stream is accorded equal significance, in the text, it is the agency

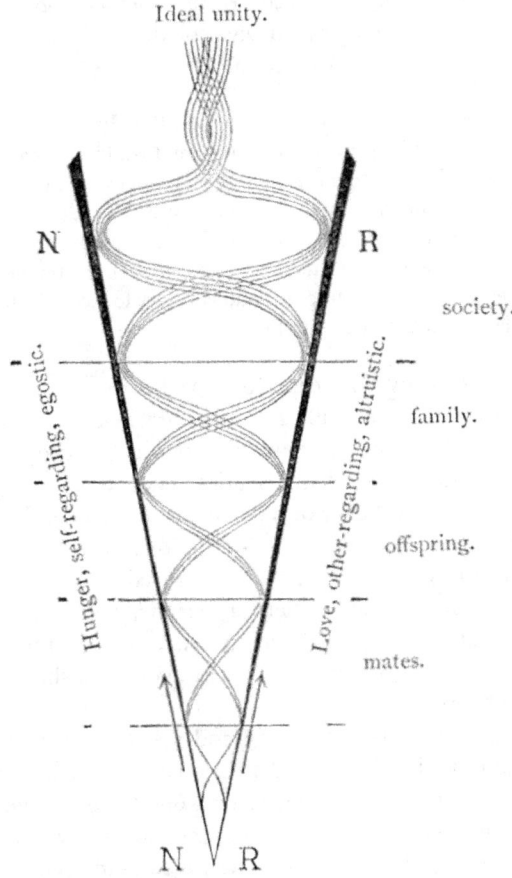

Diagrammatic Representation of the Relations between Nutritive, Self-Maintaining, or Egoistic, and Reproductive, Species-Regarding, or Altruistic Activities.

12 Geddes and Thomson's diagrammatic representation of 'Ideal Unity' in *The Evolution of Sex*, p. 280

of the altruistic impulses which is emphasised. In the attainment of his evolutionary ideal, Geddes anticipates that sexual attraction must become less, not more, selfish and that love must ultimately overcome hunger.[99] Similarly, in the book's concluding paragraphs, he asserts that 'each of the greater steps of progress is in fact associated with an increased measure of subordination of individual competition to reproductive or social ends, and of interspecific competition to co-operative association', before continuing with a rousing rejection of 'survival of the fittest' as the sole or even dominant mechanism of evolution:

> For we see that it is possible to interpret the ideals of ethical progress, through love and sociality, co-operation and sacrifice, not as mere utopias contradicted by experience, but as the highest expressions of the central evolutionary process of the natural world. The ideal of evolution is indeed an Eden; and although competition can never be wholly eliminated, and progress must thus approach without ever completely reaching its ideal, it is much for our pure natural history to recognise that 'creation's final law' is not struggle but love.[100]

While altruism is by no means conceived of as an exclusively feminine trait, women, and especially mothers, are held to have 'a larger and more habitual share of the altruistic emotions'.[101] According to the recollections of a former student, Geddes made this connection between maternity and evolutionary progress explicit in one of his lectures, which he closed with an effective re-gendering of evolution: 'I recall the thrill which went through an audience as he traced the basal feature of all life to be the sacrifice of the mother for her offspring and closed by saying, with his usual fingering of the abundant locks and the phrase over the shoulder: "So life is not really a [male] gladiator's show; it is rather – a vast mothers' meeting!"'[102]

The third and final aspect of Geddes's 1889 text that contemporary feminists found valuable was its discussion of birth control. In an extension of his critique of natural selection, Geddes questioned Darwin and Spencer's insistence that 'positive checks' to population growth, such as disease, starvation, war and infanticide, were a necessary evil, insisting instead on the evolutionary benefits of enhancing 'individuation' through a 'conscious and rational adjustment of the *struggle* into the *culture* of existence'.[103] Vital to the perpetuation of this culture was the deliberate spacing of children at least two years apart, ensuring that mothers, their health no longer destroyed by the 'cruelly exhaustive' practice of annual pregnancies, could devote more time to each child.[104] To this end, Geddes provided a brief description of the main 'artificial preventive checks to fertilisation' or birth control methods, causing *The Evolution of Sex* to be banned from at least one public library, and attracting the censure of the *Pall Mall Gazette* and *Nature*, the latter arguing that a warning should have been placed on the title page.[105]

One of his sources was clearly Jane Hume Clapperton. While he doesn't appear to have met her until a year after *The Evolution of Sex* was published, he was clearly aware of her work, citing her 1885 treatise on social reform, *Scientific Meliorism and the Evolution of Happiness*, in his chapter on family limitation, along with Charles Drysdale's *The Population Question* (1878) and Annie Besant's *The Law of Population* (1887). However, although Clapperton advocated the use of birth control methods, both as a means of population control and to facilitate sexual pleasure, Geddes was more cautious. While he dismissed the prejudice surrounding the discussion of 'neo-Mathusian proposals' as 'based in a moral cowardice', he was also anxious that birth control might lead to 'exaggerated sexuality'. Furthermore, he was concerned that this trait might become even more pronounced when passed down the generations. This meant he stopped short of recommending 'mechanical methods' and instead suggested an ethical 'prudence after marriage', in effect restricting sex to procreative purposes.[106]

Geddes's ideas on inherited sexual traits were clearly informed by eugenics, Geddes reviewing favourably Francis Galton's *Natural Inheritance* for the *Scottish Leader* in 1890 and the sociologist Victor Branford describing him in 1904 as a 'Galtonian', albeit 'a critical one'.[107] However, they were also based on an understanding of sexual behaviour as itself subject to evolutionary forces. In *The Evolution of Sex*, Geddes described how in its lowest form, the 'love of mates' manifested as the crude, physical pairings of the lowest organisms, a union in which 'there is physical attraction, and the whole process is very much a satisfaction of proto-plasmic hunger'. With the increasing intellectual, emotional and moral sensibilities of birds and mammals, however, came the development of 'what pedantry alone can refuse to call love', with 'every shade of flirtation, courtship, jealousy, and the like'.[108] Conceptualising sex in this way meant that there was therefore a risk that a lack of sexual self-control, possibly triggered by the widespread use of birth control, might result in racial degeneration, a falling back to the 'ethical level of the harlots and profligates of our streets'.[109] However, such an understanding also admitted the possibility that the evolution of sex was not over, Geddes depicting a potential future in which 'the rare fruits of an apparently more than earthly paradise of love', previously known only to poets and their heroines, would become one of the 'realities of daily life towards which we and ours may journey'.[110]

Romantic eugenics in Edinburgh's bohemia

It was in Edinburgh that Geddes attempted to realise this earthly paradise, first and foremost in his intimate relationship with his wife Anna. The couple had three children, each spaced four years apart (figure 13). Whether this was achieved through an ethical 'prudence after marriage' or 'mechanical

13 Anna Geddes with children Alasdair, Arthur and Norah, 1897

methods' is unknown, although their letters suggest a loving and passionate relationship. Anna referred to Geddes during their engagement as her 'perfect, passionate lover' and later wrote that she was 'sometimes almost dying' to see him, while Geddes expressed similar sentiments when in Boston in 1899, exclaiming 'oh, dear lassie, how I long with it all for you, and to have you in my arms again – and all, and all – and all.'[111] However, in his later book *Sex*, published in 1914, Geddes was still advocating a 'higher degree of temperance in married life' and warning of the risk of 'smothering love in physical fondness'.[112]

Geddes also tried to create the conditions for evolved sexual relations in Edinburgh, by helping to create a vibrant, intellectual and progressive space, particularly appreciated by women, in which many of the rigid, gendered conventions of respectable, middle-class Edinburgh society did not apply. The Aberdeen-born poet Rachel Annand Taylor related how visits to Edinburgh left her 'ever so much re-animated, and restored', while Fabian Eleanor Podmore wrote effusively to Anna that 'so many others besides myself must be trying to tell you & the Professor how you have helped to remake their lives & fill them with beauty'.[113]

This sense of liberation from gendered and sexual norms was particularly apparent at the Summer Meetings held in Edinburgh every August, which attracted an eclectic mix of male and female students from a variety of social backgrounds (see figure 14). In attendance one year was the New Woman writer Mona Caird, who wrote a 'charming account' of a

14 Summer Meeting in Edinburgh, 1894

Summer Meeting to the suffrage campaigner and Bella Pearce's friend Elizabeth Wolstenholme Elmy, while Edmond Demolins was a frequent lecturer and was struck by the ability, attitude and ambition of the female students.[114] In his newsletters home, he effused that 'in no other country of the world is the woman closer to man than by the mind set, the intellectual habits and the practice of life', noting in particular their independence, physical robustness and desire for intellectual self-improvement.[115] He was similarly impressed by the nature of relations between the sexes, finding them considerably more enlightened than those in *fin de siècle* France. According to Demolins, the men in Edinburgh were more reserved, less vulgar and more honourable in their treatment of women, relating that when a 'Frenchman, of a mature age' ventured 'a cheeky hint' on one of their excursions, while in France it would have raised a laugh, 'here everyone seemed embarrassed'.[116] The manners of the women he found similarly straightforward, his female hosts at a dinner treating him without 'the slightest awkwardness' or 'shade of coquetry'.[117] Indeed, in many ways the sexual culture at the Edinburgh Summer Meetings appears close to what Bella Pearce was trying to foster within ILP circles in Glasgow: a 'spirit of comradeship', born of 'joint sympathies and interests', that was devoid of flirtation or other 'unnatural sex barriers'.[118] Furthermore, at least within the surviving correspondence, there is no hint of the condescension towards women that was a feature of some articles in the *Labour Leader*.

There are two particular qualities of the subculture that can be attributed specifically to Geddes. Firstly, like Geddes, it was refreshingly unconventional. Geddes had begun his revolt against the values of bourgeois respectability when a young man, his former teacher the Scottish geologist James Geikie describing him in 1881 as 'a damned good fellow. You know – with strong radical tendencies: – hates humbug and all that sort of thing – don't set much store by Mrs Grundy – etc. etc. etc.'[119] This disregard for convention manifested itself during his engagement, in 'escapades' that Anna knew her mother would have termed 'most improper conduct'.[120] The proprieties of Edinburgh society, what Geddes called 'the current forms of dull prosperity, of soul-deep hypocrisy, so rife among us in this "east-windy, west-endy" town', were similarly ignored at the Summer Meetings, with women accorded equal freedom of movement and access to the educational programme.[121]

Yet secondly, and as importantly, the subculture also fostered high standards of 'morality'. Despite his unconventionality, Geddes believed that sexual relationships should only be conducted within monogamous, loving and permanent unions, preferably solemnised by marriage. Furthermore, in accordance with contemporary feminist critiques of male sexuality and the sexual double standard, he emphasised men's responsibility in achieving this monogamous ideal, arguing it was their duty not to sink into moral degeneracy but instead to act with sexual self-control, to obey an 'individual spirit of duty' and a 'collective soul of honour'.[122]

Geddes upheld this masculine ideal in his own intimate life, the evidence suggesting that he remained faithful to Anna and resisted any 'twilight moments' with the 'adoring women' who sat 'with rapt eyes' listening to his soliloquies.[123] He also attempted to enforce this model of manhood on the younger constituents of his progressive circle. In June 1897, three of the male residents at his Ramsay Lodge university hall of residence were caught 'living on improper relations' with two of the female servants. As Geddes had established the hall to be a self-governing institution, the transgression was summarily dealt with by a student committee, who showed 'at once a determined front against the evil doers', immediately expelling the culprits, or at least the two who confessed.[124] Nonetheless, Geddes remained devastated by the 'awful calamity', his friend the accountant Thomas Whitsun reflecting that its greater impact on Geddes was no doubt because his morals were 'very different & of a much higher grade than mine'.[125] Geddes subsequently wrote to the committee, concerned that by allowing the men liberty from an external disciplinary system he had exposed them to 'individual & collective dangers': 'For, just as our muscular tone speedily fails without active exercise, & our intellectual tone cannot exist without active mental culture, so our moral tone, without clearly formed moral purposes of one kind or another also sinks, & indeed most surely of all – most silently too, generally quite unobserved, until the necessarily resulting disaster.'[126]

The way to avoid such disasters, wrote Geddes, was by maintaining 'a moral surveillance' over the residents, clarifying that by this he meant 'not merely a mechanical control of rooms, hours, &c', but by instilling 'a moral impulse of each individual & the group as a whole'.[127] He had endeavoured to engender this impulse through the provision of masculine ideals from Scotland's mythical Celtic past, commissioning a mural series for the common room of scenes from James Macpherson's *Ossian* poems, including the awakening and symbolic rebirth of the Celtic hero Cuchullin.[128] He now suggested, as a further course of action, an edifying 'opening night' at the beginning of the winter session, a ritualistic occasion attended by 'friends of the Hall Scheme' including 'many leading citizens & distinguished men outside Edinburgh', at which the 'collegiate aims', and ultimately Geddes's masculine ideal, would be reinforced.[129]

However, the moral rectitude and social unconventionality simultaneously encouraged by Geddes were not the only features of the progressive subculture that emerged in 1890s Edinburgh. The qualities brought by its varied participants, as well as by its protagonist, deserve to be considered. In line with the master–disciple model that structured many of his relationships, the men who were closest to Geddes were often either former natural history students or else artists or writers in receipt of his patronage. As well as the artist John Duncan and the poet William Sharp, they included the sociologist and businessman Victor Branford, the geographer A. J. Herbertson and the bursar of the Outlook Tower T. R. Marr, all of whom remained lifelong friends.[130] The women were a mixture of artists, social reformers and feminists. While not members of what Leah Leneman has identified as the three Edinburgh households pivotal in the early women's movement (the McLarens, the Mairs and the Stevensons), several of them were nonetheless closely involved in a variety of feminist causes.[131] The Geddeses' closest friends were the Hill Burton family, whose female members constituted a formidable dynasty with close connections to the early campaigns for women's work, higher education and the suffrage. Patrick and Anna's peer was the artist Mary Rose Hill Burton, a founder member of the Edinburgh Lady Artists' Club and a teacher at the Old Edinburgh School of Art, who was responsible for some of the murals at University Hall and in the Geddeses' Ramsay Gardens home.[132] Mary Rose's mother, Kate, whom Geddes referred to as his 'second mother', had served with Florence Nightingale in the Crimea and was active in the Edinburgh Ladies Education Association, while her aunt, Mary Burton, had been an early campaigner for women's suffrage, accompanying the lecturer Miss Taylour on her meetings across Scotland in the 1870s.[133] Finally, the other female members of Geddes's circle about whom we have less information, while not prominent feminists, nonetheless appear to have embraced the expanding opportunities for women in the 1880s and 1890s. In her letters to Anna, Kate Cooke related her experience of being the solitary female in a practical chemistry class, while Jane Hay detailed her exploits in South Africa, where she revelled in the freedom the colonies could offer white, European women, riding twelve to eighteen miles a day, sleeping in wagons, doing her own cooking and generally 'living like gypsies'.[134]

That such individuals had a profound impact on Geddes's work can be seen by a consideration of his 1896 essay 'The moral evolution of sex'. Written with Thomson and published in the *Evergreen*, in many ways it is the companion piece to the 1889 *The Evolution of Sex*. In the intervening seven years, Geddes and Anna had had two further children, and were immersed in the feminist and progressive culture of 1890s Edinburgh, as well as possessing more personal experience of marriage, sexual relations and family life. It is to be expected, therefore, that his perspective on both the Sex Question and the Woman Question would have shifted.

In 'The moral evolution of sex', Geddes is much more understanding regarding women's desire for professional autonomy. He is no longer anxious about the ruinous impact on the family of men and women competing economically, and instead depicts the ideal 'woman-worker' as one who works with men to fulfil her own aims and ambitions. This is described by Geddes in his typically convoluted style as 'she who works not merely or mainly For men as the help and instrument of their purpose, but who works With men as the instrument yet material of her purpose'.[135] Having lived for several years in the heart of Edinburgh's Old Town, he is well informed on the wide range of occupations undertaken by working-class as well as middle-class women, including that of 'doctor and nurse, teacher and typist, dressmaker, mill girl, shop girl, and all the rest'.[136] However, despite his close relationships with women involved in the suffrage movement in Edinburgh, when discussing New Women he again displays his preference for practical action over political campaigning, implying that 'those who call themselves New and Advanced and what not, without working' are both masculine and unproductive members of society.[137] Fundamentally, what his 1896 essay reveals is an indecision over women's roles, encapsulated in his use of a bee metaphor to illustrate the differing options available to contemporary women:

> The 'Queen' [bee] is no queen but an imprisoned Mother; the 'Neuters' are no neuters, but the busy Sisters of the hive. For the first is the life-long imprisonment, the narrow home of motherhood; for the others the life of energy and of labour, for them the freedom, the sunlight, and the flowers. Here is your contrast of house-mother and new woman – sure enough as old as the world.[138]

On first impression, the life Geddes depicts for the New Women neuters, with their freedom, sunlight and flowers, is far more attractive than the lifelong imprisonment of motherhood. However, later in the text Geddes is more positive about the happiness brought to mothers by their children, while cautioning against 'over-envying' the New Woman, denigrating the worldliness of her vocation and referring to her 'poisoned sting'.[139] Overall, he appears caught between wanting to idealise women as mothers while acknowledging the legitimacy of the women's rights movement, a dilemma perhaps engendered by a conflict between his scientific understanding of women's innate, sexed characteristics, his experience of the aspirations and ambitions of the women in his circle, and his relationship with his wife.

By 1896, Geddes's views on sex had also undergone a transformation. of Geddes's earthly paradise, something no longer to be disciplined and as one in which physicality was transcended, with spiritual and romantic love evolving beyond the crude impulses of lust. In 'The moral evolution of sex', however, sex is reconfigured as a vital element in the attainment of Geddes's earthly paradise, something to be no longer disciplined and controlled but celebrated and enjoyed. In a remarkable passage, Geddes reinterprets the biblical phrase 'Consider the lilies how they grow'. Instead of, as in Luke 12:27, the lily exemplifying natural, unsought-for, God-given beauty, as a lesson against vanity or materialism, Geddes transforms the flower into a potent symbol of the natural phenomenon of sex:

> Consider then the lily: face its elemental biologic-moral fact. 'Pure as a lily' is not really a phrase of hackneyed sham-morals; for it does not mean weak, bloodless, sexless, like your moral philosopher's books, your curate's sermons. Its Purity lies in that it has something to be pure; its Glory is in being the most frank and open Manifestation of Sex in all the organic world. Its magnificent array is to show forth, not conceal: these wear their lucent argent for the passion-fragrant night, and these roll back their swart-stained robes of scarlet-orange to the sun-rich day; naked and not ashamed, glowing, breathing, warm, each flower showers forth its opulence of golden dust, stretches forth to welcome it in return. This, when we consider, is How they Grow.[140]

Geddes then translates this new openness about sex into an innovative application of eugenics. While in 1889 he had been concerned lest children inherit their parents' exaggerated sexuality, seven years later the focus of his anxiety has switched. His central concern now is not sexual licentiousness but the emotional sterility of marriages of convenience. In what could be termed a form of 'romantic eugenics', Geddes asserts that the physical and psychological health of children is determined by the emotional authenticity of their parents' relationship at the time of conception. Thus, the strength and courage of illegitimate historical heroes such as William the Conqueror and Don Juan of Austria is accounted for by the love between their mother and father. Conversely, the 'sinister devilry' of Philip II, Pedro the Cruel and 'imbecile kinglets without end' is seen as a direct result of their parents' arranged marriages. The same logic is used to explain the particular 'organic vigour' and 'ingenium perfervidum' of the Scottish race, which Geddes claims is due to the 'exceptional freedom in marriage choice, in love choice, illegitimacy and all' that he believes exists in Scotland. His central argument is that having loveless marital sex is as immoral as having loveless illegitimate sex. There may, he declared, 'be base-born children without wedlock, but there are also too many base-born with it.'[141]

As with his attitudes to the role of women, however, the contradictions in Geddes's thinking about sex remain. While he asserts the need for openness, declaring 'here as everywhere the road lies forward, not back. We must grapple with each question, whoever be shocked; not shirk it, gloss it, retreat from it, in our feeble virtue', when speaking about sex he continues to utilise metaphors from nature, rather than employing a more explicit use of language.[142] In addition, it is clear he feels free to be unconventional on the pages of the *Evergreen*, to a greater degree than he ever did in his life. The scandal at the Ramsay Lodge hall of residence happened the year after the publication of 'The moral evolution of sex'. Yet Geddes did not stop to question whether the sex between the male students and the female servants had been loving and thus morally justifiable or loveless and therefore base. Instead, his immediate assumption was that the men, by acting sexually, had acted dishonourably. While a lily's sexuality could be celebrated, the sexuality of a male student was, even for Geddes, still firmly taboo.

Conclusion

In 1912, Jean Finot lambasted Geddes and 'the numerous prophets and adepts' of his theories as the worst among recent scientists who shored up popular prejudices against women, describing *The Evolution of Sex* as 'one of those mirages which, while springing from science, are nevertheless illusory and erroneous.'[143] A year later, Geddes's friend and disciple, the progressive educationalist Cecil Reddie, was 'assaulted by Suffragettes' whilst giving a paper on sex education at Cambridge, the women ridiculing the 'Laws of Nature' Reddie had imbued from his mentor. In 1919, Geddes himself reflected back on his life and work, two years after Anna's death from fever in India and of his eldest son Alasdair in the First World War. He lamented the failure of *The Evolution of Sex* to influence scientific and popular opinion, arguing that advanced people like George Bernard Shaw had found it 'technical' and advanced women 'reactionary': 'It is as with a shop: we have stocked our goods: but where are the customers? if woman & people don't come!'[144]

To a degree, his self-assessment was overly harsh. When first published, the book was an immediate success, an American edition in 1890 and a French translation two years later securing an international reputation for its authors. Furthermore, one of its core arguments reached an even wider audience through its inclusion in Henry Drummond's 1894 *Ascent of Man*, although not in a form which Geddes would have welcomed. A Christianised account of human evolution by an evangelical Scottish theologian, the *Ascent of Man* sold 30,000 copies in Britain within five years of its publication.[145] According to Thomas Dixon, *The Evolution of Sex* was its most important source, Drummond drawing from it Geddes and Thomson's emphasis on the altruistic, self-sacrificing nature of mothers.[146] In the process, Dixon argues, Drummond developed 'their relatively sober analysis into something more colourful', ultimately using their analysis to reinforce an anti-feminist message that it was natural for women to subordinate their needs to that of their husband and children.[147]

However, several feminists took a very different message from *The Evolution of Sex*. The American settlement worker Jane Addams embraced Geddes's understanding of women's inherently anabolic characteristics, in her works *Democracy and Social Ethics* (1902) and *Newer Ideals of Peace* (1907), according women a crucial role in the ethical regeneration of American society, by virtue of their altruistic, cooperative and pacifist tendencies.[148] Geddes and Addams became close friends, in 1900 Geddes visiting her Hull House settlement in Chicago and later that year Addams lecturing for Geddes at the International School he organised for the Paris Exposition of 1900. Other feminists seized on specific aspects of Geddes and Thomson's hypotheses and subjected them to a more radical reformulation. The British social purist Frances Swiney used the anabolic/katabolic distinction to argue that women represented a higher stage of evolutionary development than men, in her *Awakening of Women* (1899) asserting that 'Anabolism implies growth, concentration, conservation, unification, cohesion and solidarity. Katabolism on the other hand, signifies division, dispersion, disintegration, decay and death.'[149] Similarly, in the *Evolution of Woman* (1894), the American suffragist Eliza Burt Gamble argued that women's anabolic qualities justified an expansion of their role in public life, as keepers of the 'industrial arts of peace, the virtues of the home and of the family, and the ultimate welfare and happiness of the state'.[150]

The changing reception accorded Geddes's work by feminists, from being embraced in the 1890s to being assaulted in the 1910s, was as much a reflection of the continuing diversity of opinion within the women's movement over biological essentialism as of *The Evolution of Sex*'s inherent progressive or reactionary nature. That Geddes himself construed his arguments surrounding sexual complementarity, female-coded altruism and birth control as radical and unconventional is clear. These ideas were further nuanced by a progressive circle of artists, writers, scientists and feminists in Edinburgh whose contribution has until now been overlooked. Yet confusion over Geddes and the impact of his ideas can also be attributed to an indecisiveness within his work and life over women, feminism and sex. Women could be 'civic mothers' but not 'queen bees' and were encouraged to become scientists and artists, but within anabolic, altruistic parameters. While in theory he encouraged egalitarian social relations, his personality ensured that his wife, children, friends and colleagues were often required to play supporting and subsidiary roles. Finally, while marriages of convenience were criticised, only the sex of the lily could be celebrated: when young male students really did have sex for pleasure, it was an occasion which caused Geddes real anguish.

Notes

1 Related by Norah Geddes to Philip Boardman, 9 January 1939, in P. Boardman, *The Worlds of Patrick Geddes: Biologist, Town Planner, Re-educator, Peace-warrior* (London: Routledge & Kegan Paul, 1978), p. 112.
2 P. Geddes and J. A. Thomson, *The Evolution of Sex* (London: Walter Scott, 1889). John Arthur Thomson (1861–1933) attended Geddes's classes in practical botany and zoology at Edinburgh University in 1881, when Geddes was an assistant to the Professor of Botany and part-time lecturer in natural sciences at the Medical School. Thomson became his lifelong friend and collaborator. He held the Chair of Natural History at Aberdeen from 1890 to 1930 and was the author of several highly popular general science books. With regard to the division of labour on *The Evolution of Sex*, it is generally accepted that Geddes provided the original ideas and Thomson summarised the existing literature and improved the lucidity of the text.
3 Advertisement for 'The Contemporary Science Series', Geddes and Thomson, *The Evolution of Sex*, p. 323.
4 F. Turner, *Contesting Cultural Authority: Essays in Victorian Intellectual Life* (Cambridge: Cambridge University Press, 1993), p. 131. See also M. Fichman, 'Biology and politics: defining the boundaries', in B. Lightman (ed.), *Victorian Science in Context* (Chicago: University of Chicago Press, 1997), pp. 94–118.
5 Quoted by Havelock Ellis in *The New Spirit* (London: Walter Scott, [n.d.]), 2nd edn, pp. 7–8. Ellis called Huxley 'one of the most militant and indefatigable exponents of the scientific spirit during the past half century'.
6 C. Eagle Russett, *Sexual Science: The Victorian Construction of Womanhood* (Cambridge, MA: Harvard University Press, 1989), pp. 3–6.
7 N. Morais, 'A reply to Miss Hardaker on the Woman Question', *Popular Science Monthly*, 21 (1882), p. 70.
8 J. H. Clapperton, *Scientific Meliorism and the Evolution of Happiness* (London: Kegan Paul, Trench & Co., 1885), p. 27.
9 The phrase is used by Thomas Dixon in *The Invention of Altruism: Making Moral Meanings in Victorian Britain* (Oxford: Oxford University Press, 2008), p. 275.
10 C. Darwin, *The Descent of Man, and Selection in Relation to Sex*, 2 vols (London: John Murray, 1871, 1901); H. Spencer, *Education: Intellectual, Moral, and Physical* (London: Williams & Norgate, 1861); G. J. Romanes, 'Mental differences between men and women', *Nineteenth Century*, 21:123 (May 1887), pp. 654–72; G. S. Hall, *Adolescence*,

2 vols (New York: D. Appleton, 1904); H. Campbell, *Differences in Nervous Organisation of Man and Woman* (London: H. K. Lewis, 1891); G. Allen, 'Plain words on the Woman Question', *Popular Science Monthly*, 36 (1889); K. Pearson, 'Woman and labour', *Fortnightly Review*, 61 (1894); H. H. Ellis, *Man and Woman: A Study of Human Sexual Secondary Characters* (London: Walter Scott, 1894). See also Eagle Russett, *Sexual Science* and A. Richardson, *Love and Eugenics in the Late Nineteenth Century: Rational Reproduction and the New Woman* (Oxford: Oxford University Press, 2003), pp. 39–44.

11 P. Geddes, 'Sex', in *Encylopaedia Britannica*, 9th edn, 24 vols (Edinburgh: A. & C. Black, 1888), vol. 21, p. 723. See also Geddes and Thomson, *The Evolution of Sex*, p. 33.

12 This is in contrast to America, where sex theorists paid far more attention to 'normal' heterosexuality. See V. Bullough, 'The development of sexology in the USA in the early twentieth century', in R. Porter and M. Teich, *Sexual Knowledge, Sexual Science: The History of Attitudes to Sexuality* (Cambridge: Cambridge University Press, 1994), p. 16.

13 R. Felski, 'Introduction', in L. Bland and L. Doan (eds), *Sexology in Culture: Labelling Bodies and Desires* (Cambridge: Polity Press, 1998), p. 4.

14 S. Sleeth Mosedale, 'Science corrupted: Victorian biologists consider "The Woman Question"', *Journal of the History of Biology*, 11:1 (Spring 1978), pp. 32–41; L. Bland, *Banishing the Beast: Feminism, Sex and Morality* (London: Penguin 1995, Tauris Parke, 2002), p. 78.

15 C. Nottingham, *The Pursuit of Serenity: Havelock Ellis and the New Politics* (Amsterdam: Amsterdam University Press, 1999), p. 150.

16 Nottingham, *The Pursuit of Serenity*, p. 149.

17 Patrick Geddes, quoted in Boardman, *The Worlds of Patrick Geddes*, p. 13.

18 Introduction to the letters of Patrick Geddes by Norah G. Mears, Geddes Papers, NLS, MS 10508, fol. 105.

19 The nicknames were awarded by Geddes's eldest brother John. Geddes was 'Deputy-Assistant-Adjutant-General' and his sister Jessie 'Correspondent in Chief'. See Introduction to the letters of Patrick Geddes by Norah G. Mears, Geddes Papers, MS 10508, fol. 166, NLS.

20 Patrick Geddes, 'Earliest recollections' [undated], quoted in Boardman, *The Worlds of Patrick Geddes*, p. 13.

21 E. Gordon, 'The family', in L. Abrams, E. Gordon, D. Simonton and E. Janes Yeo (eds), *Gender in Scottish History since 1700* (Edinburgh: Edinburgh University Press, 2006), p. 254.

22 Letter from Patrick Geddes to his brother Jack Geddes, 17 October 1863, Geddes Papers, NLS, MS 10508, fol. 1.

23 P. Geddes, 'Further researches on animals containing chlorophyll', *Nature*, 25 (1882), pp. 303–5.

24 J. A. Thomson and W. Macdonald, 'Proem', *Evergreen* (Spring 1895), p. 11; Dixon, *The Invention of Altruism*, p. 230.

25 For summaries of Comte's philosophy and a detailed analysis of its impact in Britain, see Dixon, *The Invention of Altruism*, pp. 41–89 and T. R. Wright, *The Religion of Humanity: The Impact of Comtean Positivism on Victorian Britain* (Cambridge: Cambridge University Press, 1986).

26 A. Comte, *System of Positive Polity* (1851–4), quoted in Dixon, *The Invention of Altruism*, p. 41.

27 See, for example, his 1871 essay 'Administrative nihilism', in T. H. Huxley, *Collected Essays*, 9 vols., Vol. 1: *Methods and Results* (London: Macmillan, 1893), pp. 251–89. T. H. Huxley, *Lay Sermons, Addresses and Reviews* (New York: D. Appleton, 1871), p. 140; Patrick Geddes, 'Introduction', in Susan Liveing, *A Nineteenth-Century Teacher: John Henry Bridges, M.B., F.R.C.P.* (London: Kegan Paul, Trench, Trubner, 1926), p. 1.

28 Wright, *The Religion of Humanity*, p. 261. Other examples include the sociologists Victor Branford, Leonard Trelawny Hobhouse and Lewis Mumford, and the Fabians Sidney and Beatrice Webb. According to Geddes, by 1926, despite the dwindling number of Positivist Societies, 'the man in the street [was] far more of a positivist than he knows'. See Geddes, 'Introduction', in Liveing, *A Nineteenth-Century Teacher*, p. 9.

29 Geddes, 'Introduction', in Liveing, *A Nineteenth-Century Teacher*, p. 2. In a letter written in 1886, Geddes's fiancée Anna Morton refers to their joint commitment to the 'religion of humanity', regretting that her mother was 'not young enough to make our beliefs hers'. See Anna Morton to Patrick Geddes, 14 February 1886, Geddes Papers, NLS, MS 19253, fols 5–8. Geddes would later develop an interest in theosophy and the occult, attending Theosophical Society lectures and, according to Michael Shaw, planning a society for contributors to the *Evergreen* which resembled W. B. Yeats's Order of Celtic Mysteries. M. Shaw, 'The fin-de-siècle Scots renascence: the roles of decadence in the development of Scottish cultural nationalism, c. 1880–1914' (PhD thesis, University of Glasgow, 2015), pp. 234, 241–56.

30 J. Mavor, *My Windows on the Street of the World*, 2 vols (London: J. M. Dent, 1923), vol. 1, p. 215.

31 *The Times*, 24 May 1895, in Cuttings Book, p. 4, Geddes Papers, T-GED 8/1/8, University of Strathclyde (hereafter UofS).

32 I. Zangwill, 'Without prejudice', *Pall Mall Magazine*, 8:34 (February 1896), pp. 327–8.

33 Letter from Patrick Geddes to Mr. Campbell, 1 November 1895, Geddes Papers, MS 10508A, fol. 119, NLS. In the letter, Geddes illustrates the reason behind his aversion to politics by explaining that 'I similarly won't go to temperance meetings, not because I don't want much greater temperance, but because I find in practice that the political teetotalers won't come to a real temperance Café when I build one and I must wait until I see the members of the home rule association furthering Scottish literature work for the Scottish Universities Scottish art, Scottish industries of a very greater extent before I could join them.'

34 S. Eagles, 'Appendix: Ruskin Society, partial list of lectures', in idem, 'Political Ruskin: the influence of Ruskin's political ideas and social experiments, circa 1870–1920' (DPhil thesis, Oxford, 2008), pp. 253–82. Geddes also later became honorary Vice President of the Ruskin Society of Paisley.

35 Printed report of 1894 visit by the Ruskin Society to University Hall, Edinburgh, 'The Ruskin Society of Glasgow Minute Book, 1891–9', RSG Papers, MS Gen 1093/2.

36 In a press report on Geddes's lecture on 'The Social Observatory: Its Uses and Possibilities', given to the Ruskin Society of Glasgow in February 1896, Mr Bream Pearce is reported as being present. See 'The Ruskin Society of Glasgow Minute Book, 1891–9', RSG Papers, MS Gen 1093/2.

37 C. G. Jones, *Femininity, Mathematics and Science, 1880–1914* (Basingstoke: Palgrave Macmillan, 2009), p. 112.

38 Introduction to the letters of Patrick Geddes by Norah G. Mears, Geddes Papers, NLS, MS 10508, fol. 186.
39 Introduction to the Geddes Papers by Norah G. Mears, Geddes Papers, NLS, MS 10508, fols 189–190.
40 Letter from Anna Morton to Patrick Geddes, 28 February 1886, Geddes Papers, NLS, MS 19253, fols 9–12.
41 Letters from Anna Morton to Patrick Geddes, 11 February 1886 (fols 1–4); 28 February 1886 (fols 9–12); 28 March 1886 (fols 13–16), Geddes Papers, NLS, MS 19253.
42 Letter from Anna Morton to Patrick Geddes, 28 February 1886, Geddes Papers, NLS, MS 19253, fols 9–12.
43 Letter from Anna Morton to Patrick Geddes, 11 February 1886, Geddes Papers, NLS, MS 19253, fols 1–4.
44 Letter from Anna Morton to Patrick Geddes, 28 March 1886, Geddes Papers, NLS, MS 19253, fols 13–16.
45 Letter from Anna Morton to Patrick Geddes, 28 March 1886, Geddes Papers, NLS, MS 19253, fols 13–16.
46 Lily Bell, 'Matrons and Maidens', *Labour Leader*, 9 June 1894, p. 11.
47 Introduction to the letters of Patrick Geddes by Norah G. Mears, Geddes Papers, NLS, MS 10508, fol. 185.
48 Ibid.; letter from Anna Morton to Patrick Geddes, 14 February 1886, Geddes Papers, NLS, MS 19253, fols 5–8.
49 Letters from Anna Morton to Patrick Geddes, 28 March 1886 (fols 13–16) and 3 April 1886 (fols 19–22), Geddes Papers, NLS, MS 19253.
50 Edmond Demolins's newsletter 'Le movement Social', bound in with *La Science sociale*, 1892–3, p. 80 (copy in Musée Social, Paris). I am indebted to Siân Reynolds for providing me with a copy of the newsletter and to Christelle Le Riguer for translating it.
51 R. Stephens, *The Cruciform Mark: The Strange Story of Richard Tregenna, Bachelor of Medicine (Univ.Edin.)* (London: Chatto & Windus, 1896), pp. 121–2. Riccardo Stephens was a Cornishman and occultist whom Geddes employed as the house physician for his university halls of residence in Edinburgh. Their disagreement occurred in 1895 and was over money. Stephens's novel, a gothic murder-mystery, was published the following year. See S. A. Robertson, 'Patrick Geddes', *Scottish Educational Journal*, 29 April 1932 and letter from Patrick Geddes to Dr Stephens, 26 October 1895, Geddes Papers, NLS, MS 10508A, fol. 116.
52 Jean Craigie Cunningham describes him as 'the true Answerer ... beloved of all – possessing of grace that man. woman soul, which the occultists strives painfully to attain', before continuing 'I am avowedly always a disciple of Geddes – avowedly always trying to practice his theories'. Letter from Jean Craigie Cunningham to Patrick Geddes, 1 September 1891, Geddes Papers, NLS, MS 10569, fols 4–7. See also postcard from John Duncan to Patrick Geddes, [undated], Geddes Papers, NLS, MS 10531, fol. 208.
53 Letter from Ernst Grosse to Patrick Geddes, 15 February 1891, Geddes Papers, NLS, MS 10525, fols 89–91.
54 Letter from Fanny Franks to Patrick Geddes, 13 September 1903, Geddes Papers, T-GED 9/503, UofS.

55 According to Paddy Kitchen, Anne Murray was the sister of George Murray, the Keeper of Cryptogamia at the National History Museum. P. Kitchen, *A Most Unsettling Person: An Introduction to the Ideas and Life of Patrick Geddes* (London: Victor Gollancz, 1975), pp. 74, 81–2.
56 Letters from Anne Murray to Patrick Geddes, 8 June 1885, fols 31–2 and 29 June 1885, fols 33–4, both Geddes Papers, NLS, MS 10524.
57 Letters from Alex Michael to Patrick Geddes, 18 September 1885, Geddes Papers, NLS, MS 10524, fols 47–8; 11 December 1890, MS 10525, fols 67–70.
58 Letter from Alex Michael to Patrick Geddes, 18 September 1885, Geddes Papers, NLS, MS 10524, fols 47–8. In a subsequent letter, Michael wrote to Geddes that 'You will be surprised to hear that I am married although there is nothing very surprising in the fact itself.' Patrick and Anna Geddes clearly took an interest in Michael, maintaining a correspondence with him for over a decade and sending him copies of the *Evergreen* and circulars of the Celtic Library to distribute when he moved to Dunedin in New Zealand with his family in around 1890. The relationship experienced some sort of crisis in 1898, when Geddes accused him of being 'diabolically selfish' and Michael was forced to make a 'miserable apology'. Letters from Alex Michael, 19 December 1886, Geddes Papers, NLS, MS 10524, fols 106–9; 11 August 1896, MS 10528, fols 121–4; 24 November 1898, MS 10530, fol. 268.
59 Correspondence between Patrick Geddes and Mr H. Lowerison, 2 April 1895, Geddes Papers, NLS, MS 10508A, fol. 100. Lowerison was a socialist, naturalist and educationalist who in 1901 established a mixed-sex 'Ruskin School Home' in Heacham-on-Sea in Norfolk. See K. Manton, 'Establishing the fellowship: Harry Lowerison and the Ruskin School Home, a turn-of-the-century socialist and his educational experiment', *Journal of the History of Education Society*, 26:1 (1997), pp. 53–70. See also 'Calamus 12', W. Whitman, *Leaves of Grass* (Boston, MA: Thayer and Eldridge, 1860), p. 358.
60 'Calamus 11', Whitman, *Leaves of Grass*, p. 358.
61 University of Edinburgh, Chair of Botany. Letter of Application from Patrick Geddes, 14 February 1888, quoted in Boardman, *The Worlds of Patrick Geddes*, pp. 103–4.
62 Boardman, *The World of Patrick Geddes*, pp. 145–6. Mumford also wrote of Geddes that he was 'primarily a scientist, shy of committing his thought to writing, lest the provisional and dynamic and tentative became static and absolute'. See 'Mumford on Geddes', *Architectural Review* (August 1950), p. 81, Geddes Papers, NLS, MS 10651, fols 29–32.
63 Review, 'The Evolution of Sex', *Nature*, 10 April 1890, p. 532.
64 Ibid., p. 531.
65 Patrick Geddes, 'Theory of growth, reproduction, sex, and heredity', *Proceedings of the Royal Society of Edinburgh*, 13 (1884–1886), pp. 911–31; 'Reproduction', vol. 20, pp. 407–22 and 'Sex', vol. 21, pp. 720–4, in *Encyclopaedia Britannica*, 9th edn, 24 vols (Edinburgh: A. & C. Black, 1888).
66 Geddes did not originate the terms, which according to the Oxford English Dictionary were first used by the leading embryologist Michael Foster in 1876, the same year that Geddes had studied briefly with him at Cambridge University. See C. Renwick, *British Sociology's Lost Roots: A History of Futures Past* (Basingstoke: Palgrave Macmillan,

2012), p. 195n68. Geddes himself stated in the *Evolution of Sex* that the words 'anabolic' and 'katabolic' were 'new, unfamiliar, and undeniably ugly'. See Geddes and Thomson, *The Evolution of Sex*, p. 123.

67 Geddes and Thomson, *The Evolution of Sex*, p. 271.
68 For an extended comparison of the theories of Geddes and Darwin, see Eagle Russett, *Sexual Science*, pp. 89–92.
69 Darwin, *The Descent of Man, and Selection in Relation to Sex*.
70 Richardson, *Love and Eugenics*, pp. 41–4.
71 See, for example, C. Perkins Gilman, *Women and Economics: A Study of the Economic Relation Between Men and Women as a Factor in Social Evolution* (Boston, MA: Small, Maynard, 1898).
72 Geddes and Thomson, *The Evolution of Sex*, p. 267.
73 T. Laqueur, *Making Sex: Body and Gender from the Greeks to Freud* (Cambridge, MA: Harvard University Press, 1990); L. Schiebinger, *The Mind Has No Sex?: Women in the Origins of Modern Science* (Cambridge, MA: Harvard University Press, 1989) and *Nature's Body, Sexual Politics and the Making of Modern Science* (Boston, MA: Beacon Press, 1993); Eagle Russett, *Sexual Science*.
74 This was by the French anatomist Marie Thiroux d'Arconville. It incorrectly represented the female skull as proportionately smaller than the man's and emphasised the breadth of the pelvis by greatly exaggerating the narrowness of the ribs. As Londa Schiebinger has commented, despite the new scientific emphasis on objectivity and precision, eighteenth-century anatomists, even female ones, '"mended" nature to fit emerging ideals of masculinity and femininity'. See Schiebinger, *The Mind Has No Sex?*, pp. 195–8, 203.
75 S. Shuttleworth, 'Review of "Making Sex: Body and Gender from the Greeks to Freud"', *Journal of the History of Sexuality*, 3:4 (April 1993), p. 635; K. Harvey, 'The substance of sexual difference: change and persistence in representations of the body in eighteenth century England', *Gender & History*, 14:2 (August 2002), pp. 202–23; M. Fissell, 'Gender and generation: representing reproduction in early modern England', *Gender & History*, 7:3 (November 1995), pp. 433–56.
76 Romanes, 'Mental differences between men and women', pp. 654–5, 665.
77 'The mental difference between men and women', *British Medical Journal* (20 August 1887), pp. 415–16.
78 Geddes and Thomson, *The Evolution of Sex*, pp. 267–8. Indeed, they stated that Romanes's recent discussion 'sorely disappoints us in this regard'. See also Geddes, 'Sex', in *Encylopaedia Britannica*, vol. 21, p. 724.
79 Richardson, *Love and Eugenics*, p. 35.
80 J. S. Mill and H. Taylor Mill, *Essays on Sex Equality* (Chicago: University of Chicago Press, 1970), pp. 149.
81 This is in comparison to 'essentialist' or 'separatist' feminists. S. Holton, *Feminism and Democracy: Women's Suffrage and Reform Politics in Britain 1900–1918* (Cambridge: Cambridge University Press, 1986), p. 28.
82 Letter from Charlotte Despard to Patrick Geddes, 22 November 1909, Geddes Papers, NLS, MS 19260. Geddes's reply, dated 4 December 1909, is written below the letter and is hard to decipher. What is clear is that he turns down the invitation to speak

because of what might be considered a 'very old-fashioned view', although he offers to help in other ways.
83 Geddes and Thomson, *The Evolution of Sex*, p. 267.
84 Ibid., pp. 268, 297.
85 Ibid., pp. 268-9, 271.
86 Ellis, *Man and Woman: A Study of Human Secondary Sexual Characters*, pp. 393-4. The book was the twenty-fourth volume to be published within the 'Contemporary Science Series'.
87 Geddes and Thomson, *The Evolution of Sex*, p. 37.
88 According to Darwin, male superiority was manifest across many disciplines, whether they required 'deep thought, reason, or imagination, or merely the use of the senses and hands', including poetry, painting, sculpture, music, history, science and philosophy. See E. O. Wilson (ed.), *From So Simple a Beginning: The Four Great Books of Charles Darwin* (New York: W. W. Norton, 2006), p. 1204.
89 Wilson, *From So Simple a Beginning*, p. 1205. Elsewhere in the *Descent of Man*, Darwin is more circumspect regarding the ability of natural and sexual selection to provide a universal, causal explanation for all inherited characteristics, stating, for example: 'Why certain characters should be inherited by both sexes, and other characters by one sex alone, namely by that sex in which the character first appeared, is in most cases quite unknown.' Wilson, *From So Simple a Beginning*, p. 940. According to Eagle Russett's interpretation, on the critical issue of whether intelligence was transmitted in the male line alone, 'it can only be said that Darwin waffled'. Eagle Russett, *Sexual Science*, p. 81.
90 Spencer's construction of an antagonistic relationship between individual development and reproduction, first articulated in an unsigned *Westminster Review* article of 1852, later gained great currency in the debate over women's higher education, with authorities such as Henry Maudsley and Grant Allen arguing strenuously that intellectual exertion had the potential to make women sterile. H. Spencer, 'A Theory of Population, deduced from the General Law of Animal Fertility, *Westminster Review*, n.s., 57:112 (April 1852), pp. 468-501; H. Maudsley, 'Sex in mind and in education', *Fortnightly Review*, 15:88 (April 1874), pp. 466-83; G. Allen, 'Plain words on the woman question', *Fortnightly Review*, 46:274 (October 1889), pp. 448-58.
91 Geddes and Thomson, *The Evolution of Sex*, p. 37. H. Spencer, 'The study of sociology. IV - Preparation in psychology', *Contemporary Review*, 22 (June 1873), pp. 524-32 (also published in *Popular Science Monthly*) and 'The Comparative Psychology of Man', *Popular Science Monthly*, 8 (January 1876), pp. 257-69. For a broader discussion of the strategic place the analogy between race and gender occupied in nineteenth- and twentieth-century scientific theorising about human variation, see N. L. Stepan, 'Race and gender: the role of analogy in science', *Isis*, 77:2 (June 1986), pp. 261-77.
92 P. Geddes and J. A. Thomson, *Sex* (London: Williams and Norgate, 1914), p. 208.
93 Geddes and Thomson, *The Evolution of Sex*, p. 270.
94 Ibid., pp. 270-1.
95 J. Finot, *Problems of the Sexes*, trans. M. J. Safford (New York: G. P. Putnam's Sons, 1913), pp. 135-6.

96 Sarah Grand to John Blackwood, 5 December 1892, quoted in Richardson, *Love and Eugenics*, p. 104; M. G. Fawcett, 'The appeal against female suffrage: a reply', *Nineteenth Century*, 26 (July 1889), p. 96.
97 T. Huxley, 'The struggle for existence: a programme', *Nineteenth Century*, 23:132 (February 1888), pp. 161–80; Geddes and Thomson, *The Evolution of Sex*, p. 279 (the full quote is: 'The optimism which finds in animal life only "one hymn of love" is inaccurate, like the pessimism which sees throughout nothing but selfishness'); L. A. Dugatkin, 'Survival of the nicest: the quest for a biological explanation for "altruism is intricately linked to our ideas of goodness. No wonder biologists have taken it personally"', *New Scientist*, 192:2577 (November 2006), p. 56.
98 Geddes and Thomson, *The Evolution of Sex*, pp. 280–1.
99 Ibid., p. 281.
100 Ibid., pp. 311–12.
101 Ibid., pp. 270–1.
102 S. A. Robertson, 'A Scottish tribute', *Sociological Review* (London: October 1932), p. 395. The foregrounding of altruism in the story of evolution reached its apotheosis in the influential 1902 book, *Mutual Aid: A Factor of Evolution*, written by Geddes's friend, the Russian anarchist, mathematician and naturalist Peter Kropotkin, who based his argument for communism on examples of co-operative behaviour drawn from the natural world. According to Kropotkin, the lesson from nature was: 'Don't compete! – competition is always injurious to the species, and you have plenty of resources to avoid it! … Therefore combine – practise mutual aid! That is the surest means of giving to each and to all the greatest safety, the best guarantee of existence and progress, bodily, intellectual, and moral.' Geddes later referred to it as a 'valuable account of the inadequately appreciated "other side" of the struggle for existence'. See P. Kropotkin, *Mutual Aid: A Factor of Evolution* (Harmondsworth: Penguin, 1939) and P. Geddes and J. A. Thomson, *Evolution* (London: Williams and Norgate, 1911), p. 253.
103 My italics. Geddes and Thomson, *The Evolution of Sex*, p. 292.
104 Geddes and Thomson, *The Evolution of Sex*, p. 296.
105 The *Pall Mall Gazette* 'regretted that the counsel given is associated with details in questionable taste, and concerning which a little reticence would have been advantageous.' See 'The Contemporary Science Series', *Pall Mall Gazette*, 4 August 1890 and 'The Evolution of Sex', *Nature*, 10 April 1890, p. 532. For the banning of the book from a public library, see letter from J. Butt, Eastbourne to Thomson and Geddes, 30 October 1892, Geddes Papers, NLS, MS 10525, fols 147–54.
106 Geddes and Thomson, *The Evolution of Sex*, p. 297.
107 P. Geddes, 'Mr. Francis Galton on natural inheritance', *Scottish Leader*, 14 March 1890 (I am indebted to Chris Renwick for this reference); Branford is quoted in Renwick, *British Sociology's Lost Sociological Roots*, p. 144.
108 Geddes and Thomson, *The Evolution of Sex*, pp. 264–6.
109 Ibid., p. 297.
110 Ibid., p. 267.
111 Letter from Anna Morton to Patrick Geddes, 3 April 1886, Geddes Papers, NLS, MS 19253, fols 19–22; letter from Anna Geddes to Patrick Geddes, [undated, poss. 1887],

Geddes Papers, NLS, MS 10503, fol. 28; letter from Patrick Geddes to Anna Geddes, 17 March 1899, Geddes Papers, NLS, MS 10508, fol. 31.

112 Geddes and Thomson, *Sex*, p. 139.
113 Postcard from Banabhard [Rachel Annand Taylor] to Anna Geddes, 3 December 1907, Geddes Papers, NLS, MS 10572, fol. 3; letter from Eleanor O. Podmore to Anna Geddes, 12 January [1905], Geddes Papers, T-GED 9/585, UofS. Podmore and Annand Taylor appear to have been part of the same friendship network, Eleanor Podmore referring to herself in her correspondence as 'Dreolin', the Irish gaelic for 'wren' and Rachel Annand Taylor as 'Banabhard', the Scots gaelic for 'poetess'. Frank Podmore was one of the founding members of the Fabian Society. In 1907, he and his wife Eleanor separated after what Alan Gauld refers to as 'alleged homosexual involvements'. He was also forced to resign without pension from his job at the Post Office and later appears to have committed suicide. See A. Gauld, 'Podmore, Frank (1856–1910)', *Oxford Dictionary of National Biography*.
114 Letter from E. L. W. Elmy to 'Madam' [presumably Anna Geddes], 12 June 1897, Geddes Papers, NLS, MS 10577, fol. 40.
115 Demolins, 'Le Mouvement Social', p. 83. According to Siân Reynolds, Demolins visited in 1892, 1893, possibly 1894 and 1895. See S. Reynolds, *Paris–Edinburgh: Cultural Connections in the Belle Epoque* (Aldershot: Ashgate, 2007), p. 85.
116 Demolins, 'Le Mouvement Social', p. 104.
117 Demolins, 'Le Mouvement Social', p. 85.
118 Lily Bell, 'Matrons and Maidens', *Labour Leader*, 15 September 1894, p. 7 and 1 December 1894, p. 7.
119 Quoted in Kitchen, *A Most Unsettling Person*, p. 74.
120 Letter from Anna Morton to Patrick Geddes, 14 February 1886, Geddes Papers, NLS, MS 19253.
121 P. Geddes, 'The Scots renascence', *Evergreen* (Spring 1895), p. 133.
122 Letter from the Outlook Tower to 'Gentlemen', 23 July 1897, Geddes Papers, NLS, MS 10509, fols 69–73. The letter is typed and unsigned but is written in Geddes's distinctive style.
123 Boardman, *The Worlds of Patrick Geddes*, p. 393.
124 Letter from Thomas Whitsun to Patrick Geddes, 21 July 1897, Geddes Papers, NLS, MS 10529, fols 56–7. See also letter from George F. Henderson, Ramsay Lodge to Patrick Geddes and J. Arthur Thomson, 30 July 1897, Geddes Papers, NLS, MS 10529, fols 60–2.
125 Letter from Thomas Whitsun to Patrick Geddes, 21 July 1897, Geddes Papers, NLS, MS 10529, fols 56–7.
126 Letter from the Outlook Tower to 'Gentlemen', 23 July 1897, Geddes Papers, NLS, MS 10509, fols 69–73.
127 Letter from the Outlook Tower to 'Gentlemen', 23 July 1897, Geddes Papers, NLS, MS 10509, fols 69–73. The letter is typed and unsigned but is written in Geddes's distinctive style.
128 M. Macdonald, 'Celticism and internationalism in the circle of Patrick Geddes', *Visual Culture in Britain*, 6:2 (2005), pp. 72–6; M. Ferguson, 'Patrick Geddes and the Celtic renascence of the 1890s' (PhD thesis, University of Dundee, 2011), pp. 90–1.

129 Letter from the Outlook Tower to 'Gentlemen', 23 July 1897, Geddes Papers, NLS, MS 10509, fols 69–73.
130 Victor Branford met Geddes at the University of Edinburgh and was responsible for setting up the British Sociological Society in 1904. A. J. Herbertson worked closely with Geddes during the early 1890s, before disseminating many of his ideas as an influential pioneer of geography. T. R. Marr was Geddes's assistant at the University of Dundee in 1894 and bursar of the Outlook Tower between 1895 and 1901. See H. Meller, *Patrick Geddes: Social Evolutionist and City Planner* (London: Routledge, 1990), p. 14n6 (Victor Branford), pp. 126–9 (A. J. Herbertson) and pp. 16–17n31 (T. R. Marr).
131 L. Leneman, *A Guid Cause: The Women's Suffrage Movement in Scotland* (Edinburgh: Mercat Press, 1995), pp. 11–39; L. Leneman, *The Scottish Suffragettes* (Edinburgh: NMS Publishing Ltd, 2000), pp. 18–26.
132 Entry 'Mary Rose Hill Burton', in E. Ewan, S. Innes, S. Reynolds and R. Pipes (eds), *The Biographical Dictionary of Scottish Women* [*BDSW*] (Edinburgh: Edinburgh University Press, 2006), pp. 55; J. Helland, *Professional Women Painters in Nineteenth-Century Scotland: Commitment, Friendship, Pleasure* (Aldershot: Ashgate, 2000), pp. 123–49. Mary Rose Hill Burton's father was John Hill Burton, the historiographer Royal of Scotland. The close friendship between the Geddes and Hill Burton families was cemented when Anna's younger sister Bex married Cosmo Hill Burton, Mary Rose's brother, although he died after contracting a fever a year into the marriage.
133 Letter from Patrick Geddes to Willy Burton, 5 December 1889, Geddes Papers, NLS, MS 10508A, fols 48–51; Leneman, *A Guid Cause*, p. 15; Mavor, *My Windows on the Streets of the World*, vol. 1, p. 169; entry 'Mary Burton', in Ewan et al., *BDSW*, pp. 54–5; E. Crawford, *The Women's Suffrage Movement in Britain and Ireland: A Regional Survey* (London and New York: Routledge, 2006), pp. 227, 231, 246.
134 Letter from Kate Cooke to Anna Geddes, 10 October 1886, Geddes Papers, NLS, MS 10503, fols 18–21; letter from Jane Hay to 'My Dear Folk' [Anna and Patrick Geddes], 25 January 1891, Geddes Papers, NLS, MS 10525, fols 80–5.
135 Geddes and Thomson, 'The moral evolution of sex', p. 80.
136 Ibid., p. 74.
137 Ibid., Geddes calls New Women who don't work 'buzzing drones'.
138 Ibid., p. 73.
139 Ibid., p. 73.
140 Ibid., p. 76.
141 Ibid., pp. 76–7.
142 Ibid., p. 75.
143 Finot, *Problems of the Sexes*, p. 132.
144 Letter from Patrick Geddes to Victor Branford, 9 January 1919, Geddes Papers, NLS, MS 10557, fols 74–8.
145 Dixon, *The Invention of Altruism*, p. 284.
146 Drummond does reference *The Evolution of Sex* regarding its emphasis on altruism, commenting that Geddes and Thomson, 'more clearly than any other writers, have

grasped the bearings of this theme in all directions, and they fearlessly take their stand-point from the physiology of the protoplasm'. Henry Drummond, *The Lowell Lectures on the Ascent of Man* (London: Hodder & Stoughton, 1894), p. 34. See also Dixon, *The Invention of Altruism*, pp. 283–302.

147 Dixon, *The Invention of Altruism*, p. 298.

148 J. Conway, 'Stereotypes of femininity in a theory of sexual evolution', in Martha Vicinus (ed.), *Suffer and be Still: Women in the Victorian Age* (Bloomington and London: Indiana University Press, 1972), pp. 151–2; J. Conway, 'Women reformers and American culture, 1870–1930', *Journal of Social History*, 5:2 (Winter 1971/2), pp. 164–77.

149 F. Swiney, *The Awakening of Women; or, Woman's Part in Evolution* (London: William Reeves, 1899), p. 20, quoted in Richardson, *Love and Eugenics*, p. 50. See also G. Robb, 'Eugenics, spirituality and sex differentiation in Edwardian England: the case of Francis Swiney', *Journal of Women's History*, 10:3 (Autumn 1998), pp. 97–117.

150 E. L. Milam, *Looking for a Few Good Males: Female Choice in Evolutionary Biology* (Baltimore, MD: John Hopkins University Press, 2010), pp. 24–5 and R. Jann, 'Revising the descent of woman: Eliza Burt Gamble', in B. T. Gates and A. B. Shteir (eds), *Natural Eloquence: Women Reinscribe Science* (Madison: University of Wisconsin Press, 1997), pp. 147–63.

5

Deeds of daring rectitude

In the autumn of 1890, Patrick Geddes escorted a visitor through the dilapidated and unsanitary wynds and closes of Edinburgh's Old Town. Jane Hume Clapperton was an interloper from the New Town, a respectable, upper middle-class woman who spoke with a 'delightfully cultured Scotch accent' and wore her hair up in an early Victorian cap, a signifier of her spinster status.[1] It appears to have been the first time the two had met in person, although both were familiar with each other's published work.[2] As he would do on a later occasion, Geddes perhaps enlightened his new acquaintance on his visionary schemes for the improvement of the city, darting in and out of the 'foul alleys' all the while explaining how he was 'demolishing this and reconstructing that – at once a Destroying Angel and a Redeemer'.[3]

However, a 'whiff of bad odours' as they emerged together from a close prompted Clapperton to question Geddes's approach.[4] Recognising in him and in his 'fine following of young men' a 'concentration of reform force' with real potential to enact positive change, she was 'nettled' that his time, energy and expertise were being usurped by mere 'side issues'.[5] Aesthetic improvements to the urban environment were far better left to the municipal authorities, she argued, with the work funded out of the public purse. Instead, Geddes should redirect his private resources towards the only effective solution to the chronic social conditions they were currently surveying: 'The connection of biology with economics', or the espousal of neo-Malthusian arguments on birth control.[6] Indeed, Clapperton asserted, this was something Geddes had got wrong in *The Evolution of Sex*. While he was correct to make the connection between smaller family sizes and individual and racial progress, his solution of having less sex within marriage, what he termed 'an ethical rather than ... a mechanical "prudence after marriage"', was based on a false assumption.[7] Practising 'moderation in sexual indulgence' did not in fact secure 'infrequency of pregnancy' and Geddes would have been better to have advocated the explicit use of 'artificial checks to conception' or methods of birth control. Employing 'moderation' as a euphemism for sex, she declared:

> For the ignorant, the gross the degraded there is no other means [than birth control] – moderation forsooth is perhaps the only pleasure besides drinking that the base nature can enjoy! Cut off the breeding of that type and where is the social bad result? Drinking is infinitely worse to my mind. Does this shock you I wonder I have reached the conclusion very slowly myself but the ascetic view of the sexual problem is not the right one I am convinced[8]

Whether the conclusion Clapperton had reached on the 'sexual problem' succeeded in shocking Geddes, the historical record doesn't relate. A decade later, her views would get more controversial still, in later work rejecting sexual asceticism not just for 'the ignorant, the gross the degraded', but for people of all classes, including, very specifically, women. The 'average normal woman', she would assert boldly in 1900, 'has sexual needs of commanding importance to be met and satisfied', lamenting that sex that was 'voluntary, pleasurable, healthful' was 'of comparatively rare occurrence'.[9] This was a circumstance she accorded in part to 'an obstinate prejudice' and in part to women's own awareness of the likely generative result.[10] Happily, she argued, 'science here comes to the rescue', the use of birth control allowing women and men to have more sex, form closer bonds and develop vital altruistic and socialistic emotions, while ensuring that population growth remained within sustainable limits.[11]

Articulating such views in print was highly unusual for this period. Methods of contraception, like other matters relating to sex, were discussed only in euphemisms, although even then 'preventive checks' or 'Malthusian appliances' were not topics for polite conversation. Most feminists preferred to avoid the subject, seeing birth control less as a means of securing female bodily autonomy and more as a potential facilitator of male sexual demands, *Freewoman* contributor Isabel Leatham writing in 1911 that contraception was 'a gross outrage on the aesthetic sensibilities of women and the final mark of their sexual degradation'.[12] The birth rate did decline from 1870, with the average British household size falling from six in 1860 to three by 1910; however, while the reasons for this are still debated by historians, it was certainly not due to the increased use of contraceptive devices.[13] The condom, sponge, diaphragm and cap were widely eschewed due to their cost, inconvenience and associations with sex work and venereal disease, with the most common forms of birth control being abstinence, withdrawal and abortifacients.[14]

To speak specifically of women's right to sexual pleasure was more transgressive still. Dominant discourses on femininity dictated that women appear passionless, Anna Geddes during her engagement to Patrick recounting how she had sat 'quite passive & unmoved' while Geddes kissed her.[15] Once married, sexual fulfilment was anticipated for both parties, if not always, or perhaps often, realised for women; however, this was within the context of a spiritual union, and for reproductive purposes. Explicit discussion of sexual acts or behaviours was safely sequestered to public spaces figuratively and geographically removed from the private bourgeois bedroom – the street, the brothel, the public house and the music hall. It is notable that during the 1857 murder trial of the young, middle-class Glaswegian, Madeleine Smith, it was her epistolary accounts of her unabashed enjoyment of premarital sex with her lover Pierre Emile L'Angelier that shocked the public, as much as any alleged murderous intent.[16]

Despite Clapperton's outward appearance as an 'old fashioned spinster lady', it is clear, therefore, that she was one of the era's sexually radical voices, her friend the socialist Dora Montefiore viewing her as someone who was 'thinking out the thoughts on the sex question', alongside Edward Carpenter and George Bernard Shaw.[17] Clapperton articulated these thoughts in a diverse body of work published between 1885 and 1904, including two book-length treatises on social reform, a utopian novel, and numerous pamphlets, articles and letters printed in the feminist, neo-Malthusian and periodical press. Produced over the course of almost two decades, the style and emphases of the publications vary, reflecting their differing formats, publishers and intended audiences, as well as Clapperton's growing candour and confidence as a writer. Nonetheless, collectively, they present a strikingly consistent, coherent and fundamentally radical set of ideas on sex, which Clapperton framed as a new, 'wide-reaching modern moral code', designed to replace the Christian sexual ethics which underpinned contemporary intimate relations.[18]

Analyses of her publications have featured in historical and literary studies of feminist writers at the *fin de siècle*, by scholars including Laura Schwartz, Lucy Bland, Angelique Richardson and Sally Ledger.[19] This work has proved invaluable in contextualising Clapperton's ideas within feminist freethought, the sexual politics of the women's rights movement, and New Woman writing on eugenics and socialism. However, only her novel, *Margaret Dunmore: Or, A Socialist Home* (1888), has received extended critical scrutiny, Wendy Parkins examining its representation of individual sensory and emotional experience, and Kristin Brandser Kalsem focusing on its inclusion of the use of birth control.[20] The scholarship has lacked a comparatively detailed engagement with her non-fictional publications, while the absence of an in-depth biographical study of Clapperton has necessarily precluded any elucidation of the connections between her life and work.

This chapter remedies these elisions, for the first time tracing the familial and friendship networks that were vital in the formation of her views on sex. More particularly, it argues that it was her association with secularism, with individuals such as George Arthur Gaskell, James Cranbrook, Sarah Hennell and Charles Bray, and with organisations including the Malthusian League, which facilitated the germination of her transgressive ideas, freethought providing at once a rationale, an atmosphere of open discourse and a back catalogue of sexually transgressive thought upon which to draw. As Lesley Hall notes, at the end of the nineteenth century, 'linked networks of women, not just odd rebellious individuals, were protesting in very various ways both personal and political against the established order'; paying attention to these networks solves the conundrum of how a respectable, unmarried woman, raised in an upper middle-class mercantile family in Edinburgh in the Victorian period, was able to formulate and disseminate such a progressive sexual code.[21]

Beginning with a survey of Clapperton's family background, the chapter then details the three freethinking circles critical to the evolution of her thinking: in Edinburgh, Coventry and nationally. Next, it analyses the two interrelated tenets underpinning her vision of a new sexual morality – her advocacy of methods of birth control and her belief in the right to sexual pleasure – contextualising her ideas within contemporary feminist, socialist and secularist thought. Finally, after considering the impact on her sexual philosophy of her most important friendship, with the neo-Malthusian George Arthur Gaskell, it examines the nature and extent of her influence on progressive and wider popular thought on sex.

Not one's best self

Jane Hume Clapperton was born on 22 September 1832, the tenth child of twelve of Ann Hume and Alexander Clapperton.[22] Her father came from 'humble origins', although by the time of his marriage was on course to accrue a considerable fortune as a woollen merchant in Edinburgh.[23] The family business, John Clapperton & Co, had been established in 1796, Alexander becoming a partner after the death of his older brother in 1825, and continuing to expand the business, opening a branch house in Glasgow in addition to the shop on Edinburgh's High Street.[24] He appears to have met and married Jane's mother Ann in Colinton, then a village six kilometres south-west of Edinburgh, where Ann's family were farmers and where Alexander leased a large summer house, Spy law Bank, which was described as a 'romantic retreat' in an 1820s traveller's guide to Scotland.[25]

Jane's early childhood was divided between Spy law Bank and their Edinburgh town house on Princes Street, one of the New Town's pre-eminent addresses. Education for Jane and her eight sisters was provided by a live-in governess, who in addition to lessons at home took the girls to classes in French and the 'higher branches' of knowledge. Jane's 'delicate health', however, precluded her from this latter 'excitement', a restriction which she later reflected left her often alone and exacerbated her 'natural tendencies to reflection and morbid feeling'.[26] At twelve, she was sent to a finishing boarding school in England, where the teaching was 'extremely superficial' but where, she later recollected, her passionate friendships with other girls, along with the 'bright and healthful' surroundings, 'immensely improved her health and spirits'.[27]

Her formal education complete, aged sixteen she returned to Edinburgh. Three of her sisters had already married and moved away, finding suitors from within respectable upper middle-class society. In 1838, the eldest, Eliza, had married John Rotherham, a watch manufacturer from Coventry, with Grace and Ann following suit in 1841, in a double wedding to a publisher and merchant respectively. The expectation must surely have been that Jane's life would follow a similarly conventional path, consisting of marriage, domestic routine and respectable sociability. Yet while she appears not to have explicitly rejected this future, it is clear that from an early age she experienced real anxiety over her 'destiny', the thought that she might fail to 'fulfil her life's purpose' precipitating moments of 'intense pain' during her childhood.[28]

The family's social standing in Edinburgh rested to a large degree upon its patriarch. A Liberal in politics, Alexander played a part in Edinburgh's civic life, attending public dinners and acting as Chairman of the Chamber of Commerce and Manufacturers.[29] His death in April 1849 cast a long shadow over family life. Jane recollected that old friends fell away and that life altered 'in many respects', the family moving from their substantial Princes Street home to Drummond Place in the northern New Town, abeit still an eighteen-roomed townhouse.[30] Jane's brothers took over the family firm, their standing as affluent merchants and partners in what was a considerable business concern allowing them to assume a range of public roles, John becoming a justice of the peace and Deputy-Lieutenant of the city, a 'Curator of Patronage' at Edinburgh University and a Governor of a children's charity.[31] The fate of Jane's

15 Jane Hume Clapperton, 1899

sisters, however, like the majority of middle-class girls, rested in an advantageous marriage to an appropriate suitor. One by one her siblings achieved this critical objective and moved away, first Agnes in December 1849, then Alison in 1857, Charlotte in 1859, Sophia in 1864 and finally the youngest, Sarah Openshaw, in 1865.

By the mid-1860s, Jane was in her thirties and therefore beyond the age at which she would have anticipated attracting a husband, a friend later remarking that 'people married young if they married at all in those days'.[32] Unlike Anna Morton, no charismatic lover appeared on the horizon to deliver her from spinsterhood, no oak tree for her ivy. As an unmarried daughter, it fell to her to remain with and care for her mother, whose advanced years 'made necessary a life of perfect repose'.[33] Yet, while outwardly Clapperton appeared resigned to becoming one of the era's 'surplus women', endeavouring to remain cheerful in her mother's company and donning a style of cap worn by 'single aunts ... as a sort of signal that they accepted their fate', inwardly her passionate nature was in torment (figure 15).[34] Celibacy, not freely chosen, was 'a *cruel lot*', she would later avow, society requiring unmarried women to 'hide away in obscure corners', only coming out at intervals 'to fill some gap in other people's lives'.[35] Some two decades later, her sense of loneliness and resentment during these years remained keenly felt, expressed in a short biography in the *Women's Penny Press* (1889):

> Life had dealt hardly with me, my nature was stirred to its depths, I palpitated with desire for an exchange of thought and feeling that touched realities at all points. To meet my fellow-creatures at a shallow level and talk superficially, became intolerable. Ibsen has said that he could not afford to have many friends: they were too costly a luxury; they gave him no time, no chance to be himself. But without many friends one is not one's best self. I had no superfluity nor indeed at that time enough to meet the necessities of ordinary human nature.

She imagined hundreds of people like her across Edinburgh, 'daily and hourly suffering' through a similar lack of sympathetic companionship, apportioning some of the blame to what she felt to be the particular character of her native city. Like Patrick Geddes, she chafed against Edinburgh's proprieties, finding it 'fundamentally conventional' and it affording her 'no pleasurable distraction'; unlike Geddes, her gender and its concomitant caring responsibilities precluded her from flouting these conventions.[36] Whereas Geddes possessed the freedom to sit up 'far into the night' discussing Edinburgh's social problems, lead bands of enthralled students on midnight walks up Arthur's Seat and indulge in improper 'escapades' with his fiancée Anna, Clapperton struggled. Female friendships were 'difficult' and male friendships 'impossible'; as an unmarried woman, caring for an elderly relative, she was only too aware of the damage to her reputation and no doubt to her mother's peace of mind that 'an idle rumour' or 'whiff of gossip' could cause.[37]

This period of social isolation in the 1860s would have a profound impact on her later thinking, informing her conceptualisation of a radically different model of domesticity, one not dependent upon a male breadwinner for its formation and within which men and women would be free to form 'intimate and lasting relations ... of the most varied character'.[38] For now, however, her fledgling interest in social reform followed more conventional channels. In accordance with widespread evangelical understandings of women's special role in 'home mission' work, she engaged in a range of philanthropic endeavours, becoming a Sunday School teacher, a district visitor and a superintendent at a girls' industrial school and a children's hospital.[39] Ultimately, however, it was not through these pursuits that she found the sympathetic and intellectually stimulating company she craved; instead, it was her family, seemingly an exemplar of respectability, which provided her with the connections to three radical, freethinking circles which would prove formative in the development of her ideas on sex.

Freethinking circles and sexual morality

Clapperton's first radical circle was in Edinburgh and centred around the Reverend James Cranbrook, a man the Scotsman dubbed a 'theological *enfant terriblé*.[40] Cranbrook was the minister of the Albany Street Chapel, the Congregationalist church around the corner from the Clapperton family home. In 1866 he found himself at the centre of a theological maelstrom, precipitated by his views on divine providence and the efficacy of prayer.[41] The ravages of a cattle plague, combined with fears over an imminent cholera epidemic, had led ministers across the city to exhort their flocks to confess their sins and pray 'for the mitigation and prevention of calamity', such prayers becoming 'part of the public worship of almost every congregation'.[42] Cranbrook took issue with this guidance, in a sermon on 17 October rejecting the doctrine of 'supernatural Providence' as a 'figment and relic of the days of ignorance and darkness', one which fostered a 'heathenish notion of a perpetual miracle'.[43] Instead, he argued, while God as the 'Divine Architect' had initially created the laws of nature, there was no evidence to suggest that he had subsequently violated them by supernatural intervention; indeed, science was everyday 'solving mysteries and narrowing the domain' of what had previously been considered miraculous. Furthermore, prayer, while undoubtedly beneficial to the individual soul, bringing upon it 'the fulness of the Divine blessing', was incapable of altering the course of earthly events.[44]

Cranbrook's questioning of aspects of Christian doctrine reflects the considerable heterogeneity of theological opinion engendered by the Victorian 'crisis of faith'. No longer viewed as an inevitable consequence of new scientific discoveries, the period's religious doubt is now understood more as a 'fluid contest between different sections of the intelligentsia for cultural authority, for the right to define what faith was', with adversaries in this contest coming from both within and without the Christian faith.[45] His sermon, an abridged version of which was printed in the *Scotsman* without his knowledge, caused 'vituperations' to be heaped upon him, forcing him to justify himself in the press and in the pulpit.[46] While Cranbrook retained the support of his Albany Street congregation, the affair affected him deeply, leaving him profoundly disillusioned with all forms of organised religion. Upon resigning his pastorate in February 1867, he stated he had 'done' with churches forever, calling them 'organisations which impede God's truth and human progress'.[47]

Instead, he attempted to instigate a new religious movement. Gathering around himself a group of 'liberally-minded men and women', he began to deliver weekly religious services at the Hopetoun Rooms on Queen Street, on the strict proviso that he did so as an independent teacher and that his followers 'were not pledged to receive one word he uttered as true, unless it commended themselves to their own understanding'.[48] The group also held social events, planned a scheme to help the poor and heard from invited speakers, in 1868 Geddes's formative teacher, the Darwinist Thomas Huxley, lecturing on 'The Physical Basis of Life'.[49] The venture received interest from across the country: one sympathetic clergyman described it as a 'bold, novel, and most interesting experiment of a more excellent way', while another commentator asserted that 'many a seeker after truth, and many a devout worshipper' owed much to the experiment, comparing it to the later, religiously inflected socialist organisation the Fellowship of the New Life.[50] In common with this group, Cranbrook's movement skirted the boundaries of respectability, with attendance causing some to lose 'esteemed friends'.[51] Numbers remained steady however, and after a year Cranbrook reported that 'happy progress' had been made.[52]

It is likely that Clapperton was among the band of seekers who met weekly to hear Cranbrook's sermons at the Hopetoun Rooms during 1867 and 1868. This assumption is based in part on her accounts of her relationship with him, Clapperton describing how he had taught her 'logic, political economy and metaphysics', how she had been inspired by her 'intimate intercourse' with his 'pure and elevated nature', and how his premature death in 1869 had been an 'irreparable loss and a lasting sorrow'.[53] However, it is also based on the confluence between Cranbrook's sermons and the form of 'religious agnosticism' developed and articulated by Clapperton just over a decade later, in articles in the periodical *Nineteenth Century* and in her major work *Scientific Meliorism*.[54]

Like Cranbrook, Clapperton was fully convinced by the new scientific thought, particularly the theory of evolution, which she believed offered a clear explanation for the present social state and an inspiring vision for the direction of future evolved relations.[55] However, also like Cranbrook, she envisaged a continuing and critical role for religion, believing it had a unique capacity for rousing people to act for the collective good, for instilling in them, through abstract ideas, 'a conscience or duty spirit, which compels the realization in actual life of *ideals of conduct*'.[56] Rejecting any belief in an anthropomorphised supernatural divinity, including Spencer's understanding of a 'great stream of Creative Power unlimited in Space or in Time', neither did she embrace the anthropic god of the positivists' 'Religion of Humanity', followed by Patrick and Anna Geddes, with its assertion that 'Humanity is the grandest object of reverence within the region of the real'.[57] Instead, she proposed a new '*cultus*' or form of religion, fit for the modern, scientific age. Termed the 'Religion of the Real', its 'object-matter' was not God, or a Creative Power or Humanity, but rather scientific principles: science would enlighten humankind as to the 'true ideas of the universe, society, and man', while direct emotional appeals, including 'touching pictures of suffering humanity', would inspire 'noble ideals of human character and conduct'.[58] This fusion of religion's 'emotional bearing on life' with the facts of science would trigger a rapid progress in human evolution, and result ultimately in a state of universal happiness:[59]

> Standing as we do at the beginning of an epoch of Conscious Evolution, the vista before Religion is indeed vast and magnificent, its work enormous. It has to reconcile the heart, and put into the hand of man the golden thread of science which will guide him in the labyrinth of life. It has to disclose all the grovelling instincts of humanity, and show the scientific method of their sure destruction. It has to nurse the nobler instincts, and to promote the rapid birth of the germs of a perfected Humanity ... It has to reveal the new heaven and the new earth, and to inspire mankind with the faith, the energy, the indomitable will, to move in that direction.[60]

The second radical, freethinking circle to which Clapperton was exposed was located in the West Midlands. Clapperton's eldest sister Eliza had settled in Coventry, her husband's family business, Rotherham & Sons, the largest and oldest watch manufacturers in the city.[61] Another sister, Alison, had settled in the nearby village of Berkswell, with her husband William Floyd living in what an 1874 directory described as a 'large, well-built handsome residence, surrounded by extensive grounds and gardens'.[62] It is highly likely that two such prominent local families would have known Charles Bray. A prosperous Coventry ribbon manufacturer, Bray was also a secularist and social reformer, who, with his wife Cara, provided a haven for visiting members of the liberal intelligentsia.[63] Bray later recollected fondly that everyone 'who came to Coventry with a queer mission, or a crochet, or was supposed to be a "little cracked", was sent up to Rosehill', their house on the outskirts of the city (figure 16). Guests

16 Rosehill, c. 1850s

gathered 'When the bear skin [was] under the acacia', for unrestrained talk and the interchange of ideas, visitors including Herbert Spencer, Robert Owen and Ralph Waldo Emerson, as well as their neighbour and close friend Mary Ann Evans (George Eliot).[64]

Clapperton was presumably introduced to the Brays while on a visit to her sisters and was 'generously and cordially welcomed' into their 'delightful social circle'.[65] Although she never met George Eliot, she became friends with Charles, who 'steadfastly encouraged' her writing until his death in 1884.[66] Significantly, she also became acquainted with his wife Cara and her sister Sara Hennell.[67] While Cara remained a 'reverent' if 'uncommitted' Christian, Sara's religious views closely mirrored Clapperton's own.[68] A freethinker and feminist, Sara had rejected the Unitarianism of her childhood, instead developing a singular form of natural religion that, according to Laura Schwartz, 'emphasised the continuing importance of faith in a post-Christian world'.[69] Indeed, Hennell's refusal to identify as 'Atheistic in the negative sense', and her emphasis on the need to retain doctrinal systems in order to ensure the 'conscious directing of moral life', bears a striking similarity to Clapperton's religious outlook, the two women also sharing a commitment to women's rights.[70]

In addition to her connections to these freethinking networks in Coventry and Edinburgh, Clapperton saw herself as belonging to a third network of doubters, what she termed Britain's 'considerable band of female agnostics'.[71] As research by Schwartz has shown, the nineteenth century witnessed a growing number of feminist Freethinkers who 'combined their campaigning for women's rights with a militant and antagonistic renunciation of Christianity'.[72] Such women were not typically the 'honest doubters' of the middle classes, but instead part of the organised, Secularist movement, which drew its members from the lower-middle and upper working classes. Freethinkers saw their apostasy not just as a rational response to evolution or biblical criticism but as a radical attack on the political and religious foundations of the British constitution, the movement reaching the peak of its influence in the 1880s under the charismatic leadership of Charles Bradlaugh and Annie Besant.[73]

Yet Schwartz has argued that despite their differing motivations and membership body, we should resist categorising organised Secularists and middle-class doubters as separate historical entities, and instead see them as intersecting movements.[74] Clapperton clearly occupied one point of intersection. While not a member of a Freethought organisation, neither did she attempt to disassociate herself from what some perceived to be their 'vulgar secularism'.[75] She cited a leading Secularist journal, the *National Reformer*, in her work, and, when asked to identify the female-authored books which had most influenced her, chose titles by three freethinking women, Mary Wollstonecraft, Harriet Martineau and George Eliot.[76] She also counted secularists amongst her friends. In addition to the circle around Charles Bray in Coventry, she corresponded, like Bella Pearce, with the Freethinker and feminist Elizabeth Wolstenholme Elmy, whose husband Ben Elmy was the Vice President of National Secular Society.[77] Furthermore, Clapperton traced a direct correlation between women's education, a key focus of contemporary women's rights campaigns, and agnosticism, stating that 'Love of truth, and earnest desire to follow it, have led many of the sex to cultivate their minds', and that with this cultivation had come a consciousness of the irrationality of their earlier, religious beliefs.[78] Finally, she evoked a sense of a national community of female agnostics, countering any sense of them as bitter or despondent and instead defending their collective right to 'express their opinions freely and fearlessly'.[79]

It was only with the death of her mother in 1873, however, that Clapperton felt free to exercise *her* opinions, fearlessly or otherwise. Her declaration of her agnosticism came in her first publications, two articles in the *Nineteenth Century* in 1880 and 1882, in which she pronounced that 'honesty of thought' had obliged her to cast aside her 'ancient landmarks', finding in agnosticism 'truth for delusion' and 'a standpoint from which clearness of thought and stability of feeling increase'.[80] Her sexually radical views followed shortly afterwards. The renunciation of Christianity automatically implicated Freethinkers in a reassessment of society's moral codes, including the Church's teachings on sex, marriage, monogamy, reproduction and divorce.[81] Furthermore, Freethought's guiding principle of open discourse made it possible for members to redraft these codes, conceptualising and considering radical new alternatives. These ranged from the sexual libertarianism of Scot George Drysdale, who in his controversial 1854 *Elements of Social Science* espoused promiscuous sexual experimentation and provided detailed accounts of sexual organs, intercourse and diseases, to George Jacob Holyoake's more moderate endorsement of liberal divorce laws and 'free unions'.[82] Opinion among feminists within the movement was similarly fractured. Some, like Annie Besant, took a positive view of the body and 'human passion', regarding 'true marriage', disassociated from the Church, as far preferable to celibacy, and 'physical union' as 'perfecting the union of the heart and mind', while others voiced their concerns over the implications of marriage reform for women and children's lives, given their continued economic, social and legal precarity.[83] Such nuance was lost on the public, however, with secularist lectures and publications on such topics serving to cement the association between freethought and sexual licentiousness. Such approbation disproportionately affected women in the movement, who were more vulnerable to attacks on their reputation: in 1862, the *National Reformer* reported the circulation of 'sickening' stories concerning the prominent Freethinker Harriet Law, after a 'premeditated' attack by a minister 'to ruin her character, and hence destroy her influence'.[84]

Like her fellow 'infidel feminists', Clapperton believed society required an up-to-date ethical blueprint, regarding the existing 'regulative system' to be 'no longer fitting for the age'.[85] Also like other secularist women, she experienced social censure for expressing such views, Dora Montefiore relating how her nearest relatives 'cut' her after the publication of her first book, although it is unclear who exactly was responsible for the snub: it is unlikely to have been the sisters indirectly responsible for her entrée into secularism, or indeed the nephews with whom she stayed in subsequent years.[86] For Clapperton, however, the 'present evil social state', with its moral deterioration and general unhappiness, justified her intervention.[87] It was 'more than time', she declared, 'that *all* should put their shoulders to the wheel, and, grappling with the problems of our complex social life, find true solutions that will reveal what social conduct ought to be, and give a scientific basis for a wide-reaching modern moral code, subserving general happiness'.[88]

Birth control, feminism and the Malthusian League

The first tenet of this moral code was the dissemination of information on birth control. Clapperton held the widespread promotion and use of what were variously termed 'scientific', 'artificial' or 'preventive' checks to conception to be a panacea for the most pressing problem facing British society: poverty.[89] She first articulated this view in *Scientific Meliorism and the Evolution of Happiness* (1885), a serious, detailed and lengthy work of social reform, which drew on authorities spanning the fields of natural science, utilitarianism, positivism, feminism, socialism, neo-Malthusianism and eugenics, to argue for the conscious and methodical application of evolutionary knowledge, in order to attain life's primary object, 'happiness for all at all times'.[90] Imperative to achieving this goal, Clapperton argued, was solving the 'population question', the dilemma raised by the profound demographic changes which had accompanied industrialisation. While the nation's ability to provide subsistence for its rapidly expanding populace had long been a source of anxiety – in 1798 the Reverend Thomas Malthus raising fears over population geometrically outstripping arithmetically increasing food supplies – such concerns were now amplified by new statistical evidence which revealed a disproportionately high birth rate amongst the urban poor.[91] In Clapperton's summation, while the middle and upper classes, whom she termed the 'intelligent, the thoughtful, the prudent', had begun to regulate their fertility through fewer and later marriages, the lower classes, particularly in factory towns and industrial centres, continued to reproduce at an alarming rate, resulting in endemic poverty and imminent racial degeneration:

> It is simply impossible for general well-being to be maintained in a society where the increase is greatest from the worst stock; and truly the individuals at the base of our society are not of such mental, physical, and moral type as to make it desirable, or even safe, that the greatest proportion of young life, the vital strength (we may call it) of the coming race, should spring from them![92]

The impoverished were not to blame for their lack of prudence; rather, Clapperton asserted, unscientific methods employed by past societies had allowed deleterious environmental pressures to act upon what she saw to be defective inherited constitutions, stymying the urban poor's evolutionary progress and leaving them at a stage of 'simple egoism', in which rational thought and self-control were well-nigh impossible.[93]

Identifying the cause of poverty as overpopulation, Clapperton reviewed a range of potential solutions, before dismissing each of them in turn. Celibacy within marriage was deemed a sacrifice too great, and in any case was only possible for individuals 'rare amongst the best intelligences'; philanthropy, though well intentioned, only exacerbated the problem, its various 'props' counteracting the law of natural selection that would otherwise have 'checked' the survival of the unfit; emigration was 'woefully inadequate' as it attracted those whom the nation needed to retain, namely working-class men 'above average in physical strength and mental vigour'; finally, socialism was too risky, any forcible redistribution of property jeopardising the 'liberty and fraternity' currently enjoyed by 'civilised humanity'.[94] One remedy however, was mercifully free of this litany of shortcomings: indeed, Clapperton asserted, it was 'the *only possible method*' by which society could address not merely the symptoms but the fundamental cause of poverty, and cut away 'its great, outspreading, gangrened *roots*.'[95] That method was the use of birth control.

Clapperton's analysis situates her squarely within neo-Malthusianism, the middle-class propagandist movement whose activities coalesced with the establishment in 1877 of the Malthusian League.[96] A late Victorian iteration of the long-standing advocacy of birth control within Secularism, the organisation's leadership was dominated by Charles Robert Drysdale (the 'Malthusian King', according to one League member), his partner Alice Vickery, and their son Charles Vickery Drysdale, all Freethinking liberals.[97] Membership peaked at 1,224 in 1879, with the League's official objective not to inform the working classes about birth control devices and techniques, but rather to convince doctors, educators and politicians of their economic justification.[98] Therefore, while it did recommend texts which contained practical advice on contraception, such as Annie Besant's *Law of Population* (1878) and George Standring's *The Malthusian Handbook* (1893), such information was absent from the majority of the estimated three million pamphlets and leaflets published by the League between 1879 and 1921, which consisted primarily, in Schwartz's words, of 'turgid proselytising for Malthusian economics'.[99] Its first practical advice leaflet was not released until 1913, and while advertisements for devices were permitted in its journal the *Malthusian*, no accompanying commentary was supplied.[100] Indeed, Angus McLaren has argued that it was the Malthusian League's myopic focus on excess births as the sole cause of poverty which precluded any significant support from socialists and resulted ultimately in its failure as a popular movement, one reader of the *Malthusian* articulating the frustrations of many when they wrote in 1881, 'What is really wanted ... is plain and practical advice.'[101]

The League was formed in the wake of the infamous trial in June 1877 of Annie Besant and Charles Bradlaugh, charged with obscenity for the publication and distribution of *The Fruits of Philosophy*, a sixpenny birth-control tract by an American doctor called Charles Knowlton. The couple, then the national figureheads of Secularism, while not fully endorsing the pamphlet, had deliberately invited prosecution as a test case for free speech, believing the 'fullest right of free discussion ought to be maintained at all hazards'.[102] Conducting her own defence, Besant claimed to speak 'as counsel for hundreds of the poor', her two-day testimony including numerous personal accounts testimonies of lives blighted by poverty, overcrowding and ill health.[103] For the prosecution, however, timony including numerous personal accounts of lives blighted by poverty, overcrowding and ill health.[103] For the prosecution, however, General, Sir Harding Gifford, calling it a 'dirty filthy book', its sole object 'to enable a person to have sexual intercourse, and not to have that which in the order of providence is the natural result of that sexual intercourse.'[104] Besant and Bradlaugh were found guilty, although their conviction was later overturned on a technicality: however, the case succeeded in generating a huge amount of public interest in their cause, the 'unspeakable' topic of birth control entering public discourse for the first time, in a manner comparable to the discussion of prostitution during Josephine Butler's campaigns against the Contagious Diseases Acts. The Scottish press reported on the trial, the *Aberdeen Weekly Journal* commenting astutely that 'the effect of the prosecution will be enormously to enhance the demand for the obnoxious book'. An estimated 125,000 copies of *Fruits of Philosophy* were sold between March and June of 1877, with around 2,000 people flocking in October to Glasgow's City Hall to hear Besant and Bradlaugh speak on the 'Population Question'.[105]

Clapperton was a member of the Malthusian League and fully committed to its propaganda mission, believing that 'The sway of intelligent minds over the unintelligent is immensely powerful when calmly exercised and widely directed.'[106] Both *Scientific Meliorism* and her later book on social reform, *A Vision of the Future* (1904), contain extended, neo-Malthusian explications of the cause and cure of poverty, while Clapperton also appears to have had at least indirect experience of the distribution of birth control tracts, describing how 'over-burdened mothers' had responded 'with gratitude' when a 'few ladies' had distributed Besant's *Law of Population*.[107] However, there was another dimension to Clapperton's writing on birth control. From its inception, the League had advanced a genuine commitment to a feminist analytic: a third of its Council were women, and Clapperton was one of many feminists active within its rank and file.[108] For them, contraception was not just a panacea for poverty but an issue which predominantly affected women.

The primary text in which Clapperton articulated her feminist neo-Malthusianism was the utopian novel *Margaret Dunmore: Or, A Socialist Home* (1888), her sole venture into fiction and likely the first novel in English to feature 'scientific methods' of birth control.[109] It was written in response to requests by readers of *Scientific Meliorism* that she elaborate upon her 'ideal home of the future'.[110] Socialism, she had asserted, '*must* lay hold of the *family* and fashion it anew', Clapperton proposing a network of communes or 'Unitary Homes', domestic spaces which presented a striking contrast to the patriarchal, mid-Victorian home of her childhood and early adulthood.[111] The stifling etiquette, traumatic disruptions and periods of ennui and loneliness that had been a feature of her family life in Edinburgh were to be rendered obsolete by a 'new domestic *régime*', one which would guarantee social stability, promote the freedom to form mixed-sex relationships and ensure a shared responsibility of care-giving towards the young and old.[112] The communes were to be populated by a combination of individuals, couples and family units, although all from the educated elite, Clapperton believing the poor at present too irrational and immoral to make suitable tenants.[113] In time she foresaw the communes federating, thereby achieving the ultimate aim of 'the universal and voluntary adoption of economic socialism', but by the gradual means dictated by 'conscious evolution' and not the violence and rapidity proposed by political socialism.[114]

These ideas are narrativised in *Margaret Dunmore*. Set just two years in the future, the novel tells the story of 'La Maison', a 'Unitary Home' founded by a Scots woman who bears more than a passing resemblance to Clapperton – wealthy, intellectual, agnostic and reform-minded, who has reached the age of twenty-seven without receiving 'the echo of a whisper of an offer of marriage'.[115] The diverse assemblage of individuals who sign up to the utopian endeavour include Walter Cairns, a Bradford freethinker, Henri Martin, a revolutionary French socialist and Ruth Amor, a victim of male seduction, the group settling in a house bought by Margaret in Peterloo, a reference to the 1819 Peterloo Massacre and a prior instance of cross-gender radical participation.[116] From this point on, the novel interweaves the chronicling of the emotional and intellectual lives of the protagonists as they attempt to negotiate new forms of intimacy, with an articulation of the practical arrangements underpinning La Maison's credentials as a prototype for a radically new conceptualisation of the home. Patriarchal power is replaced by governance through committees, while servants are eschewed in favour of the collective undertaking of domestic tasks by male and female inhabitants alike, a General Council ensuring the fair distribution of the commune's cooking, cleaning and childcare.[117]

The issue of birth control is explored in the novel through the relationship of a newly married couple, Vera and Joe Ferrier. From the upper middle class, but lacking the necessary capital to form a household, moving into La Maison has enabled them to marry. However, while Vera is transformed by communal living, the stimulation provided by her varied household duties turning her from 'timid, emotional, lady-like Vera' to 'an active, bustling little wife', her husband Joe remains stubbornly patriarchal, a trait explained as 'an unfit survival' of the process of evolution.[118] Joe's journey from egoistic patriarch to altruistic, fully evolved manhood a thousand years', Joe expects his wife to honour, if not obey him, acknowledging that 'some women' were 'touchy' on this latter point.[119] However, when Joe chastises Vera for placing the needs of the commune's children above his, she falls seriously ill, losing the baby she was carrying. Joe's journey from egoistic patriarch to altruistic, fully evolved manhood begins when he admits his deficiencies as a husband and a father, and voluntarily submits himself 'to authoritative dictation on a matter of purely personal conduct', or, in other words, uses birth control.[120] Vera does eventually give birth to a son, but only once her health has sufficiently recovered, Joe has developed his paternal instincts through romps with the household's 'little ones', and the couple have undertaken a serious study of 'physiology', attending the commune's public, thrice-weekly classes. The underlying principle behind their course of action is articulated by the narrator, who states: 'In La Maison the power of bringing fresh human life into existence is bound to be controlled in unfavourable conditions by unhurtful scientific methods. No massacre of innocents is permitted there, and the birth of unhealthy infants is pronounced nothing else else, *in an epoch of conscious evolution.*'[121] The counterpoint to La Maison's rational, scientifically informed approach to reproduction is provided by a rectory, unsurprising given Clapperton's secularism. Indeed, that Clapperton held ministers particularly culpable for failing to provide instruction on the population question, 'by precept or example', can be seen in her commentary in *Scientific Meliorism* on a newspaper's charitable appeal for a clergyman's widow and her ten children.[122] Clapperton laid the blame for the family's destitution firmly on the late minister, who, she argues, must have been aware of the arguments in support of birth control but nonetheless conceived children 'out of all proportion to his income', in doing so effectively 'launching paupers into an already overcrowded country.'[123] A comparable situation is presented in *Margaret Dunmore*. In a 'crowded'

Devonshire rectory, the childhood home of one of the inhabitants of the commune, a baby is born 'at intervals of never more, sometimes less, than eighteen months', the rector believing children to be a 'heritage of the Lord', with the 'fruit of the womb' His reward.[124] Yet despite the claims on his purse of his numerous offspring, he prioritises an expensive college education for his eldest son Basil, the minister described as 'a man who applied all his logic to the squaring and fitting of practice to old dogmas under new conditions, rather than to the examination of new doctrines in the light of simple truth'.[125] The consequences of his outdated approach are Basil's ignominious failure in his pursuit of a colonial career (a victim of 'highly strung nerves'), the restricted opportunities afforded the remaining children, and the feeble health of the family's 'gentle' matriarch, who later reflects that 'marriage tries a woman in every way' especially when 'the family is large'.[126]

However, if women in *Margaret Dunmore* are portrayed as the victims of male intransigence on reproductive issues, they are also represented as agents of change. The novel ends with a female-run conference on birth control, staged in the commune's new lecture hall and envisaged as the first in a wider series of events for local, working-class people on the theme of 'The Conduct of Life'.[127] Only mothers are allowed to attend, commune resident 'Mrs Plimsoll' calling it a delicate matter 'for women alone', with the conference's feminist ideology underscored by its aim not only to supply working-class women with birth control advice, but to school them in 'self-respect': in this context, this means their right to bodily autonomy and how to defend this right collectively as women, 'in cases where men are brutal and ought to be resisted.'[128] Wider dissemination of this message is aided by a female-authored tract entitled 'Plain words to Mothers', this dual-pronged strategy reflective of the real-world endeavours of Clapperton and her fellow neo-Malthusian feminists: for example, in 1910 prominent League activist Alice Vickery provided contraceptive advice to working women at a welfare centre in Rotherhithe, while, as we know, Clapperton herself knew of 'ladies' who had distributed Besant's pamphlet on birth control.[129]

Such ventures, both real and imagined, force a reappraisal of the nature and influence of the Malthusian League. While in its official publications the League pursued a socially conservative population theory, as Bland has noted, there was disparity between its official policy and the wide-ranging views and activities of its members.[130] Clapperton is a case in point, propounding Malthusian economics in both her 1885 and 1904 works of social reform, while simultaneously in these and other publications making the feminist case for women's right to family limitation to preserve their health, to mitigate the worse consequences of male 'brutality' and, as we shall see in the next section, to facilitate their sexual pleasure. Furthermore, it appears that despite the League's scruples, Clapperton, like other neo-Malthusian feminists, recognised early on the importance of disseminating practical birth control advice direct to women themselves, her fictional conference in *Margaret Dunmore* placing working-class mothers' practice of family limitation as central to the process of social transformation; 'Miss Plimsoll' states that 'when real reform begins, it will begin with the mothers'.[131] Neither was Clapperton a lone voice, with numerous Malthusian League feminists, including its leaders Annie Besant and Alice Vickery, along with Council members Mrs Heatherley and Mrs Thornton Smith, pursuing a woman-centric, practical approach, the latter speaking publicly in 1892 of the sexual vulnerability of match girls in London's East End, and of women's duty to 'speak out' and provide them with birth control advice.[132]

The outspokenness of Malthusian League feminists on the taboo topic of birth control is all the more remarkable given the antithetical views held by many within the wider women's movement. While all feminists were committed to 'voluntary Motherhood', there was widespread ambivalence towards 'artificial checks', variously seen as dehumanising, immoral, obscene (with their associations with sex work) and as potentially facilitating male sexual desire.[133] The 1877 Besant–Bradlaugh trial was ignored by all the leading feminist journals, while the suffragist Millicent Garrett Fawcett refused to testify, writing to Bradlaugh that if she and her husband were called as witnesses, 'we should effectually damage your case'.[134] When the Men and Women's Club discussed contraception in May 1887, opinion was broadly split between those who dismissed it outright as encouraging 'animalism', and those who conceded that it might have an interim role to play in the quest for female independence, framing it as 'a necessary evil awaiting a better state of self-control and higher relations between the sexes'.[135] The neo-Malthusian argument was represented at the meeting by New Woman writer Mona Caird, who commented, 'by limitation of population, pressure of numbers would be relieved and so social misery relieved': however, possibly fearing criticism, she chose not to make her support for contraception explicit in her published work.[136]

In fact, Clapperton was one of only a handful of women active within feminism who openly advocated birth control in the late nineteenth century. They included Alice Vickery, who led the Malthusian League alongside her husband until 1921; she was also a member of the WSPU and the Women's Freedom League, although her contributions went 'virtually unmentioned' in the League's paper the *Vote*, presumably due to the 'embarrassment' of her neo-Malthusianism.[137] After her trial for obscenity, Annie Besant continued to campaign for access to contraception until her conversion to theosophy in the late 1880s, while her feminist advocacy was conducted primarily within esotericism, socialism and 'new unionism', Besant instigating the 1888 London match girls' strike.[138] Lady Florence Dixie was a Scottish aristocrat and traveller who wrote articles for the *Malthusian*; she was also the author of a New Woman novel, *Gloriana, or the Revolution of 1900* (1890), and served on the Council of the Women's Emancipation Union. However, when she died in 1905, the *Englishwoman's Review* commented on the 'lack of balance in her mind', perhaps an oblique reference to her views on birth control.[139] Hypatia Bradlaugh Bonner wrote articles on 'artificial checks' and abortion in 1897–8 in her monthly paper the *Reformer:* she was also a Liberal feminist, campaigning for women's suffrage within the Women's Liberal Association.[140] Finally, Florence Fenwick Miller was a feminist Freethinker who lectured for the National Society for Women's Suffrage and was one of the first women to sit on the London School Board; both roles were jeopardised, however, by her public support for Besant and Bradlaugh during their 1877 trial.[141]

There is no evidence that Clapperton suffered censure from other feminists for her radical views. However, this may be in part because of the nature of her contributions to the wider women's rights movement during this period. While numerous and wide ranging in their scope, they didn't entail lecturing, committee or leadership roles, and she therefore had no privileges that could be withdrawn. She became a member of the Edinburgh National Society for Women's Suffrage in 1871, joining the Central National Society in 1889 and subscribing to the Women's Emancipation Union in 1894 and 1896. She also wrote on suffrage and other issues for feminist periodicals, including in 1889 the *Women's Penny Paper* and the *Pioneer*, the latter the organ of the London Pioneer Club, founded by Emily Massingberd in 1892 as a 'home for women of advanced views'.[142] In 1899, she attended the International Congress of Women in London, along with Geddes, Montefiore and fellow feminist freethinkers Wolstenholme Elmy and Fenwick Miller, producing an accompanying pamphlet entitled 'Some Evolutionary Aspects of the Woman Movement'.[143]

Clapperton, then, was part of a small coterie of feminists in the 1880s and 1890s who found no difficulty in reconciling their birth control advocacy with their work for the cause of women's rights. All bar one were either members of the Malthusian League or had close ties to it. This suggests that rather than perceiving the League as an idiosyncratic, single-issue pressure group, dwarfed and ultimately outperformed as a reform movement by socialism and feminism, its significance as the predominant space in which radical feminist thought on birth control could germinate should be acknowledged.[144]

Sexual pleasure and George Arthur Gaskell

The second tenet in Clapperton's 'wide-reaching modern moral code' was closely related to birth control, and even more transgressive.[145] In addition to ameliorating poverty, and supporting women's health and right to bodily autonomy, Clapperton saw 'artificial checks' as playing a vital role in facilitating sexual pleasure. Society had been mistaken, she asserted in *Scientific Meliorism*, in perceiving sex as 'impure' and exalting celibacy as 'the highest form of human dignity'.[146] Instead, drawing on the work of the essayist William Rathbone Greg and the philosopher (and George Eliot's partner) George Henry Lewes, along with insights from evolutionary biology, she saw sex as a legitimate human instinct, comparable to eating and drinking. Furthermore, rather than conceiving it as a shameful or selfish act, she believed it to be inherently affective and socialistic, the primary source of altruistic emotions such as tenderness and sympathy. Physical pleasure, then, was not something to evolve out of in pursuit of a 'more than earthly paradise of love', as Geddes and Thomson believed, but rather an act which facilitated evolutionary progress, enabling the human race to develop emotions that were of 'the highest, most purifying order'.[147] In this regard, her sense of the potential of selfless sex to foster social beneficence is comparable to Thomas Lake Harris's conception of 'conjugial' unions, in which the altruistic intent of couples was key to achieving divine transcendence. For Clapperton, birth control played a key role in ensuring this altruistic sex could be enjoyed without a concomitant increase in the birth rate.

Fused with such evolutionary understandings of sexual pleasure were insights drawn from psychiatric and gynaecological discourse. Given what Clapperton believed to be the passionate nature of most people, she saw societal expectations of abstinence, particularly for the young, as not just unrealistic, but potentially harmful, to both the body and mind.[148] Enforced celibacy made young men vulnerable to 'sexual evils' including 'persistent and mentally irritating cravings, self-abuse, etc.', while for young women, 'hysteria, chlorosis, love melancholy and other unhappy ailments' often turned their youth into 'an almost *insufferable* martyrdom'.[149] Far better to encourage 'an early moderate stimulation of the female sexual organs', which in addition to averting mental illness, had the happy side effect of making subsequent childbirths safer and easier.[150]

Nineteen years after her first monograph, Clapperton produced a second work on social reform in which she elaborated upon sexual pleasure's benign influence on society. However, while *A Vision of the Future* (1904) employed a more straightforward and confident tone, her core conclusions remained unchanged, Clapperton finding resonance and legitimation in the proliferating and varied commentaries on human sexuality in the 1890s, rather than revelation. The 'animal nature of sexual passion' did not imply brutality, she argued; rather, its sociable aspect had a purifying and ennobling effect, inspiring an individual tenderness which radiated out into society, leading ultimately to a 'great increase of goodness'.[151] At once evoking and inverting Christian ethics, redemption was to be found through sexual intercourse, while the 'Puritan or ascetic feeling' that insisted on its repression had led to 'heart-rending misery and unmitigated evil'.[152] The new sources which informed this understanding included literary works by Henrik Ibsen and Walt Whitman, Clapperton believing art to be 'in the van of social reform'.[153] She also drew on texts by the sexologist Havelock Ellis and his mentor James Hinton, finding synergies with Hinton's view that 'sensuous pleasure', with undreamt-of 'enhancements and multiplied powers', would underpin the morality of the future.[154]

What was distinctive in Clapperton's later work was her specific advocacy for the sexual needs of women. The vast majority of feminists during the 1900s campaigned to mitigate women's exposure to sexual danger, a more explicit engagement with questions of pleasure and identity coming later, in the pages of Dora Marsden's *Freewoman* (1911–12), although even then the conversation was short lived.[155] Earlier, Clapperton had certainly been mindful of such dangers, referencing W. T. Stead's exposé of child prostitution in the *Pall Mall Gazette*, which was unfolding as *Scientific Meliorism* went to press.[156] By around 1900, however, in a pamphlet entitled 'What Do We Women Want?', she asserted boldly that the average woman had sexual needs which were met relatively rarely.[157] Only by recognising such needs, and allowing women to have sex in 'purity, dignity and freedom', could society avoid the perpetuation of numerous miseries, including prostitution, venereal disease and loveless marriages.[158]

The specific origin of these ideas is not made manifest, her c. 1900 pamphlet devoid of references to other writers, although it was published by the Secularist and neo-Malthusian William Reynolds.[159] Explicit statements on female sexual pleasure were certainly present within the milieu of freethought, albeit universally expressed by men and not representative of the wider movement. George Drysdale, in his 1854 *Elements of Social Science*, insisted women's sexual desires were as strong as men's, commending birth control for putting 'the two sexes almost on a par in sexual freedom', while more recently S. Symes, in a letter to the *National Reformer* in 1877, had asked 'why should not young girls be allowed to make vice as safe for themselves as the young men do?'[160] Annie Besant, however, while arguing that there was 'nothing wrong in a natural desire rightly and properly gratified', stopped short of discussing women's sexual needs.[161]

However, it is also legitimate to ask how Clapperton's views on female sexual pleasure might have been influenced by or played out within her own intimate life. Her most significant friendship over the course of her life was with a man named George Arthur Gaskell. Born in 1842 in Liverpool, the eldest son of nine children, Gaskell's family belonged to the lower middle class: his father worked as a landlord, the family employed at least one servant and Gaskell's younger brothers became banking and insurance clerks.[162] After a childhood in the north-west, in various addresses in Liverpool and Bangor, Gaskell lived for a period in London before settling in the late 1870s in Bradford. In his thirties and forties, he lived in lodgings, earning a living as an oil painter, his portraits of six local worthies adorning the walls of Bradford's Free Library and Museum.[163] He was also an early socialist, the only known photograph of him taken in 1886 when out on a ramble with the Leeds and Bradford Socialist League (see figure 17).[164]

17 George Arthur Gaskell with the Leeds and Bradford branches of the Socialist League, 1886

It is likely that Clapperton met Gaskell through their shared commitment to neo-Malthusianism. Described as an 'ardent friend of the cause', Gaskell was one of a handful of individuals to sit regularly on the Malthusian League's Council, attending meetings in London throughout the 1880s and 1890s.[165] Back home in Bradford, he waged a 'unwearied' propaganda campaign, visiting the city's poorer districts to distribute tracts and give birth control advice, organising lectures by Annie Besant, writing two pamphlets – on the futility of thrift and on maternal endowments – and penning letters to the *Bradford Observer*, one disgruntled reader branding him a 'philosophical wiseacre' for promoting birth control above self-help.[166] In 1878, he even corresponded with Charles Darwin, proposing that birth control and eugenics be collectively viewed as the third great 'law of Race Preservation' after 'natural' and 'sympathetic selection'. In his reply, Darwin courteously yet firmly rejected the suggestion, in part because 'artificial checks' might encourage 'extreme profligacy amongst unmarried women'.[167]

Gaskell was clearly a formative influence on Clapperton's work, as well as a source of vital emotional support. The *Vision of the Future* is dedicated to him, while in the Preface to *Scientific Meliorism* she expresses her gratitude for his 'patient and persistent encouragement and aid', and declares herself indebted to his knowledge of evolution, socialism and sociology, describing how 'Each chapter as it was written has been submitted to him, and every point of difficulty discussed with him.'[168] Beyond these details, however, the historical record is frustratingly silent, and to get any indication of his personality or the dynamics of their relationship, one has to look instead for clues in her fictional writing.

In *Margaret Dunmore*, Clapperton uses the relationship between three characters, Margaret, Frank and Rose, to illustrate how a remodelled intimacy might work in practice within a Unitary Home. Frank is the embodiment of ideal manhood, a 'fine-looking man ... of culture and taste' with a 'single, clear, scientific, masculine intellect'.[169] He enters into an intense collaborative study of social science with Margaret (the novel's reform-minded spinster), which precipitates an emotional crisis: Frank's wife Rose becomes jealous and leaves the commune, after being warned that Frank 'is in love or on the verge of falling in love' with Margaret.[170] The situation is resolved when Frank's passionate feelings for Margaret are shown to be the result of a masculine lack of introspection, to be corrected in the future by schooling boys in 'self-observation': as Wendy Parkins has noted, emotions in the novel are depicted as 'amenable to conscious adaptation through a combination of social correction and self-scrutiny.'[171] In contradiction to Clapperton's defence of sexual pleasure in her works of non-fiction, in *Margaret Dunmore* passion is not exempt from this disciplinary regime, the 'wholesome check' given to Frank's 'barbarous' male instincts one of 'an innumerable host of delicate forces' or routine correctives, which ultimately enable marriages to survive in the commune and a more complex matrix of human relationships to flourish.[172]

Margaret eventually finds love, or at least the promise of it, with Alfred Widnell, a character who, in common with George Arthur Gaskell, is an artist and bachelor, and who has lived for several years in cramped lodgings, donating over half his salary to the poor. His arrival at La Maison provides at once a solution to the commune's lack of a cohesive plan of social reform and Margaret's need for a romantic partner, Frank describing how he has found 'A new, deep-hearted friend':

> "Yes, Margaret, a friend after *your* heart I have found: a philosopher! – not a mere anarchist, social democrat, communist, collectivist, socialist, or even Fabian; but one who is all these, and more. He has thought out the present condition of things, and has systematized a reform – I mean, a theory and practice immediately applicable! Our hiatus, Margaret, is filled by his – scientific meliorism … Oh, yes! you will like him. You will see, eye to eye, you and he, – and I shall be jealous," he added, in the playful mood that betokens perfect confidence in your friend.[173]

We can only speculate as to whether Clapperton modelled Alfred Widnell on George Arthur Gaskell, or whether her relationship with him bore any resemblance to Margaret's potential romantic entanglement with Alfred or intellectual exchanges with Frank. We do know that she defended others who engaged in 'free unions' and gave serious consideration to alternatives to monogamy, asserting that there was 'no reason why people of liberal thought should make a dogged, pious stand at monogamy while lightly dismissing promiscuity, polygamy, polyandry as disreputable forms of sex-union'.[174] We also know that she was a fierce critic of modern marriage, believing its history to be 'in short, … the history of man's domination of woman and the measures he has taken to assume, assert and establish his rights of possession'.[175] Furthermore, while it is possible that she defied societal and religious injunctions forbidding sex outside marriage and engaged in a sexual relationship with Gaskell, this would have been difficult to keep secret, especially given that from the time of her mother's death, she lived with relatives rather than establishing an independent household.[176] If the relationship had become public, it would have caused an immediate scandal, both in Edinburgh and within her feminist and secularist networks, and would inevitably have left a trace in the historical record. In any case, a letter printed in 1897 in the *Adult* suggests this is unlikely. The journal was the organ of the Legitimation League, which had just shifted its aims from securing equal rights for illegitimate children to championing 'free love'. The League had clearly invited Clapperton to join, along with other well-known commentators on sexuality including Thomas Hardy and W. T. Stead. However, Clapperton declared herself 'extremely chary' of accepting, in her answer revealing an attitude towards maintaining a public/private boundary in line with others within the era's progressive movements: while she agreed with sex freedom in principle, she considered 'hasty action on the lines of sexual freedom' to be 'injurious to the public interests'.[177]

Whatever the nature of their relationship in the 1880s, by the 1890s Gaskell's life took a different direction. His secularism morphed into a deep engagement with esotericism: in 1890 he joined the Theosophical Society and in 1895 married Ellen Sophie Atkins, a feminist who shared his interest in the occult, the couple moving to England.[178] They had no children, possibly by using birth control, possibly because of Ellen's belief, contrary to Clapperton's, that mankind was required to renounce sex in order to liberate the spirit, which had become imprisoned in the body.[179] After living together for at least nine years, a period in which they conducted joint seances and Ellen published on diverse topics including dietary reform, feminist biblical criticism and men's responsibility for the spread of venereal disease (the latter in the *Freewoman*), the couple appear to have separated, the 1911 census recording them as living apart.[180] Gaskell's friendship with Clapperton endured, however, Clapperton bequeathing him the considerable sum of £350 in her will, 'in token of sympathy with his lifelong labours both in relation to industrial freedom and to religious freedom'.[181]

Conclusion

Clapperton remained unmarried throughout her life. Although a woman of independent means, she lacked sufficient capital to establish her own household, after her mother's death living variously with her widowed sister in Edinburgh's New Town, her sisters in Coventry, and her nephews in the West End of Glasgow.[182] Yet the life she created for herself in middle and old age appears far removed from the desolation and ennui she experienced when caring for her mother in the 1850s and 1860s, and the dependency and dutifulness she saw as an inherent feature of the 'cruel lot' of spinsterhood. The 1880s and 1890s were decades of intense activity, encompassing non-fictional and fictional book writing, journalism for the periodical press and activism for her freethinking and feminist causes. She also supported socialist organisations, despite an initial scepticism akin to that of Geddes's, that 'outward equality produced by external force or authority, and not by impulse from within, could never be maintained'.[183] The subsequent socialist movement changed her mind, however, Clapperton becoming a member of the ILP and maintaining connections with the Edinburgh Fabians, asserting that 'the genesis of socialism is distinctly to be traced to the vital element in human nature – unselfish sympathy'.[184] The 1900s brought further publications on social reform and, when it arrived, participation in the militant suffrage movement. Now in her seventies, she joined the WSPU in 1907, encouraging her niece Lettice Floyd to follow suit, becoming a member of the Women's Freedom League in 1908, the following year donating sticks of rock and books for the Edinburgh stall at the WSPU Prince's Skating Rink Exhibition and acting as a hostess at a Women's Freedom League 'At Home' at the Café Vegetaria in Edinburgh.[185] Her commitment to secularism also endured. In the 1910s she became involved with the Edinburgh Rationalist Ethical Guild, a freethinking organisation whose concerns appear perfectly aligned to her own; according to Ray Challinor, its periodical the *Reform Journal* was 'devoted to attacking religion, the strict Sunday observance laws and the prevailing puritanical attitude to sex'.[186] Clapperton presided over salon meetings and through the Guild may have been reunited with her old friend Geddes, who was also a member, while also making a new acquaintance.[187] John S. Clarke was a maverick antiquarian, adventurer, lion-tamer, poet, socialist and later parliamentarian, whom she employed as her private secretary, the two becoming great friends and Clarke finding her 'one of the most wonderful women' he had ever met.[188]

Clapperton was at home in Edinburgh when she died of a cerebral haemorrhage in September 1914, just two months after the advent of war.[189] An analysis of her life and work clearly establishes her as a radical, early voice on the Sex Question. A rare example of a feminist advocate of birth control and women's right to sexual pleasure, her 'modern moral code' enhances our understanding of the range of positions taken up within the women's movement on the 'battlefield' of sexuality during the 1880s to 1900s.[190] Through her involvement in secularist networks, she was able to draw upon a tradition of feminist and libertarian views on sex, underscoring the importance of freethought as a vital space for the formation of sexually progressive discourse. Furthermore, by working as a feminist within the Malthusian League, she put forward practical measures for family limitation, going beyond the articulation of 'turgid' neo-Malthusian economics often represented as the primary output of the

League. Finally, by 'performing' respectability and approaching her subject matter seriously and eruditely, while ostracised by some members of her family, she escaped the censure dealt out to other feminist and secularist campaigners.

Gaskell was undoubtedly an important influence, Clapperton drawing upon his knowledge of a range of subjects in her writing. Less clear, however, is the nature or impact of their intimate relationship. While she anticipated a romantic liaison between 'Margaret Dunmore' and 'Alfred Widnell', how closely this equated to the course of her and Gaskell's emotional life is a matter for conjecture. Her published work makes it clear that she hated the condition of celibacy, viewed sex as a pleasurable and important element in human relations and supported others who engaged in 'free unions'. It is also clear that for other sexual progressives during this period, conducting an intimate relationship outside marriage was an important way to 'perform one's ethics', as 'part of an ideological praxis'.[191] However, a sexual relationship with Gaskell was by no means a prerequisite to the formulation of her radical views, and it could equally be the case that the 'passionate' same-sex friendships which she formed at boarding school continued to constitute an important element in her emotional life.

While Clapperton's work was reviewed widely in the periodical press, opinion varied. Some reviewers were effusive in their praise, noting Clapperton's considerable erudition. In the *Academy*, Vernon Lee, the pseudonym of feminist writer Violet Paget, found *Scientific Meliorism* to be 'the work of a woman who has listened a great deal, read much, and thought more and who has therefore the power of forcing us to listen, to think, and to read', while the *Westminster Review* held her 1904 *A Vision of the Future* to be 'a particularly brilliant piece of work' which 'ought to be brought home to every citizen'.[192] For other reviewers, however, Clapperton's prose style proved problematic, some finding it dull, pedantic and verbose, the *Saturday Review* commenting wryly that 'Miss Clapperton cannot be acquitted of a worldly weakness for padding.'[193] Her seriousness of tone appears to have deflected any charge of immorality occasioned by her radical views. While the *Westminster Review* acknowledged that *Scientific Meliorism*'s advocacy of the 'perilous doctrine of neo-Malthusianism' made it liable to 'danger of shipwreck against current morality', it nonetheless reassured its readers that birth control aside, there was nothing 'which would be unwholesome for persons of either sex who approach it sober-mindedly'.[194]

Within radical circles, Clapperton's ideas were similarly contrarily received. Clearly, Clapperton had her allies. SDF socialist Dora Montefiore described her as 'among the very remarkable women of the Victorian Age' and *Scientific Meliorism* as the 'Bible of Altruism', while the political economist James Mavor praised her simultaneously delicate and bold handling of the Sex Question.[195] According to John S. Clarke, in the 1880s she was 'lionised' by 'that coterie of advanced literateurs', including 'Herbert Spencer, Frederick Harrison, Elizabeth Linton, George Henry Lewes and George Eliot', although this account likely relies upon Clapperton's own recollection of events.[196] However, Mona Caird, Karl Pearson and Geddes and Thomson certainly cited her work, while the Australian social reformer Catherine Helen Spence drew heavily on *Scientific Meliorism* when writing her 1888–89 utopian novella *A Week in the Future*, with several sections transcribed almost verbatim.[197]

Other progressives were less enamoured, however. Edward Carpenter was sceptical of the nature and scale of change envisaged in *A Vision of the Future*, Sheila Rowbotham asserting that 'His close observation of several surges of new womanhood had inclined him to stress inner psychological and spiritual shifts over alterations in the outer structures of society and politics.'[198] Furthermore, several reviewers needed persuading of the practicality of Clapperton's proposed Unitary Homes. The *Saturday Review* stated, 'Battle, murder and sudden death could be promoted in no surer way', while the most vituperative response came from the 'scientific socialists' of the SDF, the reviewer in their periodical *To-day* calling *Margaret Dunmore* a 'perfectly preposterous book', and claiming that 'as to the "Socialist Home" – well, rather than an hour spent within those terrible walls give us an eternity beside the "Capitalistic Hearth," even as sketched by the acrid pen of Mr. Belfort Bax'.[199] Even Clapperton's friend James Mavor noted that she 'had less influence upon the men and women of her time than she might have had', Clapperton missing an opportunity to contribute in any substantial way to Karl Pearson's Men and Women's Club, one of the era's key forums for the discussion of issues relating to sex. When she attended as a guest in May 1888, she was tired and 'failed somehow to catch the thread' of the debate on the celibate ideal in Christianity, contributing little and leaving early.[200] *Scientific Meliorism* sold 'slowly and very unequally', while her earnings from *Margaret Dunmore* were 'pitifully small', with copies still remaining on her death in 1914.[201] Fifty years after the publication of her major treatise, an attempt was made by a relative to bring her work to a wider public audience: in 1937 William Dreaper published a book and series of pamphlets on the principles of 'scientific meliorism' under the auspices of the 'League of Science'; what became of this endeavour is unknown, however.[202]

Clapperton began *Scientific Meliorism* with a poem written by her muse George Eliot, in which she articulates a desire to join 'The choir invisible / Of those immortal dead that live again / In minds made better by their presence – live / In deeds of daring rectitude.'[203] It is clearly debateable whether Clapperton succeeded in joining, as Eliot undoubtedly did, the 'choir invisible' of thinkers who continue to exert a profound influence on the subsequent generation. However, her published works, given their sexually progressive views, can certainly be construed as 'deeds of daring rectitude' and her role in foreshadowing, if not perhaps precipitating, change in sexual attitudes deserves to be acknowledged.

Notes

1 D. B. Montefiore, *From a Victorian to a Modern* (London: E. Archer, 1927), p. 115.
2 P. Geddes and J. A. Thomson, *The Evolution of Sex* (London: Walter Scott, 1889), p. 299. In her utopian novel *Margaret Dunmore*, Clapperton draws upon Geddes's classification of the sciences from physical to moral: see J. H. Clapperton, *Margaret Dunmore: Or, A Socialist Home* (London: Swan Sonnenschein, Lowrey & Co., 1888), p. 204.
3 I. Zangwill, 'Without prejudice', *Pall Mall Magazine*, 8:34 (February 1896), p. 328.
4 Letter from Jane H. Clapperton to Patrick Geddes, 15 October [1890], Geddes Papers, NLS, MS10525, fols 57–8.
5 Ibid.
6 Ibid.
7 Geddes and Thomson, *The Evolution of Sex*, p. 297.
8 Letter from Jane H. Clapperton to Patrick Geddes, 15 October [1890], Geddes Papers, NLS, MS10525, fols 57–8.
9 J. H. Clapperton, 'What do we women want?' (W. H. Reynolds, u.d. [1900]), p. 4.
10 J. H. Clapperton, *A Vision of the Future based on the Application of Ethical Principles* (London: Swan Sonnenschein & Co Ltd, 1904), p. 98.
11 Clapperton, *A Vision of the Future*, p. 106.
12 Letter from I. Leatham, *The Freewoman*, 7 December 1911, pp. 51–2.
13 For the debate over the cause and timing of fertility decline in modern Europe, see H. Cook, *The Long Sexual Revolution: English Women, Sex, and Contraception 1800–1975* (Oxford: Oxford University Press, 2004); S. Szreter, *Fertility, Class and Gender in Britain, 1860–1940* (Cambridge: Cambridge University Press, 1996).
14 L. Bland, *Banishing the Beast: Feminism, Sex and Morality* (London: Penguin, 1995, Tauris Parke, 2002), pp. 189–90.
15 Letter from Anna Morton to Patrick Geddes, 3 April 1886, Geddes Papers, NLS, MS19253, fols 19–22.
16 E. Gordon and G. Nair, *Murder and Morality in Victorian Britain: The Study of Madeleine Smith* (Manchester: Manchester University Press, 2009).
17 Montefiore, *From a Victorian to a Modern*, p. 115; letter from Dora Montefiore to Hardie, c. 1898/9, quoted in C. Collette, 'Socialism and scandal: the sexual politics of the early labour movement', *History Workshop*, 23 (Spring 1987), p. 111.

18 J. H. Clapperton, *Scientific Meliorism and the Evolution of Happiness* (London: Kegan Paul, Trench & Co., 1885), p. 12.
19 L. Schwartz, *Infidel Feminism: Secularism, Religion and Women's Emancipation, England 1830-1914* (Manchester: Manchester University Press, 2013), pp. 64, 112, 121, 135, 195; Bland, *Banishing the Beast*, pp. 78, 172, 211; A. Richardson, *Love and Eugenics Eugenics in the Late Nineteenth Century: Rational Reproduction and the New Woman* (Oxford: Oxford University Press, 2003), pp. 52-3, 57, 65, 67, 92-3, 112, 138, 170, 174; S. Ledger, *The New Woman: Fiction and Feminism at the Fin de Siècle* (Manchester: Manchester University Press, 1997), pp. 50-3, 54 and 'The New Woman and the crisis of Victorianism', in S. Ledger and S. McCracken (eds), *Cultural Politics at the Fin de Siècle* (Cambridge: Cambridge University Press, 1995), pp. 36-7. Further analyses of Clapperton's writing can be found in A. Ardis, *New Women, New Novels: Feminism and Early Modernism* (New Brunswick, NJ: Rutgers University Press, 1990), pp. 118-19; C. Waters, 'New Women and socialist-feminist fiction: the novels of Isabella Ford and Katharine Bruce Glasier', in A. Ingram and D. Patai (eds), *Rediscovering Forgotten Radicals: British Women Writers, 1889-1939* (Chapel Hill: University of North Carolina Press, 1993), p. 29; D. Suksand, 'Equal partnership: Jane Hume Clapperton's evolutionist-socialist utopia', *Utopia Studies*, 3:1 (1992), pp. 95-107.
20 W. Parkins, 'Domesticating socialism and the senses in Jane Hume Clapperton's *Margaret Dunmore: Or, A Socialist Home*', *Victoriographies*, 1:2 (2011), pp. 261-86; K. B. Kalsem, 'Law, literature and libel: Victorian censorship of "dirty filthy" books on birth control', *William and Mary Journal of Women and the Law*, 10:3 (Spring 2004), pp. 533-68.
21 L. A. Hall, 'The next generation: Stella Browne, the New Woman as freewoman', in A. Richardson and C. Willis (eds), *The New Woman in Fiction and in Fact: Fin-de-Siècle Feminisms* (Basingstoke: Palgrave Macmillan, 2001), p. 224.
22 St Cuthbert's Parish Register (685-02; vol. 0340), p. 469.
23 Memorial stone, John Clapperton Esq., St John and St Cuthbert's cemetery, Gravestone Photographic Resource, grave 60741. Jane Hume Clapperton would later describe herself as being of 'the Philistine stock which has vulgarized society in its mercantile epoch'. Letter from Jane H. Clapperton to Patrick Geddes, 15 October [1890], Geddes Papers, NLS, MS10525, fols 57-8.
24 Entry for 'John Clapperton, Esq. of Spylaw', *Edinburgh Annual Register, for 1825*, vol. 18 (Edinburgh: Cadell, 1827), p. 348.
25 *The Statistical Account of Edinburghshire* (William Blackwood, Edinburgh: 1845), p. 116; *The Traveller's Guide through Scotland*, 9th edn (John Thomson: Edinburgh, 1829), p. 51.
26 'Miss Jane Hume Clapperton, Authoress', *Women's Penny Paper*, 22 June 1889, issue 35, pp. 1-2.
27 'Miss Jane Hume Clapperton', *Women's Penny Paper*.
28 Ibid.
29 Ibid.; App. 366, 369, 789, *Appendix to the Reports of the Select Committee of the House of Commons on Public Petitions* (1846), pp. 182-4, 414-15. Alexander Clapperton held a ticket for a dinner given to statesman Earl Grey (1834) and was Steward at a dinner in aid of Polish refugees (1835). His public roles included Director of the Standard Life Assurance Company and Auditor of the North British Railway Company.

30 'Miss Jane Hume Clapperton', *Women's Penny Paper*; 1871 Census. It may not have been reduced finances that prompted the move from Princes Street, since during this period the character of the street was transforming from residential to primarily commercial.

31 A 'Curator of Patronage' had the power to appoint and dismiss members of University staff. The children's charity was the Heriot Foundation.

32 S. Magarey, B. Wall, M. Lyons and M. Beams (eds), *Ever Yours, C. H. Spence: Catherine Helen Spence's An Autobiography, Diary (1894) and Some Correspondence (1894–1910)* (Kent Town, S. Australia: Wakefield Press, 2005), p. 47.

33 'Miss Jane Hume Clapperton', *Women's Penny Paper*.

34 Magarey et al., *Ever Yours, C. H. Spence*, p. 47. Clapperton's friend the SDF socialist Dora Montefiore also recollected her choice of headwear, remarking that 'she remained always in outward appearance the old-fashioned spinster lady wearing the early Victorian cap that all women of that period seemed, when over thirty, to wear'. Montefiore, *From a Victorian to a Modern*, p. 115.

35 Clapperton, *Scientific Meliorism*, pp. 110–11.

36 'Miss Jane Hume Clapperton', *Women's Penny Paper*.

37 Ibid.

38 Ibid.

39 For an extended discussion of the nature of 'Woman's Mission' in Scotland, see L. A. Orr Macdonald, *A Unique and Glorious Mission: Women and Presbyterianism in Scotland, 1830–1930* (Edinburgh: John Donald, 2000), pp. 41–103. As a district visitor, Clapperton would have assisted her minister by visiting working-class families, providing them with aid and advice (although with a heavy emphasis on self-help), and exhorting them to read the Bible, attend Church and keep the Sabbath. See the *District Visitors Manual: A Compendium of Practical Information and of Facts, for the use of District Visitors* (London: Parker, 1840), p. 27. The institutions at which she was likely to have been a superintendent are Edinburgh's Original Industrial School for Girls (founded 1847) and the Royal Hospital for Sick Children, Edinburgh (founded 1863).

40 Editorial, *Scotsman*, 16 March 1866.

41 Kathleen Chater has established that Cranbrook was articulating similar views almost two decades earlier, when preaching in Ireland during the potato famine. K. Chater, 'James Cranbrook', *Congregational History Society Magazine*, 7:4 (2014), pp. 163–4.

42 Editorial, *Caledonian Mercury*, 14 November 1865.

43 'Rev. J. Cranbrook on the Relation of Divine Providence to Prayer and Plagues', *Scotsman*, 17 October 1865.

44 Ibid.

45 M. Ledger-Lomas, '"Glimpses of the great conflict": English Congregationalists and the European crisis of faith, circa 1840–1875', *Journal of British Studies*, 46:4 (October 2007), p. 831. The seminal text on the Victorian 'crisis of faith' is R. J. Helmstadter and B. Lightman (eds), *Victorian Faith in Crisis: Essays on Continuity and Change in Nineteenth-Century Religious Belief* (Stanford, CA: Stanford University Press, 1990).

46 Cranbrook wrote a letter to the *Scotsman* and preached a second sermon on the same topic a fortnight later. 'The Rev. Mr Cranbrook and his Censors', *Scotsman*, 24 October

1865; 'Rev. James Cranbrook on Prayer in Relation to Divine Providence', *Scotsman*, 30 October 1865.
47 'The Rev. James Cranbrook on Creeds and Churches', *Scotsman*, 25 February 1867.
48 Ibid.; 'The Rev. James Cranbrook's Congregation. Social Meeting and Presentation', *Scotsman*, 27 April 1867.
49 The lecture was reprinted in the *Fortnightly Review*, 5:3 (1869), pp. 129–45.
50 'The Rev. James Cranbrook's Congregation. Social Meeting and Presentation', *Scotsman*, 27 April 1867; W. Knight, *Some Nineteenth Century Scotsmen* (Oliphant, Anderson & Ferrier: Edinburgh, 1903), pp. 201–2.
51 'The Rev. James Cranbrook's Congregation. Social Meeting and Presentation', *Scotsman*, 27 April 1867.
52 'Mr Cranbrook on the Tendencies of Modern Religious Thought', *Scotsman*, 24 February 1868.
53 *Scientific Meliorism*, p. x; 'Miss Jane Hume Clapperton', *Women's Penny Paper*.
54 J. H. Clapperton, 'Agnosticism and women: a reply', *Nineteenth Century*, 7:39 (May 1880), pp. 840–4; 'The agnostic at church. II', *Nineteenth Century*, 11:62 (April 1882), pp. 653–6; 'Chapter XXIII. Religion', *Scientific Meliorism*, pp. 409–24. The articles on agnosticism appear to be Clapperton's first pieces of journalism.
55 Clapperton, *Scientific Meliorism*, p. 27.
56 Clapperton's italics. *Scientific Meliorism*, p. 418.
57 H. Spencer, 'Retrogressive religion', *Nineteenth Century Magazine* (July 1884), quoted in *Scientific Meliorism*, p. 415; F. Harrison, 'The ghost of religion', *Nineteenth Century Magazine* (March 1884), quoted in *Scientific Meliorism*, p. 415.
58 *Scientific Meliorism*, pp. 420–2.
59 Ibid., p. 417.
60 Ibid., pp. 423–4.
61 A. C. Davies, 'Time for a change? Technological persistence in the British watchmaking industry', *Material Culture Review/Revue de la culture matérielle* [Online], 36.1 (June 1992), point 19, https://journals.lib.unb.ca/index.php/MCR/article/view/17529/22464 (accessed 3 January 2019).
62 Quoted in A. Tucker, *Suffragette Partnership: The Lives of Lettice Floyd and Annie Williams, 1860–1943* (Mercian Manuals, 2005), p. 6.
63 M. Lee, 'Bray, Charles (1811–1884), freethinker and social reformer', *ODNB*.
64 C. Bray, *Phases of Opinion and Experience during a Long Life: An Autobiography* (London: Longmans, Green and Co., 1884), pp. 70, 72–3, 76.
65 Clapperton, *Scientific Meliorism*, p. ix.
66 Ibid.
67 Eliot lived in Coventry between 1841 and 1849 when Clapperton was still a young girl. It is unlikely that Clapperton's association with the Brays' circle began before 1850, when she turned eighteen. The Brays were at Rosehill between 1840 and 1857, before moving to the adjacent Ivy Cottage. That Clapperton knew Cara and Sara Hennell is indicated by her visit to them in 1893 with the Australian feminist and social reformer Catherine Helen Spence, who wrote in her memoir that they 'took tea with two most interesting old ladies – one 82, and the other 80 – who had befriended

the famous authoress when she was poor and stood almost alone'. Magarey et al., *Ever Yours, C. H. Spence*, p. 159.
68 R. Ashton, 'Caroline Bray [née Hennell] (1814–1905)', *ODNB*.
69 Schwartz, *Infidel Feminism*, p. 56.
70 S. S. Hennell, *Christianity and Infidelity: An Exposition of the Arguments on Both Sides. Arranged According to a Plan Proposed by George Baillie, Esq.* (London: Arthur Hall, Virtue & Co., 1857), p. 163; S. S. Hennell, *On the Need of Dogmas in Religion. A Letter to Thomas Scott* (London: Thomas Scott, 1874), p. 13. In the late 1880s, both Sarah Hennell and Jane Hume Clapperton contributed numerous articles and letters to the *Women's Penny Paper*.
71 Clapperton, 'Agnosticism and women: a reply', p. 844.
72 Schwartz, *Infidel Feminism*, p. 1. I have applied Schwartz's approach of employing the capitalised forms of 'Secularism' and 'Freethought' only when referring to the organised movement. See Schwartz, *Infidel Feminism*, pp. 5–6.
73 Schwartz, *Infidel Feminism*, p. 10. For an extended discussion of the political origins, organisational culture and wider influence of Secularism, see E. Royle, *Victorian Infidels: The Origins of the British Secularist Movement, 1791–1866* (Manchester: Manchester University Press, 1974).
74 Schwartz, *Infidel Feminism*, p. 57.
75 Ibid.
76 Clapperton, *Scientific Meliorism*, p. 419; 'Miss Jane Hume Clapperton', *Women's Penny Paper*.
77 E. Crawford, 'Clapperton, Jane Hume', *The Women's Suffrage Movement: A Reference Guide, 1866–1928* (London: Routledge, 1999, 2001), p. 112.
78 Clapperton, 'Agnosticism and women: a reply', p. 841.
79 Ibid., p. 844.
80 Ibid., p. 840. See also Clapperton, 'The agnostic at church. II', pp. 653–6.
81 For an extended discussion of the question of sex within freethought, see Schwartz's chapter 'Freethought and Free Love? Marriage, birth control and sexual morality' in *Infidel Feminism*, pp. 178–216.
82 Schwartz, *Infidel Feminism*, pp. 180–2, 190. George and Charles Drysdale were born into a wealthy family who resided at 8 Royal Crescent in Edinburgh, within walking distance of the Clapperton family homes. I have yet to establish a connection between the two families, however.
83 A. Besant, *The Legislation of Female Slavery in England* (London: Besant & Bradlaugh, 1885), p. 2; Schwartz, *Infidel Feminism*, p. 194. Besant's stance shifted with her involvement in theosophy, as her critique of the sexual philosophy of Thomas Lake Harris indicates (see p. 94).
84 *National Reformer*, 14 June 1862, pp. 6–7, in Schwartz, *Infidel Feminism*, pp. 180, 186.
85 Laura Schwartz coined the phrase 'infidel feminism'. Clapperton, *Scientific Meliorism*, p. 12.
86 Montefiore, *From a Victorian to a Modern*, p. 115.
87 Clapperton, *Scientific Meliorism*, p. 9.
88 Ibid., p. 12.

89 The term 'birth control' was not used until the 1920s.
90 Clapperton, *Scientific Meliorism*, p. 1.
91 T. R. Malthus, 'An essay on the principle of population as it affects the future improvement of society' (London, 1798).
92 Clapperton, *Scientific Meliorism*, pp. 89, 94.
93 Ibid., p. 95.
94 Ibid., pp. 90–1, 92–3, 95, 97, 128–9.
95 Clapperton, *Scientific Meliorism*, p. 85.
96 For accounts of the Malthusian League, see P. Fryer, *The Birth Controllers* (New York: Stein and Day, 1965), pp. 173–89; R. Ledbetter, *A History of the Malthusian League, 1877–1927* (Columbus: Ohio State University Press, 1976); A. McLaren, *Birth Control in Nineteenth-Century England* (New York: Holmes & Meier, 1978), pp. 107–15; R. A. Soloway, *Birth Control and the Population Question in England, 1877–1930* (London: University of North Carolina Press, 1982), pp. 49–69; J. M. Benn, *The Predicaments of Love* (London: Pluto, 1992); Bland, *Banishing the Beast*, pp. 202–21; Schwartz, *Infidel Feminism*, pp. 204–7.
97 The League member to confer royalty on Charles Drysdale was J. Rothwell, who spoke at the Ninth Annual Meeting of the Malthusian League in 1886, cited in Ledbetter, *A History*, p. 58. On the predominant role played by the Drysdale family in neo-Malthusianism, see Ledbetter, *A History*, pp. 57–80. Drysdale and Vickery were in a 'free union' although presented as married to their contemporaries, presumably to avoid scandal.
98 The figure is from Ledbetter, *A History*, p. 62.
99 Ledbetter, *A History*, p. 68; Schwartz, *Infidel Feminism*, p. 206.
100 The pamphlet was entitled 'Hygienic Methods of Family Limitation', and although free, applicants had to sign a declaration that they were over 21 and married (or about to be). See Bland, *Banishing the Beast*, p. 209.
101 McLaren, *Birth Control*, pp. 107–15, quoted in Ledbetter, *A History*, p. 70. The American birth control campaigner Margaret Sanger was more positive about the work of the Drysdale family, referring to their 'quiet, unceasing service' and 'loyalty to an ideal'. Cited in Ledbetter, *A History*, p. 58.
102 C. Knowlton, *Fruits of Philosophy. An Essay on the Population Question. A New Edition with Notes* (London: Freethought Publishing Company, 1877), p. iv.
103 Cited in Kalsem, 'Law, literature, and libel', p. 545.
104 Ibid., p. 542.
105 'The Bradlaugh-Besant Case', *Aberdeen Weekly Journal*, 23 June 1877, p. 4; McLaren, *Birth Control*, p. 108; 'The population question', *The Scotsman*, 6 October 1877, p. 6.
106 Clapperton, *Scientific Meliorism*, p. 88.
107 Ibid., pp. 81–102; Clapperton, *A Vision of the Future*, pp. 79–96.
108 Bland, *Banishing the Beast*, p. 205.
109 That Clapperton chose a fictional form in which to present her 'Unitary Homes' is consistent with her view of the potential of contemporary literature to provide instruction on the 'subject of love', believing classic works by William Makepeace Thackeray, Robert Browning and in particular George Eliot provided 'pictures of modern social

life' and 'moral principles' that could and should direct and control the social conduct of young women and men. Clapperton, *Scientific Meliorism*, pp. 185-6.
110 Miss 'Jane Hume Clapperton', *Women's Penny Paper*.
111 Clapperton, *Scientific Meliorism*, p. 430; 'What do we women want?', p. 7.
112 Clapperton, *Scientific Meliorism*, p. 428; 'What do we women want?', p. 5.
113 Clapperton, *Scientific Meliorism*, p. 302.
114 Ibid., p. 433.
115 Clapperton, *Margaret Dunmore*, p. 1. Clapperton did allow herself some artistic licence, however: she was in her fifties by the time she wrote *Margaret Dunmore*.
116 The character of Walter Cairns is clearly modelled on aspects of the life of the Rev. James Cranbrook. Like Cranbrook, Cairns's unorthodox teachings lead to his expulsion from his Unitarian chapel. Cairns then hires a public hall and proceeds to lecture to 'his few earnest followers' in non-theistic or agnostic thought. Clapperton, *Margaret Dunmore*, p. 64. Women were a dynamic presence at the Peterloo Massacre, attending as part of all-female reform associations, wearing white, carrying flags and ensuring their female leaders were on the speakers' platform.
117 Clapperton, *Margaret Dunmore*, pp. 81-93.
118 Ibid., pp. 118, 119.
119 Ibid., pp. 120, 125.
120 Ibid., p. 126.
121 Ibid., p. 126.
122 Clapperton, *Scientific Meliorism*, p. 98.
123 Ibid.
124 Clapperton, *Margaret Dunmore*, pp. 13, 14.
125 Ibid., p. 15.
126 Ibid., pp. 13, 14, 164.
127 Ibid., pp. 191-2, 202-3.
128 Ibid., p. 203.
129 Bland, *Banishing the Beast*, pp. 207-8.
130 Ibid., p. 217.
131 Clapperton, *Margaret Dunmore*, p. 203.
132 *The Malthusian*, July 1892, p. 50, cited in Bland, *Banishing the Beast*, pp. 205-6.
133 Bland, *Banishing the Beast*, pp. 189-221.
134 Ibid., p. 196; Garrett Fawcett is quoted in J. A. and O. Banks, *Feminism and Family Planning in Victorian England* (Liverpool: Liverpool University Press, 1964), p. 93.
135 L. Sharpe, 'Comments on Papers in Artificial Checks on Population', June 1887 (Pearson Collection), quoted in Bland, *Banishing the Beast*, p. 214.
136 Caird was a member of the Malthusian League, donating money to them in 1907. Men and Women's Club Minutes, 9 May 1887 (Pearson Collection), quoted in Bland, *Banishing the Beast*, p. 215.
137 Bland, *Banishing the Beast*, p. 213.
138 A. Taylor, 'Besant [née Wood], Annie (1847-1933), theosophist and politician in India', *ODNB*.
139 *The Englishwoman's Review*, 15 January 1906, pp. 69-70, quoted in Bland, *Banishing the Beast*, pp. 209-11.

140 Schwartz, *Infidel Feminism*, pp. 59, 205. E. Royle, 'Bonner, Hypatia Bradlaugh (1858–1935)', *ODNB*.
141 R. T. Van Arsdel, *Florence Fenwick Miller: Victorian Feminist, Journalist and Educator* (Ashgate: Aldershot, 2001), pp. 79–80, 92–3; Schwartz, *Infidel Feminism*, pp. 61, 205. By 1896, Fenwick Miller was able to include an advertisement for a birth control manual in the *Woman's Signal*, the feminist periodical she owned and edited, without attracting criticism.
142 J. H. Clapperton, 'Mr. J. S. Stuart Glennie on the Women's Suffrage Bill. An answer', 22 June 1889 and 'An evolutionist's reply to the appeal against female suffrage', *Women's Penny Paper*, 3 August 1889. For Clapperton's contribution to *Pioneer*, see 'The pioneer', *Women's Penny Paper*, 12 October 1889 and the entry on the 'Pioneer Club' in Crawford, *The Women's Suffrage Movement: A Reference Guide, 1866–1928*, p. 126. Clapperton offered to send a prospectus for Geddes's Town and Gown Association to the Pioneer Club in 1896. See letter from Clapperton to Geddes, 19 May 1896, Geddes Papers, NLS, MS10528, fols 91–2.
143 *Portrait Album of Who's Who at the International Congress of Women* (London: The Gentlewoman, 1899); J. H. Clapperton, 'Some Evolutional Aspects of the Woman Movement' (S. I.: June 1899). In the light of this activity, it is hard to countenance Montefiore's comment that Clapperton had 'never actively identified herself with the Woman movement'. D. Montefiore, 'Jane Hume Clapperton speaks', *New Age*, 4 May 1905, p. 288.
144 Schwartz has made this case for the wider Secularist movement in *Infidel Feminism*, pp. 198–207.
145 Clapperton, *Scientific Meliorism*, p. 12.
146 Ibid., p. 173.
147 Geddes and Thomson, *The Evolution of Sex*, p. 267; Clapperton, *Scientific Meliorism*, p. 173.
148 Clapperton, *Scientific Meliorism*, pp. 303–4. Clapperton's views on sexual self-control were class-inflected: she believed abstinence rare although possible amongst those possessed of 'the best intelligences' but '*nowhere* to be found amongst the masses'. Clapperton, *Scientific Meliorism*, p. 95.
149 Despite her relative candour on sex, Clapperton felt unable to elaborate on the topic of male masturbation, stating 'To these I need not … further allude'. Clapperton, *Scientific Meliorism*, p. 321.
150 Clapperton, *Scientific Meliorism*, p. 321.
151 Clapperton, *A Vision of the Future*, pp. 100, 103.
152 Ibid., p. 98.
153 Clapperton referred specifically to Ibsen's *Ghosts* and Whitman's *Leaves of Grass*.
154 Clapperton, *A Vision of the Future*, pp. 103–4.
155 Bland, *Banishing the Beast*, pp. 250–1, 256, 265–73.
156 Clapperton, *Scientific Meliorism*, p. 303, note '*'.
157 Clapperton, 'What do we women want?', p. 4.
158 Ibid.
159 William Hammond Reynolds (1844–1911) was a publisher, Secularist and the secretary of the Malthusian League, who also handled its finances and distributed Malthusian literature. See Ledbetter, *A History*, p. 63.

160 G. Drysdale, *The Elements of Social Science; or, Physical, Sexual and Natural Religion by a Graduate of Medicine*, 7th edn (London: Edward Truelove, 1867) (first published 1854), p. 376 and *National Reformer*, 23 September 1877, p. 644. Quoted in Schwartz, *Infidel Feminism*, pp. 182, 202.

161 *National Reformer*, 23 June 1877, p. 404, quoted in Schwartz, *Infidel Feminism*, pp. 201–2.

162 'George Arthur Gaskell', b. 4 December 1842, England and Wales Christening Index, 1530–1980; England census returns, 1861, 1871.

163 'Skied', *Yorkshireman*, 28 December 1887, West Yorkshire Archive Service, Bradford, DB65/C2/34. The paper describes Gaskell as an 'artist of renown', who had donated the paintings to the art gallery. Seemingly, however, they had been 'skied' or hung in an obscure corner 'as if they were so much rubbish', until the subjects of the portraits complained.

164 Clapperton, *Scientific Meliorism*, p. x; F. Brockway, *Socialism Over Sixty Years: The Life of Jowett of Bradford* (London: George Allen and Unwin, 1946), pp. 29–30. According to Brockway, the Bradford branch of the Socialist League had less than a dozen members and was comprised of 'a cross-section of the thinking working class of that time', who met in a room in Laycock's Temperance Hotel and 'discussed continuously as they drank their tea and coffee bought in half-pint mugs as though it were beer'.

165 Ledbetter, *A History*, p. 65.

166 Ibid.; K. Ittmann, *Work, Gender and Family in Victorian England* (Basingstoke: Palgrave Macmillan, 1995), pp. 219–21. G. A. Gaskell, 'The Futility of Pecuniary Thrift as a Means to General Wellbeing' (London: R. Forder, 1890) and 'Social Control of the Birth-rate and Endowment of Mothers' (London: Freethought Publishing Company, 1890).

167 Letters from G. A. Gaskell to Charles Darwin, 13 and 20 November 1878; letter from Charles Darwin to G. A. Gaskell, 15 November 1878, printed in full in Clapperton, *Scientific Meliorism*, pp. 337–42.

168 Clapperton, *Scientific Meliorism*, pp. x–xi. The book is inscribed to Gaskell as 'the living friend by whose aid my aims have shaped themselves to Scientific Meliorism'.

169 Clapperton, *Margaret Dunmore*, pp. 9, 157.

170 Ibid., p. 162.

171 Ibid., p. 170; Parkins, 'Domesticating socialism and the senses', p. 262.

172 Clapperton, *Margaret Dunmore*, p. 195.

173 Ibid., p. 197.

174 Clapperton, *A Vision of the Future*, p. 137. For Clapperton's views on 'free unions' and divorce law reform, see her article 'Miss Chapman's Marriage Reform. A Criticism', *Westminster Review*, 130:1 (December 1888), pp. 709–17.

175 Clapperton, *A Vision of the Future*, p. 135.

176 At the time of the 1881 and 1901 census returns, Clapperton was staying first in Edinburgh with her sister Sophia Balgarnie, now a widow, and then with her nephews Alan and Lewis Clapperton in Glasgow.

177 Clapperton also believed it would be misleading for someone 'who see things in their wide relations' to support a society 'of narrower aims and issue'. Letter from Jane Hume Clapperton, *The Adult*, 1:6 (January 1898), pp. 134–5.

178 England and Wales Civil Registration Marriage Index, 1895. Ellen Sophie Gaskell joined the Hermetic Order of the Golden Dawn on 20 March 1897. 'Membership Roll of the Hermetic Order of the Golden Dawn', Library and Museum of Freemasonry, GD 2/2/2.

179 Ellen Sophie Atkins, 'The Secret of Happiness' (London: Women's Printing Society, 1894), in British Library Philosophical Tracts 1875-94. For a detailed account of Ellen Atkins and George Arthur Gaskell's lives and publications, see Sally Davis's online biographies of members of the Hermetic Order of the Golden Dawn, www.wrightanddavis.co.uk/GD/ (accessed 3 January 2019).

180 G. A. Gaskell, 'What the "Fire Elemental" told us', *Theosophical Review*, 33:196 (15 December 1903), pp. 347-54; G. A. Gaskell, 'What some "Devas" told us', *Theosophical Review*, 34:200 (15 April 1904), pp. 110-21; 'Notable nothings', *Good Housekeeping*, 26:5 (May 1898), p. 216; Ellen Gaskell, *A Woman's View of Genesis* (London: Advance Press, 1905); E. S. Gaskell, 'The unspeakable', *Freewoman*, 1:9, 18 January 1912, p. 176. In 1911 George Gaskell was living at an address in Brighton and Ellen Sophie Gaskell in Portsmouth. Although they both listed themselves as married on the census return, when Gaskell died in 1933, his sister acted as his executor, despite Ellen still being alive.

181 Jane Hume Clapperton, Edinburgh Sherriff Court Wills SC70/4/464.

182 In the census for 1881, Clapperton is listed as having a 'small independent income'.

183 Clapperton, *Scientific Meliorism*, p. 129.

184 Clapperton, *A Vision of the Future*, p. 82. Dora Montefiore describes Clapperton in 1905 as having been 'for some years a member of the I.L.P.'. See D. B. Montefiore, 'Jane Hume Clapperton Speaks', *New Age*, 4 May 1905, p. 288. When the Australian social reformer Catherine Helen Spence visited Britain in 1894, Clapperton arranged for her to speak to the Edinburgh Fabians, Spence also noting that Clapperton had been given a grant to hold 'Socialist lectures and fraternal concerts' in Coventry. Diary entries for 17 May and 30 June 1894, in Magarey et al., *Ever Yours, C. H. Spence*, pp. 268, 275.

185 Crawford, 'Clapperton, Jane Hume (1832-1914)', *The Women's Suffrage Movement*, p. 112.

186 Ray Challinor, *John S. Clarke: Parliamentarian, Poet, Lion-Tamer* (London: Pluto Press, 1977), p. 33.

187 Ibid. and letter from Arthur Woodburn to Ray Challinor, 23 March 1972, Papers of John S. Clarke, NLS, Acc7656/1/3.

188 Challinor, *John S. Clarke*, p. 34.

189 Jane Hume Clapperton, death certificate, 30 September 1914.

190 E. DuBois and L. Gordon, 'Seeking ecstasy on the battlefield: danger and pleasure in nineteenth-century feminist thought', *Feminist Studies*, 9:1 (Spring 1983), pp. 7-25.

191 D. Maltz, 'Ardent service: female eroticism and new life ethics in Gertrude Dix's *The Image Breakers* (1900)', *Journal of Victorian Culture* (2012), p. 5.

192 Vernon Lee, *The Academy*, 15 May 1886, no. 732, pp. 340-1; 'Sociology, politics, jurisprudence', *Westminster Review*, 161:6 (June 1904), p. 709.

193 'Scientific Meliorism', *Saturday Review*, 26 December 1885, pp. 847-8.

194 'Politics, sociology, voyages and travels', *Westminster Review*, 125:249 (January 1886), p. 251.
195 Montefiore, *From a Victorian to a Modern*, p. 115; Montefiore, 'Jane Hume Clapperton Speaks'; J. Mavor, *My Windows on the Street of the World*, 2 vols (London: J. M. Dent, 1923), vol. 1, pp. 225–6.
196 Quoted in Challinor, *John S. Clarke*, p. 34.
197 Clapperton was either unaware of Spence's plagiarism or unfazed by it, the two meeting in June 1894 and spending a few days visiting George Eliot's old haunts in Coventry. See 'Prologue' by L. D. Ljungdahl in C. H. Spence, *A Week in the Future* (Sydney: Hale & Iremonger, 1987), pp. 10–12 and Magarey et al., *Ever Yours, C. H. Spence*, p. 159.
198 S. Rowbotham, *Edward Carpenter Carpenter: A Life of Liberty and Love* (London: Verso, 2008), p. 326.
199 'Scientific Meliorism', *Saturday Review*, 26 December 1885, pp. 847–8; *To-day: Monthly Magazine of Scientific Socialism*, 52 (March 1888), pp. 90–2.
200 Record of meeting held on 14 May 1888, Minute Book of the Men and Women's Club (p. 142), Karl Pearson Papers, University College London (hereafter UCL), 1/5/1/2; letter from J. H. Clapperton to Maria Sharpe, 15 May 1888, The Men and Women's Club Correspondence, Karl Pearson Papers, UCL, 1/6/8.
201 Mavor, *My Windows on the Streets of the World*, p. 226; 'Miss Jane Hume Clapperton', *Women's Penny Paper*; Jane Hume Clapperton, Edinburgh Sheriff Court Wills, SC70/4/464, November 1914.
202 W. P. Dreaper, *The Future of Civilisation and Social Science: A Study Involving the Principles of Scientific Meliorism* (London: Heron, 1937).
203 Clapperton, *Scientific Meliorism*, p. v.

Conclusion

Bella Pearce's fellow suffrage campaigner Helen Fraser once overheard a comment, made with what sounds like wistful optimism, that if, during a talk by the theosophist Annie Besant at the Athenaeum, the roof had fallen in and the entirety of the audience had been 'extinguished', 'all the cranks in Glasgow would be gone'.[1] To the 'unco guid', this is what Bella and Charles Pearce, Patrick and Anna Geddes, and Jane Hume Clapperton were: 'cranks', the Victorian appellation for all those whose idiosyncratic beliefs fell outside of what was considered rational and respectable. Such individuals deliberately situated themselves on the margins of the middle class, from this position launching a series of attacks on the hypocrisies of their age's sexual and social codes.

Clearly, such 'cranks' were not confined to London. Instead, the era's sexual revolt was staged in a myriad different forms and settings across Britain, in public lectures, party meetings and impassioned conversations, as well as in utopian novels, natural history books and avant-garde Celtic journals. While the individuals detailed here were vibrantly connected to English networks, examining the Scottish case complicates our understanding of sexually progressive thought and behaviour in Britain as a whole in a number of important ways. It affirms the necessity of inserting the revolt from established religion into the historian's gaze, while also recognising that it was not unbelief but rather to the heterodox belief systems of Swedenborgianism, positivism and 'religious agnosticism', that the sexual radicals were drawn. It highlights, too, the ways in which progressive sexual ideas were linked to wider and above all older radicalisms, disrupting the established perception of the period as one of generational challenge. Finally, it emphasises the regulatory role played by the progressive organisations themselves, as well as the establishment, as feminist and socialist parties endeavoured to balance idealism with pragmatism and retain electoral appeal, despite enduring public associations between radicalism and immorality. This meant that while transgressive ideas could be mooted in New Woman fiction or secularist pamphlets, respectability retained a powerful regulatory function, limiting the expression of such ideas in both the lives and work of Scotland's sexual progressives.

What sustained them in their quest to realise a utopian ideal of reformed intimate relations were the emotional and intellectual ties fostered within their networks and subcultures. These relationships were founded not just on a shared philosophy and vision of a 'new life' but the countless events which form the texture of the everyday. Charles and Bella Pearce sent Brotherhood of the New Life wine to Elizabeth and Ben Wolstenholme Elmy; Anna and Patrick Geddes's daughter Norah stayed with the Fabians Eleanor and Frank Podmore; the Pearces looked after James Keir Hardie's song-birds in their office; Jane Hume Clapperton publicised Geddes's slum regeneration programme at the Pioneer Club in London; the WSPU campaigner Teresa Billington got married from the Pearces' house in Langside; the Geddeses' son Arthur married a young relative of the anarchist Elisée Reclus; Clapperton gave a black lace mantle to the Australian social reformer Catherine Helen Spence; the progressive educationalist Cecil Reddie sent Geddes cold cures from his school in Derbyshire. Yet, as Edith Ellis noted, fellowship could be hell as well as heaven and there were also arguments between the Scottish sexual rebels. An Edinburgh friend of the Geddeses, May Nitchie, wrote to Patrick in 1896, distraught over a recent disagreement, regretting that she had let her 'wild McGregor blood boil up as it did and not only up but over', while Patrick often clashed with the Dundee poet Rachel Annand Taylor, who resented his requests for poetry on demand, on one occasion calling him an 'insatiable egotist' and vowing to Anna that she would 'not forgive Merlin for days and days'.[2] Several of the relationships within Charles and Bella Pearce's ethical socialist network in Glasgow broke down irretrievably, not over the wider, ideological questions addressed by Bella in her column, such as the feminist challenge to the sexual double standard, or the role of women within socialism, but over more mundane matters, including internal politicking surrounding a loan made by Charles to the 1895 ILP election fund and an altercation between Hardie and the printers of the *Labour Leader*, in which Charles was closely implicated.

While the fraternity and fellowship lasted, however, the effect of escaping the narrow-mindedness of a conservative family, the rigid social rules of a respectable neighbourhood or the evangelical zeal of the 'unco guid', and joining like-minded individuals in fashioning a new code of sexual morality or ushering in an imminent, progressive age could be exhilarating. There was an excitement and a novelty in sitting up 'far into the night' attempting to solve Edinburgh's social problems; listening to Geddes unravel Scotland's ancient Celtic past atop a moonlit Arthur's Seat; discussing the 'burning questions of the day' with fellow comrades at a Women's Labour Party 'At Home'; sitting on the bear skin under the acacia tree in Charles Bray's garden for unrestrained talk with the local liberal intelligentsia; and hosting a notorious American mystic in your home and hearing fairies speak over breakfast.[3] Clapperton was able to overcome the isolation and ennui of her early adulthood through her feminist freethinking networks, Annand Taylor felt 're-charged' by her visits to Edinburgh, while Bella clearly relished the energy of both the 1890s ethical socialist movement and the 1900s women's suffrage campaigns.[4]

The danger, as Chris Nottingham has noted, is that by isolating themselves within rarefied coteries, the sexual progressives narrowed their social horizons, eradicating any internal voices of dissent, and instead creating 'the illusion that the part of society one knew was a perfect microcosm of the whole, and the world was waiting breathlessly for the latest formulation of woman's true role, or whatever'.[5] Despite his preference for practical action over political rhetoric, Geddes's reputation amongst 'the more frigid society of Edina' as a 'dreamer in stone and fresco' was not entirely misplaced, especially when it came to his conceptualisation of intimacy.[6] His idealised notions of reinstituting the love between Celtic heroes and their ladies, or poets and their muses, bore little relation to modern sexual behaviour. When the scandal at Ramsay Lodge forced Geddes to face the rather more prosaic realities of the sex lives of young male students, he was profoundly shocked, disquieting his colleague Thomas Whitsun with the intensity of his reaction. Whitsun commented, 'I confess that I feel surprised that you let this be such a slap in the face to you & the idea of such a thing happening has all along been familiar to me & I thought to you also'.[7] While Clapperton advocated birth control, female sexual pleasure and socialist and feminist 'Unitary Homes', there is no evidence she applied her theoretical conceptualisations to her own intimate life, the romantic future envisaged between the fictional Margaret Dunmore and Alfred Widnell most likely going unrealised in her relationship with the neo-Malthusian George Arthur Gaskell. Similarly, Bella Pearce's initial hopes that the 'new life' of ethical socialism would encompass a more 'natural relationship between the sexes', one based on rationality and respect rather than misogyny or flirtation, were harder to achieve than she anticipated.[8] When a prostitution scandal broke in Glasgow, Hardie chose to narrate it in the *Labour Leader* as a story of class rather than gender exploitation, a tale of rich seducers leading the daughters of working men to their ruin, while the condescension shown by ILP propagandists Jim Connell and George Samuel towards their female colleagues further indicates the masculinised culture of 1890s socialism.

The longer-term impact of their sexually radical ideas was manifold and varied. The Swedenborgian sexual mysticism of Bella and Charles Pearce was recast by Thomas Lake Harris's most well-known disciple, Laurence Oliphant, who broke with Harris in 1881 and with his wife, Alice le Strange, established a new community in Haifa, Palestine.[9] However, wider public interest in Harris, always more prurient than sincere, dwindled upon his death in 1906, with the passing of Charles himself the year before, in 1905, followed by key disciples Arthur Cuthbert in 1911 and Edward Berridge in c. 1923, further eroding the Brotherhood of the New Life's British support base. In Glasgow, while Bella claimed to be asked 'frequently' in 1923 for news of the release of Edwin Markham's much-anticipated official biography of Harris, the failure of this volume to materialise undoubtedly damaged the chances of a twentieth-century legacy for the Brotherhood.[10] By the time of Bella's death in 1929, the Glasgow network of followers had dissipated entirely, Bella's housekeeper Annie Wood dissuading the American scholars Herbert Schneider and George Lawton from visiting Scotland, for 'there are now no publishers of Harris books & no library have his books'.[11] The subsequent publication of their exhaustive joint biography of Harris and Laurence Oliphant in 1942 did little to revive interest in Brotherhood theology, with reviews in Britain treating Harris as a curiosity from history, one of many 'cranks and zealots', 'bred a century ago in the fertile American soil'.[12]

The Brotherhood belief in the compatibility of religion and sexuality may conceivably have influenced later, alternative religious practices. Research in heterodox religion in modern Scotland is burgeoning, with new work by Michelle Foot on spiritualism in Scottish art and by Michael Shaw on occult and theosophical themes in Scottish cultural nationalism.[13] Steven Sutcliffe has emphasised the significant role played by 'post-Presbyterian' traditions such as spiritualism and theosophy in twentieth-century Scotland 'as religious resources for lower middle and middle social groups'.[14] The continued survival of organisations such as the Theosophical Society of Scotland (the first Lodge was founded in Edinburgh in 1884) and the Glasgow Association of Spiritualists (founded in 1871) suggests that a groundswell of interest and support was retained in alternative religion during the interwar years, with a renewed enthusiasm for new age ideas emerging in the 1960s and 1970s. In 1962, the Findhorn colony was established on the Moray Firth coast, by the mid-1970s becoming an internationally recognised centre for the promotion and practice of alternative religious and spiritual ideas. For Sutcliffe, this demonstrates the importance of acknowledging the plurality of the religious landscape in modern Scotland, with communities such as Findhorn providing an important corrective to the narrative of pervasive secularisation.[15] To what extent alternative religion provided a space for unconventional sexual and gender expression is unclear, however.

What should also be considered is the longer-term impact of Bella Pearce's feminist sexual politics within socialism. While as 'Lily Bell' she was undoubtedly a pioneer, in the interwar years, the desire to follow both a socialist and feminist agenda continued to implicate women in a complex process of negotiation. Many socialists persisted in their assumption that feminism was a bourgeois preoccupation, some labour men retaining 'an abiding suspicion of all women's organizations as inherently middle class and divisive'.[16] While the ILP may have envisaged itself as the 'Real Women's Party', promoting policies such as equal pay for equal work and the unionisation of female workers, in reality a gap between its rhetoric and practice remained. Helen Gault, who as the women's columnist for the Glasgow socialist paper *Forward* was a direct inheritor of Bella's earlier pioneering journalism, commented archly that 'among socialists the belief in equality is only skin deep', a viewed shared by many women within the ILP.[17] Despite this, however, Annmarie Hughes believes the party compared favourably to European and other British socialist organisations, with women, by 1921, constituting up to 25 per cent of the total membership of some branches, and the Pearces' early contribution towards achieving this integration should not be overlooked.[18]

Yet while the ILP may have acknowledged its commitment to women, it was another matter entirely to embrace sexually radical ideas, especially in a climate of intense political electioneering. This reluctance can be seen in the response of the party leadership to the Workers' Birth Control Group (WBCG), which formed in 1924 to campaign for the administration of birth control advice through government-funded welfare centres.[19] Despite the group's emphasis on the economic benefits to working-class women of the limitation of family size, and their emphatic rejection of 'free love', the male-dominated Labour Party leadership still believed the proposals too controversial to be adopted. The response from the WBCG's president, Dorothy Jewson, one of the Labour Party's first Members of Parliament, was one of resignation, in 1925 commenting that 'It is no new thing for the women of the Labour Party to find questions of particular interest to themselves placed at the end of a long agenda'.[20] Women may have won the vote, first partially in 1918 and then fully in 1928, yet enfranchisement did not bring the power to transform the political system, which continued to be structured by conventional gendered assumptions.

The legacy of Patrick Geddes's ideas is more obviously apparent. He continued to publish on sex during the 1910s, in 1912 writing a sixpenny pamphlet on 'Problems of Sex' with Thomson for the National Council of Public Morals, and in 1914 writing *Sex*, another book for a popular audience, this time for the 'Home University Library of Modern Knowledge'.[21] Twenty-five years had passed since the publication of *The Evolution of Sex* and Geddes and Thomson acknowledged and incorporated new advances in the natural and social sciences, drawing on Sigmund

Freud's psycho-analytic theories of the significance of childhood sexuality and Stanley Hall's 'discovery' of adolescence as a discrete and significant phase of childhood. *Sex* was also more explicit in tone than *The Evolution of Sex*, and included a lengthy treatise on the need for sex education, as well as a whole chapter on 'sexual vice', although it kept its title in Latin and concluded somewhat banally that 'From all such anomalies one turns with relief to the opinion of Sancho Panza the wise, who liked a man to be a man and a woman a woman.'[22] Geddes and Thomson also revised their earlier prescriptions on the psychological differences between the sexes, stating simply that the day of such assumptions was over, dismissing them as 'guesses at truth without scientific precision'.[23] Overall, however, *Sex* constituted a restatement rather than a revision of their theories, the natural scientists reiterating their belief in the anabolic and katabolic origins of sexual difference, the importance of the maternal feelings in social evolution and the need for sexual self-control to achieve the 'poetic and spiritual possibilities' of the evolution of love.[24]

By 1914, the scientific study of sex was accepted as a legitimate field of study, although it wasn't until the 1930s that sexological ideas gained a broader currency in popular discourse, informing the newly available sexual advice literature. Geddes and Thomson's contribution to this field deserves to be better recognised. Yet considering Geddes's consistent emphasis on learning through practical experience rather than academic scholarship, it is also important to consider his continued influence in Edinburgh, through the cultural organisations he instigated and the networks he helped foster. Geddes left the city in 1917, living and working in India, Palestine and finally Montpelier in France, where he died in 1932. Deprived of the force of his charismatic personality, several of his projects floundered. While one of his halls of residence is lived in by University of Edinburgh postgraduate students to this day, his final Summer School took place in 1903, and the Outlook Tower, his sociological museum, closed its doors in 1905.[25] However, a number of his inner circle remained in Scotland, the painter John Duncan, after a brief period teaching art in Chicago, settling permanently in Edinburgh, continuing to paint subjects from Celtic myth and legend and in 1909 joining the Edinburgh Theosophical Society.[26] Patrick and Anna's surviving children also settled in Edinburgh, their daughter Norah becoming a landscape architect and marrying the urban planner Frank Mears, and their youngest son Arthur teaching geography at the University of Edinburgh. Other disciples moved away, however, the poet Rachel Annand Taylor relocating to London, where after her husband's breakdown she appears to have begun an intense relationship with a twenty-three-year-old man called Adrian, who 'burns his youthful time and devotion before me with all the passion of youth and the tenderness of an archangel'.[27]

The interwar period in Scotland had its own generation of sexual progressives. The anarchist and 'free lover' Guy Aldred lived in a 'free union' with the socialist-anarchist and feminist Rose Witcop between 1908 and 1921, although it is not clear exactly when the couple settled permanently in Glasgow. Aldred held strong convictions regarding marriage, dismissing it as 'serfdom' and 'rape by contract', although like most 'free lovers' he was not in favour of promiscuity, believing like Geddes that as civilisation evolved, men and women would become more rather than less monogamous.[28] When the birth control campaigner Margaret Sanger visited Glasgow in 1922 to speak at a public meeting on Glasgow Green, Aldred and Witcop hosted Sanger, subsequently publishing her pamphlet *Family Limitation*.[29]

Another group who could be considered sexual progressives were the cohort of female modernist writers now considered important contributors to the interwar literary revival known as the Scottish Renaissance. They included Catherine Carswell, Willa Muir, Nan Shepherd, Lorna Moon and Naomi Mitchison, who in their novels and essays explored themes of female sexuality, of the changing relationships between women and men, and of women's roles in modern Scotland. Catherine Carswell's first novel, *Open the Door!* (1920), depicts the quest of its protagonist Joanna to find sexual and emotional fulfilment, and, according to Margery Palmer McCulloch, is 'iconoclastic in the way female sexuality is foregrounded in the narrative', while her second novel *The Camomile* (1922) is similarly unconventional, arguing implicitly for 'a lack of hypocrisy, for openness with regard to sexual desire, and for a more equal partnership between men and women'.[30] Willa Muir wrote novels and essays which critiqued the limited roles accorded women in Scottish society, including *Imagined Corners* (1931), *Women: An Inquiry* (1925), *Mrs Grundy in Scotland* (1936) and 'Women in Scotland' (1936), while Naomi Mitchison often placed women at the heart of her historical fiction, exploring issues around sexual desire, childbearing and female autonomy.[31] While none of these authors acknowledged a direct link to Geddes's 'Celtic Renascence', his earlier insistence on the cultural legitimacy of the Scottish voice, of the need for 'Iona to educate London' not London to educate Iona, was clearly significant, Murray Pittock and Isla Jack referring to the movement in Edinburgh during the 1890s as the 'neglected root' of the 1920s and 1930s Scots Renaissance.[32]

The social change precipitated by the First World War and female enfranchisement undoubtedly affected attitudes towards women: however, the sexual and gendered norms challenged by the interwar progressives appear strikingly familiar. Social taboos on sexual activity outside marriage remained strong, as did the sexual double standard that Bella Pearce and her feminist colleagues had campaigned so vigorously against. As Roger Davidson's work on the moral agenda behind the provision of treatment for venereal disease has shown, women in the interwar period were persistently viewed as constituting the principal source of venereal infection in Scottish society, with the period witnessing the identification of a new female stereotype of social deviance, the 'problem girl' or 'amateur prostitute'. She consisted of a young, working-class woman who through her unpaid, casual sex and cavalier attitude towards taking precautions was understood to represent an even bigger threat to the nation's racial health than the seasoned prostitute. As in pre-war Scotland, women were offered a choice between 'the passive sexuality of the wife and mother, or, as sexual initiator, be stigmatized as a prostitute and the reservoir of disease'.[33]

The relative stasis in Scotland with regard to hegemonic sexual and gender norms reminds us 'just how difficult it was – and is – to translate the desire to be good into doing good for others'.[34] While the period 1880–1914 was experienced by Scotland's sexual progressives as one of transition, Bella Pearce writing in 1894 that 'Time must bring many changes, especially in the relations between men and women, which have in the past been of the most unreasonable and absurd nature', enacting that change was not straightforward.[35] As well as the challenges associated with an idealistic outlook, the progressives' manifestos were inflected by their own class, gender, race and sexual prejudices, which hindered their ability to find widespread resonance. Nonetheless, the attempts by Bella and Charles Pearce, Patrick and Anna Geddes, and Jane Hume Clapperton to realise a 'more than earthly paradise of love' in *fin de siècle* Scotland constituted genuine attempts to disrupt the hegemony of the forces of moral conservatism, and instead reimagine intimacy along egalitarian lines.

Notes

1 H. Moyes, *A Woman in a Man's World* (Alpha Books: Sydney, 1971), p. 21.
2 Letter from May Nitchie to Patrick Geddes, Autumn 1896, Geddes Papers, NLS, MS 10528, fols 131–2; letter from 'the Banabhard' [Rachel Annand Taylor] to 'Dearest Musicmaker' [Anna Geddes], Friday 12.30 [undated, poss. 1910/11], Geddes Papers, NLS, MS 10572, fol. 32.
3 Introduction to the letters of Patrick Geddes by Norah G. Mears, Geddes Papers, NLS, MS 10508, fol. 186; L. Glasier, 'The Woman's Labour Party, Glasgow', *Labour Leader*, 25 May 1895, p. 5.

4 Postcard from Rachel Annand Taylor, 3 December 1907, Geddes Papers, NLS, MS 10572, fol. 3.
5 C. Nottingham, *The Pursuit of Serenity: Havelock Ellis and the New Politics* (Amsterdam: Amsterdam University Press, 1999), p. 103.
6 I. Zangwill, 'Without prejudice', *Pall Mall Magazine*, 8:4 (February 1896), p. 329.
7 Letter from Thomas Whitsun to Patrick Geddes, 21 July 1897, Geddes Papers, NLS, MS 10529, fols 56–7.
8 Lily Bell, 'Matrons and Maidens', *Labour Leader*, 1 December 1894, p. 7.
9 J. Chajes, 'Alice and Laurence Oliphant's divine androgyne and "The Woman Question"', *Journal of the American Academy of Religion*, 84:2 (2016), pp. 498–529.
10 Letter from Bella Pearce to Edwin Markham, 1 June 1923, TLH Papers 13/307.
11 Letter from Annie Wood to George Lawton, 15 July 1930, TLH Papers 13/308.
12 D. W. Brogan, 'Odd bodies', *Manchester Guardian*, 16 June 1943.
13 M. Foot, 'Modern spiritualism and Scottish art between 1860–1940' (PhD thesis, University of Aberdeen, 2016); M. Shaw, 'The fin-de-siècle Scots renascence: the roles of decadence in the development of Scottish cultural nationalism, c. 1880–1914' (PhD thesis, University of Glasgow, 2015).
14 S. Sutcliffe, 'The quest for composure in the "post-Presbyterian" self', in C. Brown and L. Abrams (eds), *A History of Everyday Life in Twentieth Century Scotland* (Edinburgh: Edinburgh University Press, 2010), p. 185.
15 Ibid.
16 M. Pugh, *Women and the Women's Movement in Britain: 1914–1999* (Basingstoke: Palgrave Macmillan, 2000), p. 134, quoted in A. Hughes, *Gender and Political Identities in Scotland* (Edinburgh: Edinburgh University Press, 2010), p. 4.
17 *Forward*, 7 December 1919 and 1 July 1922, quoted in Hughes, *Gender and Political Identities in Scotland*, p. 39.
18 Hughes, *Gender and Political Identities in Scotland*, pp. 39–40.
19 L. Hoggart, 'The campaign for birth control in Britain in the 1920s', in A. Digby and J. Stewart (eds), *Gender, Health and Welfare* (London: Routledge, 1996), pp. 143–66.
20 Quoted in ibid., p. 155.
21 J. A. Thomson and P. Geddes, *Problems of Sex* (New York: Moffat, Yard and Co., 1912); P. Geddes and J. A. Thomson, *Sex* (London: Williams and Norgate, 1914).
22 Geddes and Thomson, *Sex*, p. 146.
23 Ibid., p. 209.
24 Ibid., p. 8. Indeed, a large section from their 1896 essay, 'The moral evolution of sex, is simply restated, with little modification. See *Sex*, pp. 193–203.
25 Postgraduates at Edinburgh University can stay in Patrick Geddes Hall at Mylne's Court.
26 C. Young, 'John Duncan (1866–1945)', *ODNB*.
27 Letter from Rachel Annand Taylor to Anna Geddes, NLS, MS 10572, fols 33–7.
28 Guy Aldred, 'Socialism, women, and the suffrage', *Voice of Labour*, 1 (1907), pp. 146, 150, quoted in G. Frost, *Living in Sin: Cohabiting as Husband and Wife in Nineteenth-Century England* (Manchester: Manchester University Press, 2008), pp. 214–15.
29 L. Leneman, *The Hidden History of Glasgow's Women: The THENEW Factor* (Edinburgh: Mainstream, 1993), pp. 144–5.

30 M. P. McCulloch, 'Fictions of development 1920–1970', in D. Gifford and D. McMillan (eds), *A History of Scottish Women's Writing* (Edinburgh: Edinburgh University Press, 1997), p. 361 and 'Interwar literature', in G. Norquay (ed.), *The Edinburgh Companion to Scottish Women's Writing* (Edinburgh: Edinburgh University Press, 2012), p. 106.

31 For extracts from W. Muir, *Women: An Inquiry* (London: Hogarth Press, 1925) and 'Women in Scotland' (*Left Review* 2:14, November 1936, pp. 768–70), see M. P. McCulloch (ed.), *Modernism and Nationalism: Literature and Society in Scotland, 1918–1939. Source Documents for the Scottish Renaissance* (Glasgow: Association for Scottish Literary Studies, 2004), pp. 193–219.

32 M. Pittock and I. Jack, 'Patrick Geddes and the Celtic Revival', in S. Manning, I. Brown, T. O. Clancy and M. Pittock (eds), *The Edinburgh History of Scottish Literature*, Vol. 2: *Enlightenment, Britain and Empire (1707–1918)* (Edinburgh: Edinburgh University Press, 2007), pp. 341, 346.

33 R. Davidson, *Dangerous Liaisons: A Social History of Venereal Disease in Twentieth-Century Scotland* (Amsterdam: Rodopi, 2000), p. 149.

34 S. Koven, *Slumming: Sexual and Social Politics in Victorian London* (Princeton, NJ: Princeton University Press, 2006), p. 22.

35 Lily Bell, 'Matrons and Maidens', *Labour Leader*, 1 December 1894, p. 7.

Select bibliography

Archival sources

British Library
    Papers of Elizabeth Wolstenholme Elmy
Library and Museum of Freemasonry
    Papers of the Hermetic Order of the Golden Dawn
Mitchell Library, Glasgow
    Strathclyde Regional Archives, Cathcart Parish School Board Records
National Library of Scotland [NLS]
    Papers of the Independent Labour Party: Francis Johnson Correspondence [FJC]
    Papers of Patrick Geddes
    Papers of John S. Clarke
University College London
    Papers of Karl Pearson
University of Edinburgh Special Collections
    Papers of Patrick Geddes
University of Glasgow Special Collections
    Papers of the Glasgow Ruskin Society
    Papers of Robert Franklin Muirhead
University of Liverpool Special Collections
    Papers of John Bruce Glasier
University of Strathclyde Special Collections [UofS]
    Papers of Patrick Geddes
The Women's Library, London School of Economics and Political Science
    Papers of Teresa Billington-Greig
    Oral history interviews with Helen Moyes
Columbia University Rare Book and Manuscript Library
    Papers of Thomas Lake Harris
North Bay Regional and Special Collections, Sonoma State University
    Gaye LeBaron Digital Collection

Newspapers and periodicals

Aberdeen Weekly Journal
Academy
Adult
Bailie
Barr's Monthly Professional and Author's Journal
Blackwood's Edinburgh Magazine
British Medical Journal
Caledonian Mercury

Contemporary Review
Eugenic Review
Evening Citizen, Glasgow
Evergreen
Fortnightly Review
Forward
Freewoman
Glasgow Evening News
Glasgow Herald
Glasgow Weekly Mail
Labour Leader
Light and Life
Longman's Magazine
Lucifer
Manchester Guardian
Medium and Daybreak
Nature
New Church Life
Nineteenth Century
North British Daily Mail
Pall Mall Gazette
Pall Mall Magazine
Path
Popular Science Monthly
Professional and Authors' Journal
Punch
Saturday Review
Scotsman
Scots Observer
Scottish Geographical Magazine
Scottish Leader
Sociological Review
Spiritual Magazine
To-day: Monthly Magazine of Scientific Socialism
Yorkshireman
Westminster Review
Women's Penny Paper

Printed primary sources

Alexander, John, *Thirty Years' History of the Church and Congregation in Prince's Street Chapel, Norwich* (Norwich: Fletcher and Jarrold, 1847)

Allen, Grant, 'Plain words on the Woman Question', *Popular Science Monthly*, 36 (1889), pp. 448–58

SELECT BIBLIOGRAPHY

Besant, Annie, 'Mysticism, true and false', *Lucifer*, 15 November 1891, pp. 177–81

Bray, Charles, *Phases of Opinion and Experience during a Long Life: An Autobiography* (London: Longmans, Green and Co., 1884)

Brockway, Fenner, *Socialism Over Sixty Years: The Life of Jowett of Bradford* (London: George Allen and Unwin, 1946)

Brotherton, Edward, *Spiritualism, Swedenborg and the New Church: An Examination of Claims* (London: William White, 1860)

Burd, Van Akin (ed.), *Christmas Story: John Ruskin's Venetian Letters of 1876-7* (Cranbury, NJ: Associated University Presses, 1990)

Carpenter, Edward, *Love's Coming of Age: A Series of Papers on the Relations Between the Sexes* (Manchester: The Labour Press, 1896)

Clapperton, Jane Hume, 'Agnosticism and women: a reply', *Nineteenth Century*, 7:39 (May 1880), pp. 840–4

Clapperton, Jane Hume, 'The agnostic at church. II', *Nineteenth Century*, 11:62 (April 1882), pp. 653–6

Clapperton, Jane Hume, *Scientific Meliorism and the Evolution of Happiness* (London: Kegan Paul, Trench & Co., 1885)

Clapperton, Jane Hume, *Margaret Dunmore: Or, A Socialist Home* (London: Swan Sonnenschein, 1888)

Clapperton, Jane Hume, 'Some Evolutional Aspects of the Woman Movement' (S. I.: June 1899)

Clapperton, Jane Hume, 'What do we women want?' (W. H. Reynolds, u.d. [1900])

Clapperton, Jane Hume, *A Vision of the Future based on the Application of Ethical Principles* (London: Swan Sonnenschein, 1904)

Coleman, Helen C., *Prince's Street Congregational Church, Norwich 1819-1919* (London: Jarrolds, 1919)

Cook, Edward Tyas, *The Life of John Ruskin*, Vol. 2: *1860-1900* (London: G. Allen, 1911)

Cuthbert, Arthur A., *The Life and World-Work of Thomas Lake Harris: Written from Direct Personal Knowledge* (Glasgow: C. W. Pearce, 1908)

Darwin, Charles, *The Descent of Man, and Selection in Relation to Sex*, 2 vols. (London: John Murray, 1871, 1901)

Drummond, Henry, *The Lowell Lectures on the Ascent of Man* (London: Hodder & Stoughton, 1894)

Du Maurier, George, *Trilby* (London: Osgood, McIlvaine, 1894)

Ellis, Henry Havelock, *The New Spirit* (London: Walter Scott, [1890])

Ellis, Henry Havelock, *Man and Woman: A Study of Human Sexual Secondary Characters* (London: Walter Scott, 1894)

Emerson, Mary S., *Among the Chosen* (New York: Henry Holt, 1884)

Eyre-Todd, George, 'Leaves from a life. V. – The genius of the outlook tower', *Scots Observer*, 20 August 1931

Fawcett, Millicent Garrett, 'The appeal against female suffrage: a reply', *Nineteenth Century*, 26 (July 1889), pp. 86–96

Finot, Jean, *Problems of the Sexes*, trans. Mary J. Safford (New York: G. P. Putnam's Sons, 1913)

SELECT BIBLIOGRAPHY

Gaskell, Ellen, *A Woman's View of Genesis* (London: Advance Press, 1905)

Gaskell, Ellen, 'The unspeakable', *Freewoman*, 1:9, 18 January 1912

Gaskell, George Arthur, 'The Futility of Pecuniary Thrift as a Means to General Wellbeing' (London: R. Forder, 1890)

Gaskell, George Arthur, 'Social Control of the Birth-rate and Endowment of Mothers' (London: Freethought Publishing Company, 1890)

Gaskell, George Arthur, 'What the "Fire Elemental" told us', *Theosophical Review*, 33:196 (15 December 1903), pp. 347–54

Gaskell, George Arthur, 'What some "Devas" told us', *Theosophical Review*, 34:200 (15 April 1904), pp. 110–21

Geddes, Patrick, 'Further researches on animals containing chlorophyll', *Nature*, 25 (1882), pp. 303–5

Geddes, Patrick, 'Theory of growth, reproduction, sex, and heredity', *Proceedings of the Royal Society of* Edinburgh (1884–1886), 13:911–31

Geddes, Patrick, 'Reproduction', in *Encylopaedia Britannica*, 9th edn, 24 vols, vol. 20 (Edinburgh: A. & C. Black, 1888), pp. 407–22

Geddes, Patrick, 'Sex', in *Encylopaedia Britannica*, 9th edn, 24 vols, vol. 21 (Edinburgh: A. & C. Black, 1888), pp. 720–5

Geddes, Patrick, 'Mr. Francis Galton on natural inheritance', *Scottish Leader*, 14 March 1890

Geddes, Patrick, 'A great geographer: Elisée Reclus, 1830–1905', *Scottish Geographical Magazine*, 21:9–10 (September–October 1905), pp. 490–6, 548–55

Geddes, Patrick, and J. Arthur Thomson, *The Evolution of Sex* (London: Walter Scott, 1889)

Geddes, Patrick, and J. Arthur Thomson, 'The moral evolution of sex', *Evergreen* (Summer 1896), pp. 73–85

Geddes, Patrick, and J. Arthur Thomson, *Evolution* (London: Williams and Norgate, 1911)

Geddes, Patrick, and J. Arthur Thomson, *Sex* (London: Williams and Norgate, 1914)

Gilman, Charlotte Perkins, *Women and Economics: A Study of the Economic Relation Between Men and Women as a Factor in Social Evolution* (Boston, MA: Small, Maynard, 1898)

Glasier, J. Bruce, *James Keir Hardie: A Memorial* (Manchester: National Labour Press, 1919)

Haddow, William, *My Seventy Years* (Glasgow: Robert Gibson, 1943)

Hall, G. Stanley, *Adolescence*, 2 vols (New York: D. Appleton, 1904)

Harris, Thomas Lake, *A Lyric of the Morning Land* (New York: Partridge and Brittan, 1854)

Harris, Thomas Lake, *A Lyric of the Golden Age* (Glasgow: John Thomson, 1870)

Harris, Thomas Lake, *The Marriage of Heaven and Earth: Verified Realities* (Glasgow: C. W. Pearce & Co., 1903)

Harris, Thomas Lake, *The Triumph of Life* (Glasgow: C. W. Pearce & Co., 1903)

Harris, Thomas Lake, *Song of Theos: A Trilogy* (Glasgow: C. W. Pearce & Co., 1903)

Hennell, S. S., *Christianity and Infidelity: An Exposition of the Arguments on Both Sides. Arranged According to a Plan Proposed by George Baillie, Esq.* (London: Arthur Hall, Virtue & Co., 1857)

Hennell, S. S., *On the Need of Dogmas in Religion. A Letter to Thomas Scott* (London: Thomas Scott, 1874)

Huxley, T. H., *Lay Sermons, Addresses and Reviews* (New York: D. Appleton, 1871)

Huxley, T. H., 'The struggle for existence: a programme', *Nineteenth Century*, 23:132 (February 1888), pp. 161–80

Huxley, T. H., *Collected Essays*, 9 vols, Vol. 1: *Methods and Results* (London: Macmillan, 1893)

Jackson, Holbrook, *The 1890s: A Review of Art and Ideas at the Close of the Nineteenth Century* (London: Cresset, 1913, 1988)

Knowlton, Charles, *Fruits of Philosophy. An Essay on the Population Question. A New Edition with Notes* (London: Freethought Publishing Company, 1877)

Kropotkin, Peter, *Mutual Aid: A Factor of Evolution* (Harmondsworth: Penguin, 1939)

Liveing, Susan, *A Nineteenth-Century Teacher: John Henry Bridges, M.B., F.R.C.P.* (London: Kegan Paul, Trench, Trubner, 1926)

Lowe, David, *From Pit to Parliament: The Story of the Early Life of James Keir Hardie* (London: Labour Publishing Company, 1923)

Magarey, Susan, Barbara Wall, Mary Lyons and Maryan Beams (eds), *Ever Yours, C. H. Spence: Catherine Helen Spence's An Autobiography, Diary (1894) and Some Correspondence (1894–1910)* (Kent Town, S. Australia: Wakefield Press, 2005)

Mavor, James, *My Windows on the Street of the World*, 2 vols (London: J. M. Dent, 1923)

McCully, Richard, *The Brotherhood of the New Life and Thomas Lake Harris: A History and an Exposition based upon their Printed Works and upon other Published Documents* (Glasgow: John Thompson, 1893)

McPhee, Carol, and Ann FitzGerald, *The Non-Violent Militant. Selected Writings of Teresa Billington-Greig* (London: Routledge, 1987)

Mill, John Stuart, and Harriet Taylor Mill, *Essays on Sex Equality* (Chicago: University of Chicago Press, 1970)

Montefiore, Dora B., *From a Victorian to a Modern* (London: E. Archer, 1927)

Morais, Nina, 'A reply to Miss Hardaker on the Woman Question', *Popular Science Monthly*, 21 (1882), pp. 70–8

Moyes, Helen, *A Woman in a Man's World* (Alpha Books: Sydney, 1971)

Mr. J. Keir Hardie versus Labour Literary Society: A Reply to the Article Signed 'Keir' in the 'Labour Leader' of August, 17th, 1895 (Glasgow: Labour Literature Society, 1895)

Oliphant, Laurence, *Masollam: A Problem of the Period* (Leipzig: Tauchnitz, 1886)

Oliphant, Margaret W., *Memoir of the Life of Laurence Oliphant and of Alice Oliphant, His Wife*, 2 vols (Edinburgh: Blackwood, 1891)

Portrait Album of Who's Who at the International Congress of Women (London: The Gentlewoman, 1899)

Robertson, S. A., 'A Scottish tribute', *Sociological Review* (London: October 1932), p. 395

Rogers, Edmund Dawson, *Life and Experiences of Edmund Dawson Rogers, Spiritualist and Journalist* (London: Office of Light, [1911])

Romanes, George John, 'Mental differences between men and women', *Nineteenth Century*, 21:123 (May 1887), pp. 654–72

Sharp, Elizabeth A., *William Sharp (Fiona Macleod): A Memoir* (London: Heinemann, 1910)

Spence, C. H., *A Week in the Future* (Sydney: Hale & Iremonger, 1987)

Spencer, Herbert, 'A theory of population, deduced from the general law of animal fertility', *Westminster Review*, 57:112 (April 1852), pp. 468–501

Spencer, Herbert, *The Principles of Biology*, 2 vols (London: Williams & Norgate, 1864, 1867)

Spencer, Herbert, 'The study of sociology. IV – preparation in psychology', *Contemporary Review*, 22 (June 1873), pp. 524–32

Spencer, Herbert, 'The comparative psychology of man', *Popular Science Monthly*, 8 (January 1876), pp. 257–69

Stephens, Riccardo, *The Cruciform Mark: The Strange Story of Richard Tregenna, Bachelor of Medicine (Univ.Edin.)* (London: Chatto & Windus, 1896)

Strachey, Ray (ed.), *Religious Fanaticism: Extracts from the Papers of Hannah Whitall Smith* (London: Faber & Gwyer, 1928)

Swan, Annie, *Courtship and Marriage and the Gentle Art of Home Making* (London: Hutchinson & Co., 1894)

Swedenborg, Emanuel, *The Delights of Wisdom concerning Conjugial Love: after which follow the Pleasures of Insanity concerning Scortatory Love*, trans. John Clowes (Amsterdam, 1768; London: R. Hindmarsh, 1794)

Symonds, John Addington, *Memoirs*, ed. Phyllis Grosskurth (1889; London: Hutchison, 1984)

Warren, Rev. Samuel M., *A Compendium of the Theological Writings of Emanuel Swedenborg* (London: The Swedenborg Society, 1896)

The Christian Watt Papers, ed. David Fraser (Edinburgh: Berlinn, 1988)

Whitman, Walt, *Leaves of Grass* (Boston, MA: Thayer and Eldridge, 1860)

Wilson, Edward O. (ed.), *From So Simple a Beginning: The Four Great Books of Charles Darwin* (New York: W. W. Norton, 2006)

Young, Arthur C. (ed.), *The Letters of George Gissing to Eduard Bertz 1887–1903* (London: Constable, 1961)

Zangwill, Israel, 'Without prejudice', *Pall Mall Magazine*, 8:34 (February 1896), pp. 327–9

Secondary sources

Abrams, Lynn, *Myth and Materiality in a Woman's World: Shetland 1800–2000* (Manchester: Manchester University Press, 2005)

Abrams, Lynn, Eleanor Gordon, Deborah Simonton, and Eileen Janes Yeo (eds), *Gender in Scottish History since 1700* (Edinburgh: Edinburgh University Press, 2006)

Alaya, Flavia, *William Sharp – 'Fiona Macleod': 1855–1905* (Cambridge, MA: Harvard University Press, 1970)

Alexander, Wendy, 'Early Glasgow women medical graduates', in Eleanor Gordon and Esther Breitenbach (eds), *The World is Ill-Divided: Women's Work in Scotland in the Nineteenth and Early Twentieth Centuries* (Edinburgh: Edinburgh University Press, 1990)

Ardis, A. *New Women, New Novels: Feminism and Early Modernism* (New Brunswick, NJ: Rutgers University Press, 1990)

Armytage, W. H. G., *Heavens Below: Utopian Experiments in England 1560–1960* (London: Routledge & Kegan Paul, 1961)

Armytage, W. H. G., 'J. C. Kenworthy and the Tolstoyan communities in England', in W. Gareth Jones (ed.), *Tolstoi and Britain* (Oxford: Berg, 1995), pp. 135–51

Aspinwall, Bernard, *Portable Utopia: Glasgow and the United States, 1820–1920* (Aberdeen, Aberdeen University Press, 1984)

SELECT BIBLIOGRAPHY

Bailey, Peter, 'Conspiracies of meaning: music hall and the knowingness of popular culture', *Past and Present*, 144 (August 1994), pp. 138-70

Ballhatchet, Kenneth, *Race, Sex and Class under the Raj: Imperial Attitudes and Policies and Their Critics, 1793-1905* (London: Weidenfeld & Nicolson, 1980)

Barclay, Katie, *Love, Intimacy and Power: Marriage and Patriarchy in Scotland, 1650-1850* (Manchester: Manchester University Press, 2011)

Barkun, Michael, *Crucible of the Millennium: The Burned-Over District of New York in the 1840s* (Syracuse, NY: Syracuse University Press, 1986)

Barr, Allan P., 'Evolutionary science and the Woman Question', *Victorian Literature and Culture*, 20 (1992), pp. 25-54

Barrow, Logie, 'Socialism in eternity: the ideology of plebeian spiritualists, 1853-1913', *History Workshop Journal*, 9:1 (1980), pp. 37-69

Basham, Diana, *The Trial of Woman: Feminism and the Occult Sciences in Victorian Literature and Society* (New York: New York University Press, 1992)

Beaumont, Matthew, 'Socialism and occultism at the fin de siècle: elective affinities', in Tatiana Kontou and Sarah Willburn (eds), *The Ashgate Companion to Nineteenth Century Spiritualism and the Occult* (Farnham: Ashgate, 2012), pp. 165-80

Bell, Susan Groag, and Karen M. Offen (eds), *Women, the Family and Freedom: The Debate in Documents*, Vol. 2. *1880-1950* (Stanford: Stanford University Press, 1983)

Benn, Caroline, *Keir Hardie* (London: Hutchinson, 1992)

Benn, J. Miriam, *The Predicaments of Love* (London: Pluto, 1992)

Bevir, Mark, 'The Labour Church movement, 1891-1902', *Journal of British Studies*, 38:2 (April 1999), pp. 217-45

Bevir, Mark, *The Making of British Socialism* (Princeton, NJ: Princeton University Press, 2011)

Blaikie, Andrew, and P. Gray, 'Archives of abuse and discontent? Presbyterianism and sexual behaviour during the eighteenth and nineteenth centuries', in Liam Kennedy and Robert Morris (eds), *Order and Disorder: Scotland & Ireland, 1600-2001* (Edinburgh: John Donald, 2005), pp. 61-84

Blaikie, Andrew, E. Garrett and R. Davies, 'Migration, living strategies and illegitimate childbearing: a comparison of two Scottish settings, 1871-1881', in Alysa Levene, Samantha Williams and Thomas Nutt (eds), *Illegitimacy in Britain, 1700-1920* (London: Palgrave Macmillan, 2005), pp. 141-67

Blaikie, J. A. D., 'The country and the city: sexuality and social class in Victorian Scotland', in Gerry Kearns and Charles W. J. Withers (eds), *Urbanising Britain: Essays on Class and Community in the Nineteenth Century* (Cambridge: Cambridge University Press, 1991)

Bland, Lucy, *Banishing the Beast: Feminism, Sex and Morality* (London: Penguin 1995, Tauris Parke, 2002)

Bland, Lucy, and Laura Doan (eds), *Sexology in Culture: Labelling Bodies and Desires* (Cambridge: Polity Press, 1998)

Bland, Lucy, and Laura Doan (eds), *Sexology Uncensored: The Documents of Sexual Science* (Cambridge: Polity Press, 1998)

Boardman, Philip, *The Worlds of Patrick Geddes: Biologist, Town Planner, Re-educator, Peace-warrior* (London: Routledge & Kegan Paul, 1978)

Bournelha, Penny, 'Women and the new fiction 1880-1900', in *Thomas Hardy and Women: Sexual Ideology and Narrative Form* (Wisconsin: University of Wisconsin Press, 1985), pp. 63-97

Bowe, Gordon Nicola, and Elizabeth Cumming, *The Arts and Crafts Movements in Dublin and Edinburgh, 1885-1925* (Dublin: Irish Academic Press, 1998)

Boxer, Marilyn J., and Jean H. Quataert (eds), *Socialist Women: European Socialist Feminism in the Nineteenth and Early Twentieth Centuries* (New York: Elsevier, 1978)

Boyd, Kenneth M., *Scottish Church Attitudes to Sex, Marriage and the Family, 1850-1914* (Edinburgh: John Donald, 1980)

Brady, Sean, *Masculinity and Male Homosexuality in Britain* (Basingstoke: Palgrave Macmillan, 2005)

Brake, Laurel, and Marysa Demoor (eds), *Dictionary of Nineteenth-Century Journalism in Great Britain and Ireland* (London: British Library/Academia Press, 2009)

Brandon, Ruth, *The New Women and the Old Men: Love, Sex and the Woman Question* (London: Papermac, 1990)

Briggs, Julia, *A Woman of Passion: The Life of E. Nesbit, 1858-1924* (London: Hutchinson, 1987)

Brown, Callum, and Jayne D. Stephenson, '"Sprouting wings"?: women and religion in Scotland c. 1890-1950', in Eleanor Gordon and Esther Breitenbach (eds), *Out of Bounds: Women in Scottish Society 1800-1945* (Edinburgh: Edinburgh University Press, 1992), pp. 95-120

Brown, Callum G., *Religion and Society in Scotland since 1707* (Edinburgh: Edinburgh University Press, 1997)

Brown, Callum G., *The Death of Christian Britain: Understanding Secularisation, 1800-2000*, 2nd edn (London: Routledge, 2009)

Bullough, Vern L., and Bonnie Bullough, *Cross Dressing, Sex and Gender* (Philadelphia: University of Pennsylvania Press, 1993)

Burgess, Moira, *The Other Voice: Scottish Women's Writing Since 1808: An Anthology* (Edinburgh: Polygon, 1987)

Burkhauser, Jude (ed.), *The Glasgow Girls: Women in Art and Design 1880-1920* (Edinburgh: Canongate, 1990)

Cameron, Anne, 'The establishment of civil registration in Scotland', *The Historical Journal*, 50:2 (June 2007), pp. 377-95

Chajes, Julie, 'Alice and Laurence Oliphant's divine androgyne and "The Woman Question"', *Journal of the American Academy of Religion*, 84:2 (2016), pp. 498-529

Challinor, Ray, *John S. Clarke: Parliamentarian, Poet, Lion-Tamer* (London: Pluto, 1977)

Cheadle, Tanya, 'Music hall, 'mashers' and the 'unco guid': competing masculinities in Victorian Glasgow', in Lynn Abrams and Elizabeth Ewan (eds), *Nine Centuries of Man: Manhood and Masculinities in Scottish History* (Edinburgh: Edinburgh University Press, 2017), pp. 223-41

Checkland, Olive, *Philanthropy in Victorian Scotland: Social Welfare and the Voluntary Principle* (Edinburgh: John Donald, 1980)

Clark, Anna, *The Struggle for the Breeches: Gender and the Making of the British Working Class* (Berkeley: University of California Press, 1995)

Clark, Anna, 'Twilight moments', *Journal of the History of Sexuality*, 14:1/2 (January 2005), pp, 139-60

Clive, Eric M., *The Law of Husband and Wife in Scotland*, 2nd edn (Edinburgh, 1982)
Cockram, Gill G., *Ruskin and Social Reform: Ethics and Economics in the Victorian Age* (London: Tauris Academic Studies, 2007)
Cocks, Harry, '*Calamus* in Bolton: spirituality and homosexual desire in late Victorian England', *Gender & History*, 13:2 (August 2001), pp. 191–223
Cocks, H. G., and Matt Houlbrook (eds), *Palgrave Advances in the Modern History of Sexuality* (Basingstoke: Palgrave Macmillan, 2006)
Collette, Christine, 'Socialism and scandal: the sexual politics of the early labour movement', *History Workshop*, 23 (Spring 1987), pp. 102–11
Conway, Jill, 'Women reformers and American culture, 1870–1930', *Journal of Social History*, 5:2 (Winter 1971/2), pp. 164–77
Conway, Jill, 'Stereotypes of femininity in a theory of sexual evolution', in Martha Vicinus (ed.), *Suffer and Be Still: Women in the Victorian Age* (Bloomington and London: Indiana University Press, 1972), pp. 140–229
Cook, Hera, *The Long Sexual Revolution: English Women, Sex and Contraception 1800–1975* (Oxford: Oxford University Press, 2004)
Cott, Nancy F., 'Passionlessness: an interpretation of Victorian sexual ideology, 1790–1850', *Signs*, 4 (1978), pp. 219–36
Cowman, Krista, '"Incipient Toryism"? The Women's Social and Political Union and the Independent Labour Party, 1903–14', *History Workshop Journal*, 53 (2002), pp. 129–48
Crawford, Elizabeth, *The Women's Suffrage Movement: A Reference Guide, 1866–1928* (London: Routledge, 2001)
Crawford, Elizabeth, *The Women's Suffrage Movement in Britain and Ireland. A Regional Survey* (London and New York: Routledge, 2006)
Cross, Whitney R., *The Burned-Over District: The Social and Intellectual History of Enthusiastic Religion in Western New York, 1800–1850* (New York: Harper & Row, 1965)
Cumming, Elizabeth, 'A "gleam of Renaissance hope": Edinburgh at the turn of the century', in W. Kaplan (ed.), *Scottish Art and Design: 5000 Years* (London: Orion, 1990)
Cumming, Elizabeth, *Hand, Heart and Soul: The Arts and Crafts Movement in Scotland* (Edinburgh: Berlinn, 2006)
Davidoff, Leonore, and Catherine Hall, *Family Fortunes: Men and Women of the English Middle Class, 1780–1850* (Chicago: University of Chicago Press, 1987)
Davidson, Roger, *Dangerous Liaisons: A Social History of Venereal Disease in Twentieth-Century Scotland* (Amsterdam: Rodopi, 2000)
Defries, Amelia, *The Interpreter Geddes: The Man and His Gospel* (London: Routledge, 1927)
Delap, Lucy, *The Feminist Avant-Garde: Transatlantic Encounters of the Early Twentieth Century* (Cambridge: Cambridge University Press, 2007)
Dempsey, Brian, '"By the law of this and every other well governed realm": investigating accusations of sodomy in nineteenth-century Scotland', *Judicial Review* (2006), pp. 103–13
Dempsey, Brian, 'Making the Gretna blacksmith redundant: who worried, who spoke, who was heard on the abolition of irregular marriage in Scotland?', *The Journal of Legal History*, 30:1 (2009)
Deutscher, Penelope, 'The descent of man and the evolution of woman: Antoinette Blackwell, Charlotte Perkins Gilman and Eliza Gamble', *Hypatia*, 19:2 (Spring 2004), pp. 35–55
Devine, T. M., *The Scottish Nation: 1700–2000* (London: Penguin, 1999)

Dinnie, Elizabeth, and Kath Browne, 'Creating a Sexual self in heteronormative space: integrations and imperatives amongst spiritual seekers at the Findhorn Community', *Sociological Research Online*, 16:1 (2011), www.socresonline.org.uk/16/1/7.html (accessed 5 June 2019)

Dixon, Joy, *Divine Feminine: Theosophy and Feminism in England* (Baltimore, MD: Johns Hopkins University Press, 2001)

Dixon, Thomas, *The Invention of Altruism: Making Moral Meanings in Victorian Britain* (Oxford: Oxford University Press, 2008)

Dowling, Linda, 'The decadent and the New Woman in the 1890s', *Nineteenth-Century Fiction*, 33:4 (March 1979), pp. 434–53

Dubois, Ellen Carol, and Linda Gordon, 'Seeking ecstasy on the battlefield: danger and pleasure in nineteenth-century feminist sexual thought', *Feminist Studies*, 9:1 (Spring 1983), pp. 7–25

Dugatkin, Lee Alan, 'Survival of the nicest: the quest for a biological explanation for "altruism is intricately linked to our ideas of goodness. No wonder biologists have taken it personally"', *New Scientist*, 192:2577 (November 2006)

Eagles, Stuart, *After Ruskin: The Social and Political Legacies of a Victorian Prophet, 1870–1920* (Oxford: Oxford University Press, 2011)

Eagleton, Terry, 'The flight to the real', in Sally Ledger and Scott McCracken (eds), *Cultural Politics at the Fin de Siècle* (Cambridge: Cambridge University Press, 1995), pp. 11–21

Eunson, Eric, *The Gorbals: An Illustrated History* (Catrine: Richard Stenlake Publishing, 1996)

Ewan, Elizabeth, Sue Innes, Siân Reynolds and Rose Pipes (eds), *The Biographical Dictionary of Scottish Women* (Edinburgh: Edinburgh University Press, 2006)

Ewan, Elizabeth, Rose Pipes, Jane Rendall and Siân Reynolds (eds), *The New Biographical Dictionary of Scottish Women* (Edinburgh: Edinburgh University Press, 2017)

Faderman, Lillian, *Scotch Verdict: Miss Pirie and Miss Woods v. Dame Cumming Gordon* (New York: Columbia University Press, 1993)

Fagley, Richard M., 'A Protestant view of population control', *Law and Contemporary Problems*, 25 (1960), pp. 470–89

Federico, Annette R., *Idol of Suburbia: Marie Corelli and Late-Victorian Literary Culture* (Charlottesville: University Press of Virginia, 2000)

Fichman, Martin, 'Biology and politics: defining the boundaries', in Bernard Lightman (ed.), *Victorian Science in Context* (Chicago: University of Chicago Press, 1997), pp. 94–118

Fissell, Mary, 'Gender and generation: representing reproduction in early modern England', *Gender & History*, 7:3 (November 1995), pp. 433–56

Foster, Lawrence, *Religion and Sexuality: The Shakers, the Mormons, and the Oneida Communities* (Champaign: University of Illinois Press, 1984)

Foster, Roy, *Vivid Faces: The Revolutionary Generation in Ireland 1890–1923* (London: Penguin, 2014)

Foucault, Michel, *The History of Sexuality*, Vol. 1: *An Introduction*, trans. Robert Hurley (1976; London: Penguin, 1990)

Friedman, Geraldine, 'School for scandal: sexuality, race and national vice and virtue in *Miss Marianne Woods and Miss Jane Pirie Against Lady Helen Cumming Gordon*', *Nineteenth-Century Contexts*, 27:1 (2005), pp. 53–76

Frost, Ginger, *Living in Sin: Cohabiting as Husband and Wife in Nineteenth-Century England* (Manchester: Manchester University Press, 2008)
Fryer, Peter, *The Birth Controllers* (New York: Stein and Day, 1965)
Gifford, Douglas, and Dorothy Macmillan (eds), *A History of Scottish Women's Writing* (Edinburgh: Edinburgh University Press, 1997)
Gilbert, R. A., *The Golden Dawn Companion: A Guide to the History, Structure and Workings of the Hermetic Order of the Golden Dawn* (Wellingborough: Aquarian, 1986)
Gordon, Eleanor, *Women and the Labour Movement in Scotland, 1850–1914* (Oxford: Clarendon Press, 1991)
Gordon, Eleanor, 'Irregular marriage and cohabitation in Scotland, 1855–1939: official policy and popular practice', *The Historical Journal*, 58:4 (2015), pp. 1059–79
Gordon, Eleanor, and Gwyneth Nair, *Public Lives: Women, Family and Society in Victorian Britain* (New Haven, CT: Yale University Press, 2003)
Gordon, Eleanor, and Gwyneth Nair, *Murder and Morality in Victorian Britain: The Study of Madeleine Smith* (Manchester: Manchester University Press, 2009)
Griffith, Freda G., *The Swedenborg Society 1810–1960* (London: Swedenborg Society, 1960)
Hall, Lesley A., 'The next generation: Stella Browne, the New Woman as freewoman', in Angelique Richardson and Chris Willis (eds), *The New Woman in Fiction and in Fact: Fin-de-Siècle Feminisms* (Basingstoke: Palgrave Macmillan, 2001)
Hall, Lesley A., *Sex, Gender and Social Change in Britain Since 1880*, 2nd edn (London: Palgrave Macmillan, 2013)
Hall, Lesley A., 'Hauling down the double standard: feminism, social purity and sexual science in late nineteenth-century Britain', *Gender & History*, 16:1 (2004), pp. 36–56
Hall, Lesley A., *Outspoken Women: An Anthology of Women's Writing on Sex, 1870–1969* (London: Routledge, 2005)
Hamilton, Sheila, 'The first generation of university women, 1869–1930', in Gordon Donaldson (ed.), *Four Centuries: Edinburgh University life 1583–1983* (Edinburgh: Edinburgh University Press, 1983), pp. 99–115
Hammerton, A. James, *Cruelty and Companionship: Conflict in Nineteenth-Century Married Life* (London: Routledge, 1992)
Hannam, June, '"In the comradeship of the sexes lies the hope of progress and social regeneration": women in the West Riding ILP, c. 1890–1914', in Jane Rendall (ed.), *Equal or Different: Women's Politics, 1800–1914* (Oxford: Blackwell, 1987), pp. 214–38
Hannam, June, *Isabella Ford* (Oxford: Basil Blackwell, 1989)
Hannam, June, 'Women and the ILP, 1890–1914', in David James, Tony Jowitt and Keith Laybourn (eds), *The Centennial History of the Independent Labour Party* (Halifax: Ryburn, 1992), pp. 205–28
Hannam, June, 'Women as paid organizers and propagandists for the British Labour Party between the wars', *International Labour and Working-class History*, 77 (Spring 2010), pp. 69–88
Hannam, June, 'Review, *The Newer Eve: Women, Feminists and the Labour Party*', *Contemporary British History*, 25:2 (2011), pp. 336–8

SELECT BIBLIOGRAPHY

Hannam, June, and Karen Hunt, 'Propagandising as socialist women', in Bertrand Taithe and Tim Thornton (eds), *Propaganda: Political Rhetoric and Systems of Belief* (Stroud: Sutton Publishing, 1999)

Hannam, June, and Karen Hunt, *Socialist Women: Britain, 1880s to 1920s* (London: Routledge, 2002)

Hardy, Dennis, *Alternative Communities in Nineteenth Century England* (London: Longman, 1979)

Harvey, Karen, 'The substance of sexual difference: change and persistence in representations of the body in eighteenth century England', *Gender & History*, 14:2 (August 2002), pp. 202–23

Helland, Janice, 'Francis Macdonald: the self as fin de siècle woman', *Woman's Art Journal*, 14:1 (1993), pp. 15–22

Helland, Janice, *The Studios of Francis and Margaret Mackintosh* (Manchester: Manchester University Press, 1996)

Helland, Janice, *Professional Women Painters in Nineteenth-Century Scotland: Commitment, Friendship, Pleasure* (Aldershot: Ashgate, 2000)

Helmstadter, Richard J., and Bernard Lightman (eds), *Victorian Faith in Crisis: Essays on Continuity and Change in Nineteenth-Century Religious Belief* (Stanford, CA: Stanford University Press, 1990).

Hine, Robert V., *California's Utopian Colonies* (New Haven, CT: Yale University, 1966)

Hoggart, Lesley, 'The campaign for birth control in Britain in the 1920s', in Anne Digby and John Stewart (eds), *Gender, Health and Welfare* (London: Routledge, 1996)

Holman, M. J. de K, 'The Purleigh Colony: Tolstoyan togetherness in the late 1890s', in Malcolm Jones (ed.), *New Essays on Tolstoy* (Cambridge: Cambridge University Press, 1978), pp. 194–222

Holton, Sandra Stanley, *Feminism and Democracy: Women's Suffrage and Reform Politics in Britain, 1900–1918* (Cambridge: Cambridge University Press, 1986)

Holton, Sandra Stanley, 'Free love and Victorian feminism: the divers matrimonials of Elizabeth Wolstenholme Elmy and Ben Elmy', *Victorian Studies*, 37:2 (Winter 1994), pp. 199–222

Holton, Sandra Stanley, *Suffrage Days: Stories from the Women's Suffrage Movement* (London: Routledge, 1996)

Howe, Ellic, *The Magicians of the Golden Dawn: A Documentary History of a Magical Order, 1887–1923* (London: Routledge & Kegan Paul, 1972)

Hughes, Annmarie, *Gender and Political Identities in Scotland, 1919–1939* (Edinburgh: Edinburgh University Press, 2010)

Hughes, Annmarie, 'The "non-criminal" class: wife-beating in Scotland, c. 1800–1949', *Crime, History & Societies*, 14:2 (2010), pp. 31–53

Hunt, Karen, *Equivocal Feminists: The Social Democratic Federation and the Woman Question, 1884–1911* (Cambridge: Cambridge University Press, 1996)

Hunt, Karen, 'Censorship and self-censorship: revisiting the Belt case in the making of Dora Montefiore (1851–1933)', *19: Interdisciplinary Studies in the Long Nineteenth Century*, 27 (2018), pp. 1–22

Ingram, Angela, and Daphne Patai (eds), *Rediscovering Forgotten Radicals: British Women Writers, 1889–1939* (Chapel Hill: University of North Carolina Press, 1993)

Ittmann, Karl, *Work, Gender and Family in Victorian England* (Basingstoke: Palgrave Macmillan, 1995)

Jackson, Margaret, *The Real Facts of Life: Feminism and the Politics of Sexuality, c. 1850–1940* (Abingdon: Taylor & Francis, 1994)

Jann, Rosemary, 'Revising the descent of woman: Eliza Burt Gamble', in Barbara T. Gates and Ann B. Shteir (eds), *Natural Eloquence: Women Reinscribe Science* (Madison: University of Wisconsin Press, 1997), pp. 147–63

Jeffreys, Sheila, *The Spinster and Her Enemies: Feminism and Sexuality, 1880–1930* (London: Pandora, 1985)

Johnson, Jim, and Lou Rosenberg, *Renewing Old Edinburgh: The Enduring Legacy of Patrick Geddes* (Glendaruel: Argyll, 2010)

Jones, Claire G., *Femininity, Mathematics and Science, 1880–1914* (Basingstoke: Palgrave Macmillan, 2009)

Kagan, Paul, *New World Utopias: A Photographic History of the Search for Community* (New York: Penguin, 1975)

Kalsem, Kristin B., 'Law, literature and libel: Victorian censorship of "dirty filthy" books on birth control', *William and Mary Journal of Women and the Law*, 10:3 (Spring 2004), pp. 533–68

Kelvin, Norman (ed.), *William Morris on Art and Socialism* (Toronto: Dover, 1999)

Kent, Susan Kingsley, *Sex and Suffrage in Britain, 1860–1914* (Princeton, NJ: Princeton University Press, 1987)

Kern, Louis J., *An Ordered Love: Sex Roles and Sexuality in Victorian Utopias: The Shakers, the Mormons and the Oneida Community* (Chapel Hill: University of North Carolina Press, 1981)

King, Elspeth, 'The Scottish women's suffrage movement', in Eleanor Gordon and Esther Breitenbach (eds), *Out of Bounds: Women in Scottish Society 1800–1945* (Edinburgh: Edinburgh University Press, 1992), pp. 121–50

King, Elspeth, *The Hidden History of Glasgow's Women* (Edinburgh: Mainstream Publishing, 1993)

Kitchen, Paddy, *A Most Unsettling Person: An Introduction to the Ideas and Life of Patrick Geddes* (London: Victor Gollancz, 1975)

Koven, Seth, *Slumming: Sexual and Social Politics in Victorian London* (Princeton, NJ: Princeton University Press, 2004)

Laqueur, Thomas, *Making Sex: Body and Gender from the Greeks to Freud* (Cambridge, MA: Harvard University Press, 1990)

Laybourn, Keith, *The Rise of Socialism in Britain c. 1881–1951* (Stroud: Sutton Publishing, 1997)

LeBaron, Gaye, 'Serpent in Eden: the final utopia of Thomas Lake Harris and what happened there', *The Markham Review*, 4 (February 1969), pp. 14–24

Ledbetter, R., *A History of the Malthusian League 1877–1927* (Columbus: Ohio State University Press, 1976)

Ledger, Sally, *The New Woman: Fiction and Feminism at the Fin de Siècle* (Manchester: Manchester University Press, 1997)

Ledger, Sally, and Scott McCracken, *Cultural Politics at the Fin de Siècle* (Cambridge: Cambridge University Press, 1995)

Ledger, Sally, and Roger Luckhurst (eds), *The Fin de Siècle: A Reader in Cultural History, c.1880–1900* (Oxford: Oxford University Press, 2000)

Ledger-Lomas, Michael, '"Glimpses of the great conflict": English Congregationalists and the European crisis of faith, circa 1840–1875', *Journal of British Studies*, 46:4 (October 2007), pp. 826–60

Leneman, Leah, *The Hidden History of Glasgow's Women: The THENEW Factor* (Edinburgh: Mainstream, 1993)

Leneman, Leah, *A Guid Cause: The Women's Suffrage Movement in Scotland* (Edinburgh: Mercat Press, 1995)

Leneman, Leah, *The Scottish Suffragettes* (Edinburgh: NMS Publishing Ltd, 2000)

Littlewood, Barbara, and Linda Mahood, 'Prostitutes, magdalenes and wayward girls: dangerous sexualities of working-class women in Victorian Scotland', *Gender & History*, 3:2 (1991), pp. 160–75

Livesey, Ruth, *Socialism, Sex, and the Culture of Aestheticism in Britain, 1880–1914* (Oxford: Oxford University Press, 2007)

Lloyd, Trevor, 'Morris v. Hyndman "Commonweal" and "Justice"', *Victorian Periodicals Newsletter*, 9:4 (December 1976), pp. 119–28

Macdonald, Murdo, 'Patrick Geddes', *The Edinburgh Review*, 88 (1992), pp. 113–19

Macdonald, Murdo, 'Celticism and internationalism in the circle of Patrick Geddes', *Visual Culture in Britain*, 6:2 (2005), pp. 70–83

Mahood, Linda, *The Magdalenes: Prostitution in the Nineteenth Century* (London: Routledge, 1990)

Mairet, Philip, *Pioneer of Sociology: The Life and Letters of Patrick Geddes* (London: Lund Humphries, 1957)

Maltz, Diana, 'Living by design: C. R. Ashbee's Guild of Handicraft and two English Tolstoyan Communities, 1897–1907', *Victorian Literature and Culture*, 39 (2011), pp. 409–26

Maltz, Diana, 'Ardent service: female eroticism and new life ethics in Gertrude Dix's *The Image Breakers* (1900)', *Journal of Victorian Culture* (2012), pp. 1–17

Maltz, Diana, 'The newer new life: A. S. Byatt, E. Nesbit and socialist subculture', *Journal of Victoria Culture*, 17:1 (2012), pp. 79–84

Mangum, Teresa, *Married, Middlebrow and Militant: Sarah Grand and the New Woman Novel* (Ann Arbor: University of Michigan Press, 1998)

Manton, Kevin, 'Establishing the fellowship: Harry Lowerison and the Ruskin School Home, a turn-of-the-century socialist and his educational experiment', *Journal of the History of Education Society*, 26:1 (1997), pp. 53–70

Manton, Kevin, 'The Fellowship of the New Life: English ethical socialism reconsidered', *History of Political Thought*, 24:2 (Summer 2003), pp. 282–304

Marshall, Ian, and Ronald Smith, *Queen's Park Historical Guide and Heritage Walk* (Glasgow: Glasgow City Council, 1997)

Mason, Michael, *The Making of Victorian Sexual Attitudes* (Oxford: Oxford University Press, 1994)

Mason, Michael, *The Making of Victorian Sexuality* (Oxford: Oxford University Press, 1995)

McCall, Alison, 'The poetry and life of Bessie Craigmyle (1863–1933), the Sappho of Strawberry Bank', *Aberdeen University Review*, 61 (2005), pp. 109–21

McCulloch, Margery Palmer, 'Fictions of development 1920-1970', in Douglas Gifford and Dorothy McMillan (eds), *A History of Scottish Women's Writing* (Edinburgh: Edinburgh University Press, 1997), pp. 360-72

McCulloch, Margery Palmer (ed.), *Modernism and Nationalism: Literature and Society in Scotland, 1918-1939. Source Documents for the Scottish Renaissance* (Glasgow: Association for Scottish Literary Studies, 2004)

McCulloch, Margery Palmer, 'Interwar literature', in Glenda Norquay (ed.), *The Edinburgh Companion to Scottish Women's Writing* (Edinburgh: Edinburgh University Press, 2012), pp. 103-12

McDermid, Jane, *The School of Working-Class Girls in Victorian Scotland: Gender, Education and Identity* (London: Routledge, 2005)

McDermid, Jane, 'School Board women and active citizenship in Scotland, 1873-1919', *History of Education*, 38:3 (May 2009), pp. 333-47

McKinlay, Alan, and R. J. Morris (eds), *The ILP on Clydeside, 1893-1932: From Foundation to Integration* (Manchester: Manchester University Press, 1991)

McLaren, Angus, *Birth Control in Nineteenth-Century England* (New York: Holmes & Meier, 1978)

Meek, Jeffrey, *Queer Voices in Post-War Scotland* (Basingstoke: Palgrave Macmillan, 2015)

Meller, Helen, *Patrick Geddes: Social Evolutionist and City Planner* (London: Routledge, 1990)

Meyers, Terry L., *The Sexual Tensions of William Sharp: A Study of the Birth of Fiona Macleod, Incorporating Two Lost Works, 'Ariadne in Naxos' and 'Beatrice'* (New York: Peter Lang, 1996)

Milam, Erika L., *Looking for a Few Good Males: Female Choice in Evolutionary Biology* (Baltimore, MD: Johns Hopkins University Press, 2010), pp. 24-5

Moore, Lindy, *Bajanellas and Semilinas: Aberdeen University and the Education of Women 1860-1920* (Aberdeen: Aberdeen University Press, 1991)

Morgan, Kenneth O., *Keir Hardie: Radical and Socialist* (London: Weidenfeld & Nicolson, 1975)

Morgan, Kenneth O., *Labour People* (Oxford: Oxford University Press, 1987)

Mort, Frank, *Dangerous Sexualities: Medico-moral Politics in England Since 1830*, 2nd edn (London: Routledge, 2000)

Mosedale, Susan Sleeth, 'Science corrupted: Victorian biologists consider "The Woman Question"', *Journal of the History of Biology*, 11:1 (Spring 1978), pp. 1-55

Nottingham, Chris, *The Pursuit of Serenity: Havelock Ellis and the New Politics* (Amsterdam: Amsterdam University Press, 1999)

Oppenheim, Janet, *The Other World: Spiritualism and Psychical Research in England, 1850-1914* (Cambridge: Cambridge University Press, 1985)

Oram, Alison, and Annmarie Turnbull, *Lesbian History Sourcebook* (London: Routledge, 2001)

Orr, Lesley Macdonald, *A Unique and Glorious Mission: Women and Presbyterianism in Scotland: 1830-1930* (Edinburgh: John Donald, 2000)

Owen, Alex, *The Darkened Room: Women, Power and Spiritualism in Late Victorian England* (London: Virago, 1989)

SELECT BIBLIOGRAPHY

Owen, Alex, *The Place of Enchantment: British Occultism and the Culture of the Modern* (Chicago: University of Chicago, 2004)

Parkins, Wendy, 'Domesticating socialism and the senses in Jane Hume Clapperton's *Margaret Dunmore: Or, A Socialist Home*', *Victoriographies*, 1:2 (2011), pp. 261–86

Pedersen, Jane Elisabeth, 'Sexual politics in Comte and Durkheim: feminism, history and the French sociological tradition', *Signs*, 27:1 (2001), pp. 229–63

Pickering, Mary, 'Angles and demons in the moral vision of Auguste Comte', *Journal of Women's History*, 8:2 (Summer 1996), pp. 10–40

Pittock, Murray, and Isla Jack, 'Patrick Geddes and the Celtic revival', in Susan Manning, Ian Brown, Thomas Owen Clancy and Murray Pittock (eds), *The Edinburgh History of Scottish Literature*, Vol. 2: *Enlightenment, Britain and Empire, 1707–1918* (Edinburgh: Edinburgh University Press, 2007), pp. 338–46

Pollock, Griselda, 'Feminism/Foucault – surveillance/sexuality', in Norman Bryson, Michael A. Holly and Keith Moxey (eds), *Visual Culture: Images and Interpretations* (Hanover, NH: Wesleyan University Press, 1994), pp. 1–41

Porter, Roy, and Mikulas Teich (eds), *Sexual Knowledge, Sexual Science: The History of Attitudes to Sexuality* (Cambridge: Cambridge University Press, 1994)

Pugh, Martin, *Women and the Women's Movement in Britain: 1914–1999* (Basingstoke: Palgrave Macmillan, 2000)

Rabinow, Paul (ed.), *The Foucault Reader* (London: Penguin, 1984)

Rafeek, Neil C., *Communist Women in Scotland: Red Clydeside from the Russian Revolution to the End of the Soviet Union* (London: Tauris, 2008)

Renwick, Chris, 'The practice of Spencerian science: Patrick Geddes's biosocial programme, 1876–1889', *Isis*, 100:1 (March 2009), pp. 36–57

Renwick, Chris, *British Sociology's Lost Biological Roots: A History of Futures Past* (Basingstoke: Palgrave Macmillan, 2012)

Reynolds, Siân, *Paris–Edinburgh: Cultural Connections in the Belle Epoque* (Aldershot: Ashgate, 2007)

Richardson, Angelique, *Love and Eugenics in the Late Nineteenth Century: Rational Reproduction and the New Woman* (Oxford: Oxford University Press, 2003)

Richardson, Angelique, and Chris Willis (eds), *The New Woman in Fiction and Fact: Fin de siècle Feminisms*, foreword by Lyn Pykett (Basingstoke: Palgrave Macmillan, 2002)

Rix, Robert, 'William Blake, Thomas Thorild and radical Swedenborgianism', *Nordic Journal of English Studies*, 2:1 (2003), pp. 97–128

Rix, Robert, *William Blake and the Cultures of Radical Christianity* (Aldershot: Ashgate, 2007)

Robb, George, 'Eugenics, spirituality and sex differentiation in Edwardian England: the case of Francis Swiney', *Journal of Women's History*, 10:3 (Autumn 1998), pp. 97–117

Rodger, Richard, *The Transformation of Edinburgh: Land, Property and Trust in the Nineteenth Century* (Cambridge: Cambridge University Press, 2001)

Roper, Michael, 'Slipping out of view: subjectivity and emotion in gender history', *History Workshop Journal*, 59, pp. 57–72

Rowbotham, Sheila, *Edward Carpenter: A Life of Liberty and Love* (London: Verso, 2008)

Rowbotham, Sheila, *Dreamers of a New Day: Women who Invented the Twentieth Century* (London: Verso, 2010)

Rowbotham, Sheila, *Rebel Crossings: New Women, Free Lovers and Radicals in Britain and the United States* (London: Verso, 2016)

Rowbotham, Sheila, and Jeffrey Weeks, *Socialism and the New Life: The Personal and Sexual Politics of Edward Carpenter and Havelock Ellis* (Pluto, 1977)

Russett, Cynthia Eagle, *Sexual Science: The Victorian Construction of Womanhood* (Cambridge, MA: Harvard University Press, 1989)

Schiebinger, Londa, *The Mind Has No Sex?: Women in the Origins of Modern Science* (Cambridge, MA and London: Harvard University Press, 1989)

Schiebinger, Londa, *Nature's Body: Gender in the Making of Modern Science* (Boston, MA: Beacon, 1993)

Schmidt, Leigh, *Heaven's Bride: The Unprintable Life of Ida C. Craddock: American Mystic, Scholar, Sexologist, Martyr and Madwoman* (New York: Basic Books, 2010)

Schneider, Herbert W., and George Lawton, *A Prophet and a Pilgrim: Being the Incredible History of Thomas Lake Harris and Laurence Oliphant; Their Sexual Mysticisms and Utopian Communities Amply Documented to Confound the Skeptic* (New York: Columbia University Press, 1942)

Schwartz, Laura, *Infidel Feminism: Secularism, Religion and Women's Emancipation, England 1830–1914* (Manchester: Manchester University Press, 2013)

Searby, P. 'The new school and the new life: Cecil Reddie (1858–1932) and the early years of Abbotsholme School', *History of Education*, 18:1 (1989), pp. 1–21

Seidman, Steven, 'The power of desire and the danger of pleasure: Victorian sexuality reconsidered', *Journal of Social History*, 24:1 (Autumn 1990), pp. 47–67

Settle, Louise, *Sex for Sale: Prostitution in Edinburgh and Glasgow, 1900–1939* (Edinburgh: Edinburgh University Press, 2016)

Shields, Stephanie A., 'The variability hypothesis: the history of a biological model of sex differences in intelligence', *Signs*, 7:4 (Summer, 1982), pp. 769–97

Showalter, Elaine, *Sexual Anarchy: Gender and Culture at the Fin de Siècle* (New York: Viking, 1990)

Shuttleworth, Sally, 'Review of *Making Sex: Body and Gender from the Greeks to Freud*', *Journal of the History of Sexuality*, 3:4 (1993), pp. 633–5

Slade, Joseph W., 'Historical sketch of Thomas Lake Harris, Laurence Oliphant and the Brotherhood of the New Life', in Jack T. Ericson (ed.), *Thomas Lake Harris and the Brotherhood of the New Life. Books, pamphlets, serials and manuscripts 1854–1942. A Guide to the Microfilm Edition* (Glen Rock, NJ: Microfilming Corporation of America, 1974)

Smith, Leonard, 'Religion and the ILP', in David James, Tony Jowitt and Keith Laybourn (eds), *The Centennial History of the Independent Labour Party* (Halifax: Ryburn, 1992)

Smith, Norah, 'Sexual mores and attitudes in Enlightenment Scotland', in Paul-Gabriel Boucé (ed.), *Sexuality in Eighteenth-Century Britain* (Manchester: Manchester University Press, 1982)

Smitley, Megan K., *The Feminine Public Sphere: Middle-Class Women and Civic Life in Scotland: 1870–1914* (Manchester: Manchester University Press, 2009)

Soloway, Richard A., *Birth Control and the Population Question in England, 1877–1930* (London: University of North Carolina Press, 1982)

Spurlock, John C., *Free Love: Marriage and Middle-Class Radicalism in America, 1825–1860* (New York: New York University Press, 1988)

Steedman, Carolyn, *Childhood, Culture and Class in Britain: Margaret McMillan 1860–1931* (London: Virago, 1990)

Stepan, Nancy Leys, 'Race and gender: the role of analogy in science', *Isis*, 77:2 (June 1986), pp. 261–77

Stevens, Carolyn, 'The objections of "Queer Hardie", "Lily Bell" and the Suffragettes' Friend to Queen Victoria's Jubilee, 1897', *Victorian Periodicals Review*, 21:3 (1988), pp. 108–14

Stoehr, Taylor, *Free Love in America: A Documentary History* (New York: AMS Press, 1979)

Suksand, D. 'Equal partnership: Jane Hume Clapperton's evolutionist-socialist utopia', *Utopia Studies*, 3:1 (1992), pp. 95–107

Sullivan, Alvin (ed.), *British Literary Magazines: The Victorian and Edwardian Age, 1837–1913* (London: Greenwood Press, 1984)

Sutcliffe, Steven, 'The quest for composure in the "post-Presbyterian" self', in Callum Brown and Lynn Abrams (eds), *A History of Everyday Life in Twentieth Century Scotland* (Edinburgh: Edinburgh University Press, 2010)

Sydie, R. A., 'Sex and the sociological fathers', *Canadian Review of Sociology and Anthropology*, 31:2 (1994), pp. 117–38

Szreter, Simon, *Fertility, Class and Gender in Britain, 1860–1940* (Cambridge: Cambridge University Press, 1996)

Szreter, Simon, 'Victorian Britain, 1831–1963: towards a social history of sexuality', *Journal of Victorian Culture*, 1:1 (1996), pp. 136–49

Taylor, Anne, *Laurence Oliphant: 1829–1888* (Oxford: Oxford University Press, 1982)

Taylor, Barbara, *Eve and the New Jerusalem: Socialism and Feminism in the Nineteenth Century* (London: Virago, 1983)

Thompson, Laurence, *The Enthusiasts: A Biography of John and Katharine Bruce Glasier* (London: Victor Gollancz, 1971)

Thor, Jowita A., 'Religious and industrial education in the nineteenth-century Magdalene asylums in Scotland', *Studies in Church History*, 55 (2019), pp. 347–62

Tucker, Alan, *Suffragette Partnership: The Lives of Lettice Floyd and Annie Williams, 1860–1943* (Mercian Manuals, 2005)

Turner, Frank, *Contesting Cultural Authority: Essays in Victorian Intellectual Life* (Cambridge: Cambridge University Press, 1993)

Ugolini, Laura, '"It is only justice to grant women's suffrage": Independent Labour Party men and women's suffrage, 1893–1905', in Claire Eustance, Joan Ryan and Laura Ugolini (eds), *A Suffrage Reader: Charting Directions in British Suffrage History* (London: Leicester University Press, 2000), pp. 126–44

Versluis, Arthur, *The Secret History of Western Sexual Mysticism: Sacred Marriage and Spiritual Practices* (Rochester, VT: Destiny Books, 2008), p. 104–13

Versluis, Arthur, 'Sexual mysticisms in nineteenth century America: John Humphrey Noyes, Thomas Lake Harris and Alice Bunker Stockham', in Wouter J. Hanegraaff and Jeffrey J. Kripal (eds), *Hidden Intercourse: Eros and Sexuality in the History of Western Esotericism* (Leiden: Koninklijke Brill NV, 2008), pp. 333–54

Vicinus, Martha, 'Sexuality and power: a review of current work in the history of sexuality', *Feminist Studies*, 8:1 (Spring 1982), pp. 132–56

Vicinus, Martha, *Intimate Friends: Women Who Loved Women* (Chicago: University of Chicago Press, 2004)

Wainwright, Emma M. 'Constructing gendered workplace 'types': the weaver–millworker distinction in Dundee's jute industry, c. 1880–1910', *Gender, Place & Culture*, 14:4 (2007), pp. 467–82

Walkowitz, Judith, *Prostitution and Victorian Society: Women, Class and the State* (Cambridge: Cambridge University Press, 1980)

Walkowitz, Judith R., *City of Dreadful Delight: Narratives of Sexual Danger in Late-Victorian London* (Chicago: University of Chicago Press, 1992)

Waters, C., 'New Women and socialist-feminist fiction: the novels of Isabella Ford and Katharine Bruce Glasier', in A. Ingram and D. Patai (eds), *Rediscovering Forgotten Radicals: British Women Writers, 1889–1939* (Chapel Hill: University of North Carolina Press, 1993)

Weeks, Jeffrey, *Sex, Politics and Society: The Regulation of Sexuality since 1800*, 3rd edn (Harlow: Pearson, 2012)

Weeks, Jeffrey, 'Remembering Foucault', *Journal of the History of Sexuality*, 14:1–2 (January/April 2005), pp. 186–201

Wright, Maureen, *Elizabeth Wolstenholme Elmy and the Victorian Feminist Movement: The Biography of an Insurgent Woman* (Manchester: Manchester University Press, 2011)

Wright, T. R., *The Religion of Humanity: The Impact of Comtean Positivism on Victorian Britain* (Cambridge: Cambridge University Press, 1986)

Yeo, Eileen Janes, *The Contest for Social Science: Relations and Representations of Gender and Class* (London: Rivers Oram, 1996)

Yeo, Eileen Janes, 'Feminizing the citizen: British sociology's sleight of hand?', in Barbara L. Marshall and Anne Witz (eds), *Engendering the Social: Feminist Encounters with Sociological Theory* (Maidenhead: Open University Press, 2004)

Yeo, Stephen, 'A new life: the religion of socialism in Britain, 1883–1896', *History Workshop Journal*, 4 (Autumn 1977), pp. 5–56

Theses, dissertations, papers

Butler, Meagan L. '"Husbands without wives, and wives without husbands": divorce and separation in Scotland, c. 1830–1890' (PhD thesis, University of Glasgow, 2014)

Carr, Rosalind, 'Gender, national identity and political agency in eighteenth century Scotland' (PhD thesis, University of Glasgow, 2008)

Duncan, Alison, '"Old Maids": family and social relationships of never-married Scottish gentlewomen, c. 1740–c.1840' (PhD thesis, University of Aberdeen, 2012)

Eagles, Stuart, 'Political Ruskin: the influence of Ruskin's political ideas and social experiments, circa 1870–1920' (DPhil thesis, Oxford University, 2008)

Ferguson, Megan, 'Patrick Geddes and the Celtic Renascence of the 1890s' (PhD thesis, University of Dundee, 2011)

Foot, Michelle, 'Modern spiritualism and Scottish art between 1860–1940' (PhD thesis, University of Aberdeen, 2016)

Kelman, Kate, 'Female 'self culture' in Edinburgh: the Ladies' Edinburgh Debating Society' (PhD thesis, Queens Margaret University College, 2002)

Lines, Richard, 'James John Garth Wilkinson 1812–1899: Author, Physician, Swedenborgian', paper, Second Bloomsbury Project Conference, UCL, 16 June 2009, www.ucl.ac.uk/bloomsbury-project/articles/events/conference2009/lines.pdf (accessed 3 January 2019)

Lines, Richard, 'Swedenborgianism and pugilism: the William White affair', paper, Third Bloomsbury Project Conference, UCL, 15 April 2011, https://www.ucl.ac.uk/bloomsbury-project/articles/events/conference2011/lines.pdf (accessed 5 September 2019)

Lintell, Helen, 'Lily Bell: socialist and feminist, 1894–8' (MA dissertation, Bristol Polytechnic, 1990)

Meek, Jeff, 'The legal and social construction of the "sodomite" in Scotland, 1885–1930' (MSc thesis, University of Glasgow, 2006)

Meek, Jeff, 'Gay and bisexual men, self-perception and identity in Scotland, 1940 to 1980' (PhD thesis, University of Glasgow, 2011)

Reilly, John Patrick, 'The early social thought of Patrick Geddes' (PhD dissertation, Columbia University, 1972)

Shaw, Michael, 'The fin-de-siècle Scots renascence: the roles of decadence in the development of Scottish cultural nationalism, c. 1880–1914' (PhD thesis, University of Glasgow, 2015)

Index

Note: page numbers in *italics* refer to illustrations; texts are listed under authors' names; 'n.' after a page reference indicates the number of a note on that page.

Addams, Jane 144
adultery 15, 16–17, 22, 33, 58
altruism 1, 20, 42, 51, 65, 86, 99–100, 102, 104–6, 132–4, 144–5, 152n.102, 155n.146, 157, 173, 177, 185
anarchism 2, 53, 68, 82, 96, 100, 152n.102, 198, 203
Atkins, Ellen Sophie 182

Berridge, Edward 95, 200
Besant, Annie 6, 81, 94, 135, 167, 168, 170, 171, 174, 175–6, 179, 180, 190n.83, 197
Billington-Greig, Teresa 67, 68, 74n.78, 78n.152, 79n.157, 198
birth control 2, 4, 6, 7, 9, 21, 99, 110, 117, 134–7, 152n.105, 156–7, 158, 169–80, 182, 183, 184, 191n.89, 191n.100, 191n.101, 193n.141, 201, 203
  Besant-Bradlaugh trial (1877) 6, 171, 175–6
  see also 'karezza'; Clapperton, Jane Hume; Malthusian League
Blavatsky, Helena 94
Bradlaugh, Charles 167, 171, 175, 176
Bray, Charles 9, 159, 165–6, 189n.67, 198
Brotherhood of the New Life 8–9, 69, 85, 89, 90, 92, 80–107, 108n.26, 109n.38, 111n.72, 114n.133, 197–8, 200
  wine production 84, 96–7
  see also Harris, Thomas Lake
Brown, James 29

Burton, Mary Rose Hill 140, 154n.132
Butler, Josephine 58–9

Caird, Mona 2, 18, 56, 58, 62, 137–8, 175, 185, 192n.136
Carpenter, Edward 2, 5–6, 28–9, 117, 158, 185
celibacy 7, 99, 162, 168, 170, 172, 177, 182, 184, 185
Chartism 6, 46, 48
chastity 15, 17, 21, 26, 32, 92
Chevallier, Alzire 93, 96, 106
Clapperton, Jane Hume (1832–1914) 2–3, 4, 6, 7, 62, 116, *161*, 156–86, 188n.34, 197–9
  birth control 134–5, 156–7, 169–77
  family 6, 159–63, 167, 172, 182, 187n.23, 187n.29, 188n.30, 194n.176
  freethought 5, 163–9, 183–4, 198
  Margaret Dunmore: Or, a Socialist Home (1888) 102, 158, 172–5, 180–1, 185, 186n.2, 192n.115, 199
  neo-Malthusianism 169–77, 180, 183–4
  philanthropy 162–3, 188n39
  Scientific Meliorism and the Evolution of Happiness (1885) 7, 135, 164, 169–72, 173, 177, 178, 180, 184, 185–6
  sexual pleasure 158, 177–82, 183, 199
  socialism 170, 172, 183, 195n.184
  'Unitary Homes' 162, 172–4, 180, 185, 199

227

INDEX

A Vision of the Future (1904) 171, 178, 180, 184, 185
'What Do We Women Want?' (c. 1900) 178
Clarke, John S. 183, 185
'coitus reservatus' *see* 'karezza'
Comte, Auguste 119–20, 132, 146n.25
    see also positivism
continence, male *see* 'karezza'
Corelli, Marie 80
Coventry 159, 165–6, 195n.184
Cowles, Louis 91–2
Cranbrook, Reverend James 9, 159, 163–4, 188n.41, 188n.46, 192n.116
'crisis of faith' *see* religion
Cuthbert, Arthur 80, 84, 88–9, 92, 94, 95, 97, 200

Darwin, Charles 116, 126, 127, 130–1, 134, 150n.68, 151n.88, 151n.89, 180
Demolins, Edmond 123–4, 138
divorce 16–17, 18, 36n.33, 58, 105, 168, 194n.174
Dixie, Florence 176
domestic violence 18–19
Drummond, Henry 104, 143–4, 155n.146
Drysdale, Charles Robert 170, 190n.82, 191n.97, 191n.101
Drysdale, George 168, 178–9, 190n.82
Duncan, John 124, 140, 202

Edinburgh 13–14, 115, 117, 120, 137–40, 159–65, 181, 182, 198, 202
Edinburgh Rationalist Ethical Guild 183
Eliot, George (Mary Ann Evans) 166, 167, 177, 185–6, 189n.67, 191n.109, 196n.197
Ellis, Edith 3, 62, 100, 198

Ellis, Havelock 2, 6, 99, 115–16, 117, 118, 130, 145n.5, 178
Elmy, Elizabeth Wolstenholme 47, 49, 56, 62, 67, 69n.8, 78n.149, 96–7, 100, 112n.98, 138, 167, 176, 198
eugenics 116, 117, 129, 135, 142–3, 169, 180
The Evergreen (1895–97) 120, 140, 143, 147n.29, 149n.58
evolutionary biology 1, 5, 103–5, 106, 116–17, 119, 126–35, 143–4, 151n.89, 152n.102, 164, 165, 167, 169, 172, 173, 177

feminism 46–7, 61, 62, 66, 68, 90, 100, 102–3, 106, 132, 140, 141, 150n.81, 167, 169, 175–7, 183
    marriage law campaigns 17, 18, 101, 105
    militancy 62, 67–8, 183
    respectability of 6, 100, 175–6, 197
    science and 117, 127, 129–35, 143–5
    suffrage campaigns 8, 44, 53, 56, 57, 59, 63, 64–9, 129, 140, 141, 176, 197, 199
    see also Male Electors' League for Women's Suffrage; Women's Emancipation Union; Women's Freedom League; Women's Social and Political Union
Fergusson, John Duncan 13
Finot, Jean 131–2, 143
Fraser, Helen 67, 68, 78n.152, 197
'free love' 2, 4, 6, 7, 43, 82, 100–1, 106, 111n.72, 112n.98, 168, 181, 184, 191n.97, 194n.174, 201, 203
    Edith Lanchester case (1895) 6, 100–1, 111n.72
freethought 2, 4, 5, 9, 82, 159, 163–9, 170, 171, 173, 178–9, 181–4, 190n.72, 190n.73, 190n.81, 193n.144, 197
    feminism 9, 167–8, 176, 190n.85
'free unions' *see* 'free love'

INDEX

The Freewoman (1911–12) 47, 98, 102, 157, 178, 182

Gamble, Eliza Burt 144
Gaskell, George Arthur 7, 9, 159, *179*, 179–82, 184, 194n.163, 194n.168, 195n.180, 199
Geddes, Anna (née Morton) (1857–1917) 4, 6, 7, 9, 121, *136*, 165, 197–8
  relationship with parents 6, 123, 138, 147n.29
  relationship with Patrick Geddes 7, 121, 123–4, 135–7, 140, 158–9, 162
Geddes, Patrick (1854–1932) 1, 4, 5, 7, 9, 10n.17, 13, 115–45, *119*, 156–7, 165, 185, 186n.2, 193n.142, 197–9, 201–2
  anabolism/ katabolism theory 104, 126–7, 129, 131, 143–5, 149n.66, 202
  birth control 134–5, 135–7, 144
  The Evolution of Sex (1889) 1, 9, 104, 115–17, *133*, 126–35, 143–4, 156, 201–2
  feminism 117–18, 129–35, 140–1, 143–5, 150n.82
  'The Moral Evolution of Sex' (1896) 7, 9, 117, 140–3
  politics 147n.33
  Ramsay Lodge scandal (1897) 139, 143, 145, 199
  reforming schemes in Edinburgh 9, 156, 202
  relationship with Anna Geddes 7, 121, 123–4, 135–7, 139, 140–1, 145, 158–9, 162
  relationship with disciples 123–5, 145
  relationship with parents 118, 146n.19
  'romantic eugenics' 142–3, 177
  Ruskin Society of Glasgow 46, 104, 121, 122, 147n.34

Sex (1914) 201–2
Summer Meetings 115, 120, 124, *137*, 137–8, 202
Gilman, Charlotte Perkins 103
Gissing, George 3
Glasgow 13, 14, 18, 23, 25, 26, 29, 32, 34, 42, 44–55, 59–60, 67, 80–1, 97, 98, 171, 182, 197
Glasgow Socialist League 29
Glasier, John Bruce 52, 55, 56, 63
Glasier, Katharine Bruce (née St John Conway) 50, 54, 62, 64, 66
Glasier, Lizzie 52, 73n.61

Hardie, James Keir 42, 46, 51, 53, 55–7, 59–61, 63, 66, 72n.45, 74n.73, 74n.74, 76n.102, 95, 97, 101, 111n.72, 112n.89, 198, 199
Harris, Thomas Lake 5, 7, 8–9, 51, *83*, 80–107, 114n.133, 177, 190n.83, 199–200
  androgynous deity 86–88, 101–2, 106, 109n.30, 109n.31
  architectural plans for an 'ideal city' 91–2, *92*, 110n.49
  'conjugial marriage' 7, 8, 86–8, 91–3, 99, 103, 106, 177
  counterparts 81, 87–8, 90–1, 93, 98, 99, 103, 105, 106
  'internal respiration' 8, 86–7
  Scotland 80–4, 94–107, 112n.88
  sex 81–2, 86–93, 105, 109n.29
  wine production 84, 96–7, 105, 198
  women 89–90, 102–3, 105
  see also Brotherhood of the New Life
Hennell, Sara 9, 159, 166, 189n.67, 190n.70
Hermetic Order of the Golden Dawn 5, 94, 111n.68, 194n.178, 195n.179
  see also occultism
heterosexuality 146n.12

INDEX

Hinton, James 99–100, 112n.95, 178
homosexuality 2, 117
   female 12–13, 29–30, 117, 160, 184
   male 4, 6, 8, 15, 22, 27–9, 125, 153n.113
   Woods-Pirie libel trial (1811–12) 12–13, 15, 29–30
Huxley, Thomas 1, 115, 116, 118–20, 132, 145n.5, 164

Ibsen, Henrik 2–3, 162, 178
illegitimacy 8, 12, 14–15, 22, 23–4, 31, 32, 34, 35n.1, 55, 58, 100
Independent Labour Party (ILP) 1, 6, 7, 8, 42, 44, 50–6, 59, 62–9, 72n.53, 73n.54, 73n.57, 73n.61, 74n.73, 96, 97, 138, 183, 195n.184, 198, 199, 201
Ireland 4, 12, 188n.41

Jackson, Holbrook 5

'karezza' 7, 92–3, 106–7, 110n.55, 110n.57
Kirk elders 14, 15, 22–3, 30, 31, 34, 118
Kirk sessions *see* Kirk elders
Kropotkin, Peter 152n.102

Labour Leader 1, 3, 7, 8, 43–4, 46–7, 48, 49–50, 55–66, 95, 96, 98, 101–2, 104, 111n.72, 123, 138, 198, 199
   circulation 62, 76n.117
   'Matrons and Maidens' 1, 8, 43–4, 48, 55–64, 66
Lanchester, Edith *see* 'free love'
Legitimation League 100, 182, 194n.177
lesbianism *see* homosexuality
Liberalism 45–6, 65, 68, 160, 176
libertinism 8, 21, 31, 32, 34
London 3–4, 6, 28, 34, 59, 67, 94, 100, 118, 120, 176, 202–3
Lowerison, Harry 125, 149n.59

Magdalene homes *see* sex work
Male Electors' League for Women's Suffrage 47, 69, 71n.30
Malthusian League 159, 170–2, 174–7, 180, 183–4, 191n.97, 192n.136, 193n.159
Markham, Edwin 80, 91, 200
marriage 1, 2, 7, 8, 15–22, 24, 30, 47, 49–50, 58, 63, 67, 82, 101, 103, 106, 123, 142, 160–1, 168, 174, 181, 203
   irregular 7, 16, 47
   national debates on 18, 58
   Scots law 15–17, 58
masculinity 1, 15, 18–19, 21, 27, 61, 150n.74, 173–4, 180–1
   new men 50
   sexuality, male 15, 21–2, 27, 33, 138–9, 172, 175, 180–1, 182, 193n.149, 199
   socialism and 43, 61, 65, 199
Mavor, James 120, 185
Men and Women's Club 100, 175, 185
Michael, Alex 125, 149n.58
Miller, Florence Fenwick 176, 193n.141
mill girls 20, 23, 25, 31
Montefiore, Dora 158, 168, 176, 184–5, 188n.34, 193n.143, 195n.184
moral conservatism 6, 12–30, 34–5, 138, 162, 168, 171, 197, 204
Morris, William 6, 34, 51
Muirhead, Bob 29, 40n.107
Murray, Anne 124–5, 149n.55
music hall 18, 22, 23, 31, 32–3, 34, 158

Nature 119, 125, 126, 134
neo-Malthusianism *see* Malthusian League
New Woman 3, 4, 50, 57, 127, 132, 141, 158, 176, 185, 197

INDEX

occultism 5, 81, 94, 102, 107, 109n.31, 111n.68, 147n.29, 148n.51, 148n.52, 182, 200
  see also Hermetic Order of the Golden Dawn
Oliphant, Laurence 82, 84, 93, 108n.14, 199–200
Oliphant, Margaret 17, 93
Oneida Perfectionists 93, 99, 110n.57
Owen, Robert 7, 166
Owenism see socialism

patriarchy 2, 7, 15, 17–19, 22, 26, 27, 33, 59, 61, 65, 82, 123, 172, 173
Pearce, Bella (née Duncan) (1859–1929) 1, 3, 4, 6, 8, 48, 42–69, 121, 123, 138, 197–201, 204
  Brotherhood of the New Life 7, 80–2, 94–107, 111n.74, 199–200
  family 5, 6, 44–5, 46
  'free love' 101
  Liberalism 45–6
  'Lily Bell' pen-name 55–6, 74n.74, 74n.78, 98, 112n.89
  'Matrons and Maidens' column 43–4, 55–63
  militant suffragism 67–8
  occultism 5, 94, 111n.68
  relationship with Charles Pearce 7, 47–50, 106
  Ruskin Society of Glasgow 6, 46–7, 121
  socialism 42–3, 50–5, 198
Pearce, Charles (1839–1905) 3, 4, 5, 6, 7, 8, 42–4, 46–56, 49, 121, 147n.36, 197–8, 200
  Brotherhood of the New Life 80–2, 84–6, 94–107, 111n.75
  children 71n.33
  family 46–7
  feminism 46–7, 50, 52, 74n.73
  occultism 5, 94, 111n.68
  relationship with Bella Pearce 7, 47–50, 106
  Ruskin Society of Glasgow 46–7, 50, 72n.45, 121, 147n.36
  socialism 50–5, 198
  'Sophia' pen-name 43, 56, 69n.8, 101
  spiritualism 85
premarital sex see illegitimacy
Podmore, Eleanor 137, 153n.113, 198
positivism 5, 6, 119–20, 132, 147n.28, 147n.29, 165, 169, 197
  see also Auguste Comte
prostitution see sex work

race 103, 104, 107, 131, 132, 142, 151n.91, 156, 169, 180, 204
racial degeneration, anxiety over 127, 135, 169
Woods-Pirie libel trial (1811–12) 13
rape 15, 33, 58, 105, 203
Reddie, Cecil 28–9, 143, 198
religion 5, 6, 8, 14, 18, 21, 24, 45, 81, 117, 164–6, 173–4, 183, 197, 200
  Calvinism 8, 13, 14
  Congregationalism 25, 163–4
  'crisis of faith' 5, 35, 163–5, 188n.45, 197
  evangelicalism 14–15, 19, 23, 25–6, 30, 80, 198
  Free Church 24, 20
  Presbyterianism 4, 5, 16, 17, 123, 200
  re-sexing of 86, 88–9, 200
  sexual regulation by 14–5, 30
  socialism and 42–3, 51, 53, 72n.51
  'Woman's Mission' 20, 162–3, 188n.39
  see also Harris, Thomas Lake; Kirk elders; occultism; positivism; spiritualism; theosophy
Religion of Humanity see positivism; Auguste Comte

Romanes, George John 116, 128–9, 150n.78
Ruskin Society of Glasgow 6, 43, 46–7, 50, 69, 72n.45, 121, 122, 147n.36

Samuel, George A. H. ('Marxian') 49, 63–4, 77n.123, 101, 199
school boards 52, 72n.53, 73n.61, 176
Schreiner, Olive 6, 29, 100
Scotland, moral identity of 4, 5, 8, 12–14, 15, 22, 30, 142
Scottish Women's Liberal Federation 45
secularism *see* freethought
separate spheres 19–20
sexed body 19, 116–17, 126–34, 150n.74, 151n.89
  see also sexual science
sexology 117
sexual cultures, working-class 31–5
sexual double standard 2, 8, 15, 16, 21–2, 33–4, 43, 44, 57–8, 63, 67, 105, 106, 138–9, 204
sexual harassment 31–2, 33, 41n.128
sexual knowledge 21, 32, 115, 134–5, 152n.105
sexual pleasure 7, 9, 99, 105, 106, 135–7, 142, 145, 157–8, 159, 177–9, 183, 184, 199
sexual regulation 8, 13, 14–30
  see also moral conservatism; sex work
sexual science 116–17, 126–35
sex work 2, 8, 22, 24–7, 28, 33, 43, 58, 67, 157, 171, 175, 178, 199, 204
  Cleveland Street scandal (1889) 6
  feminist critique of 43, 58–61, 67
  Glasgow brothel scandal (1896) 59–61, 76n.102, 199
  Magdalene homes 23, 26–7, 33

regulation in India 58–9, 61, 63, 66, 75n.89, 75n.91, 75n.92
regulation in Scotland 26–7
surveys of 25–6
Sharp, William 140
Social Democratic Federation (SDF) 44, 101, 184–5
socialism 6, 169, 170, 172, 179, 183, 194n.164, 199
  ethical/ 'new life' socialism 1, 6–7, 42–3, 44, 50–5, 65–7, 72n.51, 73n.67, 82, 99–100, 198–201
  feminism and 4, 8, 43–4, 48, 49, 50, 52, 53, 55, 57–67, 74n.71, 74n.73, 198, 200–1
  occult revival 81, 107n.8
  Owenism 6–7, 25, 82, 99
  respectability of 6–7, 82, 99–101, 106–7, 197
  see also Glasgow Socialist League; Independent Labour Party; Social Democratic Federation; Women's Labour Party (Glasgow)
Smith, Hannah Whitall 91, 108n.26
Smith, Madeleine 13, 15, 33–4, 158
social purity 26
sodomy *see* homosexuality
Spence, Catherine Helen 185, 189n.67, 195n.184, 196n.197, 198
Spencer, Herbert 131, 132, 134, 151n.90, 165, 166, 185
spinsterhood 156, 158, 161, 180, 182, 188n.34
  see also celibacy
spiritualism 6, 81, 83, 85, 93–4, 95, 98, 200
Stead, W. T. 59–60, 80, 182
Stephens, Riccardo 124, 148n.51
Swainson, William 95, 111n.73
Swedenborg, Emanuel 81, 87, 102, 106, 109n.30

Swedenborgianism 5, 6, 51, 81, 82–4, 109n.30, 197, 199
  see also Brotherhood of the New Life; Harris, Thomas Lake; Swedenborg, Emanuel
Swiney, Frances 144
Symonds, John Addington 8

Taylor, Kate 52
Taylor, Rachel Annand 137, 153n.113, 198–9, 202–3
theosophy 5, 81, 93–4, 147n.29, 176, 182, 200, 202
Thomson, John Arthur 1, 7, 13, 104, 115, 117, 119, 127, 129, 140, 145n.2, 155n.146, 177, 185, 201–2
Tolstoyan communities 72n.51, 95, 100, 111n.73
'twilight moments' 8, 33

'unco guid' *see* moral conservatism

Vickery, Alice 170, 174, 175–6, 191n.97, 191n.101

Waring, Jane Lee 80–1, 92, 93, 97–8, 106, 108n.26
Watt, Christian 18, 31–2, 34
Whitman, Walt 4, 6, 125, 178
'wife-beating' *see* domestic violence
Wilde, Oscar 3, 6, 28, 39n.97
Women's Emancipation Union (WEU) 56, 67, 69, 78n.149, 176
Women's Freedom League 129, 150n.82, 175–6, 183
Women's Labour Party (Glasgow) 43, 52, 64, 71n.29, 73n.57, 73n.61, 198
women's movement *see* feminism
Women's Social and Political Union (WSPU) 8, 44, 66, 67–9, 78n.141, 79n.157, 175, 183

Zangwill, Israel 13–14

EU authorised representative for GPSR:
Easy Access System Europe, Mustamäe tee 50,
10621 Tallinn, Estonia
gpsr.requests@easproject.com

www.ingramcontent.com/pod-product-compliance
Lightning Source LLC
Chambersburg PA
CBHW071407300426
44114CB00016B/2219